The Indian CONSTITUTION

Also by Gautam Bhatia

The Transformative Constitution: A Radical Biography in Nine Acts

Unsealed Covers: A Decade of the Constitution, the Courts and the State

The Wall

The Horizon

The Indian CONSTITUTION

A CONVERSATION *with* POWER

GAUTAM BHATIA

HarperCollins *Publishers* India

First published in India by HarperCollins *Publishers* 2025
4th Floor, Tower A, Building No 10, DLF Cyber City,
DLF Phase II, Gurugram – 122002
www.harpercollins.co.in

2 4 6 8 10 9 7 5 3 1

P-ISBN 978-93-6569-375-1
E-ISBN 978-93-6569-140-5

Typeset in 11/14.2 Adobe Caslon Pro at
HarperCollins *Publishers* India

Printed and bound at
Replika Press Pvt. Ltd.

FSC www.fsc.org MIX Paper | Supporting responsible forestry FSC™ C016779

This book is produced from independently certified FSC® paper to ensure responsible forest management.

Contents

Prologue: A Question of Power vii

1. Power Decentralized: Federalism 1
2. Power Divided: Parliamentarianism 38
3. Power Dispersed: Pluralism 75
4. Power Confronted: Institutions 115
5. Power Contained: Rights 143
6. Power Unbound: The People 177

Interlude: Yesterday's Tomorrow 207

Epilogue: State, Power, and the Future of Constitutionalism 221

Acknowledgements 239

Notes 241

Index 331

Prologue: A Question of Power

'MAY YOU LIVE IN interesting times', is an invocation that, in popular folklore, is perceived more as a curse than a blessing. But whether curse or blessing, for anyone engaging with the Indian Constitution, the period 2019–24 was certainly an interesting time.

On 5 August 2019, soon after the general election returned the Bharatiya Janata Party (BJP) to power with an absolute majority for a second consecutive term, two Presidential Orders removed the constitutional autonomy (or 'special status') of the state of Jammu and Kashmir. A law followed, which converted the state into a centrally controlled union territory. These moves were immediately challenged at the Supreme Court, sparking a long-running legal battle about the nature of Indian federalism, the purposes of constitutional autonomy, the limits of Emergency rule, the powers of the Indian President, and much else.[1] Simultaneously, within the state, a months-long internet shutdown was imposed, while members of the (political) Opposition (along with many others) were subjected to administrative detention. These moves, too, were challenged before the Supreme Court, bringing the Constitution's Fundamental Rights provisions into a clash with 'reasons of State'.

While Jammu and Kashmir stands alone as the starkest example of a constitutional-political crisis involving federal relations, it was by no means the only one. In 2023, an eight-year-long dispute between the government of the National Capital Territory (NCT) of Delhi and the central government about the distribution of legislative and executive power seemed to have been finally resolved by the Supreme Court in favour of the former, only for Parliament to swiftly pass a law taking back the power that the Supreme Court had held it did not have. The next round of constitutional challenges awaits adjudication.

Meanwhile, in the same five-year period, three state governments under the rule of the Opposition were toppled through a series of manoeuvres involving legislators resigning or parties splitting. The beneficiary was the ruling party at the Centre (the BJP), which formed the new government in each case (sometimes with the 'rebel' legislators now within its own fold, and sometimes in alliance with one of the factions in the party split). Each of these cases ended up at the Supreme Court, where bitter disputes implicated the conduct of several constitutional functionaries: the centrally appointed state governors, the speakers of the Legislative Assemblies, and the Election Commission.

Nor was this the only time that the Election Commission found itself in the eye of the storm. In early 2023, a little over a year before the 2024 general election, the Supreme Court handed down a judgment depriving the executive of the power to appoint election commissioners, and (temporarily) vesting it in a committee comprising the Prime Minister, the leader of the Opposition, and the Chief Justice of India. By the end of the year, Parliament had passed a law that replaced the Chief Justice with a member of the Union cabinet, thus restoring the executive's prerogative in selecting the composition of the Election Commission. A subsequent challenge to the law was put on ice by the Supreme Court. Thus, the 2024 general elections were contested under the auspices of an Election Commission where two out of three members had been effectively selected by the Prime Minister and a Union minister of his choice.

Constitutional conflict was not limited to states, political parties, and institutions. By the beginning of 2024, two abbreviations had entrenched themselves into national consciousness: ED, i.e., the Enforcement Directorate, and UAPA, i.e., the Unlawful Activities Prevention Act, 1967. The former is the body tasked with enforcing the provisions of India's anti-money laundering law (the Prevention of Money Laundering Act, 2002 [PMLA]). The latter is India's umbrella anti-terror legislation. What unite these two laws are their stringent bail provisions. These provisions appear to indicate a tolerance for, if not an active encouragement of, lengthy pre-trial incarceration. The frequent use of these laws saw a series of high-profile cases where members of the political Opposition arrested under PMLA and political dissidents arrested under UAPA approached the courts, challenging their arrests and seeking bail—with mixed success.

And if personal liberty often found itself at the bar of the judiciary, so did other kinds of clashes between individual, community, and the State. Challenges to home demolitions and evictions (which became endemic in 2021–23, often referred to as 'bulldozer justice'), as well as to large-scale developmental projects that would result in displacement and environmental degradation were staple features in the courts' constitutional docket.

Interesting times, indeed. But is there anything that connects these diverse struggles, other than the time period? After all, they involved very different actors, told very different stories, and involved very different parts of the Constitution.

On one popular account, these were all examples of constitutional hardball or, to invoke a more suitable metaphor, constitutional bodyline-bowling.[2] As the term suggests, constitutional bodyline-bowling refers to a constitutional actor (in this case, the central executive) testing just how far it can go under the limits established under the Constitution, and on occasion, even stretching or altering those limits.[3] Constitutional bodyline-bowling would appear to be a natural consequence of the ebb and flow of politics, which from time to time results in a powerful and dominant central executive that enjoys a large legislative majority. Indeed, India is no stranger to constitutional bodyline-bowling. The regime of Indira Gandhi in the 1970s[4]—capped by the infamous Emergency—would appear to fit the bill just as well.[5]

While there is something to say for this account of the constitutional battles during 2019–24, it remains limited in that it sees the examples cited above as separate and isolated instances.[6] I believe, however, that there is something deeper that connects them, going beyond the actions of a particular dominant central executive. These instances all constitute interconnected strands within a web of power relations that is created and sustained by the Constitution.[7] Furthermore, we are better off understanding the actions of the central executive not as tearing the web or even seeking to substantially remake it. Rather, as I will argue, these actions and the constitutional challenges that ensued, along with their judicial outcomes, help illuminate the design of the web and the manner in which its overlapping strands constitute its architecture.

Thus, while the examples I have cited above will return in the course of this book, I do not look at the 2019–24 period in constitutional history for its own sake, or as a special moment of rupture, a departure from what came before (whether in degree or in kind).[8] Rather, where I discuss these cases, I do so to the extent that they encourage us to think more deeply about the Indian Constitution's structure and design, and in particular, the Constitution as a power map.[9] To this end, these cases will be analysed on their own terms, but also as a continuation of a longer tradition of constitutional interpretation, going back to the origins (and before).

With that background, in this opening Prologue, I will outline the structure and the core argument of this book. I begin with three popular stories about the Indian Constitution and flag how the question of power is often missing from these stories **(I)**. I go on to argue that this is reflected in how we study, think, and talk about the Constitution. We do this by classifying the document into different 'silos', and studying each of these separately. I argue for a synthesis of these silos that acknowledges the deep links between what Roberto Gargarella calls the 'engine room' of the Constitution (i.e., the organization of power), and the Constitution's charter of rights and liberties **(II)**.

I then address the question of how the Constitution organizes power. I highlight six axes around which power is organized, and how each axis constitutes a terrain of contestation between different visions of power (the next six chapters will be dedicated to considering each axis in turn) **(III)**. The cases I have referred to above will feature in those discussions as part of the longer arc of constitutional history.

I briefly set out my central thesis, which will be developed through the course of my account: although the Constitution is a terrain of contestation between different visions of power, its seven-decade history has been marked by what I call a centralizing drift. The seeds of this centralizing drift, I will argue, are contained within the text and design of the Constitution itself, and over the years they have been watered and fertilized by the courts (in particular, the Supreme Court), through a set of 'inflection-point' judgments **(IV)**.

After setting out a few recurring themes of the book **(V)**, I conclude by noting that if we are to make sense of many of the constitutional developments that have taken place in the recent past, we must begin with a critical interrogation of the Constitution itself, and of the power map that it compels us to navigate **(VI)**.

I. Three Stories About the Indian Constitution

In *Between Magic and Deceit*, Gunther Frankenberg asks us to think about a constitution as narrative, as 'having an interesting story to tell'.[10] A survey of scholarship, historical sources, and judicial decisions indicates that the many stories told about the Indian Constitution can be grouped into three archetypes.

The first archetype understands the Indian Constitution to be a continuation of colonial governance forms and structures, marked by extensive borrowing from pre-Independence semi-constitutional charters such as the Government of India Act, 1935, and the retention of characteristically colonial instruments of State power, such as administrative detention and rule by decree.[11] This understanding of the Constitution was articulated within the Constituent Assembly at the time of the framing.[12] It formed the basis of early Supreme Court judgments interpreting constitutional provisions[13] and continues to be a focus of scholarly critique.[14]

The second archetype—which we can broadly call 'progressive' or 'transformative' constitutionalism—takes issue with the argument from colonial continuity. Progressive constitutionalism understands the Constitution to mark a decisive break with the colonial past, ushering in a new set of framework values to govern the Indian polity.[15] On one further—and optimistic—account, progressive constitutionalism blossomed out of Supreme Court decisions in the 1980s, and was driven by two judicial innovations: first, an expansive reading of Article 21 of the Constitution (the right to life and personal liberty), which articulated a range of civil, political, and socio-economic rights, otherwise not found in the text of the Constitution; and secondly, the development of public interest litigation (PIL), which relaxed rules of standing for approaching the Supreme Court, along with a range of procedural developments, such as the determination of facts through written expert evidence instead of oral cross-examination, judicial supervision of administration, and so on.[16]

A set of more sceptical accounts, however, points out that notwithstanding the fact that the expanded understanding of Article 21 and the institution of the PIL have both become ubiquitous in Indian constitutional jurisprudence, the actual judicial record remains patchy at best. For example, in the heyday of the PIL years and expansive Article 21 jurisprudence, the Supreme Court repeatedly upheld national security legislation in the teeth of strong constitutional challenges, deferring to the interests of the State each time.[17] Furthermore, even in the domain of socio-economic rights, the line between rhetoric and reality often appears to blur.[18] Notably, these accounts do not deny that the Constitution is a progressive or transformative document, or that progressive and transformative outcomes can be achieved through judicial interpretation of the fundamental rights chapter.[19] Rather, they view the transformative story as a chrysalis, a story that still waits to be told.[20]

A final archetype is, however, even more sceptical: it denies that the Constitution has a story to tell at all. Pointing to the plurality of voices in the Constituent Assembly, the (often) inconclusive debates, and the final (inordinately lengthy) text, this account holds that the Constitution was the result of political compromise and is better understood as a ragbag of disparate provisions cobbled together by happenstance, instead of exhibiting any unified political or social vision.[21]

It is important to note that these three archetypes are not necessarily disjunctive accounts of the Indian Constitution. It may be argued, for example, that parts of the Constitution are incoherent (a charge often labelled against the Directive Principles of State Policy), while other parts *do* bear a tangible identity.[22] Within the same Constitution, certain parts may reflect colonial continuity, while other parts may signify a transformative break. Thus, when we think about the Constitution as narrative, it is worth remembering that the document might not just tell one story, but several.

A. Silos and Synthesis

The purpose of this book is not to adjudicate between these different narratives about the Indian Constitution, but to shift the frame of reference. By way of illustration, let us briefly turn to the progressive/ transformative story. As mentioned above, accounts of progressive and transformative constitutionalism have been challenged on their own terms. Apart from questions about the judiciary's actual record, critics point out that these accounts are premised upon an optimistic—even naïve—view about the ability of constitutional interpretation to bring about lasting social change, and relatedly, an excessive focus upon the courtroom and judicial decisions as sites of transformation.[23]

There is, however, a deeper issue to consider. Ever since Granville Austin's pioneering study of the Indian Constitution, these accounts have tended to ground themselves within two chapters of the Constitution: the Fundamental Rights chapter (Part III) and the chapter on Directive Principles of State Policy (Part IV).[24] The past, present, and future of progressive constitutionalism thus comes to depend upon interpretive battles around the meaning, scope, and limitations of the substantive rights guaranteed by the Constitution—whether inside courtrooms, within the halls of Parliament, or in social movements.[25] The other 90 per cent of the Constitution might be interesting and important in its own right, but (barring a few stray provisions) has no real bearing on the Constitution's character or identity.

This is not an issue limited to the accounts I have discussed above, but extends more broadly through the field of Indian constitutional studies. In Indian law schools, constitutional law is classically taught either through three courses (federalism, Fundamental Rights and the separation of powers), or two (Fundamental Rights and the rest).[26] There is power in taxonomy: dividing up constitutional law in this fashion already presumes pre-existing, clean-cut lines between these parts of the Constitution. A look at the table of contents of a volume like *The Oxford Handbook of the Indian Constitution* reveals similar divisions between federalism, rights, and separation of powers, all of which are placed within distinctive sub-sections.[27] Standalone volumes on various aspects of Indian constitutionalism replicate this division, tending to focus either on structural issues such as federalism (and its various discontents), or on substantive rights issues (such as discrimination, the freedom of religion, the freedom of speech, and so on).

There is value in isolating various thematic parts of the Indian Constitution and subjecting them to close scrutiny. This should not, therefore, be taken as a complaint against any of the volumes mentioned in the previous paragraphs. What this does (unwittingly) accomplish, however, is a kind of 'constitutional common sense' which views these different thematic parts of the Constitution as self-contained and separated from one another.[28] This constitutional common sense then affects broader approaches to the Constitution as well, where studies about the its progressive potential become bound up with the Fundamental Rights and Directive Principles chapter.

It is here that the problems begin. As Roberto Gargarella points out in his magisterial study of two centuries of Latin American constitutionalism, 'all Constitutions contain two parts: a *dogmatic* one that includes a declaration of rights and an *organic* one that divides and organizes power' (emphasis supplied).[29] Gargarella notes that the two parts are linked to one another, and can even come into tension. For example, a '... system of concentrated power begins to conflict with the social demands generated in the name of constitutional rights—which ends up implying that a part of the Constitution begins to work against the success of the second'.[30] In the specific context of Latin American constitutional history, Gargarella notes how:

> Latin American Constitutions began, one after the other, to add these new social concerns to the old, existing legal matrix, which notably was not suppressed or significantly changed. Subsequently, the new, twentieth-century type of constitutionalism became distinguished by socially committed Constitutions, a feature that found expression in a renewed organization of rights, but also by Constitutions that remained too conservative and restrictive with regard to the organization of power.[31]

Gargarella's exhortation to constitutional scholars to focus on how constitutions organize power—what he calls 'the engine room of constitutionalism'—should give us some pause for thought, not least because of the easily visible historical similarities. While attention to the 'social question' in Latin American constitutionalism came through the drafting and adoption of new constitutions, in India, it was the result of the Supreme Court 'reading in' a range of new rights—including socio-economic rights—into Article 21 of the Constitution. Although this phase of the Supreme Court had its heyday in the 1980s, in many ways, it continues to this day.

On Gargarella's terms, the question that we perhaps should be asking is whether the substantive expansion of Part III of the Indian Constitution was accompanied by an equal attention to the manner in which the Indian Constitution organizes power, and an equal focus on the linkages between the 'organic' and 'dogmatic' parts of the Constitution. This is a question that is yet to be asked, at least in accounts about the progressive or transformative character of the Constitution and about the jurisprudence of the Supreme Court.

Departing from these accounts, therefore, this book is about the many ways in which the Indian Constitution organizes and limits power. A part of the enquiry will cover old ground: questions of federalism, bicameralism, and constitutional pluralism (to name just three) have been studied extensively. The overall approach, however, will be to ask how these thematic areas of Indian constitutionalism link to each other and back to the question of power, and how the Indian Constitution's organization of relates to its progressive or transformative potential.

With that in mind, let us now turn to the core thesis of the book.

II. The Organization of Power

Let us begin with the moment of the founding. The origins of the Indian Constitution—in the Constituent Assembly Debates, in the committee proceedings where much of the constitutional text was drafted, and indeed, in the years leading up to political independence—have been subjected to extensive scholarly treatment. For our purposes, let us examine first Uday Mehta's important insight. Mehta contrasts the Constitutions of the United States and

India along a single crucial axis: their attitudes towards (State) power. 'American constitutionalism,' Mehta points out, 'stemmed from a deep distrust of power—of which a distrust of the absolutist prince was just a single instance. The first impulse of this constitutionalism was thus to limit political power, to be suspicious of it and to constrain its reach.'[32] This is in stark contrast to the preoccupations of Indian constitutionalism, leading up to the framing: problems of mass poverty and many other social ills meant that the Constitution was understood as an instrument for the exercise, channelling, and shaping of public power, in order to solve those problems.[33]

The question, of course, was what form—or forms—this power would take. As many scholars have pointed out, on one reading of the Constitution, the dominant vision appears to be of unitary power, exercised by a strong central State designed to be the vehicle of social[34], economic[35], and political transformation, and of a constitutionalism that 'suspend[ed] suspicion of the State'.[36] A closer look at the Constitution reveals, however, that even as various parts of the document gestured towards a strong centralized State, there were other parts of it that were in tension with—and even undermined—this vision. For this reason—as I will argue throughout this book—the Constitution is best understood as a terrain of contestation between different—and at times, conflicting—ideas about the organization of power.

What might these be? I will, here, briefly set out the different axes around which the Indian Constitution organizes and channels public power, and the way(s) in which the constitutional text and structure exist as terrains of contestation between different visions of power. The succeeding chapters of this book will consider each of these axes in greater detail.

A. Federal and Unitary

Article 1 of the Constitution stipulates India to be a 'Union of States'.[37] At the outset, thus, the Constitution commits to a federal structure, where legislative and executive power is divided between two units. The 73rd and 74th Amendments to the Constitution have added a third tier of governance—the Panchayats—albeit under substantial control of the state governments. That said, the Indian federation has a well-known and extensively studied 'Central bias' (the precise meaning of this will be discussed in greater detail in Chapter 1), where the federal impulse is checked by various overarching, umbrella provisions that allow the Centre to override the states in various important domains.

B. Concentrated and Distributed

The Indian Constitution envisions a parliamentary and bicameral form of government, with an executive that is—at least formally—accountable to the legislature, and an upper house (Rajya Sabha, the council of states) that enjoys law-making powers alongside the directly elected Lok Sabha, the lower house. Over the years, the evolution of Indian parliamentary democracy—through devices such as the anti-defection law, which penalizes voting against the party whip with instant disqualification—has gradually strengthened the hand of the executive, at the cost of Parliament. While the anti-defection law was introduced into the Constitution through a constitutional amendment in the 1980s, there are provisions in the original Constitution that also undercut this horizontal distribution of power. Two such provisions (and we will discuss others) include the power of the executive to issue ordinances that have the 'force of law' (effectively, rule by decree, or 'Henry VIII' powers) and a bar on the upper house from enforcing amendments to bills that the speaker of the lower house has classified as 'money bills'.

C. Homogeneity and Plurality

Constitutional pluralism is a philosophy that acknowledges that constitutions ought to reflect the full breadth and diversity of the societies that they are meant to govern.[38] Constitutional pluralism argues that within an overarching framework of governance and an overarching normative value system, a constitution must nonetheless accommodate diverse political, social, and cultural structures, and diverse ways of living. Under the Indian Constitution, the most visible and controversial example of this was Article 370, which—at least in formal terms—granted substantial autonomy to the state of Jammu and Kashmir. While often spoken of as a case of 'asymmetric federalism', I would classify the former Article 370 as one instance of a broader constitutional recognition of pluralism. Similar forms of pluralism are found in the various special arrangements for other states (Articles 371A – I), and even more clearly, in the administrative arrangements governing indigenous areas in Schedules V and VI, which arguably form mini-constitutions of their own. Along this axis of power, constitutional pluralism is to be distinguished from constitutional homogeneity, which views with suspicion any departure from a uniform governing structure, or one specific way of organizing power, under a constitution as a whole.

D. Electoral and Guarantor

In modern constitutional democracies, the legitimacy of government is traced to periodic elections. While classical constitutional theory views the judiciary as the *non-elected* branch of government that is designed to keep a check upon the elected branches, there is also an increasing understanding that there are a range of tasks that ought to be performed by institutions or bodies that are independent *of* the elected branches, but are structured differently from the judicial branch. The best example of this is an independent electoral commission, whose task it is to ensure that elections—i.e., the bases of democratic legitimacy—are conducted fairly. For this purpose, the commission naturally must be independent of the elected bodies themselves. The concept of these fourth branch—or 'guarantor'—institutions is not unknown to the Indian Constitution, with provisions for an election commission, a comptroller and auditor general, and a commission to look into the welfare of Scheduled Castes and Scheduled Tribes. Once again, however, constitutional silences speak as loud as the text: in Chapter 4, we shall consider a range of guarantor institutions that are conspicuous by their absence from the Constitution.

E. The State and the People

In the previous section of this Prologue, I discussed how a focus upon the substantive rights chapters of the Constitution, to the exclusion of those parts of the Constitution that deal with the organization of power, gives us an incomplete chapter of the Constitution's transformative potential. That said, enforceable fundamental rights are, of course, one form of organizing power. In their classical form, they define and shape the power relationship between the State and the individual. In considering the Indian Constitution's Fundamental Rights chapter, one provision stands out amongst a litany of standard rights-and-restriction guarantees: an express constitutional sanction of administrative detention, or detention without trial.[39] It is important to note that administrative detention is not limited to cases of declared Emergencies, but is made a part of the 'regular' criminal justice system. In Chapter 5, we will discuss (among other things) how this provision—and its interpretation—have contributed to a constitutional common sense the 'state of exception' has blurred into the state of normalcy, leading to a situation where civil rights under the Constitution have been effectively subordinated to a government-articulated conception of 'the reasons of State'.

F. Representative and Direct

The Preamble of the Indian Constitution begins with a familiar phrase: 'We the People … do adopt, enact, and give to ourselves this Constitution.'[40] Apart from this titular invocation, however, what role does the Constitution envisage for 'the People'? A look towards other constitutions reveals a number of ways in which the designated authors of the constitution ('the People') have a role to play in its working. Examples include, for instance, the requirement of a referendum for a constitutional amendment[41], a guarantee of public participation in the law-making process[42], and a right of recall.[43] It is striking, however, that after the invocation in the Preamble, 'the People'—as a collective entity—disappear from the text of the Indian Constitution. Thus, the only form of public power that the Constitution of India appears to recognize is through periodic adult suffrage. It is also deemed to be the single instrument to exercise public control over representatives. In Chapter 6, we shall discuss these issues and more, about the role of the people within the Constitution, and how it interacts with the role of representative institutions.

III. The Centralizing Drift

As the previous section has indicated, the constitutional text is a terrain of contestation between different visions and articulations of power. In this context, the core argument of this book will be as follows: in the seven decades of the working of the Constitution, there has been a gradual drift towards the entrenching of its first set of characteristics: unitary, concentrated, representative, electoral, homogenous, and Statist power, at the cost of federal, distributed, direct, guarantor, plural, and individual power. This shift that I call, in short, the 'centralizing drift', has come about in different ways, which shall be discussed in detail in the succeeding chapters. I provide a brief summary here.

First, there is the constitutional text itself. As Nirvikar Singh points out in the context of federalism, the Constitution is chock-full of 'escape clauses' that skew the terrain of contestation at the outset.[44] Whether it is overriding central powers in Centre-state fiscal relations, the use of 'notwithstanding' clauses scattered throughout the Constitution, or wide-ranging gubernatorial power in the Schedule VI Areas, these escape clauses seemingly constrain and counteract the Constitution's own impulses towards the distribution and diversification of power. We shall see through the course of this book that such 'escape clauses' are not limited to federalism but pervade the Constitution. Whether it is Presidential power to appoint the officers of fourth-branch institutions (including, even, an interim power to appoint the members of the Election Commission!), or the provisions on administrative detention, the constitutional text, as well as its silences, indicate that this is an executive-trusting document.[45]

Secondly, it is important to note that 'escape clauses' are not self-interpreting. Their scope and limitations are subject to judicial adjudication. Consequently, this book will attempt to show that—much like the framers of the Constitution were faced with choices about how to organize power—the judiciary (specifically, the Supreme Court) has been faced with a set of choices about how to interpret the Constitution's scheme of organizing power. When faced with these choices, the Supreme Court has often chosen to further facilitate or accelerate the Constitution's centralizing drift. I call these judgments, discussed in the succeeding chapters, *constitutional inflection points*: they are events that definitively entrench the centralizing drift, while significantly weakening the decentralizing vision of power that is also present within the constitutional text.

Thirdly, this book will discuss how these judgments decided not just the issues before them, but also contributed towards shaping a 'constitutional common sense' (a term explained below) in favour of the centralizing drift. This 'constitutional common sense' goes beyond specific legal issues and pertains to broader questions about the organization of power under the Constitution.

Fourthly, the very fact that the constitutional text is a terrain of contestation, and that the cases we will study presented the judiciary with a choice, indicates that the centralizing drift is not inevitable.[46] This book will also, therefore, engage in a critique of these inflection-point judgments, and gesture towards a path that could have been taken, but was not. Further, in some of the themes under discussion, the judiciary has not—or not yet—explicitly endorsed the centralizing drift. In those cases, the alternative path remains not yet entirely foreclosed.

Fifthly, in the Epilogue to this book, I will advance some tentative conclusions about how the centralizing drift serves to impede the Constitution's progressive vision. As Gargarella has correctly pointed out, there is no necessary *conceptual* connection between centralization of power and (for example) the protection of rights. In theory, a powerful central executive may indeed be an effective guarantor of rights.[47] In fact, in the Indian context, as Khosla notes, there was a clear line of constitutional thinking that sought to strengthen the powers of the central executive in order to free individuals from *local* patterns and institutions of dominance.[48] At the same time, the lessons of history demonstrate that a greater and greater concentration of power in a single entity or office is invariably a threat to the meaningful exercise of individual freedom, or of social transformation. This is especially true when we look at how the centralizing drifts along various axes of power reinforce and entrench each other, creating a structure of power that becomes, in essence, unaccountable. The final chapter will be dedicated to highlighting some of these overlaps, and their consequences for the future of Indian constitutionalism.

IV. Four Themes

In the course of this book, we will examine the Indian Constitution as a 'power map'. The journey will take us through different parts of the Constitution, through judicial decisions across decades, and through different phases of constitutional history. There are, however, a few recurring themes that run through the story. While their full exploration will unfold through the course of the succeeding chapters, I will here spell out some of their contours.

The first theme is that of *colonial continuity*. There is a long-standing debate, briefly discussed in the first section of this chapter, about whether, and the extent to which, the Indian Constitution marked an active break with the colonial period.[49] This is a question that any account of the nature of the Indian Constitution must grapple with. This book is no exception. Our study, however, will focus on colonial constitutionalism from the perspective of the organization of power, and interrogate the similarities and differences when compared to the Indian Constitution's approach to power. In the process, we will see that certain constitutional provisions and themes, that do not often feature in the 'colonial continuity' debate, will come to the forefront. In certain other contexts, we may be prompted to reconsider our intuitions about the relationship between British colonial constitutionalism and Indian post-colonial constitutionalism.

The second related theme is that of the 'Frankenconstitution'. Around a decade ago, Kim Lane Scheppele used the memorable term 'Frankenstate' to describe constitutional orders where different provisions—individually reasonable when taken by themselves—were nonetheless 'stitched together' to create a monster.[50] The idea of the Frankenstate—or, in our case, the Frankenconstitution—will help to illuminate some of the more obscure latitudes of the Constitution's power map. As we shall also see, in many cases, colonial constitutionalism and the Frankenconstitution are two sides of the same coin. It is colonial constitutionalism that first introduced distortions, which post-colonial constitutionalism subsequently adopted—and often—evolved.

The third theme is that of a *constitutional common sense* (briefly flagged above), or what recent scholarship refers to as a 'constitutional culture'[51] or 'constitutional imaginary'.[52] By 'constitutional common sense', I mean a set of assumptions, beliefs, and ideas[53], widely shared and internalized among the community of judges, legislators, administrators, civil servants, and lawyers, about how the Indian Constitution does, and *should*, organize power.[54] It is precisely because constitutional common sense is internalized that it is rarely articulated[55], but it frequently constitutes an 'inarticulate major premise' of a judicial opinion.[56] Indeed, often, its impact lies not simply in how it shapes adjudication but further upstream: constitutional lawyers tend to refrain from even placing certain arguments before the court, regardless of their conceptual soundness, based on a mutual—and unspoken—understanding that those arguments lie outside the domain of 'constitutional common sense'.[57] For these reasons, the *identification* of constitutional common sense often requires a degree of intellectual excavation. One of the tasks of this book will be to attempt this excavation through a close reading of judicial opinions, sprinkled with a dose of the practitioner's standpoint.[58]

The final theme is that of the relationship between *constitutional law and politics*. The focus of this book is on the text, structure, and design of the Indian Constitution, its history, and its interpretation by the courts. How this relates to politics is a matter of some debate. While I will flesh out the relationship in greater detail in the succeeding chapters, here I want to limit myself to what will (hopefully) be an uncontroversial claim: constitutional law does not determine or exhaust the domain of politics, but it's not irrelevant to it either. The design and interpretation of the Constitution shapes and influences politics, in that it *facilitates* certain exercises of political power and *constrains* others. And the relationship is mutual: political actors (the legislature and the executive, among others) advance their own understanding of the Constitution, and political action (especially when it is long-lasting and unchallenged) affects constitutional law and interpretation.[59] Constitutional law and politics thus act upon each other in an ongoing and iterative process. The shape of that process is often influenced by the relative strengths of various actors (the judiciary, the executive, the legislature, fourth-branch institutions, and so on). While this account may appear almost truistic in its abstraction, I will attempt to flesh it out in more detail in the succeeding chapters.

V. Conclusion

I began this chapter with a set of constitutional struggles that took place between 2019–24. The promises and perils of immediacy aside, the reason for flagging these struggles should now be clear. Their role in this book is not to serve as the bases for a critique of executive-judiciary relations in the recent past. Rather, it is to help illuminate the deep structures of the Constitution. The task of this book to critically interrogate the Constitution itself, in how it organizes and distributes power, and not its interpretation by one set of judges, or its use/abuse by one executive. Therefore, it is important to note that my starting point is not that of a veneration of the Constitution, nor one that sets up a dichotomy between the Constitution on the one hand, and its interpretation/abuse on the other. My starting point, rather, is to chart a course through the Constitution's power map, and to attain a better understanding of the Indian Constitution as a conversation with power.

1

Power Decentralized: Federalism

IN DECEMBER 2023, THE state of Kerala took the Union of India to court. In a suit filed before the Supreme Court, Kerala challenged the Union's decision to impose a 'net borrowing ceiling', which set a cap upon the amount that the state could borrow from its consolidated fund. This cap was 3 per cent of Kerala's gross domestic product for 2023/2024. The state argued that the net borrowing ceiling encroached upon its freedom to balance its own budget and would have a devastating effect upon its ability to carry out a range of economic functions, from paying its employees to implementing social welfare schemes. In essence—although Kerala did not say it in so many words—the Union was using a net borrowing ceiling to enforce fiscal austerity and usurp the state's autonomy in determining its budgetary priorities.

Debates around budget cuts and government borrowing are familiar to observers of contemporary political economy. In *State of Kerala vs Union of India*, this debate was constitutionalized.[1] Kerala's case turned upon a little-discussed article of the Indian Constitution: Article 293, which sets out the fiscal relationship between the

Union and the states when it comes to government borrowing.[2] Article 293, Kerala argued, when interpreted in accordance with the Constitution's federal scheme, did not permit the Union to impose the net borrowing ceiling in the manner that it did.[3] The Union of India argued, on the other hand, that its obligations to manage national public finance and the 'fiscal health' of the country authorized it to oversee, and set limits upon, the debts incurred by state governments.[4]

A technical legal dispute around the interpretation of Article 293 thus masked a deeper disagreement about the architecture and design of the Indian Constitution—in particular, its federal structure. It was a disagreement about the extent of *power* that the Constitution granted to one constituent unit of the federation (the Union) to oversee and control the economic and fiscal policies of the other (the states). A two-judge bench of the Supreme Court recognized this when it noted that the case raised important constitutional questions about fiscal decentralization, debt management, and the role of states in shaping national economic policy.[5] As Article 293 had never been authoritatively interpreted before, the two judges referred the case to a larger bench for adjudication.[6] Even as they did so, however, the judges declined to grant Kerala substantive interim relief. Among other reasons, they found themselves prima facie convinced by the Union's arguments that 'there would be grave consequences for the fiscal health of the country' if Kerala was allowed to continue borrowing until the case was decided.[7] If, on the other hand, the state eventually prevailed, it could pay its dues at a later date, with any extra financial burden being passed on to the Union.[8]

The Supreme Court insisted that its order was not an adjudication on the merits of the case, but only a prima facie consideration of the issues.[9] Yet that is precisely what is telling: the Court's instinctive move to privilege the Union's claims to stewardship of the national economy, over the state's claims to fiscal autonomy reveals a *baseline assumption*—'constitutional common sense' —in Indian constitutional jurisprudence about what the federal structure is for, and of the roles played by the Union and the states within that structure. It is this constitutional common sense—which often translates into an unexamined, almost reflective approach to constitutional interpretation—that will be the subject of our discussion in this chapter.

Article 1 of the Constitution stipulates that 'India, that is Bharat, shall be a Union of States'.[10] The text of the Constitution's opening provision thus sets out the two primary constituents of the republic: the Union and the states. A significant part of the Constitution is concerned with the division of powers between the Union and the states: legislative power, executive power, administrative power, and (as we have just seen) financial power.

The shape and form of this division of power has been contested throughout independent India's history, right up until the December 2023 dispute between the state of Kerala and the Union of India. Indeed, in the decades immediately after Independence, much of constitutional law was shaped through tussles between the Union and the states over clashing exercises of power and authority. And, as we have just seen, much of constitutional law continues to be shaped in that context. A study of the Indian federal structure—as it has evolved over time—is therefore essential to understand one crucial way in which the Constitution organizes public power.

A complete study of federalism under the Indian Constitution is the task of several volumes.[11] In this chapter, I will confine myself to examining certain issues that speak to the broader themes of this book, concerning the Constitution as a contested terrain of power. I will begin with a look at some of the constitutional provisions at the heart of India's federal design and examine the popular claim that the Indian Constitution is 'quasi-federal', with a 'central' bias. I will argue that as an interpretive matter, this central bias—to the extent that it exists—offers up two possible readings of Indian federalism: a centralizing reading and a federalizing reading **(I)**.[12]

I will then consider an early Supreme Court judgment that in my view constitutes an 'inflection point' in the evolution of

Indian federalism: *State of West Bengal vs Union of India*. In *State of West Bengal vs Union of India*, the Supreme Court endorsed the centralizing reading of the Constitution. This reading—I shall argue—proceeded upon a set of contested premises, but has been crystallized and entrenched by the Court's jurisprudence in the years following the judgment, contributing to federalism being one of the sites where the 'centralizing drift' discussed earlier in the Prologue is most pronounced **(II)**.

This 'centralizing drift' infects multiple parts of the Constitution. In the third section of this chapter, I shall demonstrate how it was at the heart of the series of controversial constitutional measures that were utilized to 'amend' Article 370 of the Indian Constitution in 2019, remove the autonomy of the state of Jammu and Kashmir, and downgrade its status to a union territory. In my analysis of the 'Article 370 Case', I will also show how the alternative understanding of Indian federalism, advanced by Justice Subba Rao's dissenting opinion in *State of West Bengal vs Union of India*, could have been applied to a concrete constitutional dispute, with very different consequences **(III)**.

In the concluding section, I will flag a range of other disputes (apart from the fiscal dispute discussed above) where the contest between the centralizing and the federalizing readings of the Constitution continues to play out, and continues to contribute to the Constitution's overall centralizing drift. While decades of encrusted jurisprudence have relegated the federalizing interpretation to the margins of interpretation, its existence continues to light the way to a future that was once possible, and might—with the passage of time—become possible once again **(IV)**.

A final caveat: as is true for all the axes of power discussed in this book, the terrain of the Constitution is not exhaustive of the question of power. There is the domain of politics, about which the Constitution often has very little, if anything, to say. In the case of federalism, in particular, the relationship between the Centre and the states has depended at least as much on the prevailing political balance of power at any given time, rather than the constitutional text and constitutional interpretation. Indeed, the latter has often followed the former.[13] At the same time, however, as we discussed in the Prologue, the constitutional terrain *is* important, in that it facilitates the exercise of certain forms of power and throws up barriers or roadblocks for others. The Constitution and politics, therefore, are in conversation, even when the latter underdetermines the former.

With this in mind, let us turn to the specifics.

I. Words and Silences: Federalism and the Text of the Constitution

Let us begin with the constitutional text. As enacted, the Constitution contemplates a federal structure of governance, existing at two levels: the Centre ('Union') and the several states ('provinces', before Independence). In the 1990s, the 73rd and 74th amendments to the Constitution added a 'third tier' of governance—at the level of the district or the 'panchayat', and the urban municipality—which, nonetheless, in important and material respects, remains under the control of the states.[14]

Having set out the two constituent levels of governance, the Constitution then proceeds to distribute power between them through a model that largely follows the colonial Government of India Act of 1935.[15] The Union and the states are allocated legislative power: under Schedule VII, three lists set out the areas or 'fields' under which the Union and the states are exclusively or jointly competent to legislate. The Constitution also stipulates that the executive power enjoyed by the Union and the states is co-extensive with their legislative power. Financially, the Constitution allocates different sources of revenue, from which the Union and the states can raise money through taxation.[16] Lastly, when it comes to administration, the Constitution grants to both the Union and the states control over their respective civil services.[17]

This distribution of power is not, however, symmetric. In many fields, the Constitution skews the balance of power towards the

Union. The following provisions—all of which have been analysed in some detail in existing literature—set out the nature of the skew. The Union Parliament can destroy and create states, as well as alter their boundaries (Article 3); while legislative power is divided between the Union and the states, residuary power lies with the Union (Entry 97, List I, Schedule VII); in cases of the exercise of concurrent legislative power, Union laws receive primacy wherever there is conflict (Article 254); major bases of taxation (such as income tax, taxes on non-agricultural property and so on) are assigned to the Union, and—to compound the situation—the borrowing and fiscal powers of states are constrained by the Union, especially in cases of outstanding debt (Article 293);[18] the titular (albeit with a degree of discretionary power) executive heads of states (governors) are appointed by the Union (Article 155); and state governments can be dismissed by the Union on the ground that constitutional machinery in a state has broken down (Article 356).[19]

I will not here dwell at length upon the specific character of these provisions because, as I have noted above, there already exists a substantial volume of literature that deals with them.[20] It suffices here to say that these provisions were the result of conscious design on the part of the framers of the Constitution. For different reasons, both Jawaharlal Nehru and Dr B.R. Ambedkar expressed their preferences for a 'strong central authority'.[21] The Constituent Assembly's Union Powers Committee (which was chaired by Nehru) set out internal peacekeeping, economic coordination at scale, and international relations as the reasons why it was desirable for the Constitution to depart from the more federal structure that had been proposed by the earlier Cabinet Mission Plan.[22] In addition, scholars have pointed to various complementary reasons for the federal 'bias' of the Constitution, from the Independence-era need to construct a national political economy[23], to concern for the well-being of minorities under state governments more prone to capture by entrenched local power[24], to fears of secession and the accompanying desire for a national citizenship.[25]

All of this is an *explanation* for the federal structure—complete with skew—as it exists within the Indian Constitution. But what I want to focus on here is the *consequence* of the Constitution's skew towards the Union. Because, while the reasons for the skew are reflected in the provisions outlined above, where in certain domains state power is evidently subordinate to Union power, neither they nor the provisions themselves are exhaustive of the full gamut of power relations between the Union and the states. As we shall see later in this chapter, the Constitution inevitably contains numerous gaps and silences that have been and continue to be terrains of contestation between Union power and state power. Nor do the reasons for the skew amount to an interpretive approach for how these power relations *should* be understood in the absence of an explicit provision (as we shall see, this was the debate in *State of West Bengal vs Union of India*).

Thus, a profusion of terminology, especially beloved of scholars and courts—that India is a federation with a unitary 'bias', or a 'quasi-federation'—ultimately obscures more than it reveals.[26] To the extent that it indicates the existence of provisions explicitly in the Constitution, it is rather banal. To the extent that it indicates how the relationship between the Union and the states *should* be understood in other cases, it says nothing at all. Indeed, and on the face of it, the Constitution's federal skew presents us with two at least equally plausible approaches to interpretation.

On the one hand, one could argue that the Constitution's overall design indicates a preference towards a 'strong' Centre. Consequently, when in doubt, constitutional provisions should be interpreted in a way that *preserves* the Union's powers, rather than taking them away (and vesting them in the state).

But equally, one could argue with as much plausibility that the 'skew' in favour of the Union demonstrates that where the Constitution intended to depart from symmetric distribution of power in favour of the Union, it has done so explicitly. Consequently, in all other cases—cases involving interpretive gaps and silences—constitutional provisions should be read so as to preserve the Constitution's federal character (i.e., in favour of state power).

Let us call these two approaches the centralizing and the federalizing approach. The history of constitutional federalism in India has been a contest between the centralizing and federalizing approaches. In the next section, we shall study one judgment that marked an 'inflection point' in the history of this contest: *State of West Bengal vs Union of India.* Here, the Supreme Court implicitly endorsed the centralizing approach—the approach that remains dominant to this day.[27]

II. State of West Bengal vs Union of India

A. The Majority Judgment

In 1957, Parliament passed a law called the Coal Bearing Areas Act of 1957. Under the framework of the act, the central government issued notifications intending to acquire land, which was held by the state of West Bengal, for coal prospecting and mining. The state government approached the Supreme Court, challenging both the law and the notifications. Its primary argument was that Parliament lacked the constitutional power to acquire state property.

The key issue was the interpretation of Entry 42 of List III of Schedule VII of the Indian Constitution. Put simply, Schedule VII sets out the 'fields' under which the respective legislatures—Union and state—are competent to pass laws.[28] Fields under List I are within the exclusive competence of the Union legislature. Fields under List II are within the exclusive competence of state legislatures. List III is the Concurrent List, where both the Union and the state legislatures possess the competence to enact laws (with Union law prevailing in case of a conflict).

Entry 42 of List III—the Concurrent List—was the only plausible field under which the Union legislature could draw its competence. The entry reads: 'acquisitioning and requisitioning of property'.[29] The state of West Bengal argued, however, that Entry 42 ought to be interpreted with an implied exclusion: that is, 'acquisitioning and requisitioning of property *except state property*'.

What was the justification for 'reading in' these additional three words, which were not expressly present in the text of the provision? The state of West Bengal advanced many arguments. For the purposes of this chapter, one argument is particularly important: that the concept of federalism implies that within their respective spheres—as assigned by the Constitution—the Union and the states are sovereign entities, and that one sovereign cannot forcibly acquire the property of another sovereign.

The case was heard by a six-judge bench of the Indian Supreme Court. In view of the importance of the issue for the federal structure, the Court invited all the states of India to make submissions (many of them did). Eventually, by a majority of five to one, the Court upheld the constitutional validity of the law, and rejected the state of West Bengal's arguments.

The majority of the Supreme Court arrived at this conclusion by examining the history of Indian federalism, and then drawing out certain constitutional consequences from that history. The administration of British India, it noted, had been 'unitary and highly centralized'.[30] There was a gradual process of devolution that began with constitutional reforms in 1919. Later, under the 1935 Government of India Act, provincial governments (elected on limited franchise) controlled certain fields of administration (with the writ of the governor-general—the agent of the crown—nonetheless remaining supreme). Finally, at the time of Independence:

> ....the Constitution ... was erected on the foundations of the Government of India Act, 1935 ... [while] in some respects a greater degree of economic unity was sought to be secured by transferring subjects having impact on matters of common interest into the Union List ... particularly in the field of economic unity.[31]

What implications did the majority draw from this schematic history? First, it observed that 'the result was a Constitution which was not true to any *traditional* pattern of federation'.[32] By 'traditional', the Supreme Court appeared to imply federalism, US-style, where a number of independent states had voluntarily come together and ceded a part of their sovereignty to form a federation. According to the Court, this was the 'truly federal form of government'.[33] In contrast, the Indian situation involved 'the withdrawal or resumption of all the powers of sovereignty into the people of this country and the [subsequent] distribution of these powers', between the Union and the states.[34] This was reflected in the fact that states had no constitutions of their own, had no power to alter the Indian Constitution, and—particularly important, according to the Supreme Court—the distribution of powers between the Union and the states was weighed in favour of the Union. To substantiate this, the Court set out the several provisions that we have alluded to above, which demonstrated the centralizing 'skew' of the Constitution. For these reasons, the majority concluded:

> That being the extent of the power of the Parliament it would be difficult to hold that the Parliament which is competent to destroy a State is on account of some assumption as to absolute sovereignty of the State incompetent effectively to acquire by legislation designed for that purpose the property owned by the State for governmental purpose. The parliamentary power of legislation to acquire property is, subject to the express provisions of the Constitution, unrestricted. To imply limitations on that power on the assumption of that degree of political sovereignty which makes the States coordinate with and independent of the Union, is to envisage a Constitutional scheme which does not exist in law or in practice. On a review of the diverse provisions of the Constitution the inference is inevitable that the distribution of powers-both legislative and executive-does not support the theory of full sovereignty in the States so as to render it immune from the exercise of legislative power of the Union Parliament-particularly in relation to acquisition of property of the States.[35]

Thus, because the Court could find no 'positive interdict' against the Union legislating to take away state property, and because an 'implied interdict' flowing from state sovereignty as a necessary consequence of federalism had already been rejected, the state of West Bengal's arguments were turned down, and the law upheld.[36]

A close reading of the majority judgment in *State of West Bengal vs Union of India* reveals that the Supreme Court synthesized the structure of the Constitution, and a particular historical story about its origins, into a legal conclusion. The historical story was that modern India had always been a unitary state, with devolution of power to provinces being exceptional rather than the norm. The structural account was that multiple provisions of the Constitution encoded Union supremacy in legislative, executive, administrative, and financial domains. The legal conclusion that the Court drew from this—as a matter of course—was that any interpretive dispute between the Union and the states, on a question of power, was to be resolved in favour of the Union. This, in essence, is what I call the *centralizing approach to Indian federalism.*

B. The Centralizing Approach in Indian Constitutional Jurisprudence

State of West Bengal vs Union of India was not the first articulation of the centralizing approach to Indian federalism. Three years before, in *Babulal Parate vs State of Bombay*, the Supreme Court held that if a proposal for altering state boundaries under Article 3 was substantially amended by the Union Parliament, after consultation with the state legislature, there was no constitutional obligation upon the former for further consultation with the latter—no matter how substantial (or even radical) the amendment was.[37] The Court specifically rejected an argument—drawn from democratic theory—that substantial alterations to Article 3 proposals should not be implemented before a state's elected representatives were given an opportunity to express their views on them.[38]

While the Court purported to limit its interpretation to a strict, textual reading of Article 3, assumptions about Indian federalism were, however, never far from the surface. In language strikingly similar to what the *State of West Bengal vs Union of India* majority would use, the Court noted that the 'Indian Union' as a sovereign and independent entity preceded the states, that that it was 'significant' that Article 3 alterations to state boundaries did not need to go through the (stricter) constitutional amendment procedure.[39] We have noted above that these seemingly uncontroversial factual assertions nonetheless smuggle in a range of normative assumptions into the enquiry, where the Constitution's existing 'skew' in favour of the Union is taken as a justification for interpreting silences and ambiguities in favour *of* the Union.

This same centralizing approach—that was the basis of the judgments in both *Babulal Parate* and *State of West Bengal vs Union of India*—has since informed the Court's jurisprudence on a range of issues.[40] A complete analysis would need the space of a full book,[41] but we can here take a few illustrative examples, from a range of domains.

i. Federalism and Article 3

The Mullaperiyar dam is the site of a long-running dispute between the states of Kerala and Tamil Nadu. It is situated within the state of Kerala, but electricity from the dam is generated and used by the state of Tamil Nadu. In 2006, the dispute between the two states came to a head before the Supreme Court, when Kerala's refusal to allow the raising of the dam's water level from 136 feet to 142 feet—following a recommendation of the Central Water Commission (a body under the aegis of the Union water ministry)—was at issue.[42] The state of Tamil Nadu relied upon an 1886 agreement between the state of Travancore (Kerala's predecessor state) and the then-colonial government, read alongside Section 108 of the States Reorganisation Act of 1956, which had created the state of Kerala. Section 108—put simply—stipulated that the agreements between predecessor states and the central government pertaining to 'irrigation, power, or multi-purpose projects' would remain in force by default.[43] The state of Kerala argued that Section 108 was unconstitutional to the extent that it deprived state legislatures from legislating on water, which fell under List II of Schedule VII, and therefore, came within state legislative competence.

The question before the Supreme Court was this: when the Union legislature exercised its powers to create new states and reorganize existing state boundaries under Article 3 of the Constitution, to what extent—if any—could it stipulate or constrain future legislative action by those new and modified states? Under Article 4 of the Constitution, a state reorganization law under Article 3 could also contain 'such supplemental, incidental, and consequential provisions … as Parliament may deem necessary'[44] and no such law would be deemed to be an 'amendment' of the Constitution under Article 368.[45] Seizing upon this combined reading of Articles 3 and 4, the Court held that a composite law—such as the States Reorganisation Act—was an exercise of 'paramount' and 'supreme' power by the Union legislature, and was therefore 'unfettered' by questions of legislative competence and the division of powers under Schedule VII. Thus, to the extent that stipulating the continuance of prior agreements was 'incidental' or 'consequential' to the reorganization of states, the law was valid even if it covered fields that were otherwise squarely under List II of Schedule VII.

From where did the Court get this idea of 'paramount' or 'supreme' power—phrases that seem particularly jarring in the context of a constitutional democracy? We do not know, but it is notable that the Constitution itself prescribes no hierarchy between Articles 3 and 4 on the one hand, and Article 246 on the other. There is nothing in the text of the Constitution that grants state reorganization laws a status superior to that of ordinary laws when it comes to respecting the division of powers between the Union and the states. The Court tried to get around this by observing that because the state of Kerala owed its own existence to the State Reorganisation Act of 1956, 'it would be incongruous to say that the provision in an Act which gives birth to a State is *ultra vires* a legislative entry which the State may operate after it has come into existence'.[46] This is patently illogical: it means that those states that existed at the time of the framing of the original Constitution have the full protection of the federal scheme, while states that were formed later do not—with no intelligible difference between the two categories.

The Court's finding, however, betrays a deeper set of assumptions. As we have seen before, while a federal polity may be skewed one way or another, what ultimately matters is that *within* their constitutionally defined domains, the central and federal units are sovereign. Therefore, the fact—that under Articles 3 and 4 the Union legislature has the power to create new states and modify the boundaries of existing states—*should not change the proposition* that whether predecessor or successor, these states at all times retain their constitutionally defined domains of legislative and executive sovereignty, except where expressly denuded of them.

The Court's judgment is thus a classic example of the centralizing drift. It used the existence of a skew towards the Union within the text of the Constitution (i.e., the power of the Union legislature to create or modify states) as a justification for entrenching greater Union power *not* expressly within the text of the Constitution (i.e., the accompanying power to dictate or constrain the legislative power of new states even under List II). The Court could just as easily have noted, for example, that while the Union legislature undoubtedly had the power under Article 3 to create new states, that power was, in turn, limited: the power to create a new state could not extend to overriding the federal scheme, and imposing a prior constraint upon how that new state—once created—could exercise its legislative power.[47]

ii. Federalism and human rights

In 1997, in *Naga People's Movement of Human Rights vs Union of India*, the Supreme Court upheld the constitutional validity of the Armed Forces (Special Powers) Act (AFSPA), a law that empowers the Union government to grant certain 'special powers' to the armed forces in declared 'disturbed areas'.[48] These special powers include shoot-to-kill authorization with respect to anyone acting in contravention of certain laws (including laws prohibiting assembly), arresting and searching premises without warrants, destroying property, and immunity from prosecution.

The AFSPA judgment is remembered primarily for the Supreme Court's vindication of armed forces' impunity, but it is also worth remembering that one of the grounds of challenge to the law was that of federalism: namely, that 'public order' was a state subject, and that AFSPA was, in essence, a law enacted for the maintenance of public order (by using the armed forces to do so).[49] It was argued by counsel challenging AFSPA that while Entry 2A of List I of Schedule VII authorized the Union to legislate on the deployment of armed forces 'in aid' of civilian authority, principles of federalism required that the phrase 'in aid' be understood as a referring to a situation where the armed forces were deployed at the state's request, and under its supervision and control.

The Supreme Court rejected this interpretation. It stated that Entry 2A contemplated a situation where the central armed forces and the state civilian authority would work in 'cooperation'.[50] The Court saw evidence of this cooperation in the fact that the shoot-to-kill authorization was only triggered upon a prohibitory order issued by the state's civilian authorities, and that the various other powers conferred by AFSPA still left a residue of public order functions in the hands of the state.[51] This is an odd interpretation of 'cooperation', but an even odder interpretation of 'in aid of'. One wonders if A can truly be said to be 'aiding' B if A unilaterally decides when aid is required, and what kind of aid is required.[52]

The Supreme Court tried to palliate its reading by noting that it would be 'desirable' for the state government to be 'consulted' before the central government exercised its powers to declare an area a 'disturbed area', thus triggering the application of AFSPA.[53] In other words, having upheld the grant of an overriding power to the central government that severely undermined the federal scheme, the Court satisfied itself with exhorting the government to use it responsibly. The Court's observations are representative of a theme that we shall come across repeatedly in this book: when asked whether the Constitution ought to be interpreted in a way that upholds or entrenches extraordinary power, instead of confronting the question squarely, the Court suggests or hopes that the power holder will exercise that power correctly. In other words, instead of grappling with how the Constitution's power map might be reconciled with the Constitution's overarching principles, the Court takes extraordinary executive power as a given, and sees its role as providing non-binding advice about how the power holder might consider using it.

Indeed, and to no one's surprise, the Court's pious expression of 'desirability' has not been borne out in practice. This is amply demonstrated by the history of AFSPA—where, notwithstanding requests by state governments, the central government has refused to remove the law. More importantly for the purposes of this chapter, *Naga People's Movement of Human Rights vs Union of India* also illustrates the close connection between federalism and civil rights under Part III of the Constitution. The unilateral power of the Union executive to deploy armed forces within state borders—as opposed to placing this decision in the hands of more directly responsive state governments—has contributed to a situation of impunity and widespread rights violations over many decades.[54]

iii. Federalism and legislative relations

The interplay between the entries in the separate lists has also been at the heart of another contentious federal issue: the legislative relationship between the Centre and the states. Consider, for example, the judgment of a Constitution Bench of the Supreme Court in *I.T.C. Limited vs The Agricultural Produce Market Committee*.[55] The dispute arose over the clashing claims of the Centre and the state to raise revenue from the production and sale of tobacco. Purportedly acting under the authority of Entry 52 of List I—which allows the Union Parliament to legislate on 'industries, the control of which by the Union is declared by Parliament by law to be expedient in the public interest'—Parliament passed the Tobacco Board Act of 1975.[56] This law appeared to clash with the Agricultural Produce

Market Act passed by several states, according to which state governments could levy a market fee upon the purchase and sale of tobacco (which had been classified as 'agricultural produce'). These laws had, in turn, been passed under the authority of Entries 26–28 of List II, which authorized state legislatures to enact legislation on trade and commerce, production, supply and distribution of goods, and markets and fairs.[57]

Counsel for the states argued that the principles of federalism required the Court to give a narrow meaning to the word 'industry' in Entry 52, so that it excluded, for example, the growing and production of agricultural produce, such as raw tobacco. This—it was pointed out—was necessary for Entries 26–28 to retain any meaning. Any other alternative would allow the Union Parliament, under Entry 52, to take over vast swathes of legislation, and the power of raising of revenue, which ordinarily belonged to the states.

The Supreme Court responded by splitting the enquiry into two parts: first, to examine, as a standalone constitutional question, whether the Union Parliament possessed the legislative competence under Entry 52 of List I to pass the Tobacco Board Act; and secondly, if the answer to the first question was 'yes', then whether there was an irreconcilable clash between the Tobacco Board Act and the Agricultural Produce Market Act ('repugnance'), which necessitated the state law giving way to the Union law.[58]

On the first question, the Court held that the established doctrine of interpretation was that entries in the Lists had to be given their 'widest amplitude', and not a narrow or restricted meaning.[59] Upon this reading, the term 'industry' was to be given a broad meaning, which would include the growing and production of 'agricultural produce' as well.[60] Responding to the objection that this would denude the powers of states under List II, the Court held that the argument was not relevant to the question of how to *interpret* the entries in the Lists, but would be considered when looking at whether both the central and the state laws could coexist (the second stage of analysis, or the question of 'repugnance'). In this case, the Court found that because the central and the state laws were directly contradictory, the state law had to yield.[61]

However, if you look a little deeper, this seemingly innocuous 'splitting' of the question bears within it the assumptions of the centralizing approach to federalism. When the Court stated that entries in the legislative lists had to be given a broad meaning, that necessarily increased the scope of overlap between central and state laws rather than reducing it. And in cases of overlap, the Constitution skews towards the Centre by privileging the Union law over the state law. Thus, by the very act of separating the analysis into two phases—and in the first phase, by enunciating the seemingly neutral doctrine that entries in the List must be given a wide and liberal interpretation—the Court entrenched the centralizing approach within the field of legislative relations.

It is important to note that the doctrine that entries in a legislative list ought to be interpreted broadly and liberally makes sense in the case of a unitary Constitution, where a narrow reading would denude the representative body of law-making power altogether. However, in a federal Constitution, where power is divided between the Centre and the states, and where the skew favours the Centre in cases of conflict, the same doctrine turns into a *normative approach that further entrenches the existing central skew*. This is in stark contrast to the federalizing approach that was suggested by counsel for the state: namely, that the reconciliation should not be left to the second stage—where the central and state *laws* are considered, but at the first stage, where the scope of the legislative *entries* is considered.[62]

We can therefore see how, in the very selection of interpretive doctrine towards the legislative lists, the Supreme Court made a clear (if somewhat disguised) choice between the centralizing and federalizing approaches to Indian federalism.[63]

iv. Federalism and revenue

As we have seen at the beginning of this chapter, when considering the dispute between the state of Kerala and the Union of India, the central 'skew' in the constitutional scheme extends to the means and methods of raising revenue (a skew that has recently been further entrenched through the 101st Constitutional Amendment, which introduced the General Sales Tax, or the GST).[64] This means that the Union will always have substantially more money than the states, necessitating a procedure for redistribution (or financial transfers) between the Union and the states.

In a federal relationship, it is inevitable that a significant disparity in finances—accompanied by discretion vested in the more powerful party to decide how to transfer those finances—will perpetuate and entrench a significant disparity in political power.[65] Indeed, in certain postcolonial countries such as Kenya, control over finances was the first step towards a dismantling of the federal structure and the effective establishment of a unitary State.[66] For this reason, Article 280 of the Constitution contemplates the existence of a (theoretically) independent Finance Commission, the task of which is to lay out the inter se allocation of tax revenue between the Centre and the states, and also the principles that will determine Centre–state financial transfers.[67]

The Finance Commission has had a chequered history, partially because even as it is supposed to be independent, it is nonetheless the (Union) Parliament that is responsible for deciding the qualifications of members and their process of selection.[68] More than that, however, right from the inception of the Constitution, its role as the body tasked with determining the principles governing Centre–state transfers was undermined through the parallel existence of the Planning Commission, a non-constitutional body under the control of the Union cabinet.[69] The constitutionality of Centre–state transfers, made on a discretionary basis outside of the Finance Commission, was always controversial. In *Bhim Singh vs Union of India,* these came to be challenged before the Supreme Court.[70]

The case concerned the constitutionality of the Members of Parliament Local Area Development Scheme (MPLADS)—a scheme through which members of Parliament are granted Union funds for developmental work in their constituencies. While this judgment is often studied under the theme of the separation of powers, there was a strong federal component to it as well, outlined below.

One key ground of challenge was that discretionary Centre–state transfers outside the scope of Article 280 were unconstitutional.[71] On the other hand, the Union contended that MPLADS was valid by virtue of Article 282 of the Constitution, which authorizes 'the Union or a State [to] make any grants for any public purpose'.[72] In response to this, it was argued that Article 282 was an emergency provision that could be invoked in order to meet unforeseen, one-time exigencies, but could not be used to validate regular Union–state financial transfers. This argument was supported by reference to the Constitution's structure—Article 282 came under a heading titled 'miscellaneous provisions'—but also on the basis that the 'fiscal equilibrium' maintained by the Constitution would be distorted through discretionary fiscal transfers that sidestepped the Finance Commission.[73]

The Supreme Court rejected this argument, and held that Article 282 did indeed validate MPLADS. Its reasoning was more or less a mirror version of *State of West Bengal vs Union of India*: i.e., that India was not 'strictly federal' but 'quasi-federal', and that the Union had extensive powers over the states. The Court then echoed the reasoning of the *I.T.C Ltd. vs The Agricultural Produce Market Committee* line of judgments, by noting that 'every Article of the Constitution has to be given its widest meaning'.[74] On this basis, the Court held that as long as it was for a 'public purpose'—which was also to be interpreted broadly—a Centre–state transfer would fall within the scope of Article 282.[75]

Once again, however, we see that a seemingly neutral doctrine—that of giving constitutional provisions their broadest possible meaning—is anything but neutral in the context of federalism. This is because, as we have discussed, the existing constitutional scheme creates a more powerful Union and weaker states—including in the domain of raising revenue. In this situation of unequal power, a purely discretionary right granted to the Union to decide upon financial transfers to the states perpetuates and entrenches the more powerful position that the Union already enjoys.[76] Article 280 and the Finance Commission—in theory—is designed to mitigate this imbalance of power by constraining this discretion, and evolving principles that are not immediately reducible to the domain of partisan politics (which will be dominated by the Union). Thus, the effect of the Supreme Court's judgment in *Bhim Singh vs Union of India* was to legitimize non-Article 280 Union–state transfers, and validate the further entrenching of the power difference by holding that discretionary transfers were alternatives to transfers that had to go through the Finance Commission and Article 280. In this way, in yet another domain, *Bhim Singh vs Union of India* is an example of the Supreme Court's endorsement of the centralizing approach to Indian federalism.

C. The Road Not Taken

We have seen how, in *State of West Bengal vs Union of India*, a majority of the Supreme Court adopted the centralizing approach as a self-evident conclusion flowing from history and from the structure of the Constitution.

And yet, was the conclusion quite as self-evident as the majority made it sound? I suggest not.

First, on history. The history of Indian federalism is substantially older and more complex than the majority's straightforward account of a unitary colonial state that engaged in discretionary and incremental devolution to provinces that were created by its own sufferance. As Katharine Adeney notes, in the Indian subcontinent, proto-federalism—in the sense of a division of de facto sovereignty between different territorially defined levels of government—existed well into the Mughal period and beyond.[77] Consequently, both as a function of the State's ability to exercise control over vast swathes of territory, but also as a normative aspect of state-building in India, the existence of 'regional *political* and administrative units, units that might be more or less autonomous, were an abiding aspect of India's political consciousness' (emphasis supplied).[78] This continued during the Company era, where the Presidencies developed 'distinctive regional identities and distinctive approaches to the problems confronting them'.[79]

In British India, representative government—which came into being in a partial fashion with constitutional reforms in 1909—began with responsible provincial legislatures (at the Union level, governance was entirely autocratic).[80] A (limited) Union legislature was birthed many years later,[81] with plans for a federation mooted repeatedly by colonial administrators.[82] With the appearance of responsible provincial legislatures, demands for provincial autonomy too became part of the political lexicon of colonial India, and featured substantively in constitutional debates leading up to the period of Independence.[83]

Indeed, detailed proposals for an all-India Federation—that would include the princely states, which had their own distinctive histories and relationships with the British Empire[84]—were central to the debates around the Round Table Conference in London in 1930–32, though without yielding much in the way of concrete results.[85] The eventual 1935 Government of India Act did enshrine the concept of 'provincial autonomy', albeit with a set of overriding central powers that were to eventually find their way into the Constitution.[86] However, the pre-constitutional existence of independent provincial identity is revealed most tellingly in the fact that in substantial part, the Constituent Assembly was composed of members nominated by provincial legislatures, who spoke as representatives of their provinces.[87]

The Supreme Court's fundamental premise, therefore—that the Indian Constitution was based on the 'legal theory' that all sovereign power was transferred from the British to 'the People' and then 'distributed' between the Union and the states—is too quick and too superficial a reading of the historical record. And its implication—that provincial identity was submerged within a broader unitary identity at the time of the framing—is at best *one* possible inference from a complex historical record. Indeed, as H.M. Seervai notes in his critique of the majority judgment:

> Theoretically, it was possible for our Constituent Assembly to have adopted a unitary Constitution. But the actual working of provincial autonomy in the Provinces of Br. India, where ministries responsible to the Legislature had functioned effectively, made such a step impracticable, because the Provinces would have refused to give up the powers they had enjoyed from 1937 till the Indian Independence Act, 1947.[88]

The same is true for the majority's inference from constitutional structure. I have made this point above, but it bears repeating. The fact that the Constitution has multiple provisions encoding Union supremacy in key domains (what Nirvikar Singh and Govinda Rao call 'escape clause federalism') *does not necessarily* imply that Union supremacy is the norm even where there are no provisions (constitutional silences) or where there is scope for interpretive debate (constitutional ambiguities).[89] Indeed, it could equally well be argued—and would flow from the alternate reading of Indian federal history that I have advanced above—that the very act of expressly setting out those domains in which the Union was meant to prevail actually encoded the *federal principle*: namely that, save as where expressly specified, the Constitution would have to be interpreted in such a way so as to promote the decentralization and federation of power, not its concentration.[90]

The persuasiveness of this reading is evident from an analysis of Justice Subba Rao's dissenting opinion in *State of West Bengal vs Union of India*. Noting that there was no reason why the American experience of federalism should be taken as a global default, Justice Subba Rao observed, alternatively, that:

> ... pre-existing independent States may not be given any appreciable power under a constitution, while newly formed States may enjoy larger power under another constitution. *A federal structure is mainly conceived to harmonize existing conflicting interests and to*

> *provide against future conflicts*. India is a vast country: indeed, it is described as a sub-continent. Historically, before the advent of the Constitution, there were different Provinces enjoying in practice *a fair amount of autonomy and there were innumerable States with varying forms of government ranging from pure autocracy to guided democracy*. There were also differences in language, race, religion etc. There were also foreign pockets expected sooner or later to be incorporated, with the main country. In those circumstances our Constitution adopted a federal structure with a strong bias towards the Centre. Under such a structure, while the Centre remains strong to prevent the development of fissiparous tendencies, the States are made practically autonomous in ordinary times within the spheres allotted to them (emphasis supplied).[91]

This is what I have referred to above as the *federalizing* approach. The federalizing approach is based upon the following historical and normative assumptions that run counter to the assumptions of the majority. First, as a matter of history, a federal structure—and the federal impulse—was a part of Indian constitutional evolution in the run-up to the framing of the Constitution (what Seervai refers to as the existence of a 'federal situation' in India);[92] secondly, the heterogeneity within the Indian Union provides us with a normative reason for supporting and upholding the federal structure; thirdly—and therefore—interpretive disputes within the Constitution's already skewed federal framework are meant to be resolved in favour of expanded state power and limited Union power. Thus, as Justice Subba Rao noted, in words that encapsulate the federalizing approach:

> The Indian Constitution accepts the federal concept and distributes the sovereign powers between the co-ordinate constitutional entitles, namely, the Union and the States. This concept implies that one cannot encroach upon the governmental functions or instrumentalities of the other, unless the Constitution expressly provides for such interference.[93]

As we have seen, however, Justice Subba Rao's approach has not commanded sustained acceptance by the Court. This does not mean that the centralizing approach has held unchallenged dominion either. For example, *S.R. Bommai vs Union of India* is a crucial judgment where a nine-judge bench of the Supreme Court departed from prior precedent and placed substantive limitations upon when the Union could invoke Article 356 of the Constitution and dismiss state governments on the basis that constitutional machinery had broken down in the state. A significant basis of the Court's ruling was respect for the federal structure and the sovereignty of states in their own spheres.[94] It is a documented fact that resort to Article 356 reduced significantly after the *S.R. Bommai* judgment, and on occasion, the Court has restored state governments upon finding that the Union illegally resorted to Article 356.

Another potential counter-example is the judgment of the five-judge bench of the Supreme Court in *NCT of Delhi vs Union of India*, a dispute between the government of Delhi and the Union government over control of various aspects of the governance of the national capital.[95] By a majority judgment, the Supreme Court interpreted Article 239AA of the Constitution—that divided up power between the government of Delhi and the Union government—in a manner that bolstered the federal structure and prevented the subordination of the former to the latter—at least rhetorically.[96] However, the vagueness in the final holding led to its immediate dilution by a smaller bench.[97]

While a few years later, another five-judge bench finally reaffirmed its earlier holding in more categorical terms, its findings were immediately overridden, first by an ordinance and then by a legislative amendment to the Government of the National Capital Territory of Delhi Act, which placed effective power back in the hands of the Union executive—this time through legislation, rather than executive instructions (which had been the subject of challenge in the initial case).[98] At the time of writing, the Supreme Court has declined to rule on whether the amendment violates its previous judgment and whether it is consistent with the federal structure, thus leaving status quo—and Union control—intact.[99] It is, therefore, too early to definitively say whether the *NCT of Delhi vs Union of India* cases represent a true example of the federalizing approach.

These few counter-examples aside, it is safe to say that the centralizing approach has been dominant (albeit not without internal resistance). In the next section, we shall look at the interpretive consequences that follow from this, in the context of one of the starkest federal controversies in recent times.

III. Federalism and Implied Limitations

On 5 August 2019, the central government and the Union Parliament embarked upon a series of constitutional manoeuvres with respect to Article 370 of the Indian Constitution, which guaranteed an enhanced degree of autonomy to the state of Jammu and Kashmir.[100] In the chapter on asymmetric federalism, I shall discuss the case of Jammu and Kashmir at greater length. Here, I want to consider the issue from the perspective of federalism more generally; and, in particular, how the 'centralizing approach' to federalism has effectively deprived Indian constitutional jurisprudence of the conceptual vocabulary to address—and tackle—what was evidently a clear case of abuse of Union power.

Simplifying matters greatly, Article 370 of the Indian Constitution—as it then stood—guaranteed the 'special status' of Jammu and Kashmir. It also aimed to prevent its own evisceration by making the consent of the elected government of Jammu and Kashmir mandatory for any amendment of the terms of the article (and therefore, as a corollary, any change to the relationship between Jammu and Kashmir and the rest of India).[101]

The central government got around this barrier by a simple stratagem. A year and a half before the events of 5 August 2019, the government of Jammu and Kashmir had lost its majority in the legislature and had fallen. Instead of fresh elections being scheduled in short order, what happened, instead, was that the central government had taken over the state through the imposition of President's Rule under Article 356 of the Constitution (meant, as we have seen, for situations where a state's constitutional machinery breaks down).[102] As long as Article 356 is in operation, a state's government *is* the central government (acting through the President). Thus, as the state of Jammu and Kashmir was under President's Rule, the central government interpreted the term 'government of Jammu and Kashmir' in Article 370 to mean itself. Thereupon, it took its *own* consent, and amended Article 370 to remove the formal autonomy enjoyed by the state.

Once that was achieved, the scene shifted to the Union Parliament, where the government had a brute majority. Parliament passed a law that stripped Jammu and Kashmir of statehood, and turned it into a union territory (i.e., territories within India that—to various degrees—are directly controlled by the central government).[103] In doing so, Parliament purported to act under Article 3 of the Constitution that—as we have seen—authorizes Parliament to create and extinguish states, or alter their boundaries, subject only to consultation with the legislature of the affected state.[104]

The events of 5 August 2019, therefore, raised two stark federal questions. The first was whether Article 356 of the Constitution imposed any limits upon what the Centre could do to a state while it was acting as a—supposedly temporary—stand-in for the elected state government. And the second was whether, acting under Article 3, the Union Parliament could unilaterally degrade a state into a union territory, under central control. Importantly, both these questions involved constitutional silences. The language of Articles 356 and 3 does not place express, *substantive* limitations upon the actions of the central government and of the Union Parliament. Any substantive limitations, thus, would have to be *implied*, as a matter of principle. That, in turn, would depend upon what the Supreme Court in *State of West Bengal vs Union of India* had called 'the legal theory' of Indian federalism, and what I—in this chapter—have labelled the distinction between the centralizing and federalizing approaches to Indian federalism.

Under the centralizing approach, the answers would be straightforward. The Constitution, after all, places no express restrictions upon the Union executive under Article 356, or upon the Union Parliament under Article 3. This ends the debate. Under the centralizing approach, the default interpretation is that the power to do something *is* with the Union, unless explicitly constrained.

The federalizing approach, however, would yield a more complex set of solutions to the problems at hand—solutions that (I suggest) are closer to our intuition about what a fair balance between central and state powers under the Constitution ought to look like.

On the first question, the federalizing approach would begin by asking *why* the power under Article 356 exists in the first place. The location of Article 356 within the 'Emergency Provisions' chapter of the Constitution suggests the answer. It exists to deal with exceptional situations, where the governance of a state has broken down so badly that it is impossible to continue with things in a constitutional manner. The job of the Union—in such situations—is therefore *restorative*: in other words, to step in until 'normal service' can be restored.[105]

The task of restoration must be distinguished from the task of substitution. During President's Rule, the Union does not replace the state government in the same way that a new government replaces the old after an election. The Union is a caretaker, holding the fort until the owners are in a position to move back in.

The rationale underlying Article 356 therefore places certain *implied limitations* upon what the Union can do during the period of President's Rule. In particular, it cannot initiate changes or alterations to a state's governance or structure that its elected legislature would not be able to undo when—eventually—normal service is restored (think of it as a caretaker deciding to sell two floors of a house to another person). Because if the Union had *that* power, then it would effectively place the states at the absolute and permanent mercy of the

Union. As in the case of Jammu and Kashmir, a period of President's Rule (or 'Emergency') could be used to alter the basic structure of a state, or strip a state's legislature of its own powers, leaving it unable to take any effective action even upon the restoration of 'normalcy' (and the restoration of the elected legislature as the democratic, law-making organ for the state). This would, however, make a mockery of the idea that the Union only takes over a state's governing apparatus in an 'emergency'—an emergency that is meant to be an unavoidable, but temporary, departure from the basic principle that at all other times, the Union and the states remain sovereign in their respective spheres.

It is here that we can see how the intellectual force of this argument lies in Justice Subba Rao's dissenting opinion in *State of West Bengal vs Union of India*. Implied limitations upon Union power under Article 356 flow from the core idea—articulated by Justice Subba Rao in his dissent—that however much the structure of the Constitution 'skews' towards the Centre, this does not negate the core federal principle that, by *default*, and in their respective spheres, the federal organs (Union and state) are mean to be sovereign.

Let us now consider Article 3. One may look at the text of the article and ask: if the legislature can unilaterally create new states, alter the boundaries of existing states, merge one or more states into each other, or even extinguish a state—why can't it degrade a state into a union territory (i.e., in other words, bringing a prior constituent unit of the federation under direct Union control)? The answer to this, however, is that in all the illustrations set out under Article 3, while the character of an individual state might be altered, there is no change to what Seervai calls the 'federal situation'. In other words, both before and after an alteration that is envisaged by the express terms of Article 3, India remains—as Article 1 of the Constitution requires—'a union of states'.

The power to unilaterally degrade a state into a union territory contravenes this fundamental injunction—i.e., that whatever the fate of an individual state, the *federation* must continue to exist.

Conceptually, the power to degrade a state into a union territory contains within it the power to convert India from a Union of states to a Union of union territories under central control (because—again—conceptually, what can be done to one state can be done to all). Once more, therefore, this is a question of implied limitations: the power of the Union (in this case, the Union Parliament) under Article 3 is limited by the principle that one constituent of the federation—the Union—cannot alter (or in this case, erase) the *federal structure* itself, although it can alter (or even erase) another constituent of the federation (i.e., any given state).[106]

As with Article 356, we can see that the interpretation of Article 3 is not exhausted by its text. Both provisions are terrains of contestation, and the contestation is about power. In a constitution that already empowers central organs over state organs, how ought we to read constitutional gaps, constitutional ambiguities and constitutional silences? In a manner that further entrenches this power imbalance (the centralizing approach), or in a manner that mitigates or counteracts it (the federalizing approach)? The answer depends, ultimately, on what one believes the constitution is *for*, and how it ought to speak to the question of concentrating and distributing power.

In its judgment upholding the abrogation of Article 370, however, the Supreme Court evaded its responsibility of answering these questions.[107] On the issue of Article 356, the majority judgment performed a linguistic sleight of hand. It reframed the question before it as being whether, under Article 356, the Union could not make *permanent* changes—and held that it could. But in doing so, the majority elided two different senses of the word 'permanent': *physical* permanence (I dam a river and electricity is produced: obviously, that is a 'permanent' change that cannot be undone), and permanent—that is, irreversible—alterations to the *constitutional structure*. It was only the latter kind of 'permanence' that—as we have seen above—was excluded from the scope of power conferred by Article 356. The Court, however, did not engage with this crucial distinction, and returned no finding on it.[108]

On the issue of Article 3, the Court's evasion was even more blatant and egregious. Chief Justice Chandrachud, writing for the majority, accepted the 'assurance' of government counsel that at some indeterminate point in the future, the statehood of Jammu and Kashmir would be restored, and on the basis of this 'assurance', declined to decide the constitutional question before him.

The questions that we have flagged above thus remained unanswered. And as we can perhaps now see more clearly, it appears that the Court either lacked, or chose not to draw upon, the conceptual vocabulary to answer them.[109] This is the vocabulary of the federalizing approach, and I would suggest that the Jammu and Kashmir case shows how the federalizing approach accords more closely with a basic sense of equality, fairness, and the rule of law. The events of 5 August 2019—the 1.5-year-long compelled absence of the elected state legislature, the constitutional manoeuvres that were accomplished by the same entity taking its own consent to bring about the desired constitutional changes, and the forcible degradation of the state of Jammu and Kashmir into a union territory directly controlled by the central government—were classic examples of abuse of power, going some distance beyond 'constitutional bodyline-bowling'. And, in another way, these were all illustrations of how the 'skew' in the constitutional scheme—exemplified through provisions such as Articles 3 and 356—was exploited by the more powerful constitutional actor (the Union government and, by extension, the government-controlled Parliament) to assert even greater dominance over the federation's other constitutive entity—the states—by making an example of one particularly recalcitrant state.

An interpretation of the Constitution that favours such moves only serves to accelerate the centralizing drift that we have discussed—i.e., greater and greater concentration of power at the Centre (and primarily, the Union executive) at the direct cost of all other constitutional institutions (in this case, the states). What I have attempted to show in this section is that an alternative interpretation—one that seeks to *federate* power rather than concentrate it (hence, the 'federalizing approach') —is plausible, and has indeed been articulated before by the Supreme Court, albeit in dissent. With the Court declining to engage with this interpretive approach in the Article 370 case through evasion and elision, it remains to be seen whether it will find favour with the 'wisdom of a future day'.

IV. On the Road to a Unitary State

We began this chapter with a look at the dispute that erupted between the state of Kerala and the Union of India at the close of 2023, and the Supreme Court's interim order that denied immediate relief to the state of Kerala. We are now in a position to identify the fundamental interpretive assumption underlying the Court's prima facie decision to privilege the Union's claims as the steward of the national economy over the state's claims to internal economic (and, by extension, political) autonomy. This is none other than the centralizing approach to federalism, which we have teased out from the text and structure of the Constitution, and from inflection-point judgments over the seven decades of the working of the Constitution.[110]

Kerala's suit is not the only instance of strained federal relations in recent times.[111] In early 2020, the state of Chhattisgarh invoked Article 131 of the Constitution to challenge the National Investigation Agency (NIA) Act of 2008, before the Supreme Court.[112] In essence, the NIA Act authorized the central government—through the NIA—to take over the investigation and prosecution of certain 'Scheduled Offences' (provided for in the act), from the state government, regardless of whether there was a cross-state border element involved. Chhattisgarh argued that the act was destructive of the federal scheme, as policing (and, therefore, the investigation of offences), was within List II of Schedule VII—i.e., within the exclusive jurisdiction of the states.

Chhattisgarh's constitutional challenge did not come in the abstract. As we have observed earlier in this chapter, in our discussion of AFSPA, there is often a direct link between federalism and the protection of civil rights. Indeed, one of the most notorious civil rights cases in recent years has been the Bhima-Koregaon case. In 2018, following violence at the annual commemoration of the 1818 Battle of Koregaon, many prominent political dissidents and civil society activists were arrested and incarcerated under the Unlawful Activities Prevention Act (UAPA). At the time of writing, many of them remain in prison, without trial, while others have been granted bail (albeit after spending multiple years in jail).[113] Notably, one crucial element of the case was the central government's decision to *transfer* proceedings from the Maharashtra police (within whose jurisdiction the violence occurred) to the centrally controlled NIA.[114] Among other things, this would ensure that the case would remain linked to the balance of political forces at the Centre (and who controlled the central executive), rather than the balance of political forces within the state. And, perhaps unsurprisingly, in the decade and a half of its existence, the NIA has been accused on more than one occasion of political bias in its functioning.[115]

It is here, however, that the historically expansive judicial reading of Schedule VII Lists would work against federalism. Indeed, Chhattisgarh's plaint was not the first bite at the cherry. In 2012, the NIA had been challenged on federalism grounds before the Bombay High Court.[116] The High Court rejected the challenge by tracing the competence of the Union to Entry 8 of List II, which states 'central bureau of intelligence and investigation',[117] as well as Entries 1 and 2 of the Concurrent List ('criminal law and criminal procedure').[118] The court specifically cited the principle of broad and liberal construction of the entries in the lists, and the doctrine of pith and substance (which involved 'splitting up' the analysis in the manner discussed above), as well as the judgements in the *AFSPA* and *POTA* cases, to justify its conclusion.[119] As should be obvious by now, the High Court's judgment is an exemplar of the centralizing approach to federalism that has crystallized into 'constitutional common sense' since *State of West Bengal vs Union of India*: indeed, as we can see, it brings together multiple centralizing interpretive techniques that we have discussed in this chapter.[120]

Staying with the subject of policing, consider—along similar lines—the Union government's October 2021 notification that extended the jurisdiction of the Border Security Force (BSF) from 15 kilometres to 50 kilometres from the international border, in the states of Punjab, West Bengal, and Assam. Under the BSF Act of 1968, policing functions—otherwise a state subject, as we have just seen—are vested in the centrally controlled BSF, with the ostensible objective of preventing trans-border crime and protecting national security along India's international borders.[121] State governments that were governed by parties of the (political) Opposition at the time objected to the government's notification, pointing out—among other things—that this would bring almost a third of the area of these states under Union policing. Once again, however, the centralizing judicial approach to federalism would result in restricting these objections to the political domain, with their success—or failure—hinging primarily upon the balance of political forces at the time. As the judgments in *Naga People's Movement for Human Rights* and *Kartar Singh* have shown us, the Supreme Court has been particularly resistant to federal concerns once the Union invokes 'national security' as the basis for justifying legislative competence—even if this potentially means stretching the idea of a 'border' beyond its common-sense meaning.[122]

Consider, next, the bitter political controversy that erupted in 2020 and 2021 over the Union government's attempts to pass what colloquially came to be known as 'the farm laws': legislation that—in effect—sought to erode various state-level structures that insulated agriculture from the full effects of the market economy. Year-long protests eventually compelled the Union government to 'withdraw' the three laws, but it is important to note that a significant part of the conflict centred on the real meaning of Indian federalism. Under Schedule VII, 'agriculture' is a state subject, while 'trade and commerce in … foodstuffs' is in the Concurrent List.[123] The constitutional question, thus, would turn on the interpretation of the entries of the lists where—as we have seen—the Supreme Court's doctrine of broad and liberal construction has further entrenched Union power at the expense of state power. In this context, it is striking that protests against the laws continued even after the filing of constitutional challenges before the Supreme Court, indicating—among other things—a lack of confidence in the Court as an arbitrator of Union–state relations.

Finally, consider the long-standing and continuing controversy over the prescription of a uniform nationwide examination or admission to undergraduate medical programmes (commonly known as 'NEET'). The introduction of NEET in 2013—replacing state-specific entrance examinations—was met with bitter criticism, especially on grounds of federalism and the rights of states to prescribe their own syllabi and set their own examinations, taking into account interstate diversity and heterogeneity, and how medical education directly taps into a state's public healthcare system.[124] While the Supreme Court struck down NEET in 2013, it rejected the federal argument, relying upon a prior judgment called *Dr. Preeti Srivastava vs State of Madhya Pradesh*.[125] That judgment had accorded a wide interpretation to Entry 66 of List I, which authorized Parliament to legislate with respect to 'co-ordination and determination of standards in institutions for higher education'.[126] The Supreme Court relied upon that to hold that Entry 66 included the authority to set a common entrance examination—but that NEET was unconstitutional on substantive fundamental rights grounds.[127] In any event, subsequently, the judgment was recalled by a five-judge bench of the Supreme Court (acting in review jurisdiction), and NEET was allowed to proceed. At the time of writing, the examination continues to be controversial, with allegations of large-scale leakage of papers, and rigging. The legal trajectory of the challenges to NEET reveal, however, how the centralizing approach to federalism operates within the domain of education, where homogenization is accorded primacy over a more decentralized responsiveness to local conditions—especially in subjects such as medicine, where the technical (medical science) and the social (public healthcare) are inextricably linked.[128]

These examples (and there are many more) demonstrate how federalism in India is a continuing site of contestation between Union power and state power, and how the legacies of past constitutional events affect Centre–state relations in the present. To be sure, it is not my case that this contestation of power is exhausted by the constitutional text and by the judgments of the courts. As the trajectory of the farm laws in particular show us, political forces can even be better guardians of state interests than the Constitution and the courts. That said, however, the impact of the constitutional text—and its interpretation by courts—plays a significant role in impacting the balance of power. It is therefore important to study what the Constitution says and what the courts have done.

On doing that, what we find is that in crucial respects, the Constitution 'skews' towards the Union when it comes to distributing power between the Union and the states, through a variety of textual devices: notwithstanding clauses, escape clauses, residuary powers, emergency provisions, and so on. With a few exceptions, the judgments of the courts have entrenched and amplified this skew, contributing to the 'centralizing drift' that we have seen across different domains. In this chapter, I have tried to show that while this approach—the centralizing approach to federalism—is dominant, it is not inevitable. Judgments such as Justice Subba Rao's dissent in *State of West Bengal v Union of India* indicate an alternative 'federalizing' approach to constitutional interpretation.

There are, however, two barriers that remain. The first is that—as we shall see in other parts of this book—on a bare reading, the text of the Constitution encourages the centralizing approach to Indian federalism. After all, it is easy enough to look at the entire portmanteau of constitutional provisions, from Article 3 to Article 356, and conclude that state power does not really count for much in the constitutional scheme. In this chapter, I have tried to show why that bare reading deserves some rethinking on taking a deeper look at the Constitution's text, structure, and history. The alternative—the federalizing approach—however, can appear counter-intuitive at first brush, and requires the filling in of gaps and silences through interpretive doctrines, such as that of implied limitations. In other words, the federalizing approach—when it comes to the court—places a significantly greater interpretive burden upon the judiciary than the centralizing approach, a burden that for a variety of reasons (including the balance of political forces), it may not be willing to take upon itself. We therefore come back to a common theme of this book: constitutional provisions do not preclude a pushback (judicial or otherwise) against the centralizing drift, but they do erect a barrier against such a pushback.

The second issue is that interpretation, of course, has its limits. Even if all the judgments that we have discussed in this chapter—from *State of West Bengal vs Union of India*, to *Babulal Parate*, to *I.T.C. vs The Agricultural Produce Market Committee*—were decided the other way, we would still be left with a constitution in which Articles 3 and 356, and everything in between, are realities. It is questionable whether a constitutional text so skewed from the outset could ever satisfactorily prevent a centralizing drift. A skewed balance of power, after all, tends to protect, entrench, and aggrandize itself, rather than the other way around.[129]

In this context, the history of interpretation that we have discussed in this chapter might serve as a valuable guide for what *not* to do, should there come a day when the balance of power between the Union and the states (and beyond) is substantively reconsidered.

2

Power Divided: Parliamentarianism

IN DECEMBER 2023—THE LAST full parliamentary session before the General Election of 2024—146 members of Parliament, across both houses, were suspended for the session. Every suspended member belonged to the Opposition. The ostensible reason for the suspension was that these MPs had created disorder in the assembly and violated house rules, in the course of asking for an investigation into a parliamentary security breach. Amidst rows of empty seats, (what remained of) Parliament proceeded to pass far-reaching legislation without debate. This included a complete overhaul of the nation's criminal laws, a new telecommunications act, and a law for bringing the selection of the Election Commission back under the control of the executive.[1]

The mass suspension of Opposition MPs, seemingly at will[2], by the speaker of the lower house and the chairperson of the upper house (two formally independent constitutional offices, but in reality, little more than nominees of the executive[3]), created a furore about the undermining of Parliament by the executive. In truth, however, the suspensions were perhaps only the most visible manifestation of a decades-long phenomenon: that of the decay and marginalization of Parliament, in the performance of its core functions in a parliamentary democracy—those of representation, deliberation, legislation, and oversight.[4]

Indeed, parliamentary decay is one of the most oft-heard subjects of lament in Indian political conversation. The indicators are stark and difficult to dispute. The number of days that Parliament is in session in a year has declined steadily since Independence. Complex bills are passed in a matter of minutes or seconds. Debates have grown rare, legislative scrutiny by Parliamentary committees even rarer. The Upper House is frequently taken out of the conversation altogether, through the device of classifying a bill as a 'money bill'. On top of everything, when faced with parliamentary uncertainty, the executive appears to have a ready-made solution at hand: issuing ordinances while Parliament is not in session.

These laments often focus on the quality of the politicians who govern us. This, in my view, is a partial mistake. Many of the problems that Indian parliamentary democracy presently faces are structural, and more a function of constitutional design rather than an abuse of it. They have less to do with the wills or intentions of individuals (without discounting the agency of the parties involved[5]), and more to do with the manner in which the Constitution creates, distributes, and channels power between the legislature and the executive.[6]

Let us examine how.

During the framing of the Constitution, one of the most important sets of debates revolved around the system of government that the new republic would have. The framers chose the Parliamentary system. This was unsurprising, as the representative institutions that had been established by the British regime during the colonial era reflected—albeit often in a distorted way—British parliamentarianism, or the 'Westminster system of democracy'.[7]

Westminster parliamentarianism involves a certain blurring of the separation of powers when it comes to the relationship between the executive and the legislature. The Prime Minister tends to play a dual role as the (effective[8]) leader of the executive, as well as the (effective) leader of the largest party in the house.[9] The legislative agenda invariably originates from the government—or the cabinet—and then comes before Parliament for approval.[10] Thus, even though in formal terms the executive—or the Council of Ministers—is collectively responsible to Parliament, when it comes to actual functioning, Westminster systems often have an inbuilt centralizing drift, a drift towards the subordination of the legislature to the executive.[11]

At the same time, however, parliamentary democratic systems often contain a set of rules and principles, the effect of which is to shift a degree of power *away* from the executive-in-Parliament and distribute it among a range of other bodies.

First, there is power within the party—or, what is more specific to our discussion, power within the parliamentary party (i.e., the set of legislators from a particular political party, in Parliament, at any given time). In order to have legislation passed in Parliament—and barring exceptional cases—the executive will need the support and the votes of their party.[12] Intra-party dissent, therefore, can stymie the government's legislative agenda, and can even, at times, unseat the Prime Minister.[13]

Secondly, there is power within the house—or, in other words, the power enjoyed by the parliamentary Opposition. In the parliamentary system, this is a limited power.[14] There are exceptional cases where the Opposition can unite with dissenters within the majority party, and defeat the government's legislative agenda. For the most part, however, the Opposition's power lies in its ability to subject the government's record to public scrutiny, whether on the floor of the house, or during evaluation of bills in parliamentary committees.[15]

Thirdly, in bicameral parliamentary systems where Parliament is divided into a lower house and an upper house, there is the checking power of the upper house. At the Union level, the Indian parliamentary system is bicameral. The upper house—the Rajya Sabha—is the Council of States, with commensurate law-making powers (other than in the case of money bills). There is always a possibility that the majority party in the Lok Sabha might not have a majority in the Rajya Sabha. Bicameralism, thus, is a third potential counterbalance against executive dominance in India's parliamentary system.

In this chapter, we shall consider the distribution and balance of power within the Indian Parliament, along the axes discussed above.[16] Before we begin, however, three important caveats: first, as we have discussed throughout the course of this book, the Constitution does not exhaust many of these issues.[17] Relevant to the context of this chapter, for example, the Constitution does not determine the extent to which internal democracy exists within Indian political parties, or their 'de-institutionalization'.[18] Likewise, it is state elections and not the Constitution (at least, not directly) that determine the composition of the Rajya Sabha, and whether the upper house can serve as an effective, external check upon the lower house. As we shall see, however, what the Constitution does do is to create an overarching framework within which certain kinds of political action is possible—or facilitated—and other kinds of political action is prohibited, or at least, made prohibitively difficult.[19] Again, as in the other chapters of this book, we find that the Constitution does this both through its textual provisions, and through its silences.

Secondly, some of the discussions below are premised upon a political situation where the single largest party is also the majority party in the house (or, at least, close to a majority). Cases involving coalition governments, where the single largest party falls substantially short of a majority are slightly different, as smaller coalition parties can exercise a constraint upon the executive that is purely political in nature.

Finally, and most importantly, there is one significant distinction between the Westminster system of parliamentary democracy as it originated in England and the Indian version: the existence—in the Indian case—of a single written Constitution (with judicial review). Thus, in the case of England, many of the rules and procedures governing the functioning of Parliament are the product of long-standing, often uncodified, constitutional conventions.[20] The Indian Constitution, however, complicates the situation somewhat: while the constitutional conventions of parliamentary democracy do play a role, as we shall see, they have to be interpreted alongside the constitutional text and constitutional silences.

Indeed, as Khosla has pointed out, in the Indian context, the absence of a shared understanding of the content of constitutional conventions triggered both a desire for greater codification, as well as ensuring that over time, it would be the constitutional text that came to dominate over norms and conventions.[21] We shall consider the consequences of this in the first section of this chapter.

With these caveats in place, we will begin with the history. Although the parliamentary system of government was the choice of the Constituent Assembly for newly independent India, this was accompanied by a dose of scepticism. In particular, there was scepticism about the extent to which the need for rapid national development—something that required a strong executive—could be reconciled with full-blooded parliamentarianism. Parliamentarianism under the Indian Constitution, thus, is a grudging kind of parliamentarianism, and the Indian Parliament was born defanged in certain significant ways. While the specifics of this will be discussed subsequently, the point to note is that this defanging is not accidental, but the result of conscious constitutional design[22] **(I)**.

We will then move to certain concrete issues in the order that we have discussed above. We shall first consider intra-party dissent, and the impact of Schedule X of the Constitution. Schedule X was not a part of the original Constitution. It was introduced via amendment, in order to stop the practice of political defections. We shall examine Schedule X in two contexts. First, we shall look at how it has strengthened the party *leadership*, at the expense of the *legislator*. In the context of the governing party, this means a significant dilution of the ability of the party's legislators to challenge the government within Parliament. And secondly, we shall examine some additional complications when it comes to the operation of Schedule X in a *federal* context, where the purpose of anti-defection law evolves into protecting a (state) party leadership not so much against its own legislators, but against destabilization from the *Centre.* We shall examine, in particular, how recent Supreme Court judgments have undermined Schedule X's ability to play this role, and thereby contributed to a centralizing drift at intersection of the federal and parliamentary axes of power **(II).**

We shall then consider the political Opposition. Here, silences speak. The Constitution's failure to entrench Opposition rights has weakened the powers that it might be able to exercise in Parliament. This is exacerbated by another silence: the Constitution does not mandate—or contain any provisions to ensure—the speaker's independence from the ruling party. The absence of express Opposition rights—coupled with a partisan speaker—weakens another important counterweight to executive power within Parliament **(III).**

Thirdly, we shall consider the upper house. Here, again, we find that the absence of speaker impartiality weakens the power of the Rajya Sabha by simply taking it out of the equation if a bill is certified as a money bill. At the time of writing, the question of whether or not the speaker's certification is subject to judicial review is still pending before the Supreme Court. Even if it were to be held, however, that the Court does have the power of review, its previous record on checking other forms of abuse within the house—such as ordinances (see below) and speaker misconduct in other situations—makes it questionable, at best, whether this particular form of oversight will practically deter misclassification of bills. In addition to the issue of money bills, we also find that, when it comes to the functioning of the Rajya Sabha, its chairperson is the vice president of India, an individual who will often (though not always) be the nominee of the government in power. This continues to provide the executive with at least an indirect lever of control over the upper house (in ways that shall be discussed), even when the 'numbers' might not be in its favour (**IV**).

Finally, there is one situation where the political executive can bypass all the checks and balances described here: its own legislators, the political Opposition, and the upper house. This is the government's ordinance-making power, or what Shubhankar Dam memorably terms 'Presidential legislation', and what we can call 'rule by decree'. The Constitution's ordinance-making power allows the executive to legislate in conditions of emergency but makes no provision for preventing its abuse. In 2017, the Supreme Court reiterated that ordinances were not equivalent to laws, and that the ordinance-making power was not to be used as a substitute for the legislative process. While this opened the possibility of judicial review, in the years since that judgment, precisely zero ordinances have been struck down on this ground. The fault here is not entirely that of the Court, but in some part in the design of the Constitution itself, which at best only authorizes post-facto review of something that has a very limited shelf life, i.e., up to six months. **(V)**

On a combined reading of constitutional provisions, constitutional silences, and judicial decisions, therefore, the 'centralizing drift' within Parliament—qua its character as the highest representative law-making body of the people of India—is clear. It is a shift that entrenches the power of the executive and weakens the various arms of the legislature that might check that power. Indeed, it is worth asking whether, in effect, India presently functions under a de facto presidential (or at least, semi-presidential) system of government, but with none of the checks and balances, or 'veto points', that characterize many presidential systems. **(VI)**.

I. Grudging Parliamentarianism

On 4 November 1948, Dr B.R. Ambedkar rose to introduce the Draft Constitution to the Constituent Assembly. The first issue he addressed was about the form of government enshrined in the draft document. He presented this as a direct choice between two alternatives: the British Parliamentary system and the American Presidential system. The former, he noted, gave a nation a more *responsible* executive, but at the cost of stability (as the executive could, at any moment, theoretically lose the confidence of the legislature, and fall). The latter provided a more *stable* executive, but sacrificed the 'daily and periodic' assessment of executive responsibility that came with the parliamentary systems (through 'questions, resolutions, no-confidence motions' etc.). The Drafting Committee, informed by the views of the Constituent Assembly as well as the reports of its various specialized committees, such as the Union Constitution Committee and the Provincial Constitution Committee, had chosen the parliamentary system, 'prefer[ing] more responsibility to stability'.[23]

Ambedkar's characterization of the binary between British parliamentarianism and American presidentialism, and the Indian Constitution opting for the former, was echoed by other members of the assembly. Apart from Ambedkar's normative defence of parliamentarianism, there was a common consensus amongst its supporters that this was a system that Indians had grown used to working with—and even, towards the end, operating themselves—over many decades of colonial rule. Parliamentary forms and procedures were familiar to those who would take the reins after Independence, and so it made administrative sense to retain this system of government under the new Constitution. As K.M. Munshi observed, for example:

> ... during the last 100 years, the Indian public life has largely drawn upon the traditions of the British Constitutional law. Most of us, and during the last several generations before us, public men in India, have looked up to the British model as the best. For the last thirty or forty years, some kind of responsibility has been introduced in the governance of this country. Our Constitutional traditions have become Parliamentary and we have now all our provinces functioning more or less on the British model. As a matter of fact, today, the Dominion Government of India is functioning as a full-fledged Parliamentary Government. After this experience why should we go back upon the tradition that has been built for over

> 100 years, and try a novel experiment which was, as I said, framed 150 years ago and which has been found wanting even in America?[24]

Thus, in the view of the dominant current of the Constituent Assembly, parliamentarianism was both normatively desirable, and also something that Indians had become accustomed to, in their experience with working representative institutions under colonial rule.[25]

Both positions, however, are not quite as simple as they appear.[26]

As early as 1861, with its first major legislative enactment after the Revolt of 1857, the British crown experimented with granting limited—and tightly controlled—representation to Indians within the structures of colonial governance.[27] The nature and scope of representation was incrementally increased over the years, in response to increasing pressure from the growing Indian nationalist movement.[28] It was in 1919—with the Government of India Act—that the first *parliamentary* structures appeared: responsible legislatures, elected on the basis of (very limited) franchise, and empowered to legislate (on a limited range of subjects).[29] These structures were extended by the Government of India Act of 1935, which, of course, provided a significant part of the blueprint for the eventual Indian Constitution.[30] When the members of the Constituent Assembly referred to their experience with parliamentarianism, it was the 1935 Act that they had in mind, under the aegis of which the Indian National Congress had formed ministries in multiple provinces.

The 1919 and 1935 Acts, however, did not introduce anything akin to British parliamentarianism in India. What they introduced was a simulacrum—or, at best, a distortion—of parliamentarianism, oriented towards preserving imperial interests in the colony: the form without the substance. Parliamentary structures in colonial India subscribed to a model that the British brought in (with minor variations) across their colonies. It was built upon what the Kenyan constitutional lawyer Githu Muigai has described elsewhere as two pillars: the subordination of the legislature to the executive, and the subordination of the colonial parliament to the imperial parliament.[31] Thus, for example, under the 'dyarchy' model introduced by the 1919 Act at the provincial level, only certain subjects were 'transferred' to the legislatures, while 'reserved' subjects remained with the British executive. At the central level, the British governor-general retained veto powers, as well as legislative powers.[32]

Under the 1935 Act, while provincial autonomy was expanded, governors retained reserve powers, as well as the powers of 'emergency' legislation (through issuing ordinances), and suspending the elected legislature.[33] At the central level, overriding powers remained with the governor-general: he had control over the introduction of certain kinds of financial bills;[34] over certain topics of debate in the assembly;[35] law-making powers through 'Governor-General's Acts';[36] and finally, executive powers through a number of provisions that empowered him to 'act in his discretion' in a range of domains (such as financial stability, the interests of minorities, and so on). Further, in case of doubt, it was the governor-general's prerogative to decide whether something fell within his discretion or not—the very definition of personal power.[37] And through the governor-general's power to reserve bills for the consideration of the British monarch, *ultimate* control—to use Githu Muigai's framing—always lay with the imperial metropolis in London.[38]

Indeed, as Ambedkar noted in a trenchant critique of the act published in 1939, in many ways, it marked a regression from dyarchy. Not only did the governors exercise personal, discretionary power over reserved subjects, but the act's bifurcation of governmental and administrative authority also meant that elected ministers could lay down policy, but had no effective way of overseeing its implementation.[39] Furthermore, Ambedkar noted the many ways in which the 1935 Act enforced executive supremacy over the legislature[40] and curtailed its power to function meaningfully *as* a legislature.[41] Thus, at all times, representative governance was conducted under the twin shadows of the central (British) executive in India, and the imperial metropolis in London.[42]

It might therefore be worth questioning the commonly held belief that the parliamentary system of government adopted by the Constituent Assembly was the logical culmination of the gradual advancement and deepening of representative institutions in the last decades of colonial rule. Parliamentarianism in India, as we have seen, was practised under the thumb of a top-heavy executive, and under the permanent threat of takeover by that executive.

Why does this matter? It matters because, to repeat a point made above, parliamentary systems—with the fusion of legislature and executive—have an inbuilt tendency toward executive drift, or executive dominance over the legislature. To counteract this drift, there are certain internal safeguards, which we have highlighted above, and will discuss in greater detail below. In Britain, these safeguards evolved over a long period of time, through multiple struggles, and took the form of *constitutional conventions:* that is, uncodified but binding norms of behaviour, which would be extremely costly for political actors to disobey.

In the distorted version of parliamentarianism that came to colonial India, however—as it did to other British colonies—these conventions had little place or relevance. Indeed, as we have seen, the British were not concerned with ensuring that parliamentarianism in the colonies would enable the legislature to keep the executive in check. Quite the opposite: their primary concern was that representative legislatures not act in ways that would undermine core British interests, embodied in the office of the chief executive, or the governor-general.[43] This concern—as described above—was articulated through multiple legal provisions in the 1919 and 1935 Government of India Acts (some of which—such as the Ordinance-making power—were retained in the final Constitution).[44]

In the absence of constitutional conventions, the only other way to protect the stature of Parliament under the new Constitution would have been through express codification. Indeed, this was a logic that underpinned a substantial part of the Constitution. We have noted above Madhav Khosla's observation that the inordinate length and detail of the Indian Constitution, and its focus on spelling out the most granular administrative details within the text, is explained by the fact that in the absence of widely held constitutional conventions, the framers wanted to leave as little to chance (and to potential abuse) as possible.[45]

But what is particularly striking is that when it comes to Parliament, the zeal for codification that Khosla describes is notably by its absence. As we shall see below, the Constitution is virtually silent on some of the most crucial features of parliamentarianism: the position of the speaker, the existence of a leader of the Opposition, the rights of parties that form the Opposition, the obligations of the ruling party within Parliament, and so on.[46] Indeed, it is when dealing with Parliament that the Constitution makes its *only* reference to uncodified conventions.[47] This did not go unnoticed in the Constituent Assembly: in the debates on the structure of government, Kazi Syed Karimuddin specifically noted how the absence of parliamentary conventions had led to an experience where 'political opponents are practically crushed, neglected and ignored'.[48]

I want to suggest that this refusal to codify was not merely accidental, or an oversight, but a matter of constitutional *design*. Even though Ambedkar's motion on the draft Constitution suggests a clean choice between two alternatives, made as early as 1947, the history was considerably messier.[49] Up until 1949, the draft Constitution envisaged a semi-presidential system for the provinces (future states), with an elected governor who—akin to the Government of India Act of 1935—would retain the power to take over the government, to be exercised at his discretion.[50] Furthermore, the choice of a parliamentary system remained controversial throughout the proceedings of the Constituent Assembly, eliciting strong resistance—and last-minute backdoor-change attempts—deep into 1948.[51]

Notably, scepticism about full-blooded parliamentarianism was prevalent not only among votaries of presidentialism, but also within the Indian National Congress's top leadership, including those who piloted parliamentarianism through the Constituent Assembly Sub-Committees. The most significant of these figures was Jawaharlal Nehru himself. As Nazmul Sultan notes, Nehru's embrace of the developmental state necessitated the simultaneous marginalization of the legislature, which—according to him—'was slow and cumbrous and unsuited to a period of rapid change'.[52] As Sultan therefore observes:

> Nehru embraced the growing marginalisation of the legislature in the mid-twentieth century. The engine of postcolonial state-form was located not in the legislative body but in a foresighted executive that would work in conjunction with the experts. In contrast, the role of universal suffrage and legislative representatives was to keep the planners in touch with the people and allow the latter to have some control over the process, albeit via the means of elections.[53]

Or, as Udit Bhatia puts the point in more specific terms, when considering the attitude of Nehru and Ambedkar towards the legislature: '… [the] masses' backwardness necessitated a centralized executive, capable of delivering radical reform unencumbered by parliamentary delays and localist concerns. Executive dominance over parliament through the backing of the party machinery was deemed a necessary response to the problem of backwardness.'[54]

This, in turn, impacted how the role of the parliamentarian was viewed: that is, not in the classical sense of engaging in deliberation and law-making, but in participating (strictly as a junior partner)[55] in the overall developmentalist project of the Constitution, which was led by the executive.[56]

Consequently, while Ambedkar was, of course, correct in noting that the Constituent Assembly chose British parliamentarianism over American presidentialism, history shows that not only was the version of parliamentarianism that had been practised in colonial India an attenuated form, but even among the votaries of enshrining parliamentarianism into the new Constitution, there was no great enthusiasm for correcting for these attenuations (albeit for different reasons). It is this history, I think, that best explains why such a garrulous Constitution falls mysteriously silent when it comes to something as important and fundamental as Parliament. And it is a silence that, as we shall see in the rest of this chapter, has important consequences.

II. Dissent within the Party: Schedule X

A. Leadership and Legislators

We will begin, however, not with a silence, but with text: in fact, an entire new Schedule that was introduced into the Constitution three and a half decades after its enactment.

The issue of 'defections'—i.e., an elected legislator leaving their party for another party, while still in office—has plagued India right from the birth of constitutional democracy. In *theory*, a defection is a question for a legislator's conscience. A legislator who genuinely believes that their party no longer represents the interests of the constituents who elected them can choose to 'cross the floor of the house' and join another party that does. In *theory*, therefore, a legislator's ability to defect is a check upon their party leadership, and a tool for ensuring that the leadership remains at least nominally responsive to elected legislators.

The *practice*, of course, is very different. Defections are secured—and governments overturned—through offers of money, offers of ministerial positions, and threats, but rarely are they the culmination of ideological dissent.[57] As early as 1969, for example, a Parliamentary Committee on Defections noted that between March 1967 and February 1968, there were at least 438 defections, and that a significant percentage of defectors were included in the Council of Ministers of the very governments that they helped to bring about, through their defections.[58]

Attempts to control the practice of defections through a Constitutional amendment commenced in 1973. These attempts finally succeeded when in 1985, Parliament amended the Constitution and introduced Schedule X. Colloquially known as the 'anti-defection law', the ostensible purpose of Schedule X is to check the practice of party defections. It does so by making the party whip binding. According to Schedule X, the disobedience of 'any direction' given by the party triggers the disqualification of the legislator from the House.[59] The power to adjudicate disputed defections vests in the speaker of the house.[60]

Variants of the 'anti-defection law' exist in a range of other jurisdictions, such as Pakistan, Bangladesh, and Fiji.[61] Their impact upon the individual legislator's ability to dissent through voting against their party is obvious.[62] However, as Udit Bhatia points out, the effect goes beyond simply votes—the knowledge that one has no choice but to vote according to the directions of the party leadership has an upstream, chilling effect on dissent and diversity of opinion within the party, even outside the floor of the house.[63] There are a range of reasons for this: the tendency of individuals to adjust their preferences to a known, eventual outcome; the downsides of taking a public, contradictory stance in both opposing party policy, but then also voting for it in Parliament; and a reduced need for the party leadership to publicly justify its policy in a bid to persuade dissenting members, as it knows that the dissent cannot be carried over to where it matters: the floor.[64]

Anti-defection laws, therefore, undermine both intra-party dissent and the quality of deliberation within Parliament (the latter is evident through the rapidly decreasing amount of time that Parliament takes to scrutinize and enact legislation).[65] In other words, they negatively impact some of the core characteristics of classical parliamentary democracy.

In *Kihoto Hollohan vs Zaichilhu*, the constitutional validity of Schedule X was challenged before a Constitution Bench of the Supreme Court. For the purposes of this chapter, three important arguments were made, some of which flow from the points we have discussed above: first, that the very idea of an anti-defection law violated the basic structure of the Constitution, as it unduly fettered a legislator's freedom of conscience and speech, and their ability to independently represent their constituents in the house; secondly, that in any event, this version of an anti-defection law violated the basic structure of the Constitution, as it made a partisan official—the speaker—in charge of adjudicating disqualification cases; and thirdly, even if the Schedule X was constitutionally valid, it needed to be read down so that it would not completely submerge the identity of the individual legislator into the identity of the political party.

Specifically, it was argued that this could be accomplished by limiting the term 'any direction' to situations where the survival of the government was at stake, such as a vote of no-confidence, or a vote on the budget. In other cases, where voting against the whip would not have the direct effect of bringing down the government, Schedule X would not apply. Indeed, such an interpretation had already been accepted by the Punjab and Haryana High Court, in *Prakash Singh Badal vs Union of India*.[66]

By a narrow 3:2 majority, the Supreme Court rejected all three arguments. On the first issue, the Court held that Schedule X responded to a specific problem—that of unprincipled defections—and that consequently, a balance needed to be struck between the individual legislator's freedom of conscience in the house, and the preservation of democratic integrity through punishing unprincipled defections. It was not for the Court to second-guess the legislature's belief that such a balance was needed, and that certain rights in the house would need to be curtailed in order to achieve it.[67]

So far, the Court's reasoning is uncontroversial enough. It is the Court's ruling on the second and third issues, however, that saw a significant centralizing drift within Parliament, through Schedule X. The Court upheld the speaker's power to adjudicate disqualification disputes, on the basis that in the Westminster Parliamentary tradition, the office of the speaker was a high office of great dignity, and that the speaker was *supposed* and *meant* to act impartially.[68] The Court's reasoning here was not only curious, but also self-contradictory. In upholding the anti-defection law, the Court had relied upon the political reality of large-scale unprincipled defections over the ideal of freedom of conscience in the house. However, in upholding the speaker's powers, it referred to the ideal of the speaker's office in the Westminster systems, instead of how that office actually functioned in Indian legislatures.[69] In particular, the majority ignored the fact that in India, the structural features guaranteeing speaker independence are absent: for example, the speaker is not required to resign their party membership (as was the case, for example, in the UK House of Commons), or snap their ties with the ruling party.[70]

The central flaw in the reasoning of the majority is best expressed in its own words. 'It is inappropriate to express distrust in the high office of the Speaker,' the majority noted, 'merely because *some of the Speakers* are alleged, or even found, to have discharged their functions not in keeping with the great traditions of that high office (emphasis supplied).'[71] But as we noted in the beginning of this chapter, the issue was and is not about the *individuals* who occupy a constitutional position, but about the structures of incentives and disincentives, checks and balances, that characterize the position. In other words, the issue is not that some speakers have been partisan, but that as a matter of constitutional design, the Constitution not only lacks safeguards against speaker partisanship, but—through its silences—actively facilitates it. And that is why granting the speaker adjudicatory powers in case of disqualifications for defection is constitutionally problematic.[72] Indeed, these contradictions were noted in some detail in the dissenting opinion in *Kihoto Hollohan vs Zachillhu*, which also questioned why the standard constitutional method of dealing with parliamentary disqualification—i.e., adjudication by the President or governor, on the recommendation of the formally independent Election Commission—had not been followed in the case of defections.[73]

Finally, on the third issue, the majority refused to read down the term 'any direction', and reversed the judgment of the Punjab and Haryana High Court. In doing so, the Court employed a somewhat familiar tactic. It noted that the term would have to be read 'in harmony' with the objects and purposes of Schedule X. What did this mean? According to the Court, it meant that:

> ...the direction given by the political party ... the violation of which may entail disqualification ... would have to be limited to a vote on motion of confidence or no confidence in the Government or where the motion ... relates to a matter *which was an integral policy and programme of the political party on the basis of which it approached the elaborate* (emphasis supplied).[74]

But what did this mean, and who was to decide what constituted an 'integral policy and programme' of the party? According to the Court, the party leadership would decide: the direction or the whip would have to expressly state that non-compliance would result in disqualification under the Schedule X.[75] In effect, any direction or whip triggered Schedule X, as long as it clearly stated so.

Kihoto Hollohan, therefore, is an inflection point in the constitutional history of the power relations between the party leadership and individual legislators, within the house. Let us accept that curtailing political defections is a legitimate goal, which requires some degree of centralization of power, away from the legislator and in the hands of the party leadership. *Kihoto Hollohan,* however, did not just greenlight the *principle* of an anti-defection law, but it also greenlit a specific *version* of the anti-defection law that entirely effaced the identity of the legislator into the identity of the party, and effectively ended the legislator's power to check the leadership.[76] It did so by extending the scope of Schedule X to potentially all votes in the house, and by upholding the speaker as the adjudicating authority.

Notably, the second of these two rulings entrenches not just a centralizing drift towards the party leadership, but towards the leadership of the *ruling* party (which, effectively, translates to the political executive): the speaker's formal lack of independence means that they are, to all intents and purposes, handpicked by the leadership of the ruling party in the house, and therefore beholden to them. This was not only recognized by the dissenting opinion in *Kihoto Hollohan* but has been proven by the march of time. Speakers have repeatedly behaved in partisan ways in disqualification cases, and this pattern of partisanship has been observed by the Supreme Court as well.[77]

Notably, the version of the anti-defection law upheld in *Kihoto Hollohan* was not the only version possible. As we have seen above, the Punjab and Haryana High Court had already shown, through a simple act of interpretation, how the purpose of the anti-defection law (governmental stability) could be served, while leaving the space for individual dissent open; and, as the dissenting opinion in *Kihoto Hollohan* noted, there were already existing models that did not place the power to adjudicate on disqualification cases in the hands of a non-independent officer. But through its decision, the *Kihoto Hollohan* closed these windows, and endorsed a reading of anti-defection that entrenched and accelerated the centralizing drift within the Legislature.

B. Anti-Defection: The Federal Wrinkle

While the previous sub-section has engaged in a critique of the anti-defection law from the perspective of the relationship between the party leadership and its legislators, the story is incomplete without noting that Schedule X has failed in one significant respect. It has failed to check the toppling of *state* governments through political defections (or other related devices). This failure implicates the federal scheme and is attributable, in no small part, to the interventions of the Supreme Court.

As illustrations, consider three high-profile 'toppling' of Opposition-led state governments that took place during the tenure of the BJP government at the Centre, between 2019 and 2024: Karnataka, Madhya Pradesh, and Maharashtra. While the facts were different, each case tested the purpose and limits of Schedule X.

In the Karnataka and Madhya Pradesh cases, legislators from the ruling party/coalition resigned their positions. The effect of these resignations was that the strength of the house came down, the ruling party/coalition lost its majority, and the Opposition in the state legislature (which was the ruling party/coalition at the Centre) now held the numerical majority. What was obvious at the time—and remains obvious—is that these resignations were intended to do an end-run around the anti-defection law. Legislators resigning from the ruling party/coalition were able to bring the government down without being hit by the anti-defection law. Subsequently they could join the new ruling party, re-contest elections on their new party's ticket, and soon return to the Assembly. Indeed, this is precisely what happened.

In the Karnataka case, the toppling of the state government was facilitated by an interim Supreme Court order that held that the assembly members whose resignation applications were pending before the speaker would not be required to participate in the trust vote/floor test. In effect, this amounted to an interim suspension of Schedule X with respect to these members, who would otherwise have been disqualified had they disobeyed the party whip in a floor test. It also had the effect of bringing down the numbers of the house (in the manner outlined in the previous paragraph), and toppling the government. While the Court claimed that the purpose of the Order was to 'balance' the competing claims of the parties, a 'balance' that has the effect of bringing down a government—and thus making the case practically infructuous—is, to put it generously, a failed balance.[78]

Subsequently, in its final judgment, the Court sanctioned this mechanism of bypassing Schedule X by holding, first, that a resignation could be rejected by the speaker only if there was evidence that it was obtained under 'coercion' (no other 'extraneous circumstances' could be taken into account), and secondly, that disqualification for defection would not bar an individual from standing in the next election.[79] The effect of this—in both Karnataka and Madhya Pradesh—as we have noted above, was that legislators resigned without consequence (even a disqualification, as in Karnataka, had no effect, as they had already left Parliament), switched parties, stood in the ensuing by-election, and were returned to the Assembly. One would be hard-pressed to imagine a more thorough gutting of the purposes of Schedule X!

The Madhya Pradesh case saw the additional element of the centrally appointed governor, who, purportedly on being informed of the resignations, directed the chief minister to face an immediate floor test.[80] The fact that the governor was a nominee of the ruling party at the Centre, which was also the opposition party in the state, raised obvious issues of federalism as well. Despite specifically noting that the *timing* of a floor test would tend to favour the political balance of power that existed at the time, the Court nonetheless upheld the discretion of the governor to order a floor test, notwithstanding the fact that the Speaker was in the process of considering the resignation applications, as well as petitions for disqualification.[81] The result was to create a precedent where the central ruling party's nominee in the state (the governor) could—through the timing of a floor test—further weaken Schedule X.

This was, indeed, what happened in the final example—that of Maharashtra—where a split in one of the parties (the Shiv Sena) in the ruling coalition led to competing claims about which was the 'real' party. While the (deputy) speaker was considering disqualification petitions moved by the Shiv Sena leadership against their 'rebel' legislators, the governor ordered a floor test. Once again, the toppling of the state government was facilitated by interim orders of the Supreme Court, similar to Karnataka—one order prevented the speaker from taking action on the disqualification petitions by extending the time period for the 'rebel' legislators to respond to the disqualification notices that he had served on them; another order directed the floor test to go ahead. The result was that Schedule X was effectively suspended with respect to these 'rebel' legislators during the period of the floor test. With his numbers in the house now down, the chief minister was compelled to resign. The 'rebel' legislators—still claiming the mantle of the 'real' party—then entered into a coalition with the state Opposition (which was as we have seen, the ruling party at the Centre), and formed a new government.

One year later, in its final judgment, the Supreme Court went on to hold that the governor's direction of the floor test was illegal, but that nothing could be done now, as the chief minister had resigned before the floor test could take place.[82] There was a heavy irony to this, as at the time of the interim hearing, the Court had stressed that it could always 'turn the clock back' if needed.

While these cases may appear to turn around technical aspects of Schedule X and other allied provisions of the Constitution, that is not all there is to them. A recurring theme of this book has been the relationship between constitutionalism and power, and the role of the Constitution in creating maps that determine both how power is exercised, but also how it is contained. The purpose of Schedule X was to contain a particular form of the exercise of power by placing fetters upon the ability of legislators to 'defect' from their political parties—defections that were engineered through either promises or threats, made by those already holding State power.

We have critiqued Schedule X on grounds both of its conceptual premises, and for its design. With that said, however, the toppling of three Opposition-led state governments within the five-year period discussed here, accomplished *precisely* through large-scale switching of political allegiances (the very thing that Schedule X was designed to prevent, whether or not one calls it a 'defection'), reveals both a paradox and a thoroughgoing failure.

The paradox is this: while Schedule X is designed to strengthen the party leadership at the expense of the legislator, these two do not exhaust the balance of political forces. In the cases we have examined, there are three forces: the ruling (state) party leadership, its legislators, and the ruling (central) party leadership (which is also the Opposition (party) in the state)—which often acts through the office of the (centrally-appointed) governor.[83] And it is the latter two that have banded together to find ways around the Schedule X—not, as we have seen, in service of intra-party democracy, but in service of toppling and substituting the government.[84] The element of federalism, therefore, complicates our understanding of Schedule X (and reinforces one of the themes of this book, which is the intersection of various power axes). While one of its purposes is to strengthen the party leadership at the expense of the legislator, it has another purpose: that of protecting the federal structure—in particular, institutionally weaker state governments from a more powerful, and often predatory, adversarial central government.[85]

This, in turn, brings us to the failure: that is, the failure of the Schedule X to temper political power; especially, the superior power enjoyed by the ruling party at the Centre (including, but not limited to, control over functionaries such as the governor, and other instruments of pressure, such as investigative agencies)—over ruling parties in the states, which grants the former certain tools to destabilize or topple the latter. The Supreme Court's interventions—both through its interim orders and its judgments on resignations and the governor's powers—have entrenched this failure further, and have contributed to a centralizing drift where these tools have been strengthened, instead of being contained.

III. Dissent within the House: The Opposition

A. Constitutional Silences and Opposition Rights

In the previous section, we saw how Schedule X strengthened the party leadership at the expense of the individual legislator. Let us now move to the house, where at any given time multiple parties exist—the strongest, of course, is the majority party, which, like other parties, can no longer be effectively checked internally due to Schedule X. Checks upon the majority party's power, therefore must be external: either from coalition partners (if there is an effective, governing coalition), or from the Opposition (if the majority party is also the single ruling party).

This, then, brings us to the Opposition. Parliamentary democracies have a range of conventional tools to exercise a check upon the power of the majority party. These include, for example, a dedicated position of the leader of the Opposition (with certain speaking rights in the house), constitutionally recognized 'Opposition Days', the existence of Parliamentary committees to scrutinize draft legislation (with guaranteed Opposition presence), parliamentary questions, the right of the Opposition to constitute commissions of enquiry (if supported by a threshold percentage of the house) and so on.[86] The basic idea is that while the majority party's victory in the elections grants it the right to formulate policy and to legislate, the exercise of this power must at all times be subject to public-facing scrutiny and debate. As elected representatives of the people, parties in the Opposition are particularly well-placed to carry out this role.

What, then, does the Indian Constitution have to say about the Opposition? The answer unfortunately is: 'absolutely nothing'. The Constitution does not even recognize the formal position of the leader of Opposition (a subject of some controversy in recent years)[87] to say nothing of recognizing specific Opposition rights.[88] As Ramkumar and Singh point out, this is in stark contrast to a number of more contemporary Constitutions that expressly recognize both.[89] Instead, the position of the leader of the Opposition is provided for through ordinary legislation—and there, it is made conditional on recognition by the speaker—whose own lack of independence (as we have seen), in essence, renders the very existence of the leader of Opposition conditional upon the will of the executive.[90]

The constitutional silence is not accidental. We have noted above the general absence of constitutional codification when it came to Parliament (in stark opposition to the rest of the Constitution), the corresponding reliance on uncodified conventions, and the possible reasons for that choice. More specific to this section, in the Constituent Assembly, efforts to constitutionalize the post of the leader of Opposition were explicitly rejected, with the Assembly demonstrating a certain degree of contempt about the possibility of a constructive and meaningful Opposition.[91]

The Constituent Assembly's reticence to recognize constitutionally entrench Opposition rights emerges in even sharper relief when we consider the fact that colonial legislatures had provided almost no breathing room to the Opposition. As Syed Kazi Karimuddin noted in the early stage of the Constituent Assembly—soon after the initial decision to adopt Westminster parliamentarianism for the new Constitution—'we have seen in the past that in the working of the Provincial Constitution in the Provinces the Opposition was neglected, ignored and sometimes punished'.[92] One would have imagined that past experience would have made the Constituent Assembly particularly solicitous about entrenching the rights of the Opposition within the parliamentary structure, instead of leaving it to parliamentary conventions that had never developed in the first place.[93] However, the 'distortion' of parliamentarianism under the 1935 Act which we have referred to above was something that the Constituent Assembly seemed more inclined to continue rather than transform—at least when it came to the Opposition.[94]

This, coupled with historic judicial deference towards the parliamentary process, ensures that the ruling party (which, because of Schedule X, is effectively the ruling party leadership, or the executive) controls not only the content of legislation, but also the procedure of the house itself: from the decision of when to start (and when to end) parliamentary sessions, the decision on whether or not to send bills to Parliamentary Committees, and so on.[95,96] This is why, for example, attempts to compensate for the legislature's limited role in law-making through the creation of subject-specific Parliamentary committees has been mixed at best,[97] with the effectiveness and role of these committees depending on how seriously the executive branch is willing, or inclined, to take them.[98]

The result, thus, is an Opposition that is disempowered even more than it is in a well-functioning Westminster system, and its ability to participate (in law-making, in deliberation, and in oversight) is largely contingent upon the strength, will, and generosity of the ruling party (which, as we have seen, invariably means the executive). This, in turn, has given rise to other distortions in the parliamentary process, such as the well-documented and often-lamented phenomenon of the Opposition 'disrupting' proceedings in the House, and stymying legislative business. As Khaitan notes, it is the very powerlessness of the Opposition in what is a legislative 'state of nature' that incentivizes extra-parliamentary disruptions as the chosen method for Opposition legislatures to communicate their points of view to the public.[99] At the end of 2023, this led to yet another distortion, with which we began this chapter: the mass expulsion of MPs from both houses of Parliament by the respective chairs (speaker and vice president), ostensibly on the grounds of quelling disruption and letting parliamentary business go on uninterrupted. We can therefore see how one set of distortions reinforces another, in an overall web of parliamentary decay.

B. A Partisan Referee: The Speaker

Executive control over Parliament is enabled by the fact that much like Opposition rights, the Constitution also fails to guarantee the independence of the parliamentary 'referee', i.e., the speaker.[100] In the previous section, we discussed how the speaker's affiliation with the majority party creates a problem when it comes to the discharge of the adjudicatory function under Schedule X.

But of course, the speaker's powers extend to far more than adjudicating disqualification petitions for defection. Under the classic Westminster parliamentary model, the speaker exercises complete control over the proceedings of the house. This includes, for example, the power to suspend legislators and remove them from the house, the power to decide how voting will be conducted, the power to order that legislative proceedings not be broadcast at any point, the power to expunge statements from the official proceedings of the house, and so on.[101] In the Indian context, as we have seen, the speaker has the power to recognize (or not) a leader of the Opposition. Reddy and Bhargava, therefore, classify the speaker's powers (and responsibilities) under three categories: *facilitation* (of the debates and discussions of the house, i.e.,

Parliament's deliberative and representative function, which includes admitting motions for debate); *disciplining* (through suspension or expulsion, or adjourning the house); and *adjudication* (that is, the quasi-judicial functions that we have noted in the paragraph above).[102]

These powers and functions assume, and require, neutrality. It is precisely the extent of the speaker's control over the house that necessitates strong institutional safeguards guaranteeing their independence;[103] and it is precisely such safeguards that are missing from the text of the Indian Constitution.[104] The result has been a well-documented trend of Speaker partisanship recognized both in scholarship[105] and by the Supreme Court, as recently as 2023.[106] And the final consequence of this is a further tightening of executive control over the house, exercised *through* the speaker, in ways that we have discussed above (i.e., the speaker's quasi-judicial functions in adjudicating defections, or his powers over the proceedings of the house), and shall discuss below (in the context of bicameralism).

Before we proceed further, it may be worth pausing to note a particular irony here. In his critique of the 1935 Government of India Act, Ambedkar identified the 'two most important ways open to a legislature to for influencing the conduct of the administration … [that] is by discussion of the Budget, and by asking questions.'[107] On the flip side, he identified two ways in which the executive could avoid its responsibility to the legislature: by curtailing its powers, and by influencing its composition.[108] By Ambedkar's own standards, the Indian Constitution is defective on at least three out of four of these counts, through its omissions and its silences. Exercising its control over the speaker, the executive is in a position to determine what questions are 'selected' to be asked on the floor of the house, what meaningful powers the legislature exercises (through composition of committees etc.) and even the composition of the house (through adjudication of disqualification petitions and, at times. expulsions).[109] It appears that trenchant critique of the 1935 Act turned into sanguine acceptance of similar, distorting features under the Constitution, creating a stillborn parliamentarianism, the consequences of which have lingered on into the twenty-first century.

IV. Dissent within Parliament: The Second Chamber

The combination of Schedule X, the absence of Opposition rights in the Constitution, and the failure to insulate the speaker from the majority party, ensures that while in theory Parliament is meant to act as a check upon the executive, in practice, it is the executive that effectively controls Parliament. Our arguments so far, however, have been confined to the lower house. At the federal level, at least (and in some of the states), the Indian parliamentary structure is bicameral. With its veto power over bills (except money bills, which we shall discuss below), the upper house (the council of states, or the Rajya Sabha, at the federal level) thus acts as another, external check upon parliamentary majorities.

In the previous chapter, we noted that the judgment of the Supreme Court in *Kuldip Nayyar* snapped the connection between a Rajya Sabha legislator and the state that the legislator purportedly represented. The council of states, thus, is not so much a check on the lower house in the context of protecting the interests and rights of the states. However, as the composition of the Rajya Sabha depends upon the legislative majorities in the states, to the extent that the political opposition has representation in the state legislatures, the Rajya Sabha can serve as an Opposition-led check upon the lower house, exercising the power of scrutiny (and even veto) that the Opposition does not have in that house.

Needless to say, the political situation at any given time will determine whether and to what extent the Rajya Sabha can effectively perform this task. Concurrent majorities in the lower house and the upper house—or even the reliable support of upper house parties that are not formally allied with the ruling party—can stymie any checking role the Rajya Sabha might perform. Both these situations have not been entirely uncommon in Indian political history. Nonetheless, at the very least, the constitutionally entrenched

Rajya Sabha precludes parties with *only* a lower house majority from controlling the entire legislative process.

A. Money Bills

There is, however, one significant exception to this rule. Under Article 110 of the Constitution, a 'money bill', as defined by the Article, need not be passed by the Rajya Sabha in order to become law.[110] On its own terms, the money bill provision is innocuous enough, and is familiar to most parliamentary democracies. The basic idea is that as far as laws proposing taxes or the spending of public money are concerned, it is the direct representatives of the people—the lower house—that should have the final say.

An immediate question presents itself: what is to stop the majority party in the lower house from simply evading the scrutiny—and veto—of the upper house by classifying contentious bills as 'money bills'? After all, technically, virtually all substantive laws will require—directly or indirectly—*some* kind of public expenditure. Parliamentary democracy gives the following answer: a 'money bill' is only a valid money bill if the speaker of the house certifies it to be so.[111]

We can now immediately see the problem. The question of whether or not a bill is a 'money bill'—and thereby, the entire participation of the upper house in the law-making process—hinges upon 'certification' by the speaker. As we have seen above, structurally, and by *design*, in the context of the Indian Constitution, the speaker is not independent of the ruling party and is not insulated from it. To the extent, therefore, that the speaker is beholden to the ruling party, a 'money bill' in effect is little more than the ruling party in the lower house certifying the correctness of its own classification.

This is not a theoretical problem. The most notorious recent example of this was the classification of the Aadhaar Act—a law that established India's national biometric identification system—as a money bill, thus preventing the Rajya Sabha from adding certain crucial privacy-protective amendments to it.[112] The justification for this was that the infrastructure of the Unique Identification

Authority of India (UIDAI) was paid for from the public exchequer: a justification that, if taken to its logical conclusion, would shield most bills from Rajya Sabha vetoes. Bizarrely, a majority of the Supreme Court—while upholding the Aadhaar Act—failed to express a clear opinion on whether the speaker's classification of a bill as a money bill could be subject to judicial review.[113] The dissenting opinion, on the other hand, was clear on both points: that the speaker's certification *could* be reviewed, and that the Aadhaar Act had not validly been passed as a money bill.[114] Within a year of this, however—and following upon a slew of copycat laws that had been passed as money bills in order to exclude an Opposition-controlled Rajya Sabha—the Supreme Court doubted its own previous verdict, and referred the question for decision to a seven-judge bench. At the time of writing, a verdict is awaited, while bills continue to be (mis-)classified as money bills.

B. Procedure

An additional point needs to be briefly noted. According to the Constitution, the chairperson of the Rajya Sabha—i.e., the individual who plays a similar role as the speaker of the Lok Sabha—is the vice president of India.[115] At first blush, this may seem to be a more independent position than that of the speaker, and to an extent it is. Once again, however, political reality tells a different story. The 'indirect election' procedure for electing the President and vice president of India ensures that for the most part, the nominee of the ruling party will prevail (this has been the case on most—although not all—occasions in Indian history). Thus, an incoming government at the Union level (if it is a new government) might well, for a time, be faced with a vice president who is the nominee of the previous ruling party. However, as presidential and vice-presidential elections take place every five years, it is almost nailed on that at some point, the chairperson of the Rajya Sabha will, effectively, be the nominee of the ruling party of the Lok Sabha (and thus, as we have seen, of the political executive).

This immediately raises all the concerns that have been raised with respect to the speaker of the Lok Sabha. Indeed, incidents such as Rajya Sabha chairperson denying a division of votes for a particularly contentious set of bills—and then declaring them passed through a 'voice vote'—demonstrate that much like a partisan speaker, a partisan Rajya Sabha chairperson can reduce Opposition rights to a nullity.[116] The extreme example of this, of course, is mass expulsions, with which we began this chapter: the mass expulsions from the upper house in the December 2023 session of Parliament were at the instance of the vice president.

Once again, it is important to note that this is something baked into the design of the Constitution. Much like failing to insulate the speaker from the ruling party, stipulating that the chairperson of the Rajya Sabha will be the vice president is a *design choice* that facilitates the centralizing drift within the distributed parliamentary structures that the Constitution purports to establish.

V. Executive Law-making: Ordinances

So far, in this chapter, we have considered how constitutional text, constitutional silences, and judicial decisions have all contributed to a centralizing drift within Parliament, leaving the political executive with extensive control over the legislative process. There is one set of circumstances, however, where the Constitution removes even the formal constraints upon the executive and clothes it with direct, law-making power. Article 123 of the Constitution authorizes the President (on the aid and advice of the council of ministers) to promulgate ordinances while Parliament is in recess. The President may promulgate an ordinance if 'satisfied that circumstances exist which render it necessary ... [to] take immediate action'.[117] Such ordinances are deemed to have the 'same force and effect' as laws enacted by Parliament.[118] The only requirement is that once Parliament reassembles, the ordinances passed during recess must be laid before both houses, and will cease to exist if both houses pass resolutions of disapproval, or in any event, at the conclusion of six weeks.[119] Article 210 replicates these provisions for the states.[120]

The exercise of legislative power by the executive is not unknown in comparative constitutional law. It is commonly known as 'decree power' and is found—with some degree of frequency—in Latin American presidential systems (and elsewhere as well).[121] While decree powers can come in various shapes and forms, the fact that they predominantly exist in presidential systems is telling in itself.[122]

Indeed, the 'transplant' of the ordinance-making power from Britain into colonial India, at the very moment that it was giving way to representative institutions in the former, reflected the desire (as we have discussed before) to ensure that representative structures would remain subordinate to the authority of the imperial executive.[123] Ordinances—in their character as executive law-making—came into being exactly alongside representative institutions in colonial India, with the 1861 Indian Councils Act. Section 23 of that act authorized the governor-general 'in cases of emergency, to make and promulgate … ordinances for … peace and good government'.[124] These ordinances were to ordinarily last for six months. The power was retained in the 1915 Government of India Act in more or less the same language,[125] and used on a frequent basis during the First World War.[126] It was retained, once more, in the 1935 Government of India Act, with altered language.[127] As Dam notes, although the requirement of 'emergency' (later dropped) was meant to constrain the power of the governor-general to legislate through ordinances, in practice, the word 'emergency' was interpreted liberally, and determined by the subjective satisfaction of the governor general.[128] Unsurprisingly, thus, ordinances gradually morphed into a system of parallel law-making, rather than emergency law-making.

While the leaders of the freedom movement criticized legislation by ordinance during the colonial era, when it came to the framing of the Constitution, notwithstanding strong criticism, the ordinance-making power was retained (along with many other powers that those leaders had criticized with equal vehemence up until that point).[129]

It was argued in the Constituent Assembly—and later, by the Supreme Court—that the intent behind the ordinance provision was to equip the executive with law-making power in cases where there simply wasn't time to wait for Parliament to reassemble and enact legislation.[130] We have already seen that the 'emergency' requirement under colonial legislation had not acted as any meaningful fetter upon the governor-general. What is crucial to note, however, is that the text of Article 123—which was borrowed from the 1935 Government of India Act—does not even limit the scope of the ordinance-making power to cases where a formal emergency has been declared under the Constitution. Rather, it is contingent upon the 'satisfaction' of the President that 'circumstances' exist, which make 'immediate action' necessary. None of these terms can be defined by any precise definition. Thus, as Dam notes, over the years, much like in the colonial period, Article 123 has become a parallel source of law-making, which the executive uses simply to bypass the need to go through Parliament—that is, executive rule by decree.[131] In other words, the broad language of Article 123 and its valorization of the President's subjective satisfaction of circumstances needing 'immediate action'—normalizes the use of what, in theory, is *justified* on the grounds of only being an emergency power.[132]

Judicial decisions have not helped. Until 2017, the only pushback to the ordinance regime came in *D.P. Wadhwa vs State of Bihar*, where a clearly abusive practice—the multiple re-promulgation of ordinances over many years, effectively making the legislature completely redundant—was flagged by the Court as unconstitutional.[133] In other cases, however, the Court had exacerbated the problem by holding, for example, that ordinances were equivalent to 'temporary legislation'. Therefore, even after an ordinance lapsed, the things done during the time it that had been in force, along with the legal effects thereof, would continue.[134] Through these judgments, the Supreme Court gave judicial sanction to the idea that in legal terms, an ordinance stood on the same pedestal as a law made by Parliament.[135]

This position was eventually reversed in 2017, in *Krishna Kumar Singh vs State of Bihar*, where the Supreme Court issued two important findings.[136] First, it held that the President's satisfaction about urgency was subject to judicial review, albeit on the relaxed threshold of there needing to exist some material on the basis of which urgency was justified.[137] Secondly, it held that ordinances were not to treated as equivalent to temporary laws. Consequently, the default position was that once an ordinance lapsed, things that had been done during its existence—along with their legal effects—would also come to an end, *unless* it was either impossible, or significantly difficult, to reverse them.[138]

There is no doubt that *Krishna Kumar Singh vs State of Bihar* is an important judgment that recognizes that the ordinance-making power is exceptional, and deserves to be treated as such. Ultimately, however, defective constitutional design and the reality of India's constitutional practice leaves its efficacy open to question. The shelf life of a specific ordinance is around six months or less. Rarely, if ever, does the Indian Supreme Court hear and decide a constitutional challenge within that time period.[139] Indeed, in the eight years since the judgment in *Krishna Kumar Singh*, at the time of writing, not a single ordinance has been struck down on the basis that there were no urgent circumstances that warranted its promulgation. As pointed out above, for example, the Aadhaar (Amendment) Ordinance was promulgated in 2019, specifically with a view to getting over the Supreme Court's 2018 decision in *Justice K.S. Puttaswamy vs Union of India*. One would be hard-pressed to explain what the urgent circumstances were that did not allow the President to wait until Parliament reconvened. A challenge to the ordinance, however, on precisely this ground, went unheard, and then became infructuous, once the ordinance was replaced by an act.[140]

Secondly, in *Krishna Kumar Singh*, the Supreme Court's formulation of the category of things—and legal effects—that *would* survive an ordinance lapsing (or, presumably, being struck down) was not entirely precise. Limiting this category to things that were literally physically irreversible might have created a degree of deterrence when it comes to indiscriminate use of ordinances. In the event, however, we still wait to see how this might play out in practice.

Ultimately—to repeat a running theme of this book—judicial decisions cannot negate constitutional design. The fact remains that Article 123 exists, it authorizes legislation by executive decree, and the threshold for triggering it remains within the sole discretion of the political executive. Judgments like *Krishna Kumar Singh* can attempt to mitigate the abuse of such a provision, with varying degrees of success. But the problem—it should be clear—lies in the language and structure of the provision itself, and the manner in which it vests legislative power within the executive. It is the language and structure of Article 123 that, ultimately, disempowers Parliament and facilitates a parallel track of executive law-making, leaving litigation and judicial interpretation attempting to plaster over the edges and paper over the cracks.

VI. Conclusion: An Imperial Presidency in All but the Name

Ever since they evolved into the recognizable forms of government that we know today, the debate between the relative merits of the parliamentary and presidential (and semi-presidential) systems has been unceasing.[141] Partisans of parliamentarianism invoke the deliberative character of Legislative Assemblies, while supporters of presidentialism point to how their preferred system allows for swifter, more decisive action when necessary. Critics of presidentialism, in turn, argue that it allows for dangerous degrees of concentration of power; to this, supporters often counter that a functioning presidential system has a series of 'choke points' or 'veto points' that preclude any such outcome (in the United States, for example, the Congress and the Senate can stymie a president's legislative agenda). On the other hand, parliamentarianism itself can be criticized on similar grounds: the lack of a clean-cut separation between the executive and legislature encourages the concentration of power. The counter to this is what we noted at the beginning of the chapter: parliamentarianism has inbuilt corrective mechanisms such as intra-party dissent, a guaranteed space for the Opposition, and so on.[142]

It is not our task here to adjudicate between the two systems of government, or their various hybrid forms. It is worth asking, however, whether the Indian system is presently a hybrid presidential/parliamentary system that incorporates the worst of both worlds.

In the Prologue, we briefly flagged Kim Lane Scheppele's conception of the 'Frankenstate'. Scheppele takes the example of the 1920 Weimar Constitution. This constitution authorized the President to impose an emergency, subject to parliamentary ratification. It also allowed the President to dissolve Parliament once. Taken individually, both these provisions had justification, but when combined, they worked so that the President first dissolved Parliament and *then* imposed an (unchecked) emergency—thus undermining the entire constitutional order. Scheppele thus defines a 'Frankenstate' as one where 'perfectly legal and reasonable constitutional components are stitched together to create a monster'.[143]

Indeed, in our specific context, scholars of parliamentarianism in post-colonial nations have noted how the distorted forms of representative governance imposed by the British resulted in distorted legislative structures even after Independence, often leading to a 'reversal in the ... relationship between ... legislative and executive branches of government'.[144] Have the structures of representative democracy in India similarly evolved into something of a Frankenstate? *Formally*, India remains a parliamentary system, at both the central and the state level. This parliamentary system is encoded into the Constitution, and elections are contested at a constituency level, often on a party ticket, for a seat in Parliament. And the legislature and the executive are expressly separated in the Constitution.

In practice, however, we have seen that power is increasingly concentrated in the political executive. A number of things contribute to this. Schedule X strengthens the party leadership over individual legislators. Executive-controlled speakers enable executive control over the house, including over the Opposition (to the point of having the power to recognize the leaders of Opposition), that in any case has no constitutionally guaranteed rights to fall back upon. Such speakers can also remove the upper house from the equation altogether, by classifying bills as money bills. In Scheppele's terminology, there might be some justification for each of these aspects when taken alone: the anti-defection law to prevent floor-crossing and parliamentary instability; the impossibility of codifying what is essentially a parliamentary convention (speaker's independence); the relatively marginal role of the upper house vis-à-vis the lower house, because of its indirectly representative character.

However, when these are all put together and operate in a manner where each reinforces the other, it is easy to see that in effect there has been a dilution of '"horizontal" links of accountability'[145], and a concomitant centralization of power in the political executive. In breadth and scope, this arguably resembles the kind of power wielded by executive presidencies across history[146]—but with none of the safeguards or veto points that characterize some of these systems, and with severe democratic costs to boot.[147]

In the Indian context, it is the Prime Minister who comes to occupy that 'presidential' role within what is formally still a parliamentary system, but to all effects and purposes, and in terms of power, reflects the pathologies of presidentialism, albeit without the safeguards that either presidentialism or parliamentarianism have to offer. As we have seen, much of this is enabled both by the Constitution's own text and silences, which facilitate—or at least tolerate—a centralizing drift *within* the legislature, towards the executive. And so, even the grudging parliamentarianism that came into being with the Constitution has, over the years, through political action and judicial interpretation, decayed and degraded into the forms of a Frankenconstitution.

3

Power Dispersed: Pluralism

ON 5 AUGUST 2019, the President of India issued two orders: Constitutional Order (C.O.) 272 and Constitutional Order (C.O.) 273, applicable to the state of Jammu and Kashmir. These orders formally brought to an end a unique experiment in asymmetric federalism within the Indian Constitution.[1]

As the name suggests, asymmetric federalism imagines a heterogenous and plural federal structure, where different constituent units of the federation enjoy varying degrees and forms of power, autonomy, and relationships with the central authority.[2] Louis Tillin notes that asymmetric federalism might be justified on two grounds. At a *normative* level, it is argued that in diverse countries, the federal structure ought not to be homogenous, and ought to reflect diversity rather than corral it.[3] At a *functional* level, it is argued that asymmetric federalism is a pragmatic solution to accommodate a plurality of group-based claims within the overarching framework of a nation-state.[4]

Both the normative and the functional arguments have, from time to time, been invoked to justify—and interpret—asymmetric federalism within the Indian Constitution.[5] While keeping both articulations in mind, it is also important to think of asymmetric federalism through the lens of power. In one sense, the link is trivial: constituent entities that are the beneficiaries of asymmetric federalism enjoy greater power vis-à-vis their relationship with the Union. This is a simple case of distributing power through decentralization.

There is also, however, a deeper sense in which asymmetric federalism is concerned with the question of power. Both at a concrete level, but also at the level of discourse and of imagination, an asymmetric federation opens up the possibility of diverse and plural ways of organizing collective political life, and of self-governance, within the same state. This stands opposed to constitutional *homogeneity*, which argues for a uniform set of arrangements and a uniform imagination of the nation-state, regardless of actual diversity and pluralism.

We shall take up the link between asymmetric federalism and power in the conclusion to this chapter. However, as we consider the different contexts in which asymmetric federalism has evolved in the course of our constitutional history in the succeeding sections, it is important to keep this connection in mind.

Until 5 August 2019, the clearest example of asymmetric federalism within the Constitution was Article 370, which set out the constitutional relationship between the Union of India and the state of Jammu and Kashmir.[6] At the time of Independence, the then princely state of Jammu and Kashmir was able to negotiate for itself a higher degree of autonomy (as a condition for accession to the Indian Union) than its compatriot princely states within the future Indian Union. It was this autonomy that was codified into Article 370, and then undone in 2019 by two Presidential Orders.

It would be a mistake to argue, however, that C.O. 272 and 273 radically altered the status quo. From its origin, even as it purported to recognize asymmetric federalism in the case of Jammu and Kashmir, Indian constitutionalism was never entirely comfortable with the idea. This is evident in the ambiguously worded text of

Article 370; in its application to the state, starting as early as 1952; and in the Supreme Court judgments that interpreted it over the years. A combination of these three factors—within the backdrop of power politics and State coercion—had, in effect, ended Jammu and Kashmir's asymmetric federal experiment long before the events of 5 August 2019.[7]

This chapter will study the troubled history of asymmetric federalism in India. It will begin with a historical overview of the debates in the Constituent Assembly about the character of the nascent Indian State, and how these debates contributed towards the shaping of the Constitution as a terrain of contestation on the issue of asymmetric federalism **(I)**. It will then consider the exemplar of Jammu and Kashmir, noting the historical origins of Article 370 and its early career alongside the workings of another historically unique body, the Constituent Assembly of Jammu and Kashmir. It will argue that through two 'inflection point' judgments in the 1960s and '70s—*Sampat Prakash* and *Mohd Maqbool Damnoo*—the Indian Supreme Court interpreted the silences and ambiguities in Article 370 in a manner that strengthened Union power and weakened asymmetric federalism under the Constitution; and that, finally, there is a direct road from the Court's interpretation of Article 370 to its effective abrogation in August 2019 **(II)**.

This chapter will go on to examine asymmetric federalism in two other contexts within the Indian Constitution. At the level of the states, while there has been no example equivalent to that of Jammu and Kashmir, at present, no fewer than nine states of the Union enjoy 'special powers' (Articles 371A-I). However, with two qualified exceptions (Nagaland and Mizoram, which we shall discuss) these special powers are either of a purely administrative character, or come accompanied with a federal override or 'kill switch', thus making them attenuated examples of asymmetric federalism at best **(III)**. And finally, there are Schedules V and VI, which form 'mini-Constitutions' of a sort: a separate governing code for indigenous (Adivasi) territories within India. Much like the constellation of sub-articles that branch out from Article 371, however, Schedules V and VI suffer from precisely the same problem of being subjected to the federal kill switch **(IV)**.

As the conclusion will argue, all three cases are illustrative of a phenomenon that we have discussed throughout this book. The Constitution's vision of power is a contested one, with impulses towards heterogeneity and diversity constantly countered—within the text itself—by strong centralizing tendencies. Specifically, while the Constitution purports to recognize pluralism in terms of constitutional arrangements, it undermines that recognition by a counter-push towards homogeneity and uniformity. Asymmetric federalism in India thus suffers from the same centralizing drift that characterizes the other axes upon which power under the Constitution is organized. **(V)**

I. A Patchwork Quilt: On the Eve of the Constitution

As the framers of the Indian Constitution set about the task of crafting a State out of the erstwhile British colony, they were faced with numerous challenges. Prominent among these was the diversity of the Indian State that was yet to be born. Politically, India was a patchwork of territories that included the erstwhile British Dominion and more than 500 'princely states' that had been formally sovereign but effectively under British domination.[8] Linguistically, India was home to a profusion of languages, many of which were territorially specific, and were spoken by a great number of people. Religiously, even after Partition, Muslims constituted a significant minority (alongside many other religions). Socially, there were peoples within India—especially the Adivasis—whose ways of life, social organization, and institutions of self-governance were all different from the rest of the country. And geographically, there were distinct territories in the northeastern part of the country that had never been politically united with the 'mainland', and were heterogenous on each of the axes highlighted above.

In what ways—and to what extent—would the Indian Constitution reflect, articulate, and accommodate this diversity? It is important to note that the Constitution was drafted in the shadow of Partition (along with its horrendous religious violence) as well as the integration of the princely states (an accomplishment that was not free from coercion and violence either). Understandably, the need to 'hold together' the Indian State, and prevent it from splintering apart, was one of the priorities for the framers. For this reason, therefore, on some of the issues, the constitutional settlement was a foregone conclusion. Asymmetric arrangements on grounds of religion (such as, for example, electoral quotas) were rejected out of hand as a pernicious legacy of British divide-and-rule policies.[9] And while the Constituent Assembly spent a significant amount of time debating the 'language question', the debate itself was conducted primarily on the terrain of linguistic *rights*, and not (as it has been elsewhere) on the terrain of language constituting distinct *peoples*, with distinct rights to political autonomy. This would eventually culminate in the linguistic reorganization of Indian states, starting in 1956, a point we shall return to in the Epilogue.

With respect to the other issues, what stands out from the Constituent Assembly Debates is that at no point did the framers of the Constitution articulate a substantive *theory* of asymmetric federalism as a mechanism to articulate and accommodate Indian diversity. The provisions of the Constitution that eventually came to embody aspects of asymmetric federalism were debated in isolation, and driven by distinct—often political—imperatives. For example, Article 370 of the Constitution (which we shall discuss in the next section) owed its existence not to any principled convictions about asymmetric federalism, but simply to prevailing geopolitical conditions, which allowed the ruler of Jammu and Kashmir to negotiate more favourable terms for his state than any other princely state. And it was, at least in part, this history that contributed to its final unravelling in 2019, without any significant resistance from either the Indian Parliament or the Supreme Court.

On the other hand, while the discussions about Schedules V and VI did involve principled debate, this was of a very thin variety. Assimilationists warned of the possibilities of secession, and the creation of 'tribalstans' if territorially bounded areas were given special rights. On the other hand, while B.R. Ambedkar and his fellow travellers on this point ('the accommodationists') did note distinctiveness as the basis of asymmetric federal arrangements, with a few exceptions,[10] this was often couched in paternalistic terms, pointing to the need to protect 'tribals' and their way of life from absorption by the more 'sophisticated' mainstream Indian social and cultural community.[11]

This situation continued even after Independence and the framing of the Constitution. Political demands that were left unresolved at the time of the framing—such as, for example, the claims of the Mizos and the Nagas to sovereignty and independence—were eventually, and after significant violence, resolved by inserting asymmetrically federal arrangements into the Constitution (through the addition of sub-clauses to Article 371). Article 371 itself, however—as we shall see later in this chapter—has no organizing principle or theme, with its many sub-clauses having been enacted at different points in India's constitutional history, primarily in response to political imperatives.

The upshot of this is that while the Indian Constitution has a number of provisions that—in technical terms—can be labelled 'asymmetrically federal', there is no normative or principled *idea* of asymmetric federalism that holds them together. The absence of this idea—the absence of a constitutional 'common sense' around asymmetric federalism—has, I would suggest, stymied the development of any consistent jurisprudence around the issue. It has rendered Indian asymmetric federalism a fragile and vulnerable modus vivendi at the best of times, and ultimately contributed to a centralizing drift.

Let us now consider how this has happened, across the board.

II. Asymmetric Federalism and the Long Erosion of Article 370

A. History and Origins

As pointed out above, on the eve of Independence, India was a patchwork of territories that had been under the direct control of the British, and an assortment of more than 500 nominally independent princely states.[12] The relative size and power of most of these States precluded any significant problems with their absorption into the Indian Union through Instruments of Accession signed between their rulers and representatives of the Indian government.[13] There were a few exceptions. For example, Hyderabad acceded to the Indian Union only after sustained violence.[14] Another exception was Jammu and Kashmir, whose size and strategic location gave it substantially more bargaining power than most of the other princely states.

As a result, the Instrument of Accession that the ruler of Jammu and Kashmir entered into with the Indian government was of a different character. According to the instrument, Jammu and Kashmir acceded to the Indian Union in respect of three subjects: foreign affairs, defence, and communication.[15] Beyond this, the precise character of the relationship between Jammu and Kashmir and the Union was to be determined by the (future) Constituent Assembly of Jammu and Kashmir.[16] Jammu and Kashmir, thus, was the only state in the Indian Union that would have its own Constituent Assembly, and its own (state) Constitution.

How would affairs be conducted until the time that the State Constitution was framed? This question was answered by Article 370 of the Indian Constitution. Article 370, as it originally stood, set out the 'temporary' arrangement that would govern the relationship between the state and the Union. It provided for two situations: where a matter was covered by the Instrument of Accession (i.e., it related to foreign affairs, defence, and communication), the President could make laws for the state after consulting with the then maharaja.[17]

For all other matters, the President could make laws only with the concurrence of the maharaja.[18] The Indian Constitution itself could only be extended to the state on similar terms: after consultation with the head of the state of Jammu and Kashmir if the constitutional provision related to a topic in the Instrument of Accession, and only with his concurrence if it did not.[19]

This was, of course, in stark contrast to the situation in the rest of the Union, where—as we have seen in the previous chapter on federalism—legislative competence was divided up in accordance with the terms of Schedule VII. The 'temporariness' of this state of affairs was indicated by Article 370 itself, which made the recommendation of the Constituent Assembly of Jammu and Kashmir a necessary precondition for any changes to—or abolition of—Article 370 itself.[20]

In its original form, therefore, Article 370 was based upon the following principle: first, that the state of Jammu and Kashmir would frame its own Constitution for self-governance; and secondly, that barring the three subjects mentioned above, on any other issue, the federal Constitution could only be extended to the state *with its consent*. Let us call the second principle the requirement of *double consent*, i.e., that in an asymmetrically federal relationship, substantial changes to the nature of that relationship cannot be made without the consent of *both* parties to the relationship.[21]

B. Practice: Presidential Orders as Constitutional Amendments

The Indian Constitution—along with Article 370—came into force in 1950. The Constituent Assembly of the state of Jammu and Kashmir commenced its work in 1951 and finished it in 1956, with the enactment of the Constitution of Jammu and Kashmir. In the meantime, the President of India had already issued a series of Presidential Orders (the most significant one being the 1954 Presidential Order),[22] which had extended a number of provisions of the Indian Constitution to the state.[23]

The completion of the work of Jammu and Kashmir's Constituent Assembly, and the enactment of the Constitution of Jammu and Kashmir, raised certain important questions about the continued relevance of Article 370 and the future of asymmetric federalism. Under status quo, the President (in effect, the Union government) possessed law-making power for the state of Jammu and Kashmir (with the prerequisite of consultation in some cases, and concurrence in others, with Jammu and Kashmir's head of state). Needless to say, this was an anomalous situation, made further anomalous by the fact that Jammu and Kashmir now had its own Constitution. Under those changed circumstances, did the President's power to legislate for Jammu and Kashmir continue, or did it lapse?

Noorani argues, for example, that the latter position is self-evidently correct. The unique set of arrangements set up under Article 370 were meant to be temporary, holding the field only until the Constituent Assembly of Jammu and Kashmir framed the Constitution for the state. Once that was done, the future relationship between the state and the Indian Union would be governed by that Constitution, and not by further Presidential Orders. For Noorani, this was the only position that respected the negotiated settlement between Jammu and Kashmir and the Indian Union, which had culminated in the accession of the former to the latter. It was buttressed by the history of the framing of Article 370, the Constituent Assembly Debates, and the reticence of first Indian President, Rajendra Prasad, to use Presidential Orders as the default form of law-making for Jammu and Kashmir.[24]

There remains, however, a gap between Noorani's argument and the actual constitutional text, which is somewhat more ambiguous. The proviso to Article 370(3) stipulated that the recommendation of the Constituent Assembly of the state of Jammu and Kashmir would be a necessary precondition for Article 370 to stop existing. The state's Constituent Assembly, however, made no recommendation of the kind after it finished its work and dissolved itself. What followed from this? According to Noorani, the absence of Constituent

Assembly recommendation made no difference. The very text of Article 370 necessarily implied that the regime of Presidential Orders that it established was meant to cease as soon as the state's Constitution came into existence, and the Article 370 regime was to be replaced by the legal regime established by that Constitution.[25]

The counter-argument, however, was that Article 370 stipulated only one legitimate method for its own cession: a recommendation by the state's Constituent Assembly. If that body had made no recommendation, the only conclusion was that Article 370 was meant to continue, a parallel track for Union law-making, alongside the state's own Constitution, *with the blessing of the state's (now defunct) Constituent Assembly*. As we shall see, when the question came before the Supreme Court, it chose the latter interpretation. The effect of this was to weaken the asymmetric federal relationship between Jammu and Kashmir and the Indian Union, and pave the way for its eventual abolition.

C. Inflection Points: Sampat Prakash and Mohd Maqbool Damnoo

In 1967, government employees and teachers in Jammu went on strike after their demands for improved terms were rejected by the state government. In a familiar turn of events, the state government responded by placing Sampat Prakash—one of the leaders of the strike—under preventive detention. Sampat Prakash challenged his detention before the Supreme Court (*Sampat Prakash vs State of Jammu and Kashmir*). One of his arguments impugned the constitutional validity of the Jammu and Kashmir Preventive Detention Act of 1964, which authorized a regime of preventive detention that did away with the procedural safeguards mandated by Article 22 of the Indian Constitution.[26] At the heart of the argument was Article 35(c) of the Indian Constitution, which had been extended to the state of Jammu and Kashmir through Presidential Order (C.O.) 48 of 1954, passed under Article 370. Article 35(c) barred any Fundamental Rights challenge to a preventive detention law, within the state of Jammu and Kashmir, for a period of five years from 1954.

In 1959, however, through another Presidential Order, the time period of five years was extended to ten years. In 1964, ten years was extended to fifteen years (effectively creating a continuing constitutional black hole in Jammu and Kashmir, where preventive detention laws simply couldn't be challenged at all[27]). *Sampat Prakash* argued that both Presidential Orders were unconstitutional, as they were issued after the Jammu and Kashmir Constitution had come into force.

The Supreme Court rejected this argument. It held that the state's Constituent Assembly had made no recommendation for the abolition of Article 370 (and indeed, during its functioning, had recommended that the Article continue to apply, with one modification).[28] In effect, therefore, the Court held that 'Article 370 has never ceased to be operative and there can be no challenge on this ground to the validity of the Orders passed by the President in exercise of the powers conferred by this Article'.[29]

Sampat Prakash made a second argument trying to restrict the scope of presidential legislation and amendment under Article 370. He argued that when Article 370 authorized the President to extend various provisions of the Indian Constitution to the state of Jammu and Kashmir 'subject to such exceptions and modifications as the President may by order specify', it was limited to a *one-time* extension, and not a license for continual presidential (i.e., executive) tinkering with the constitutional provisions applicable to the state. In other words, having extended a provision (or provisions) of the Indian Constitution to Jammu and Kashmir, the President did not then retain a continuing power to amend them through Article 370 orders whenever he saw fit. As a corollary, *Sampat Prakash* also argued that in any event, the power to make 'modifications and exceptions' to a constitutional provision did not include the power to completely alter them (for example, placing preventive detention statutes beyond the pale of judicial scrutiny was not a simple 'amendment' or 'modification' of the Constitution as applied to Jammu and Kashmir, but a wholesale abrogation of a crucial constitutional right).

Once again, the Supreme Court read the text of the Constitution in a manner that negated these arguments. It compared Article 370 to a typical administrative law provision, which authorized a 'rule-making authority' to alter or amend the rules that it had framed from time to time (even if, as in this case, the 'rules' were actually constitutional provisions that were being amended!).[30] And it went on to hold that in accordance with past precedent, the power to 'amend' or 'modify' included the power to make 'radical transformations'.[31]

Sampat Prakash vs State of Jammu and Kashmir, therefore, did two things. First, it held that even after the passage of the Jammu and Kashmir Constitution, the President (i.e., the Union government) retained the power to alter the constitutional and legal structure of Jammu and Kashmir; and secondly, that this power was potentially unlimited in scope.

What were the implications for asymmetric federalism? In formal terms, an important safeguard remained: i.e., the requirement, under the proviso to Article 370(1)(d), and Article 370(2), of the concurrence of the state government (what we have called the principle of 'double consent'). But in effect, as Noorani and others point out, this requirement had become effectively meaningless as, ever since the ouster and imprisonment of Sheikh Abdullah in 1953, governments in Jammu and Kashmir ceased to be genuinely independent from the Union government.[32] In such a situation, the political imbalance of power ensured that the terms of Article 370—far from maintaining asymmetric federalism—placed Jammu and Kashmir in a *worse* situation than other states. Here, the Constitution could be altered through a simple 'collusive' arrangement between the government of Jammu and Kashmir and the Union government (where the former was under the effective control of the latter), instead of the two-thirds legislative supermajority requirement applicable to the rest of the country under Article 368 of the Constitution.[33]

Effectively, therefore—and this is crucial—the Supreme Court's interpretive choices in *Sampat Prakash vs State of Jammu and Kashmir* ensured that Article 370, and the principles of asymmetric federalism that it embodied, would be shaped by, and *subordinated* to, the political balance of power between the Union and the state.[34] On the other hand, the interpretation that the Court rejected would have sought to preserve asymmetric federalism—in the sense of Jammu and Kashmir governing itself by its own constitution—by *insulating* the asymmetrically federal relationship from the political balance of power. It is in this fundamental sense that the judgment in *Sampat Prakash* was an inflection point not just in the relationship between the state of Jammu and Kashmir and the Union, but in the contestation around asymmetric federalism on the terrain of Indian constitutionalism.

A few years later, in *Mohd Maqbool Damnoo vs State of Jammu & Kashmir*, the formal guarantee of asymmetric federalism was weakened still further. Once again, the case involved the question of preventive detention under the 1964 Jammu and Kashmir Preventive Detention Act (as amended in 1967). Unlike Sampat Prakash, Mohd Maqbool Damnoo was not even informed of the grounds of his detention, on the basis that doing so would be prejudicial to the public interest. He too challenged the constitutional validity of the Preventive Detention Act—this time, its 1967 amendment. Damnoo argued that the amendment was invalid because it had not been assented to by the Sadar-i-Riyasat—the elected head of state of Jammu and Kashmir, according to the state's Constitution.

However, what stood in the way of this argument was the fact that in 1965, through a Presidential Order under Article 370, references to Sadar-i-Riyasat under Article 370 (and other relevant provisions of the Indian Constitution) had been replaced by 'Governor'. This change was fundamental: while the Sadar-i-Riyasat was an elected head of state, the state governor—under the Indian constitutional scheme—was a central government nominee.

Damnoo argued that the office of the Sadar-i-Riyasat was the lynchpin of the (asymmetrically federal) relationship between the state of Jammu and Kashmir and the Union of India. Replacing that office with a Union government-appointed nominee was a change so fundamental that it could only be brought about through the convening of a fresh Constituent Assembly.[35]

The Supreme Court rejected this argument, holding that the governor was the legal successor to the Sadar-i-Riyasat, and that, therefore, the changed text of provision only reflected the changed reality. The fact that 'the Governor is not elected as was the Sadar-i-Riyasat ... would not make him any the less a successor to the Sadar-i-Riyasat. Both are heads of the State'.[36]

The effect of this—other than the fact that Mohd Maqbool Damnoo remained in detention—was that a crucial pillar of the asymmetric federal relationship between the state of Jammu and Kashmir and the Union of India ceased to exist. And this alteration was hugely significant, given the long and troubled history of the position of the governor in Indian federalism. Right from 1953 to the present day, governors—as Union government nominees—have frequently intervened in state politics in order to promote the central government's interests.[37] And while this has been true in states across the country, it is even *more* true in a state like Jammu and Kashmir, where there have been long periods of direct central government rule—often *through* the governor, accompanied by credible accusations of vote-rigging in the shadow of violence.[38] Indeed, as we shall see, the eventual and formal nullification of the asymmetric federal relationship between Jammu and Kashmir and the Union of India was enabled, in some part, by the removal of a counter-balancing force—a head of state directly accountable to the people of the state—in Article 370.

D. The Events of 5 August 2019 and their Aftermath

On 5 August 2019, two Presidential Orders—purportedly passed under Article 370—formally brought the asymmetrical federal relationship to an end. Through C.O. 272—purported to be passed under Article 370(1)(d)—the phrase 'Constituent Assembly of the State', under Article 370(3), was replaced by the phrase 'Legislative Assembly of the State'.[39] Under the new position, therefore, the 'Legislative Assembly of Jammu and Kashmir' could make a recommendation for the cession of Article 370. Following this, C.O. 273—purporting to follow on from the changes brought about by C.O. 272—stipulated that existing Article 370 would be replaced by a single clause, which stated that, henceforth, all the provisions of the Indian Constitution would apply, ipso facto, to Jammu and Kashmir.[40]

In the constitutional challenge to C.O. 272 and 273, the Supreme Court struck down the replacement of 'Constituent Assembly' with 'Legislative Assembly', and therefore invalidated C.O. 272. Nonetheless, however, it upheld C.O. 273 and—thereby—upheld the abrogation of Article 370 *as a unilateral act by the Union executive*.[41] While we shall discuss the Court's reasoning below, I want to first note that there is a direct line between the 'inflection point' judgments in both *Sampat Prakash vs State of Jammu & Kashmir* and *Mohd Maqbool Damno vs State of Jammu & Kashmir*, and the eventual abolition of the asymmetric federal relationship between Jammu and Kashmir and the Union of India.

First, *Sampat Prakash vs State of Jammu & Kashmir* held that the regime of presidential legislation (and constitutional amendment) remained in force, even after the passage of the Jammu and Kashmir State Constitution—the document that, originally, was intended to determine the relationship between Jammu and Kashmir and the Union. This *legal* finding entrenched the existing—and continuing—*political* reality, where Presidential Orders, which did not meet with any meaningful resistance from politically powerless state governments, effectively eroded Jammu and Kashmir's autonomy over time. Notably, C.O. 272 was itself a Presidential Order under Article 370(1)(d)—the very thing that Sampat Prakash had argued was precluded once the Jammu and Kashmir Constitution came into force.

Secondly, *Damnoo's* finding that the replacement of 'Sadar-i-Riyasat' with 'Governor' was a valid recognition of an existing reality (instead of completely resetting the constitutional relationship between Jammu and Kashmir and the Union) had profound consequences. Both C.O. 272 and 273 would have been impossible without this alteration. The Presidential Orders of 5 August 2019 were passed at a time when Jammu and Kashmir's Legislative Assembly had not been in existence for over a year and a half: the previous government had fallen after the collapse of the coalition in power, and no fresh elections had been held since then. At this point, therefore—with the state first under governor's, and then under President's Rule, the 'government of the state' (the body that had to accord its 'concurrence' to the Presidential Orders) was, effectively, the governor himself.

The C.O. 272, therefore, was based on the absurd logic that the nominee of the Union government could give consent to the Union government's orders: the very definition of a *unilateral* change to the *federal* relationship that was, in theory, supposed to be based upon the consent of *both* parties to that relationship. As we have seen, however, the road to this absurd logic was paved by the decision in *Mohd Maqbool Damnoo vs State of Jammu & Kashmir*, which saw no problem with the Union government nominee being the formal 'representative' of the state of Jammu and Kashmir when it came to future alterations or modifications of the relationship between the two parties.

Indeed, it was a similar logic that, ultimately, constituted the basis of the Supreme Court's judgment ratifying the events of 5 August 2019. During the course of arguments, it became evident that the Union government's defence of its actions was erected upon two pillars. First, the Union argued that Article 370 was in the nature of a political compromise, necessitated by the specific events that prevailed at the time of the framing of the Constitution. Consequently, Article 370 possessed no special sanctity and its undoing was—in simple terms—a political response to a changed political situation.[42]

As a matter of history, this is undoubtedly accurate—indeed, this is precisely the point made at the beginning of this chapter. Of course, what was missing in the Union's argument was *what follows when a political settlement takes a constitutional form*. That is, once a political compromise is written *into* a nation's Constitution, does it not acquire a normative valence that goes beyond the events that brought it into being?

The second pillar of the Union government's defence turned on one word: *integration*. The Union argued that the purpose of Article 370 had been to incrementally *integrate* Jammu and Kashmir into India, which—for various political reasons—had not been possible at the time of Independence. Echoing Prime Minister Jawaharlal Nehru's comments about Article 370 serving as a 'tunnel' through which the provisions of the Indian Constitution were meant to pass into Jammu and Kashmir, the Union therefore argued that the events of 5 August 2019 were simply the logical culmination of a process that had begun with the framing of Article 370: a culmination that was the abolition of Article 370 *itself*.[43]

'Integration', however, is not a self-interpreting word. What, precisely, did the Union mean by it? Dig a little deeper, and it becomes clear that, in the Union's arguments, integration simply meant *homogeneity*. The constitutional integration of Jammu and Kashmir was thus a ripping away of its autonomous status, in order to make its constitutional position within the Union *equivalent* to that of other states.[44] In the constitutional vision that the Union presented to the Supreme Court, there was no space for pluralism—*except* by the will of the Union, and on the terms of the Union.

It was a vision that the Supreme Court accepted. Its ratification of C.O. 273 was based upon a theory that the *goal* of Article 370 was to achieve the integration-homogenization of Jammu and Kashmir.[45] The Presidential Order of abrogation, thus, was treated as the culmination of the incremental extension of the Constitution to the state of Jammu and Kashmir over the previous seven decades, and as the *logical end point* of that history.[46] In this fashion, the

Court was able to dispense with the principle of double-consent, ignore the silencing of the people of Jammu and Kashmir in the process of abrogation,[47] endorse executive unilateralism, and ratify the abolition of the experiment in constitutional pluralism that had been Article 370.[48]

It is important to note that the Supreme Court had a choice. The case for asymmetric federalism and pluralism as constitutional *principles*—and as a part of the normative architecture of Article 370—was categorically made before the Court.[49] This was a different way of imagining integration: integration, in the submissions of the petitioners, did not mean equivalence. Rather, in a diverse and heterogenous society, integration was entirely consistent with pluralism.[50] Article 370 provided the constitutional form in which integration-as-pluralism could be imagined.

In *Re: Article 370 of the Constitution*, faced with a choice between the more capacious understanding of integration as pluralism, and integration as homogeneity, the Court chose the latter. In doing so, however, and even as we critique the judgment on its own terms, it is important to keep in mind that the judgment was consistent with the Court's own history, and continued the Court—and the Constitution—along the path that had been defined by previous inflection-point judgments. In other words, the history of asymmetric federalism in India—as exemplified by Article 370 and the position of Jammu and Kashmir within the Union—did not suddenly end on 5 August 2019. Rather, it is a history of contestation: a history where constitutional silences and ambiguities were resolved by the Supreme Court to entrench a centralizing drift, which in turn fed on, and was fed by, a political reality of diminished effective autonomy enjoyed by the state of Jammu and Kashmir. It was this history that finally culminated in the constitutional changes of 5 August 2019. But, as we have seen, it is a history that could well have taken a different turn and led to a different future for asymmetric federalism, at least in the context of Article 370.

III. Article 371 and Centrally Managed Asymmetric Federalism

Interestingly, however, the strident argument made by the Union for integration-as-homogeneity was belied by the Constitution's own design: in particular, Article 371. Article 371 of the Constitution and its various sub-clauses contain 'special provisions' for as many as nine states of the Indian Union: a bouquet of asymmetric federalism arrangements that take a diverse variety of forms. For better understanding, let us group these special provisions into three heads.

A. Administrative Asymmetric Federalism

The first form provides for different administrative regimes, often in specific areas within the chosen states. For example, Article 371 authorizes the President in turn to authorize the governors of Maharashtra and Gujarat to establish 'development boards' in those states.[51] Similarly, Article 371-D authorizes the President, by order, to make detailed provisions for the state of Andhra Pradesh concerning reservations, organization of employment cadres, and the setting up of an administrative tribunal for resolving disputes, whose operation is not subject to superintendence by the jurisdictional High Court.[52]

To this list, we should perhaps also add Article 371C of the Constitution, which deals with Manipur. This provision authorizes the President to constitute a committee of the Legislative Assembly of the state that has members elected from the Hill Areas, and also allows for the Union executive to issue directions to the state for the administration of these areas.[53] As the Constitution does not itself entrench devolution of power in Manipur (unlike the states we will discuss below), this has been sought to be accomplished through laws such as the Manipur District Councils Act (and its various amendments). These laws have, however, proven highly controversial, as they devolve only very limited (and primarily advisory) power to tribal authorities, while retaining most of the *real* power within the hands of the district administration and the state government.[54] However, the absence of constitutional entrenchment and the non-extension of Schedule VI to the Hill Areas of Manipur despite multiple recommendations[55] makes it difficult to advance claims for internal self-determination within the terrain of the Constitution, as it stands today.[56]

B. Legislative Asymmetric Federalism

This is the second form of asymmetry, which provides for different legislative structures in certain states. For example, Article 371-I provides that the Goa Legislative Assembly shall consist of not less than thirty members.[57] The state of Sikkim, which acceded to the Indian Union in 1975, has a series of both transitional and permanent provisions concerning the composition of its Legislative Assembly.[58]

C. Constitutional Pluralism

The third set of special provisions is of the greatest interest for our purposes, and comes closest to the idea of constitutional pluralism, and to the detailed constitutional arrangements that existed under the original Article 370.[59]

The most vivid and far-reaching example of constitutional pluralism is Article 371A, concerning the state of Nagaland. Constitutional asymmetry with respect to Nagaland, in the post-colonial era, was born alongside Independence.[60] In June 1947, the Naga National Council (NNC) and Governor of Assam Akbar Hydari signed a nine-point agreement that began by recognizing 'the right of the Nagas to develop themselves according to their freely expressed wishes', and went on to provide (among other things) for a legislative veto by the NNC with respect to central or provincial laws that 'materially affect the terms of this agreement or the religious practices of the Nagas'.[61] However, the death of Hydari and the framing of the Constitution saw the application of the more modest Bordoloi Committee Report and the Constitution's Schedule VI to

Nagaland.[62] This, in turn, led to an NNC-organized plebiscite where (according to the NNC) an overwhelming majority of Nagas voted for Independence.

The 1950s then saw an escalation of the situation into military hostilities and the beginnings of what is referred to as 'India's longest insurgency'.[63] Attempts to devise a political solution to the problem began with the creation of a new administrative unit (Naga Hills and Tuensang Area), which would be administered by the governor while, simultaneously, repression through legislative instruments such as AFSPA continued.[64] This eventually evolved into what came to be known as the Sixteen-Point Agreement between the central government and the NNC.[65] In a bid to defuse the demands for Independence, the Sixteen-Point Agreement promised the creation of Nagaland 'as a state *within the Indian Union*' (emphasis supplied)—but, crucially, with asymmetric statehood provisions that included a much more far-reaching veto upon central legislation at the instance of the future Legislative Assembly of Nagaland.[66]

This settlement was constitutionally entrenched as Article 371A of the Indian Constitution, enacted in 1962: the first example of asymmetric federalism after Article 370 in the original Constitution. As the brief history reveals, therefore, Article 371A (imperfectly) embodies a political compromise between the Government of India and the long-standing movement for Naga independence and sovereignty, by extending to Nagaland a form of 'negotiated and shared sovereignty', which is, in some ways, reminiscent of the old Article 370 regime.[67] For example—as noted above—Article 371A precludes central laws in relation to the 'religious or social practices of the Nagas', 'Naga customary law and procedure', and 'ownership and transfer of land' from applying to the state of Nagaland, without the consent of the Nagaland Legislative Assembly.[68]

It is perhaps no surprise that the other far-reaching provision that entrenches constitutional pluralism under Article 371 is the result of a similar conflicted history. During the colonial period, the state of Mizoram—then known as the Lushai Hills—was subjected to indirect rule through a system of chiefs.[69] At the time of Independence, in their submissions to the Bordoloi Committee, the Mizo Union raised demands similar to those of the Nagas: a right to secede after a ten-year period, and failing that, control over land tenure, the administration of justice, and immigration.[70] These were, unsurprisingly, rejected, and the Lushai Hills received the more modest devolutionary benefits of Schedule VI (discussed in the following pages).

Through the 1950s and early 1960s, the political claim was for internal statehood. However, the refusal of the Union to grant statehood, along with fears of linguistic and cultural domination by Assam (of which the Lushai Hills were formally a part) triggered more radical demands for independence, starting in 1965. An armed struggle began from 1966, which continued with varying degrees of intensity until the mid-1980s.[71] As in the case of Nagaland two decades ago, it was finally brought to an end through a negotiated settlement (this time between the government and the Mizo National Front). One of the key features of the settlement was the accession of Mizoram to a full-fledged state *with special constitutional safeguards*.[72] These were entrenched into the Constitution through Article 371G.

Thus, as with Nagaland, the second instance of constitutional pluralism in the constellation of Article 371 provisions was also the culmination of a long history that involved demands for independence, extreme State coercion, and eventual negotiation to break what was both a political and military stalemate: that is, a *political compromise that took the form of constitutional entrenchment*, to use a formulation we have considered in the previous section, when discussing Article 370.[73]

The similarities with Article 370 do not end there. It can be seen that as a matter of constitutional design, in certain ways, these provisions are reminiscent of the spirit that animated Article 370, and the principle of *double consent*. With respect to certain matters that are within the competence of the Union legislature, under India's federal scheme, the consent of the state's representatives would nonetheless be required before Union law could be applied in that state.[74]

That does not mean, however, that constitutional pluralism under Article 371 is equivalent to that under the erstwhile Article 370. The concessions that these articles make to asymmetric federalism are weakened by the creation of a governance structure in which the nominee of the central government—the governor—comes to occupy an overriding personal power, reminiscent of the executive in colonial times. For example, in the same provision that purports to extend constitutional pluralism to Nagaland, the governor is granted 'special responsibility with respect to law and order' in the state of Nagaland, to be exercised in his 'individual judgment', as long as, in his opinion, internal disturbances continue in the state; and that furthermore, the determination of whether or not a matter requires the 'individual judgment of the Governor' is also to be decided by the governor.[75] Note that this language has been *directly* taken from the governor-general's discretionary powers under the 1935 Government of India Act, which we discussed in the previous chapter!

At the time of their insertion into the Constitution in 1960, these provisions were meant to be 'transitional', until the ongoing military struggle ceased.[76] However, as recently as 2020, their potential invocation by the governor of Nagaland was the subject of political controversy, demonstrating that without an explicit sunset clause, transitional arrangements entrenching Union power—ostensibly to deal with a temporary emergency—crystallize into permanence.[77] Thus, in sum, as Kham Khan Suan Hausing argues, despite achieving certain limited success in accommodating Naga claims to self-determination within the conceptual apparatus of asymmetric federalism, 'as these arrangements [nonetheless] flow from a centralized federal framework, there are increasing pressures to re-concentrate powers both at the State and at the Centre'.[78] One can see, therefore, that even in the strongest provisions of Article 371, the shadow of the centralizing drift looms large: a centralizing drift marked by a historical reluctance on the part of Indian constitutionalism to embrace pluralism as a normative ideal.

Apart from the provisions that we have discussed, overriding gubernatorial powers exist with respect to other states as well. Article 371H has similar provisions, down to the governor's power to decide—without challenge—when a matter requires the exercise of 'his individual judgment'.[79] Similar discretionary power likewise exists for the state of Sikkim, with the governor authorized to 'act in his discretion' in order to discharge his 'special responsibility for peace and for ensuring the social and economic advancement of different sections of the population of Sikkim'.[80]

If we, therefore, consider the sub-clauses of Article 371, taken together, they constitute what we may call 'centrally managed asymmetric federalism'. In other words, while the Constitution acknowledges the link between constitutional pluralism and a heterogenous nation, the pluralism that it envisions is to be articulated not through state *autonomy* (as was the case with Article 370, in its original form), but at the *discretion of the central government*, acting either through the President or through the governor. This is asymmetric federalism at the sufferance of the Centre: the form and character that it takes, and even how long it last, depends upon presidential or gubernatorial orders. In many ways, therefore, many of the states under Article 371 and its sub-clauses are in a constitutionally *weaker* position than the other states of the Union, as their 'special provisions' are subject to modification, alteration, or erasure by decree.

It is instructive to think about these provisions in light of the interpretation that the Supreme Court accorded to Article 370 in *Re: Article 370*, which we discussed in the previous section. Recall that the Court maintained that the President held unilateral power, under Article 370(3), to abrogate the constitutional status of Jammu and Kashmir. In doing so, the Court not only dispensed with the principle of double consent, but subjected Jammu and Kashmir's constitutional status to *executive* fiat. That is, constitutional alterations could be made at the instance of the executive, without even the need for parliamentary ratification. One of the great ironies of this interpretation was, of course, that it placed Jammu and Kashmir's constitutional status at a weaker position than those of other states, where parliamentary sanction under Article 3 is required for any alteration of status.[81]

However, when we consider the Court's interpretation alongside the constitutional design discussed immediately above, a pattern begins to emerge: that of a constitutional *suspicion* of asymmetric arrangements or pluralism, and an attempt to bring and keep such arrangements *within* the control of the central executive (and, on occasion, Parliament). Indeed, this 'federal override' also characterizes the final site of asymmetric federalism in India that we shall discuss, the territories of Schedules V and VI. It is to these territories that we shall now turn.

IV. The Federal Kill Switch: Schedules V and VI

Schedules V and VI of the Indian Constitution are titled 'Provisions as to the administration and control of Scheduled Areas and Scheduled Tribes'[82] and 'Provisions as to the Administration of Tribal Areas in the States of Assam, Meghalaya, Tripura and Mizoram' (as amended), respectively.[83] As their titles suggest, these schedules set out an alternative structure of governance for specific areas—and peoples—within the Indian Union.[84]

A. History

The history of the 'Scheduled Areas' has its origins in the colonial period. As a legal category, 'Scheduled Areas' were invented in 1874, under the Scheduled Districts Act,[85] and 'referred to areas covered in forest land, and occupied by those identified by the colonial state as hill and forest peoples who were categorised as tribes'.[86] The Scheduled Districts Act marked an important inflection point in longstanding British attempts to bring the recalcitrant (and often rebellious) 'frontier' within imperial governance, a process characterized by coercion and violence.[87]

In the course of time, these areas came to be known as 'excluded areas' or 'partially excluded areas'.[88] As these terms suggest, there were areas where the laws, rules, and regulations applicable to the rest of British India were excluded, and a 'special administrative regime' prevailed.[89]

As Stephen Legg points out, therefore, even as dyarchy brought with it the first vestiges of representative governance to British India, the Excluded Areas marked a territorial zone insulated from the 'encroachment of democracy'.[90] This was crystallized in the 1935 Government of India Act's listing of areas of 'modified' and 'partial' exclusion, which became a precursor to Schedules V and VI in the Indian Constitution.[91]

Under the colonial regime, this exclusion was partially based on the paternalistic—albeit contested—logic of 'protecting' certain 'primitive'[92] forms of life from the inevitable dominance or erasure that would come with representative majoritarian and electoral politics.[93] Thus, these areas were placed under the effective direct rule of the governor, in both the 1919[94] and the 1935 Government of India Acts.[95] Among other things, the governor had the discretion to order that certain legislation would not apply—or would apply only with modifications—to such areas, based on *his* judgment about what was suitable or unsuitable for the people living there.

For exactly the same reason, the growing nationalist movement resisted the legal regime of exclusion, seeing it as another colonial tactic of divide and rule. The Indian National Congress thus was politically opposed to the 1935 Government of India Act's listing of Scheduled Areas, and opposed to including such areas in the final constitutional settlement—especially when, in the Cabinet Mission Statement, the structure of the 1935 Act with respect to excluded areas was largely replicated.[96]

By the time of the framing of the Constitution, however, the Congress—that now dominated the Constituent Assembly—

was nonetheless compelled to agree to the continued existence of Scheduled Areas, owing in no small part to a strengthening of political consciousness among the Adivasis in the run-up to Independence, and their unification under the leadership of Jaipal Munda.[97] There was, however, significant contestation around the exact shape and form that Scheduled Areas would take under the Constitution. While Munda and others articulated a demand for meaningful and effective *territorial autonomy*, a majority of the Constituent Assembly was explicitly hostile to these claims, casting them as precursors to, or proto-claims of, separatism.[98] For a majority of the Constituent Assembly, certain rights or protection around land and livelihood constituted the limits of what could be granted. These limits—often expressed through terms such as 'assimilation' or 'amalgamation'—ended well short of political and territorial autonomy.[99]

This contestation emerges with particular clarity, for example, in the debates over the role and functions of the proposed Tribes Advisory Council under Schedule V. In the Interim Report of the Sub-Committee on Excluded and Partially Excluded Areas, two crucial points were made. First, the sub-committee noted that the colonial mechanism of granting the governor overriding powers in such areas was undemocratic, and ought not to be retained. And secondly, the sub-committee recommended the setting up of a Tribes Advisory Council (TAC), 'whose primary function would be to review the suitability of laws passed by the provincial legislature on "special subjects" such as "(1) social matters, (2) occupation of land including tenancy laws, allotment of land and setting apart of land for village purposes, and (3) village management including the establishment of village panchayats"'.[100] On these matters, the TAC would have the power of veto, while on other matters, it would retain an advisory role.

In the final version of Schedule V, however—and over strenuous objections from Munda[101]—the role of the TACs was reduced to that of *solely* advisory body, and subject to the overriding power of the centrally appointed governor.[102] As Munda pointed out, this reversed both recommendations of the initial report, which were founded on the principle of autonomy: 'The whole pattern of the original draft was to bring the Tribes Advisory Council into action. It could initiate, originate things, but, somehow or other, the tables have now been turned.'[103]

Furthermore, through another amendment—also subjected to criticism—the obligation to establish a TAC was limited only to Scheduled *Areas* (which hadn't yet been declared), as opposed to Scheduled *Tribes*.[104] To round it off, through one final amendment, Parliament was granted the power to amend Schedule V through ordinary legislation, without having to obtain the supermajorities required for normal constitutional amendments. In essence, therefore, the autonomy of the Scheduled Areas was made subject to the will of a simple majority in (a structurally executive-dominated) Parliament.

The primary justification for this—in the words of B.R. Ambedkar, who moved the amendments—was to avoid the creation of a 'state within a state': the classic articulation of constitutional homogeneity.[105] This sentiment was echoed by other members of the assembly,[106] and constituted the dominant tenor of the debates around Schedule V.[107] Essentially, the difference boiled down to the aspirations of Jaipal Munda and others for the Constitution to *constitutionally entrench* meaningful autonomy for Scheduled Areas by giving the TACs genuine and *enforceable* powers, and minimize the scope of central and provincial discretion on the one hand; and the majority of the assembly—led by Ambedkar and K.M. Munshi—that saw Schedule V as embodying a principle of limited devolution, subject always to the tutelage of the executive, on the other.[108] One can see, in this debate, echoes of the early colonial period, where the British responded to demands for political autonomy by granting certain limited consultative roles to Indians in the legislative and executive councils, while retaining overriding power to themselves. That colonial logic was now turned inwards, by the framers of the Constitution, upon the peoples of the nascent Union. The similarity was noted by Munda, but—ultimately—the force of numbers carried the day, and it was the watered-down version of Schedule V that finally entered the Constitution.[109]

The fate of Schedule VI also saw a similar trajectory, where demands for independent status, or the reservation of significant law-making powers—that were submitted to the Sub-Committee on the North-East Frontier (Assam) Tribal and Excluded Areas during a wide-ranging process of public participation—were nonetheless rejected for a more contained and 'managed' version of autonomy.[110] A perusal of the sub-committee's first report reveals a fascinating range of pluralistic arrangements that were suggested by the people, some of which we have discussed above: a full draft Constitution that emerged from the Lushai Hills, and which limited the role of the Union government to defence;[111] from the Naga Hills, a proposal of an interim government for ten years, followed by a referendum;[112] from the Khasi and Garo Hills, a draft federal Constitution; and from the Mikir and North Cachar Hills, demands for control over land, local customs, and the administration of justice.[113]

However, while recording these submissions, the sub-committee nonetheless dismissed most of them as the views of a 'small group of people', and hinted at 'instigation by certain elements'.[114] Much like Schedule V, the draft recommendations of the sub-committee, therefore, ultimately resembled a kind of *revocable devolution* rather than *constitutionally entrenched political autonomy* (the District Council was the proposed unit of devolution, and its powers were revocable at the instance of the state government).[115]

The philosophy of the sub-committee is perhaps most starkly evident in its discussion about the control over mines and minerals (a valuable mineral resource). While the demands from the people were for powers of *control and management* over resources such as mines and minerals, the sub-committee dismissed these out of hand, and recommended central control, with provisions for revenue-sharing with the local councils.[116] As with the larger debate around asymmetric federalism, the constitutional imagination here was limited to certain specific and isolated material benefits that could be granted (at the discretion of the Centre), but no meaningful redistribution of power.[117]

The same limited imagination was, unsurprisingly, carried over into the Constituent Assembly Debates, which debated Schedule VI immediately after passing the watered-down version of Schedule V. Attempts to secure greater autonomy in the Constituent Assembly were met with familiar objections, pitting 'isolation' against 'assimilation'.[118] Indeed, as Schedule VI went some degrees further in the direction of autonomy by establishing autonomous districts, where Autonomous District Councils exercised a greater degree of devolved powers than in Schedule V, opposition in the Constituent Assembly was significantly more strident. Speaker after speaker rose to condemn the creation of 'Tribalstans' and accuse Ambedkar, Gopinath Bordoloi, and the other sponsors of Schedule VI of encouraging separatism;[119] so much so that Jaipal Munda expressed public shock at the 'amount of venom' in the debate.[120]

What is interesting to note, however, is that the defenders of Schedule VI made a set of defensive arguments in response. Rather than endorsing autonomy as a *normative* principle—as an aspect of the philosophy that would underpin the emerging Constitution—they argued, for example, that the Autonomous Districts were not meant to be permanent;[121] that fears of secession were adequately addressed by subjecting the legislative power of the proposed District Council to 'the control and assent of the Governor';[122] and that the 'unifying features' of the schedule (such as the executive power of the state extending to the autonomous districts) took care of the criticisms of 'segregation'.[123] In other words, the terrain of the debate around Schedule VI was not that of constitutional pluralism, but how the design of Schedule VI placed enough (centrally controlled) *checks* upon devolution to ensure that it would not transform into 'separatism' or 'secessionism' (or, we could perhaps say, into meaningful constitutional autonomy and internal self-determination). From the drafting moment, thus, the defence of pluralism and autonomy as constitutional values were conceded to a dominant register of homogeneity.

While we shall consider the design of the Schedules V and VI more closely in the next sub-section, this historical account demonstrates that much like the other forms of asymmetric federalism that we have examined in this chapter, constitutional pluralism as a *principle*, and as a normative blueprint for constitutional design, was unable to find firm purchase in the process of drafting the Constitution. Apart from the Committee Reports and the Constituent Assembly Debates (noted above), this reveals itself in the text of the Constitution, where elements of pluralism (falling well short of meaningful autonomy) are patchy, partial, and grudgingly conceded. In the words of Tewari, they are 'notional and a consequence of political expediency'.[124] And it reveals itself, as well, in jurisprudence, where, over the years, constitutional common sense appears to view homogeneity as the normative default, and pluralism as an exception, to be construed strictly. The next two sub-sections will discuss these two elements, respectively.

B. Constitutional Text and Design

In light of the history that we have discussed above, it should not be surprising that, as with the various sub-clauses of Article 371, the specific provisions of Schedules V and VI starkly illustrate the system of centrally managed asymmetric federalism.[125] Let us first consider the text of Schedule V. Part A of Schedule V, for example, vests in the Union the power to issue directions to the states for 'the administration of the said areas'.[126] At the heart of Schedule V, however, is Paragraph 5, which authorizes the governor, subject to the assent of the President, and 'notwithstanding anything in this Constitution',[127] to decide which laws apply to Schedule V Areas, and if so, with what exceptions and modifications.

In other words, on one reading, Paragraph 5 grants to the central government's executive nominee, overriding power when it comes to the administration of Schedule V Areas.[128] This includes the colonial-era phrase,[129] the 'regulations for the peace and good government of any area in a State which is for the time being a Scheduled Area'.[130] What constitutes a Scheduled Area is, itself, at the discretion of the President, who can, through executive order, create or erase Scheduled Areas.[131] This was a late addition to the Schedule, which was strenuously objected to in the Constituent Assembly by Jaipal Munda and others.

And finally, the edifice of Schedule V (as we have noted above) itself rests upon rather shaky foundations, with Paragraph 7 stipulating that the Schedule may be amended, varied, or repealed through a simple majority in Parliament, with any such amendments not counting as amendments to the Constitution, and therefore exempt from the supermajority rules under Article 368.[132]

In the previous section, we have examined the constitutional history and the Constituent Assembly Debates that led to the drafting of Schedule V. When we consider the text in light of these antecedents, the conclusion drawn by Parmar appears to be straightforwardly true: 'along with the importation of the idea of control over peoples and areas, the rationales and sensibilities that informed the colonial language were also carried over into the Constitution.'[133]

Schedule VI, by comparison, contains a far more detailed set of provisions that, on the face of it, accords substantive autonomy to Scheduled Areas in Assam, Meghalaya, Tripura, and Mizoram.[134] Schedule VI arose out of the report of the Sub-Committee on the North-East Frontier (Assam) Tribal and Excluded Areas (also known as the Bordoloi Committee), and was subject to extensive debate in the Constituent Assembly. As discussed above, a perusal of the debates shows the competing constitutional ideologies that were at issue: between a normative register of pluralism and effective autonomy on the one hand, and protectionism with a view to ultimate homogeneity and assimilation on the other.[135]

This tension is reflected in the scheme of Schedule VI. It stipulates the existence of elected district and regional councils, which have the power to make laws with respect to the allotment and use of land, the management of forests, marriage and divorce, and social customs, among other things.[136] Over the years, and in practice, the autonomous district councils (ADCs) have emerged as important legislative and administrative bodies within Schedule VI Areas, implementing—to some degree—the ideals of asymmetric federalism that Schedule VI purports to further.[137]

If, however, we consider as the exemplar of asymmetric federalism the requirement of *double consent* that characterized original Article 370, i.e., that there can be no substantial changes to the asymmetrically federal arrangement without the consent of *both* parties—we find that the constitutional text both grants, but also hedges and constrains, the power of the ADCs to a substantial degree. Their power, for example, is subject to Paragraph 15 of Schedule VI, which states:

> If at any time the Governor is satisfied that an act or resolution of a District of a Regional Council is likely to endanger the safety of India or is likely to be prejudicial to public order, he may annul or suspend the resolution and take such steps as he may consider necessary including the suspension of the Council and the assumption to himself of all or any of the powers vested in or exercisable by the Council.[138]

As in the Emergency provisions, the governor's resolution is to be laid before the state legislature for approval.[139]

I call this the federal kill switch. In other words, the autonomous powers of the district and regional councils formally exist at the sufferance of the executive (and subject to further ratification by the state legislature), and can be 'switched off'.[140] Indeed, Paragraph 16 of Schedule VI provides for two other kill switches: the dissolution of a district or regional council by the governor, on the basis of the report of a commission that the governor himself constitutes, and an emergency-like provision, which authorizes the governor to assume to himself the functions of a council, if—in the opinion of the governor—'a situation has arisen in which the administration of an autonomous district or region cannot be carried on in accordance with the provisions of this Schedule'.[141]

Thus, when we view Schedules V and VI as a whole, the contours of contestation around asymmetric federalism emerge with some clarity. These are summed up in what I have called *centrally managed asymmetric federalism*, in the context of Article 371: that is, on the one hand, the Constitution recognizes pluralism, and provides for the autonomous governance of certain Scheduled Area. *However*, at the same time, this autonomy is conditional upon the goodwill and the discretion of the governor and the state legislature. In other words, while the principles of asymmetric federalism and constitutional pluralism are part of the Constitution, it is the executive and the state legislatures that retain control over the *terms* on which these principles are articulated in constitutional practice.

C. Judicial Doctrine

Finally, and beyond the federal kill switch that appears in the text of Schedules V and VI, important interpretive disputes flowing from the textual ambiguity have been resolved by the judiciary *against* the asymmetrically federal structures. A striking example of this is *District Council of United Khasi and Jaintia Hills vs Sitimon Sawian*. This case involved one of the most crucial determining factors of genuine asymmetrically federal autonomy: control over land. The interpretive question before the Supreme Court was whether the District Council's power over 'allotment, occupation or use, or the setting apart of land'—guaranteed by Paragraph 3 of Schedule VI—included the power over *transfer* of land. The Supreme Court held that it did not, on the basis that the legal term 'transfer' was distinct from 'allotment', 'occupation or use', and 'setting apart'.[142]

What is particularly striking about this case, however, is the Court's reasoning. It was argued that, in accordance with the well-established principles governing legislative competence, words or phrases that set out the categories under which a legislative body could act ought to be interpreted broadly and liberally, so as to prevent fetters being cast upon legislative power. Indeed, as we have discussed at some length in Chapter 1 of this book, this was the exact doctrine that the Supreme Court had itself laid down while interpreting the entries in Schedule VII: it had repeatedly held that Schedule VII ought to be construed 'broadly' and 'liberally', and the role of the Court ought to be to save legislation rather than strike it down.

In this case, however, the Supreme Court held that those principles did not apply to interpreting Schedule VI, and the powers of the ADCs. Why? Because, according to the Court, 'the power of legislation conferred on bodies like the District Councils, which concerns us, must be confined strictly within the limits prescribed by the plain language used and the doctrine of wide construction visions conferring plenary nature of legislative power'.[143] But on what basis did the Court draw this distinction between plenary and non-plenary power? It reproduced the text of Schedule VI, and noted that the 'power [of district councils] to make laws is expressly limited by the provisions of Schedule VI which has created them and they can do nothing beyond the limits which circumscribe their power.'[144]

Yet this begs the question. Every form of legislative power is limited by the provisions of the Constitution, every legislative body is a creature of the Constitution, and no such body can anything 'beyond the limits which circumscribe its power'—whether it be the district council, state legislature, or Union Parliament. The only difference is that the limitations are found in different parts of the Constitution: under Schedule VI for district councils, and under Article 245 and Schedule VII for the Union and state legislatures.

Thus, as in so many cases that we have studied in this book, the Court smuggled in unstated normative premises—a 'constitutional common sense'—into a seemingly uncontroversial textual reading of the Constitution. The normative assumption, or the 'common sense', was that even though they were the institutional articulation of asymmetric federalism under the Indian Constitution—and popularly elected to boot—the district councils were hierarchically inferior to the Union and state legislatures. For this reason, the exercise of their legislative powers would be construed strictly, and with a view to containing it, rather than expanding it.

The Supreme Court's judgment in *Sitimon Sawian* might not have the significance of an 'inflection-point' judgment—as it was concerned with a very specific interpretive problem—but it does complement the idea of 'centrally managed asymmetric federalism' that we have attributed to Schedules V and VI. The Court's insistence on reading the power-conferring clauses strictly and narrowly—in opposition to its own interpretive doctrine—demonstrates a refusal to take the asymmetrically federal aspects of the Constitution as seriously as the symmetrically federal, and to contain the power flowing to the former from the latter. Thus, whether in the constitutional text or through judicial interpretation, we can observe Indian constitutionalism's continuing discomfort with asymmetrical federalism, and the consequences for power that flow therefrom.

V. Conclusion

In the Constituent Assembly, Jaipal Munda articulated a vision of Schedules V and VI in the language of 'tribal republics'.[145] He emphasized that the flag of the tribe would not be lowered for the flag of the nation, but rather, the two would coexist.[146] In doing so, Parmar observes, Munda was extending to the Constituent Assembly an invitation 'to imagine the nation differently'.[147]

This invitation, however, was not taken up by the Constituent Assembly, where the dominant register in which the nation-state was envisaged was one of *homogeneity*. To the extent that difference was tolerated or recognized in the Constitution with respect to the erstwhile 'Scheduled Areas', it was the function of political pressure, and justified in the name of *temporary* protection *with a view* to ultimate assimilation.[148]

The specific debates around Schedules V and VI fit into a broader pattern, summed up by Kham Khan Suan Hausing, in his analysis of the evolution of asymmetric federalism across multiple domains, in pre-Constitutional history. Hausing notes that:

> Despite its steadfast commitment to the right to self-determination of ethno-linguistic groups—a commitment which drove the reorganization of its provincial branches in 1927 and was reiterated by the Nehru Committee Report of 1928—the Indian National Congress reversed its stand in the 1940s. Faced with a strident two-nation theory, communal riots and an imminent partition, the Constituent Assembly of India constituted two important commission/committee in 1948, namely, the Dhar Commission (Linguistic Provinces Commission headed by M.L. Dhar) and the JVP Committee (Jawaharlal Nehru, Vallabhai Patel and Pattabhi Sitamaryya) which put an indelible stamp on giving primacy to political expediency to strengthen the unity, integrity, and security of India. The 'language factor' and for that matter the right to self-determination would subsequently form the basis for reorganizing Indian federal polity only as a matter of administrative and political expediency.[149]

This paragraph, I would suggest, gets to the heart of both the character and the limitations of asymmetric federalism in the Indian Constitution. In its strongest form, asymmetric federalism disentangles the concepts of *State* and *nation*: that is, it recognizes that a diverse and plural State, as a political entity, may be made up of several distinct nations (that are constituted by ethnic, linguistic, or other cultural bonds), and that these nations have their own rights to internal self-determination within the State.

Indeed, some modern Constitutions explicitly acknowledge this. The most famous example, perhaps, are the Constitutions of Ecuador and Bolivia, which declare their respective States to be 'plurinational'.[150] Unsurprisingly, the concepts of plurinationalism and autonomy are deeply linked.[151] Thus, Article 2 of the Constitution of Bolivia notes the 'pre-colonial existence of nations and rural native indigenous peoples', and follows up by acknowledging 'their free determination, consisting of the right to autonomy, self-government, their culture, recognition of their institutions, and the consolidation of their territorial entities'.[152] In concrete terms, this translates into—among other things—provisions for 'autonomia indigena originaria campesina', i.e., rural native indigenous autonomy;[153] this is understood as a constitutionally sanctioned 'opportunity for indigenous municipalities across the country to create their own autonomous territories ... based on [their] own models of social and political organization, representation, and authority'.[154]

Critiques of the plurinational constitutional project have noted that the autonomy clauses represent a dilution of indigenous demands for self-determination, and continue to place the nation-state at the apex of a constitutional hierarchy.[155] Plurinationalism has also sat uneasily with a State-led model of resource extraction, where many of the resources in question lie in indigenous territories—thus incentivizing the limitation, or claw-back, of meaningful territorial autonomy.[156] That said, the recognition of the right to autonomy is, at least, a partial acknowledgment that constitutional orders ought to acknowledge—and account for—territorial pluralism within the spatial boundaries of the nation-state.[157]

As Hausing notes, however, for a number of historical reasons, despite the extent and degree of diversity within the Indian Union, a constitution imagined along the lines of plurinationalism was a non-starter. Instead, the framers of the Indian Constitution were committed to the idea of India that, along a spectrum, was closer to the *nation-state* than to the *state-nation*.[158] In other words, demands for internal self-determination within the territorial boundaries of the Indian State were to be treated not as *national* demands, but as demands for a certain set of administrative and governmental arrangements, to be granted within the existing limits of a uniform federal structure (such as, for example, the linguistic reorganization of states in 1956, or the creation of new states such as Telangana), or—in cases where this was not possible—to be granted subject to central oversight and control, and to withdrawal at any moment. Anything that went beyond this was the result of the State's hand being forced by political exigencies: as in the case of Kashmir during accession, and Mizoram and Nagaland after Independence. In these cases, the asymmetric federal provisions that were negotiated sat (and continue to sit) somewhat uncomfortably within the constitutional scheme, and at odds with its dominant ideology.

And finally, as with the other axes of power that we have discussed in this book, asymmetric federalism is a terrain of contestation. Much like the other axes, however, the terrain is uneven. To start with, the potential of asymmetric federalism is sharply limited by the text of the Constitution. It exists in scattered provisions, located in different parts of the Constitution, lacking structural coherence, normative unity, and an overarching theory and purpose. And where it does exist, it is hedged in by various caveats, qualifications, and central or state-level overrides.

The constitutional text—along with the constitutional history that we discussed in the first section of this chapter and summed up above—has contributed to the absence of an overall constitutional 'common sense' of asymmetric federalism as an organizing principle of Indian constitutionalism. This, in turn, has enabled—or at least made possible—a jurisprudence of erosion as in the case of Article 370, where the constitutional silences enabled the Supreme Court to play a significant role, with its 'inflection point' judgments in *Sampat Prakash* and *Mohd Maqbool Damnoo*, and the culmination of that judicial path in *Re: Article 370*. When we place this alongside the 'centrally managed asymmetric federalism' of Article 371, its equivalent in Schedules V and VI (also further limited by Supreme Court judgments), and the federal kill switch in those schedules, we can observe the centralizing drift upon the terrain of asymmetric federalism within the Indian Constitution: a drift articulated in a language of power that privileges homogeneity and a single national narrative over heterogeneity and pluralism.

As Jaipal Munda eloquently objected, when confronted with the text of Schedule V, '[this] plan is not for unity but for *uniformity*' (emphasis supplied).[159] This narrow understanding of the nation, characterized by the elision of 'unity' and 'uniformity', would harden into an unexamined constitutional common sense which, seventy-five years later, would constitute the implicit major premise of the Supreme Court's judgment upholding the abrogation of Article 370: that the ultimate 'purpose' of the asymmetrically federal arrangements under Article 370 was 'integration', and the only understanding of 'integration' was 'uniformity'.

Indeed, the resemblance between Munda's treatment by the Constituent Assembly and the treatment of Article 370 (and the people of Jammu and Kashmir) by the Supreme Court is striking. Under the Indian Constitution, pluralism thus lives out a precarious existence between the shadowy interstices of 'unity' and 'uniformity'.

4

Power Confronted: Institutions

IN JULY 2019, THE Indian Parliament passed a set of amendments to the Right to Information Act (RTI).[1] The RTI Act had been enacted fourteen years ago, in 2005. It was the culmination of a sustained decades-long social movement focused upon transparency and probity in affairs of State.[2] At the heart of the RTI Act was an *infrastructure* dedicated to the effective implementation of the right to information. The primary responsibility for maintaining this infrastructure was vested in information commissioners—at both the central and the state levels—whose task was (among other things) to ensure that citizens were not arbitrarily denied information in the keeping of public bodies.[3]

In order to ensure their independence from the government, the RTI Act provided a set of safeguards concerning the tenure, salaries, and removal procedures of information commissioners that, in certain limited respects, placed them on par with two constitutional bodies: the Election Commission and the judiciary.[4] The 2019 amendments diluted this independence by extending greater governmental control over these conditions and the terms of employment of the information commissioners.[5] Somewhat ironically, the stated justification for these amendments was that the office of the information commissioner—being a mere creation of a statute—could not be on par with the constitutionally entrenched election commission and judiciary.[6] Effectively downgrading the status of information commissioners was argued to be a rebalancing of sorts, to ensure that bodies not explicitly envisaged by the Constitution were not insulated from the executive in the same manner as the judiciary and the Election Commission.

A few years later, however, it became clear that even constitutional entrenchment did not create particularly effective insulation. In March 2023, in *Anoop Baranwal vs Union of India*,[7] the Supreme Court ruled that for the last seventy years, Parliament had failed to discharge its constitutional obligation of enacting a law to deal with the appointment of election commissioners.[8] The Court put into place an interim arrangement whereby the selection of the election commissioners would be conducted by a committee comprising the Prime Minister, the leader of the Opposition, and the Chief Justice of India.[9]

Soon after, Parliament did (finally) act: in December of the same year—and in response to the Supreme Court's judgment—it enacted a law replacing the Chief Justice with a Union minister.[10] The cabinet (i.e., the executive) was thus granted the decisive say in the appointment of election commissioners. The law was immediately challenged on the ground that it was contrary to the judgment in *Anoop Baranwal*, as that judgment made clear that Parliament's discretion in enacting a law on the appointment of election commissioners was constrained by the constitutional requirement that the appointments process must secure the *independence* of those commissioners. The question was of some urgency, as India's general election was scheduled for the summer of 2024. Pending a final decision, however, the Supreme Court refused to stay the operation of the new act.[11] Consequently—as we noted in the Prologue to this book—the 2024 general election was conducted by an Election

Commission in which two out of three members of the commission had been appointed by the Union executive.

This chapter will examine the position—and the role—of bodies such as the Information Commission and the Election Commission in our constitutional democracy. I begin by pointing out how it is now reasonably well-established, in jurisdictions across the world, that constitutional democracy is sustained and improved by authorizing non-elected bodies to exercise certain forms of public power. Furthermore, these non-elected bodies ought to be constitutionally entrenched and thus insulated from interference by the executive, or by simple parliamentary majorities.

I then note the various justifications offered for the existence of these bodies: technocratic expertise, accountability, political neutrality, etc. For the purposes of this chapter, I will be focusing on two specific justifications (and therefore, by extension, on institutions whose existence can be traced to these justifications). Keeping with the theme of this book, these justifications have to do with power. I argue, first, that certain institutions exist to provide the necessary infrastructure in order to effectively implement and fulfil constitutional rights—and, in particular, implement these rights in a way that rebalances the power differential between the individual and the State. Furthermore, as these rights are enforceable *against* the State (most often against the political executive), the bodies tasked with putting these into practice must be effectively independent *from* the executive. And secondly, many of these institutions provide opportunities or nodes of popular participation in the exercise of public power that go beyond periodic voting in elections **(I)**.[12]

Unlike some of the other jurisdictions that I shall flag in this chapter, the Indian Constitution does not, however, as a general rule, explicitly recognize the wielding of *non-electoral public power*. In other words, barring a few exceptions, it does not constitutionally entrench non-elected public institutions. The creation of such institutions—such as the Information Commission, for example—is thus left to the discretion of Parliament, through legislation. But, as we have just seen, this is exactly what makes such institutions particularly fragile and vulnerable.[13] Simply put, it is much easier to stymie or otherwise undo their functioning by amending the law than it would be if they were constitutionally entrenched. Let us call this the *non-entrenchment problem*.

Does the non-entrenchment problem mean that short of significant constitutional overhaul, we must be resigned to such institutions existing in a forever-twilight zone? Not necessarily. I shall examine one possible response: the Supreme Court's judgment in the often-discussed *Vineet Narain vs Union of India* case where the Court held that the functions performed by the Central Bureau of Investigation (CBI) necessarily implied a degree of independence from the political executive. *Vineet Narain* is an example of how a statutory body performing constitutional functions requires a level of protection, independence, and insulation that is otherwise reserved only for constitutionally entrenched institutions **(II)**.

In *Vineet Narain*, however, the Court did not frame its analysis in the language of constitutional principle. I shall therefore attempt to articulate the unarticulated major premise of that judgment. Drawing upon the concept of a 'constitutional statute'—and using, once again, the example of the RTI Act—I shall argue that even though certain bodies are created by statute, *once created*, they ought to be treated akin to constitutionally entrenched institutions, with substantive limits being placed upon executive or parliamentary interference in their functioning. This, I will suggest, flows directly from the Fundamental Rights chapter, and from the proposition that certain rights are unenforceable without the existence of specific infrastructure designed to implement them **(III)**.

In other words, therefore, there exists a path—not yet foreclosed—by which constitutional silences can be interpreted in favour of a redistribution of public power in a way that can make substantive rights more meaningful. Even so, however, there are two serious barriers upon this path. The first is the presence of absence:

constitutional silences require courts to do substantial interpretive work. Institutions whose foundations are built on silence are potentially more fragile than those that are explicitly entrenched.

Secondly—as seen in the example of the Election Commission, flagged above—even in the case of entrenched bodies, the Constitution's vision of independence is a limited one, and constrained by direct or indirect executive control. Parliament's attempts to get around the judgment in *Anoop Baranwal*, and the Supreme Court's own interim order allowing Parliament to do so, were both facilitated by the sparse wording of Article 324 of the Constitution. Let us call this the *thin entrenchment problem* (IV).

A combination of the non-entrenchment problem and the thin entrenchment problem leads to the conclusion that even if the doctrine of constitutional statutes was to succeed, the composition and functioning of 'fourth branch' or 'guarantor' institutions remain vulnerable, and susceptible to executive control. It is therefore questionable how much *genuine* rebalancing of power can happen within the current constitutional framework, which—as a matter of structure and design—is an 'executive-trusting' document, and facilitates a centralizing drift in the relationship between the political executive and non-electoral institutions (V).

I. Public Power and Non-Elected Bodies

Traditional separation of powers theory envisages State power to be divided between the 'three wings of State', or the 'three branches'—the legislature, the executive, and the judiciary. The purpose of this is to prevent the concentration of power and ensuring a system of mutual checks and balances.[14] What this schematic picture means in practice has always been contested.[15] In any event, it has perhaps never been an entirely accurate representation of the actual exercise of public power in a State.[16] And with the rise of the modern administrative State, delegation of power is common enough for the term 'fourth-branch institutions' to become a part of the comparative constitutional lexicon.

The growing importance of such non-elected bodies is reflected by the fact that more recent constitutions specifically guarantee their existence and independence. A good example of this is the well-known Chapter IX of the South African Constitution. The opening provision of Chapter IX—Section 181 of the Constitution—lists six institutions that 'strengthen constitutional democracy'. These are: the Public Protector; the Human Rights Commission; the Commission for the Promotion and Protection of the Rights of Cultural, Religious and Linguistic Minorities; the Commission for Gender Equality; the Auditor General; and the Electoral Commission.[17] In a similar manner, Article 248 of the Kenyan Constitution provides for a number of 'Commissions and Independent Offices', with Article 249 going on to note that the objectives of these bodies include the promotion of constitutionalism and ensuring that State organs observe 'democratic values and principles'.[18] For this reason, the Kenyan Constitution explicitly stipulates that these bodies must be 'independent and not subject to direction or control by any person or authority'.[19]

In scholarly literature, various justifications have been offered for the existence of such fourth-branch institutions. One straightforward argument is *functional* in nature. This is the argument of technical expertise, or 'functional specialization'.[20] The modern administrative State performs a range of functions, many of which require specific technical expertise. It is too much to expect the political executive to directly perform all these functions. Consequently, these functions can be delegated to specifically constituted bodies to implement on a day-to-day basis.[21]

While the argument from technical expertise holds true for a range of bodies, it evidently does not tell the whole story. When we think of bodies such as an election commission, an information commission, or a human rights commission—to name just a few—we do not think *simply* of administrative efficiency or technical competence.[22] Something more is at work. Ackerman takes the example of independent election commissions and argues that this 'something more' is essentially the protection of democracy from the attempts of electoral power holders to entrench themselves in power. What Ackerman calls the 'democracy branch' provides mechanisms 'to ensure the continuing force of [the Constitutional] ideal of democracy despite the predictable efforts of reigning politicians to entrench themselves against popular reversals at the polls'.[23] Ackerman argues that the range of powers an election commission might have depends on how 'thin' or 'thick' a particular constitution's idea of democracy is; for example, is it restricted to simply the conduct of periodic polls, or does it also include more substantive commitments, such as the prevention of gerrymandering?

Taking Ackerman's point further, 'thicker'—or more substantive—conceptions of democracy are not limited to periodic elections, but involve a continuing range of interactions between the people and their representatives.[24] It is for this reason, for example, that Chapter IX of the South African Constitution establishes bodies other than the election commission, under the rubric of 'strengthen[ing] constitutional democracy'. This broader view understands one important role of these bodies as performing a checking function upon the actions of the three wings of State, in situations where the wings cannot check *each other*.[25] In the words of Heinz Klug, 'integrity institutions' perform the role of '*temper[ing]* ... the abuse of power' in a way that traditional separation of powers doctrine cannot accomplish.[26]

This is often framed in the language of *accountability*, and as a function of substantive democracy: bodies such as a comptroller and auditor general (CAG), a human rights commission, an information commission, and so on 'check government power by providing a legitimate and authoritative account of government's record, which can be used by citizens and Parliament in scrutinizing government's performance'.[27] As we can see, this is a form of accountability that is qualitatively distinct from the accountability that comes from judicial review of legislative and executive action, or executive responsibility towards Parliament.

As Tarunabh Khaitan points out, however, the institutions under consideration do not *merely* perform a negative checking function. In many cases, they are tasked with carrying out substantive positive action, and provided infrastructure for doing so (the election commission is a good example of this). Khaitan, therefore, argues that a specific set of institutions ought to be classified as 'guarantor institutions'. By guarantor institutions, he means 'a tailor-made constitutional institution, vested with material as well as expressive capacities, whose function is to provide a credible and enduring guarantee to a specific non-self-enforcing constitutional norm (or any aspect thereof)'.[28]

The concept of guarantor institutions is a valuable one. For the purposes of this chapter, I propose to concretize the term a little further. I want to consider the subset of guarantor institutions that is specifically required because many rights in a constitution are not self-executing. To be effective in any meaningful sense, rights need what we can call an *infrastructure of enforcement or implementation*. To take once again the classic example of an election commission: the constitutional right to vote is meaningless without an infrastructure in place for conducting free and fair elections. The particular way in which this is instantiated is through a well-funded and independent body, known as the election commission.[29]

It should equally be obvious that the details of the 'infrastructure of implementation' are often not located within the constitutional text itself. There are two reasons for this. First, there may be more than one acceptable way to set up the infrastructure of implementation in a manner that a right is indeed effectively implemented.[30] For instance, independence can be achieved either by making an appointment process non-partisan (i.e., excluding political actors altogether), or making it multi-partisan (i.e., striving towards a balance of political forces by including members from both the ruling party and the Opposition in an appointments commission).[31] Now, if there is more than one reasonable way of effectively implementing a right, then it also follows that a constitution should not prescribe a *specific* form:

that is a choice that should be left to the legislature. Secondly, and relatedly, 'the infrastructure of implementation' requires the threshing out of a whole set of granular details—from the structure and composition of the body, to the terms and tenure of its officers, and various other specific issues—that are better suited to the legislative process rather than to constitutional decree.[32]

It follows from the above discussion that the bodies or institutions that we shall discuss in this chapter have three characteristic features.

First, they are integral parts of an 'infrastructure of implementation', which is required in order to effectuate a constitutional right. It is crucial to note that the right is either an individual or a collective right, and is enforceable against the State. For this reason—as Khaitan also points out—these bodies will often be tasked with constraining or otherwise limiting State action.[33] Or, in language closer to the themes of this book, these bodies are part of an infrastructure designed to *rebalance* power between the State and the public (as we shall see, this is particularly true for bodies such as an information commission).[34]

Secondly, while the Constitution may (or may not) explicitly entrench these bodies, the specific details pertaining to their structure, composition, and functioning must necessarily be instantiated through legislation.

Thirdly, while there is substantial play in the joints when it comes to what specific shape or form legislation might take, the first feature that we have outlined above does—or at least, ought to—place some constraints upon legislation. For example, to the extent that the purpose of such bodies is to implement constitutional rights against the executive, their structure cannot be such that the executive has control over appointments or tenure. In other words, functional independence, or 'independence from actors who are likely to have the ability and the willingness to frustrate the norm in question', is necessarily implied.[35] Some scholars, indeed, see this fundamental point as the whole reason why these institutions need to exist in the first place. As Tushnet argues, 'the reason for creating these institutions rather than relegating their work to the

Montesquiean branches [i.e., the executive, the legislature, and the judiciary] is that those branches are placed in a situation of conflict of interest when particular cases challenging democratic functioning arise.'[36] If this is true, then placing these institutions under the control of one of the 'Montesquiean branches' would defeat the purpose of their existence.

Finally, in addition to these three characteristic features, there is a fourth element that I want to highlight. Apart from their checking or tempering functions, guarantor institutions—as Christina Murray astutely points out—provide another set of nodes, or entry points, for *public participation in the exercise of public power*.[37] This is a form of public participation that is not always possible in large representative democracies, which have seen an increasing distancing between representatives and their constituents, other than during election periods.[38] Of course, not all guarantor institutions have public participation as part of their explicit or implied remit. Some, however, undoubtedly do. Information commissions, for example, enable public participation in State affairs by facilitating greater transparency and freer flow of information between the State and the citizenry. Human rights commissions allow for participation through testimonies and fact-finding reports; and so on.[39]

Thus, to draw upon a distinction that Gargarella makes, classical separation of powers theory was premised upon *internal* checks and balances, with the institutions that wielded public power checking each other. A system of *external* checks and balances, on the other hand, involves a part of this checking role being performed by the people. We will have occasion to discuss the role of the people more thoroughly in a later chapter.[40] Here, it is important to note that guarantor institutions, when functioning well, allow for a form of *mediated external checking*, where people often have a direct opportunity to participate—through these institutions—in checking or tempering State power.

Now, what follows from this discussion about guarantor institutions, whose characteristic features are common, whether or not they are specifically entrenched? I would argue that because of the special constitutional character of such institutions, statutes designed to establish them and provide for their structure and working themselves constitute a specific category, which we can call 'constitutional statutes'. The implications of this are discussed in the subsequent sections of this chapter.

A note of caution to conclude this section, before we proceed: the independence of fourth-branch institutions can be a double-edged sword. The most striking example of this is the discourse around the 'independence' of central banks, which serves as a justification to insulate large swathes of the national economy from democratic control and oversight.[41] The relationship between central banks, the executive, and the public is a fraught and complex issue, including in India, and requires a full-fledged account of its own.[42] Here, I will limit myself to noting that central banks do not fall within the category of fourth branch or guarantor institutions, for the purposes of this chapter. Two of the four elements—an infrastructure of rights implementation and nodes of public participation—do not apply to central banks (indeed, the entire justification of central bank independence is primarily framed in technocratic terms). It is worth keeping in mind that the arguments that follow are made from the perspective of *deepening* democratic participation through the vehicle of guarantor institutions, and not (as in the case of banks) *excluding* it.

II. Independence outside the Constitution: The Case of the CBI

A reading of the Indian Constitution reveals that unlike its more recent counterparts elsewhere in the globe, there is very little scope for constitutional entrenchment of non-electoral bodies that wield public power. Chapter V of the Constitution creates and sets out the responsibilities of the CAG, who is tasked with auditing the government's accounts.[43] In addition, the Constitution provides for Union and State Public Service Commissions, as well as National and State Commissions for Scheduled Castes and Scheduled Tribes.[44]

In the constitutional scheme, however, these commissions are viewed as adjuncts of the executive, established in order to aid the executive to perform its functions. This is reflected by the fact that appointment to these commissions is at the instance of the President (i.e., in effect, the political executive).[45] The final commission is one that we have discussed above: the Election Commission. Recognizing the different stature that the Election Commission occupies, the Constitution provides some additional safeguards for election commissioners. It prohibits the terms of their service from being varied to their disadvantage, and requires the process for their removal to be equal to—and as onerous as—the process for the removal of a judge (i.e., impeachment proceedings that garner supermajorities in both houses of Parliament).[46] The question of appointments, however, is a contested one, and we will consider it in some detail in the succeeding sections.

The Constitution does not explicitly entrench any other bodies of the kind that we have discussed above. Over the years, these bodies have been established through legislation. The Protection of Human Rights Act, for example, established the Human Rights Commission.[47] The CBI was established by the Delhi Special Police Act.[48] The Information Commission is a part of the Right to Information Act.[49] The Data Protection Act envisions the existence of a Data Protection Authority.[50]

As is obvious, however, the absence of a constitutional foundation places these bodies in a relatively more precarious position than their constitutional counterparts. This is why, for instance, in downgrading the independence of information commissioners, the government attempted to wield the Constitution as a sword, arguing that the relative differences between constitutional entrenchment and non-entrenchment effectively allow for immense legislative discretion when it comes to the shape and form of the Information Commission. Similarly, in the Data Protection Law, the proposed data protection authority is notably under the control of the executive. Once again, however, the focus of the critique against this has had to be primarily framed in the language of bad policy, rather than the language of unconstitutionality.[51] Explicit constitutional entrenchment thus provides a guarantor institution with 'a greater likelihood of institutional durability, certainty and predictability than one created by ordinary legislation'—*and* vice versa.[52]

At this stage, it appears that we are looking at a somewhat bleak picture. When it comes to confronting State power through the medium of independent guarantor institutions, the Indian Constitution is defined by silence. The text is limited to creating executive-controlled administrative bodies, a partially independent CAG, and a somewhat more independent Election Commission. Anything more takes us to the vagaries of statutory enactment, modification, and erosion, with strong social movements (perhaps) serving as the only bulwark.

But this is not, perhaps, the end of the story. It is here that I want to introduce the idea of a 'constitutional statute': an idea that is incipient in Indian jurisprudence, but is yet to be developed fully. Consider, for example, the 'landmark' case of *Vineet Narain vs Union of India,* which considered the status of the Central Vigilance Commission (CVC) and the CBI, neither of which at the time had any statutory foundation.[53] *Vineet Narain* arose out of an allegation that the CBI was not doing its job under political pressure. After passing a series of interim orders effectively placing various investigations under its direct supervision, in its final judgment, the Supreme Court made the following observations:

> In view of the common perception shared by everyone including the Government of India and the Independent Review Committee (IRC) of the need for insulation of the *need for insulation of the CBI* from extraneous influence of any kind, it is imperative that some action is urgently taken to prevent the continuance of this situation with a view in ensure proper implementation of the rule of law. *This is the need of equality guaranteed in the Constitution. The right to equality*

> *in a situation like this is that of the Indian polity and not merely of a few individuals.* The powers conferred on this Court by the Constitution are ample to remedy this defect and to ensure enforcement of the concept of equality.[54] (Emphasis supplied.)

In other words, therefore, the independence of the CBI—as a body tasked with investigating offences that often involved powerful and politically influential people—flowed from the constitutional principles of equality and the rule of law. Having noted this, the Court then passed legislative guidelines under Article 142 of the Constitution, which would hold the field until a suitable statutory framework was established. In doing so, the Court specified that these guidelines were being passed in order to implement equality and the rule of law.[55]

And what of the guidelines themselves? Apart from insisting that the CBI be given a statutory basis, the Court also laid down a number of guidelines to ensure independence. These included setting out the appointments process, specifying that the tenure of director would be two years, putting brakes on transfers, and so on.

In sum, then, *Vineet Narain* laid out two propositions. First, the Court found that the purpose of the CVC and the CBI was to, inter alia, guarantee the constitutional principles of equality and the rule of law, by ensuring that the highest and most influential of people would be brought to book if they broke the law. Flowing from this, the Court laid down a set of guidelines to ensure the independence of the officers in these posts. And secondly, the Court's opinion was that fixed tenure and constraints upon transfers were crucial aspects of guaranteeing such independence.

Twenty years later, the *Vineet Narain* case got a sequel of sorts: the notorious *Alok Verma* judgment, which was handed down by a three-judge bench of the Supreme Court in late 2018.[56] The core issue in that case involved the transfer of the then CBI director, Alok Verma. By this time, there *was* a statutory framework in place: the CVC Act had been brought into force, and the Delhi Special Police Establishment Act, 1946, (DSPE Act) had been amended to include the CBI director. The Supreme Court's guidelines—including those on independence—had been legislatively enacted. The question in *Alok Verma* involved the interpretation of that statutory framework.

After going through the history of the CVC and the CBI, the Court noted the submission of Alok Verma's counsel:

> Shri F.S. Nariman and Shri Dushyant Dave, learned Senior Counsels, who have argued the case for Shri Alok Kumar Verma, Director, CBI and Common Cause have contended that *the history of the institutional framework surrounding the CBI* leading to the statutory enactments in question *and the views expressed in the judgment of this Court in Vineet Narain* (supra), including the operative directions under Article 142 of the Constitution, can leave no doubt *that the judicial endeavour should/must always be to preserve, maintain and further the integrity, independence and majesty of the institution i.e. CBI.* This is the core intent behind the statutory enactments and the amendments thereto, details of which have been noticed. *The Director of the CBI is the centre of power in an abundantly powerful organization having jurisdiction to investigate and to prosecute key offences and offenders having great ramifications and consequences on public life. There can be no manner of doubt that the Director who has been given a minimum assured tenure of "not less than two years" must be insulated from all external interference if the CBI has to live up to the role and expectations of the legislature and enjoy public confidence to the fullest measure.* This is how the provisions of the cognate legislations i.e. the CVC Act, 2003 and DPSE Act, 1946 (as amended), must be interpreted, according to the learned counsels. It is specifically urged that the embargo under Section 4B(2) of the DSPE Act which mentions that the Director *shall not be transferred except with the previous consent of the Committee* must be construed in the broadest perspective to include any attempt to divest the Director, CBI of his powers, functions, duties, etc. in any manner whatsoever and not necessarily relatable to the transfer of the incumbent as is understood in ordinary parlance. According to the learned counsels, unless such a meaning is attributed to the provisions of Section 4B(2) of the DSPE Act, the legislative intent

> would be rendered futile *and so would be the entire judicial exercise culminating in the operative directions of this Court in Vineet Narain* (supra).[57] (Emphasis supplied.)

This paragraph deserves close study. The account here started with the functions being performed by the body in question: the CBI, 'a powerful organisation having jurisdiction to investigate and to prosecute key offences and offenders having great ramifications and consequences on public life'. The fact that the CBI performs this function then led to the argument that its director's independence from the political executive (something normally reserved for constitutional functionaries) was a *necessary implication* flowing from that function. This independence was meant to be guaranteed by a fixed tenure, constraint upon transfers, and so on. And most notably, these requirements existed independent of the fact that the officials in question were not formally constitutional functionaries, and also, independent of the specifics of the statutory framework in place. Rather, they flowed from the constitutional imperative, with the task of the statutory framework being to supplement and give effect to them (which is exactly why, in the absence of a statute, the Supreme Court passed legislative guidelines in *Vineet Narain*; without the above analysis, the Court could not have done what it did).

Notably, in *Alok Verma's* Case, the Supreme Court agreed with this argument. It noted that the statutory framework of the CVC Act and the DSPE Act were a 'sequel' to the directions in *Vineet Narain* (which, in turn, flowed from the constitutional function being performed by the CBI).[58] The Court noted that specifically, *Vineet Narain's* observations on independence and insulation, grounded in the right to equality and the rule of law, 'hold a special field'.[59] The Court then applied these principles to interpret the DSPE Act and found that Alok Verma's transfer was not in accordance with law.[60]

Reading together the judgments in *Vineet Narain* and *Alok Verma*, what clearly emerges is the fact that even though the CBI is not—and never has been—provided for in the Constitution, its role and functions require a guarantee of independence in a manner broadly similar (although, of course, different in the particulars) to constitutional functionaries. Thus, although the CBI is technically a statutory body, neither it, nor the statute that provided for it, are to be understood as *merely* statutory in character, but something more. What this something more might be, we shall examine in the next section.

III. The Non-Entrenchment Problem and the Idea of Constitutional Statutes

Based upon the arguments in the previous sections, I want to lay out the concept of a 'constitutional statute' under the Indian Constitution.[61] A constitutional statute is based upon the idea that many fundamental rights guaranteed by the Constitution have both a negative and a positive dimension. The negative dimension is fulfilled by the absence of State interference (such as, for example, the negative dimension of the right to free speech is fulfilled as long as I am not censored). The positive dimension requires the State to undertake some kind of *action* to make the right effective.[62] In many cases, this action will *require* the establishment of an 'infrastructure of implementation', without which the right's positive dimension will remain unfulfilled.[63]

A range of possible alternatives open to the State for implementing the positive dimension of a right means that it is difficult to achieve this through the judicial process.[64] Judicial proceedings here would necessarily require the judiciary to direct Parliament to *legislate* (or to legislate itself), raising concerns pertaining to both expertise and legitimacy.[65] At best, the Court may find the State to be in breach of its positive obligation to legislate, but not more than that.

However, once the State *has* legislated—i.e., once the 'infrastructure of implementation' is in place, through a law—the doctrine of constitutional statutes has a role to play. So, a legislative framework that clearly falls short of what the infrastructure of implementation requires (such as, for instance, making the implementing body entirely subservient to the executive) can be struck down—or otherwise interpretively modified—by the Court.[66] More importantly, the doctrine of constitutional statutes can be invoked to prevent legislative *backsliding*, or retrogression: that is, once a legislative framework for implementing a constitutional right *is* in place, the legislature cannot simply regress from it without, at the very least, providing a satisfactory alternative.

To examine how the doctrine of constitutional statutes might work in practice, consider the famous judgment of the South African Constitutional Court in *Hugh Glenister vs President of the Republic of South Africa.*[67] *Glenister* concerned a constitutional challenge to certain amendments to the South African National Prosecuting Authority Act and South African Police Service Act. The effect of these amendments was to alter the structure and functioning of South Africa's anti-prosecution authority (earlier known as the Directorate of Special Operations or DSO, and after the amendments, the Directory of Priority Crime Investigation or DPCI).

By a narrow majority, the constitutional court held the amendments to be unconstitutional. It did so on the following grounds. First, it held that a confluence of constitutional provisions cast an affirmative obligation upon the State to 'create a sufficiently independent anti-corruption entity … [including] the rights to equality, human dignity, freedom, security of the person, administrative justice and socio-economic rights, including the rights to education, housing, and health care'.[68] Note that the obligation was not expressly written into the Constitution, but *derived* from the positive component of various rights, which—in the opinion of the constitutional court—could not be effectively enjoyed unless corruption was checked.[69] In the words of the court, the obligation flowed from the 'architecture of [the] Constitution.'[70]

Secondly, the constitutional court held that the requirement of independence had to be fleshed out keeping in mind that in many cases, the anti-corruption entity's work would require it to investigate members of the political executive. For this reason, the regulatory framework would have to guarantee an 'adequate level of structural and operational autonomy, secured through institutional and legal mechanisms, to prevent undue political interference'.[71]

Thirdly, it weighed with the constitutional court that the newly constituted DPCI was subjected to significantly greater control than its predecessor, the DSO. The manner in which the DSO's institutional autonomy had been guaranteed thus ensured that the constitutional court was not operating with a tabula rasa, but had a standard of comparison.

Fourthly, on the specifics, the constitutional court held that the absence of security of tenure (with provisions for discretionary dismissal) and remuneration, the power vested in the executive to issue guidelines for the functioning of the DPCI, and oversight by the political executives, all created a situation where the DPCI lacked 'insulation from a degree of management by political actors that threatens imminently to stifle the independent functioning and operations of the unit'.[72]

And fifthly, in fleshing out its concrete conception of institutional independence, the constitutional court drew upon the structure of South Africa's Chapter Nine Institutions, which—as we have seen above—are specifically entrenched within the constitution to 'strengthen constitutional democracy', and are required to be 'independent and impartial'.[73] In other words, the constitutional court placed the DPCI—that was not constitutionally entrenched, but owed its existence to the State's *derivative* obligation to give effect to the Bill of Rights—on par with institutions that *were* constitutionally entrenched. What was common to both, of course, was that whether or not they were constitutionally entrenched, they broadly conformed to the concept of guarantor institutions, or institutions that are part of the infrastructure of rights implementation.

Thus, although the South African Constitutional Court did not ground its findings of invalidity within a specific constitutional doctrine (such as the doctrine of constitutional statutes), its reasoning broadly proceeded along the lines that we have outlined in this section.[74]

With this in mind, let us now return to India. It is easy to see how the doctrine of constitutional statutes is applicable to the case of the amendments to the RTI Act. It has long been established that the right to information is a constitutional right, implicit within the right to freedom of speech and expression.[75] This right is fundamentally about power: it is, by now, widely agreed that opacity in government disempowers the citizen, while free and easy access to information fundamentally recalibrates the power relationship between the government and the individual in a more egalitarian direction.[76]

The right to information has both a negative (i.e., prohibition of denial of information) as well as positive dimension. The latter cannot be made effective without an infrastructure of implementation. This infrastructure is set out in the RTI Act. And because the right to information is not only enforceable against the State, but at its heart, is about taking power *away* from the State and vesting it in the public, it follows—as a necessary implication—that the infrastructure of implementation must be substantively independent from the political executive. Amendments that seek to undermine that independence—once it has been set out in the statute—are therefore unconstitutional.

The argument, of course, is not limited to the Information Commission, or to more familiar bodies such as the Human Rights Commission or the (already entrenched) Election Commission. Another important candidate for inclusion within the list of constitutional statutes is the Personal Digital Data Protection Act. As with the Right to Information Act, the Data Protection Act or DPA seeks to implement the positive component of a constitutional right (the right to privacy). As with the RTI, questions of power—and the balance of power between the State and the individual—are central to the implementation of this right. The more the State is allowed to 'database' its citizens (i.e., collect and store data, merge databases, profile citizens), the more power it holds—and can wield—over citizens. And as with the RTI, the DPA proposes to establish an *infrastructure of implementation*, at the heart of which is the Data Protection Authority. The doctrine of constitutional statutes thus requires the authority to be functionally independent as a precondition of fulfilling its constitutional obligations.[77]

Thus, in sum, the doctrine of constitutional statutes—as set out above—seeks to preserve the integrity of non-electoral bodies (that, following Khaitan above, we have called 'guarantor institutions'). Through that, it seeks to maintain the balance of power between the State and the public. The doctrine is particularly important where the purpose of the guarantor institution is to stand between the public and the State and prevent an entrenchment or aggrandizement of State power. The right to information and the protection of personal data are classic examples of these.

IV. Weak Entrenchment and the Case of the Election Commission

In the previous sections, I have considered the 'non-entrenchment problem': that is, the Indian Constitution's failure to constitutionally entrench fourth-branch institutions, and how the doctrine of constitutional statutes might be deployed to address this problem.

Even if it were to succeed, however, the doctrine of constitutional statutes cannot do more than bring certain non-entrenched fourth-branch institutions *on par* with their entrenched counterparts. This immediately brings up the question: how effective is the Constitution in protecting the independence and autonomy of those institutions that it *does* entrench within the text?

To answer this, let us turn to the Election Commission.

Article 324 of the Constitution stipulates that the superintendence, direction, and control of elections will be vested in an Election Commission.[78] Article 324(2) states:

> The Election Commission shall consist of the Chief Election Commissioner and such number of other Election Commissioners, if any, as the President may from time to time fix and the appointment of the Chief Election Commissioner and other Election Commissioners shall, *subject to the provisions of any law made in that behalf by Parliament*, be made by the President.[79]

It is perhaps not entirely surprising that in the seven decades after the Constitution's birth, Parliament failed to enact any law, leaving appointments—by default—in the hands of the President. The Election Commission itself has had a chequered history, with its reputation for independence and impartiality more a function of the personalities of individual chief election commissioners, rather than the manner and process through which they are appointed.[80]

It was in this context that the *Anoop Baranwal* case came to the Supreme Court.

The judgment of the Supreme Court in *Anoop Baranwal* is complex and requires some unpicking. First, as a matter of constitutional history, the Court studied the Constituent Assembly Debates on the question of the appointment of election commissioners. It found that while there had been agreement in the assembly that the Election Commission must be independent and free from executive interference, there had been no consensus on how this was to be achieved. Proposals requiring parliamentary supermajorities, or instruments of instruction to the President, were put forward, but none of them carried enough support from the assembly. For this reason, the framers of the Constitution left it to Parliament to decide, by law, and drafted Article 324 as they did.[81] But it also followed, therefore—according to the Court—that Article 324 carried with it a constitutional expectation *both* that Parliament would pass a law, *and also* that the design of such a law would guarantee the independence of the election commissioners from the executive.[82]

The Court then buttressed its historical argument with a structural argument. The constitutional right to vote would be meaningless without the existence of a body that was placed in charge of conducting free and fair elections (what, in this chapter, I have referred to as the 'infrastructure of implementing' a constitutional right).[83] Under the Indian Constitution, this body was the Election Commission. There was, therefore, a direct link between the right to vote, and the role and functions of the Election Commission.[84] This was further borne out by the range of functions vested in the commission, through statute:

the allocation of party symbols, the recognition or de-recognition of political parties, adjudicating 'splits' within parties, enforcing the Model Code of Conduct during elections and penalizing parties for on-compliance, and so on.[85]

The constitutional history, the role of the Election Commission in implementing the constitutional right to vote, and the vast powers vested in it to do so, led the Court to find that the continuing absence of legislation (and therefore, the default position of presidential appointments) was unconstitutional.[86] The Court sought to remedy this through a judicially mandated interim arrangement. The arrangement was a familiar one, as we have seen above: a committee consisting of the Prime Minister, the leader of the Opposition, and the Chief Justice of India.

A study of the *Anoop Baranwal* judgment reveals that the Court's reasoning was consistent with our discussion in this chapter. The Election Commission is a fourth branch, or guarantor institution, whose task is to create and oversee the infrastructure of implementation of a constitutional right (in this case, the right to vote). The commission's role, therefore, requires *structural* and *institutional* independence from the executive (a player in the very game that the commission is meant to referee). Appointments are a crucial facet of structural and institutional independence. Consequently, an arrangement where appointments to the Election Commission are under the control of the executive is unconstitutional—a position for which the Court found substantial support in the Constituent Assembly Debates. In essence, therefore, the Court drew out an *implied guarantee of institutional independence from the executive*, based on constitutional history, design, and structure.

Understanding this also makes clear that Parliament's legislative response was contrary to *Anoop Baranwal*. It is, of course, true that *Anoop Baranwal* itself made clear that its three-member committee was a temporary arrangement, until Parliament discharged its constitutional obligation to legislate under Article 324(2). However, the entire *basis* of *Baranwal* was that an Article 324(2) law would have to sufficiently guarantee the independence of the Election Commission. While there could be many different ways of guaranteeing this (from a non-partisan selection body to a multi-partisan selection body), it is evident that *executive* control over selections violates that guarantee.[87]

The problem, however, is that none of this is set out in the constitutional text. As with the unentrenched institutions that we have discussed in the previous sections, institutional independence that depends on *implied* limitations and structural readings is relatively easy to displace.

The fate of the *Anoop Baranwal* judgment reflects this. The December 2023 law was justified on the basis that the Court, in *Anoop Baranwal*, had noted that its three-member committee was a 'pro-tem measure', and that the final responsibility for legislation lay with Parliament. In its pre-general election March 2024 order refusing an interim stay upon the law, a two-judge bench of the Supreme Court repeated this justification,[88] without going into the *reasoning* of *Anoop Baranwal*.[89] The judgment, thus, was effectively nullified.

This, then, is the peril of what we have called *weak entrenchment*. Even for those fourth-branch institutions that are specifically recognized by the Constitution (whether it is the Election Commission or the CAG), the constitutional text does not stipulate or guarantee their independence. On the contrary, by expressly providing for Presidential appointment as the default (albeit a temporary default), the Constitution facilitates and enables a reading (both by the Court, but also by the other branches) that executive control over fourth-branch institutions is not inconsistent with the constitutional scheme. This, in turn, makes judgments such as *Anoop Baranwal* not only outliers, but also easier to get around through legislation (by Parliament) or interpretation (by the Court itself).[90]

V. Conclusion: Enduring Barriers

In this chapter, I have argued that notwithstanding constitutional silences, there is interpretive scope, upon the Constitution's terrain, for securing the independence and autonomous functioning of 'guarantor institutions', whose task it is to implement constitutional rights and mitigate the power imbalance between the State and the public. I propose that this can be done through an interpretive doctrine called the doctrine of constitutional statutes.

The establishment of the doctrine in Indian constitutional jurisprudence, however, faces two serious barriers.

The first barrier is the constitutional text itself. As we have seen, a large number of the guarantor institutions under consideration are simply not in the Constitution. Indeed, at first blush, the Constitution presents an executive-dominated (or, to repeat a term we have used previously, 'executive-trusting') vision of non-electoral institutions that wield public power: the Public Service Commissions and the Scheduled Caste and Scheduled Tribe Commissions are under executive control, and the procedure for appointment for the CAG is also under executive control.

Thus, guarantor institutions have been brought into existence (and in some cases are not yet in existence) through legislation, which may (or may not) be the culmination of social movements. At the first instance, therefore, the doctrine needs a judicial leap of faith to establish itself as a constitutional doctrine. The length of the leap of faith is widened when we consider that a number of rights in question are themselves implicit, and not explicitly set out in the Constitution: the right to information flows from the right to freedom of speech and expression; the right to data protection is a facet of the right to privacy, which in turn flows from the rights to life, personal liberty, and freedom of speech, expression, and conscience. The doctrine of constitutional statutes thus requires the Court to constitutionalize an institution that is not explicitly in the Constitution, on the basis that it is tasked with implementing a right that is also not explicitly in the Constitution; and to do so without falling into the trap of judicial legislation. For the reasons advanced above, I believe that it is *possible* for the Court to do so; but the gaping constitutional silences—silences that exist by design—make it a challenge.

The challenge is compounded by the fact that where the Court has dealt with the issue—in *Vineet Narain* and in *Alok Verma*—it has done so in piecemeal fashion, without articulating a constitutional principle that could then be extend to other cases (and indeed, the outcome in *Alok Verma* suggests that constitutional doctrine is rendered more or less irrelevant when the balance of political forces is overwhelmingly skewed). Thus, *Vineet Narain* and *Alok Verma* are important cases in that they demonstrate how the argument could work in practice, but leave a significant amount of intellectual work still to be done.

Indeed, the absence of intellectual foundations underlying the independence of fourth-branch institutions was evident in the 2023 case of *Dr. Jaya Thakur vs Union of India*, where periodic extensions were granted to the director of the Enforcement Directorate (ED).[91] This was initially done through executive orders, but then, on a challenge being filed, it was accomplished through legislative enactment. The law stated that the initial two-year tenure of the ED director could be extended on a year-by-year basis, subject to the recommendation of the CVC Committee. The constitutional challenge proceeded exactly along the lines of prior cases involving the independence of the CBI and the CVC (discussed above): i.e., that granting periodic extensions allowed the executive to have a 'carrot-and-stick' relationship with the director and severely undermine their independence. The Court, however, rejected the argument and upheld the law, on the basis that the recommendation of the CVC Committee provided adequate safeguards against arbitrary extensions.[92]

What was missing from the Court's analysis, however, was the understanding of the role of the ED as a fourth-branch institution, with sweeping powers and responsibilities—and which, therefore, made its institutional independence a *constitutional* principle. Had the Court engaged with that argument, it would also have been forced to confront the fact that the vigilance commissioners were themselves selected by a committee that was dominated by the

Union cabinet. Thus, the interposition of the CVC Committee only made executive control over the ED indirect, much less removing or abolishing it. The Court's task was made easier, however, by the fact that the CVC Committee was itself a product of the *Vineet Narain* judgment, which we have considered above. We can see, therefore, a continuing, executive-trusting trajectory with respect to fourth-branch institutions, which flows from the absence of principled reasoning, even in judgments such as *Vineet Narain*.

The second barrier is that even if the argument were to succeed in its entirety, how much difference it would make to constitutional *practice* is still an open question. The reason for this, once again, takes us back to the Constitution. Even when it comes to constitutional bodies (such as the Election Commission), there is insulation from arbitrary dismissal and insulation when it comes to tenure, but not so for appointments (what we have referred to in this chapter as *thin entrenchment*). It is for this reason that the historical verdict on India's Election Commission has been distinctly mixed. There are periods in India's post-Independence history where, by common consensus, it has acted independently of the political executive and the ruling party. But equally, there have been periods where it has been perceived to be thoroughly under the control of the executive. This is, at least in part, due to the very qualified and partial independence that the Constitution allows it.

This is also why the Court's eventual attempt to secure institutional independence for the Election Commission through *constitutional interpretation* was stymied through a combination of (the executive-dominated) Parliament and a different, subsequent bench of the Supreme Court itself. The Supreme Court in *Anoop Baranwal* replaced presidential appointments with a three-member committee as a temporary measure pending legislation on the basis that the Constitution required Parliament to legislate for an independent Election Commission. However, the absence of any express language requiring the latter allowed both Parliament and the later Court to focus only on the 'temporary' nature of the *Anoop Baranwal* arrangement, and restore executive dominance through a new committee with the Union cabinet in the majority. While this is undoubtedly a bad faith reading of *Anoop Baranwal*, it is a reading that is enabled by the text and structure of the Constitution.

Weak entrenchment is not, of course, limited to the Election Commission. As we have seen above, the appointment of the CAG is also under the control of the executive, and the CAG has likewise enjoyed a chequered reputation in our history.[93] And finally, it is particularly noteworthy that until the time that the judiciary seized the formal power of appointing judges for itself in *The Second Judges Case*, the constitutional text granted it to the executive (with only a fragile convention, requiring the President to defer to the views of the Chief Justice, sustaining an even more fragile practice).

Thus, the flaw here—to the extent that one agrees that there is a flaw—is evidently with the constitutional design. Even when it does establish explicitly independent institutions wielding public power, the Constitution does not seek to insulate them from the executive when it comes to the selection of who will run those institutions, or create avenues for effective public participation in the process of appointments and functioning.

In the last analysis, therefore, the doctrine of constitutional statutes—and the role of 'guarantor institutions' as independent sites where State power can be tempered and confronted—will be limited by the limited vision of the Constitution itself. After a certain point, it will run up against the predominantly *statist* and centralized vision of the Constitution, which continues to view with suspicion attempts to distribute or disperse power, or to have institutions that stand outside the State, and can—on behalf of citizens—effectively confront State power. Judicial interpretation (a possibility that, in its own right, appears increasingly distant at this time) can take us this far, but no further.

5

Power Contained: Rights

THROUGH THE COURSE OF this book, we have examined public power and its various manifestations: distributed between different levels of the State, mediated through institutions, and exercised individually or collectively. But stripped of its adornments, there is power in its raw, most unvarnished form: the power of the State over the human body, which often translates into the power to deprive the body of life, or of physical liberty. This is a form of power that all Constitutions must urgently address, and it is this form of power that we shall discuss in this chapter.

Modern democratic Constitutions address the coercive power of the State through the vehicle of civil and political rights. In keeping with the idiom of this book, the axis of power is between the State and the individual. A bill of rights is the shield that *constrains* the exercise of State power upon the individual. The terrain of contestation, thus, is the domain of rights: the interpretation and exercise of rights determines the balance of power between the State and the individual.

This chapter shall be structured as follows. We will begin by examining public power in the language of what the State is permitted to do to an individual's body. In law, this power is written into the criminal codes (especially the criminal procedure code).[1] In the pre-Constitutional era, this power was written *only* into the criminal codes, a body of law that both empowered the State, but also—in theory—spelt out its limits. The colonial logic of viewing Indians as citizens to be controlled invariably influenced the dominant register of the Code of Criminal Procedure and allied legislation as power-enabling rather than power-constraining instruments. The framing of the Constitution, *in theory*, was meant to change this, by encoding protections of life and liberty within Articles 20 to 22 of the Constitution. How these constitutional guarantees would rub up against the existing logic of the criminal codes, then, became the terrain of contestation in post-Constitutional India **(I)**.

We will then examine how this contestation has played out in Indian constitutional history. As with other chapters in this book, this history will be told through the story of inflection points. We will begin by analysing the notorious Article 22, which accords constitutional sanction (or even sanctity!) to the practice of 'preventive detention'. We will see how the Indian Supreme Court, when given the chance, refused to subject preventive/administrative detention to the touchstone of due process and other constitutional safeguards, effectively creating an 'authoritarian enclave' within the Constitution. At present, Article 22 is seemingly an exceptional provision, whose *use* has been normalized by the executive, but whose *scrutiny* by courts remains within the idiom of the state of exception **(II)**.

Next, we will look at the vital—and oft-ignored—criminal procedure safeguards guaranteed by Article 20 of the Constitution. In a classical sense, these provisions were meant to erect constitutional walls around the individual, to keep out the coercive power of the State. We will examine how, through a process of interpretation, the courts have removed key bricks from the constitutional architecture, leaving a swathe of citizens vulnerable and unprotected against State power. The logic underlying this interpretation has been the logic of *preserving* the coercive power of the State over as wide a domain as possible, and limiting any constitutional encroachment upon this power to the smallest terrain that is interpretively consistent with the text of these provisions **(III)**.

Finally, we shall consider what has long become the most famous provision of the Indian Constitution: Article 21 and its guarantee of life and personal liberty which, over the years, has come to protect everything *but* life and personal liberty. We will examine how the standards for the deprivation of liberty—originally enacted under colonial statutes, during a state of war—have become a part of the permanent statutory regime, and how judicial interpretation has read down constitutional due process safeguards to the level of that colonially inspired statutory regime, instead of subjecting the law to constitutional standards. **(IV)**.

By way of conclusion, we shall consider a recent judgment of the Supreme Court concerning a challenge to the Prevention of Money Laundering Act (PMLA), where many of these strands of jurisprudence come together. The Supreme Court's PMLA judgment—as Abhinav Sekhri points out—does not create new jurisprudence, but it is, in a way, a highlight reel or a replay of the Court's 'greatest hits' over the years. It demonstrates most starkly the centralizing drift in the domain of rights: a centralizing drift, one fears, that has become so embedded within constitutional common sense that its reversal—under the provisions of *this* Constitution—is little more than a dream **(V)**.

I. State, Power, and the Individual

This chapter is about power in its most basic sense: the power of the State to imprison, to detain, to restrict, to confine, and to otherwise impinge upon an individual's bodily integrity. This power is normally organized through a set of criminal laws (the law of crimes, the law of procedure, and the law of evidence).[2] Traditionally, the (uncodified) common law of England evolved numerous safeguards, incrementally and over time, against the abuse of State power. These included, for example, prohibitions against general warrants,[3] the right against self-incrimination, and so on.[4]

British codification of criminal law in India, in the latter half of the nineteenth century, incorporated a few of these common-law safeguards, in some form. For example, under the Evidence Act, confessions to police officers were made inadmissible.[5] The British were also clear, however, that they were dealing with a subject population, and not a citizenry whose rights (evolved and entrenched over time) had to be protected. Thus, the core function of the criminal codes was not to constrain State power, but to maintain order by enabling it.[6] For example, in the debates around the Criminal Procedure Bill of 1872, the lieutenant-governor of Bengal specifically noted that the purpose of criminal law in India—unlike in Britain—was *not* 'securing the liberties of the people', and for that reason, various 'English prejudices' (such as, for example, the right against self-incrimination) needed to be 'cleared away'.[7] This was reflected in the text of the statutes. Thus, general warrants were explicitly *permitted* under the Code of Criminal Procedure, 1898[8], and many other common-law safeguards were simply absent.[9]

In addition to the three criminal laws—the Indian Penal Code, the Code of Criminal Procedure, and the Indian Evidence Act—colonial regulation (and enabling) of coercive State power took place through a web of rules, regulations, and temporal, subject-specific, or even extraordinary legislation. Preventive—or administrative—detention, without trial, was permitted as far back as 1818[10], through the Bengal Regulation, and legalized, at various points, through seventeen different pieces of legislation.[11] Temporary 'extraordinary' laws were passed during the two World Wars. In the interwar period—primarily to quell the nationalist movement—the colonial government enacted the Rowlatt Act of 1919, which did away with numerous existing procedural safeguards.

In each case, the departure from the basic standard of legal protection under the existing regime was justified either on the touchstone of emergency, or the special circumstances in the colony.[12] As Nasser Hussain notes, therefore, racial difference supplied a ground for having a 'permanent' state of necessity, an 'exceptional' power whose exercise was—in the circumstances of the colony—no more exceptional, but a norm[13], where the overarching logic was that of social control.[14] This gave the baseline or threshold set of protections a fragile, almost ephemeral quality, subject to regression at any moment.

It is this last issue that the framing of a constitution is meant to obviate. The entrenchment of a rule against general warrants, a right against self-incrimination under the US Constitution[15], or an indefeasible right to *habeas corpus* under the Kenyan Constitution[16], for example, are guarantees against the possibility of regression—were these rights left only to legislative majorities (or judicial decisions). And these guarantees are often drawn from specific historical experience.

As with many other constitutions, the Indian Constitution also encodes a set of safeguards against the exercise of the State's coercive power over the body: Articles 20 to 22. The language of these provisions, however, betrays a tension underlying the constitutional design, which has come to define the terrain of contestation in post-constitutional debates about State power and the individual. While Article 20 contains a set of familiar safeguards—the right against ex post facto criminal laws, against double jeopardy, and against compelled self-incrimination—Articles 21 and 22 are distinctly more ambiguous.

Article 21 purports to protect the right to life and personal liberty, but only in a thin sense, by insisting that any deprivation of these rights must be in accordance with *procedure established by law*.[17] The absence of a due process right in Article 21 triggered a significant outcry in the Constituent Assembly, following which B.R. Ambedkar claimed to have addressed the problem by introducing due process into the first two clauses of Article 22.[18]

What do these two clauses say? They too are framed as safeguards. First, a person may not be arrested without being informed of the grounds of their arrest, and must be allowed to consult and be defended by a legal practitioner of their choice. Secondly, a person who is arrested or detained in custody must be produced before a magistrate (that is, a judicial authority) within twenty-four hours, whose task it is then to determine the legality of the arrest/custody, as well as to authorize (or refuse) its further extension.[19]

Immediately after, however, Articles 22(3) to 22(7) construct a regime of preventive detention, where the application of these safeguards is categorically excluded.[20] This makes India one of the very few countries in the world where preventive detention is explicitly authorized by the constitutional text.

The constitutional design thus appears as a web of safeguards and permissions, rights and restrictions, creating significant scope for contestation. The issue, however, is not limited to the text of the constitutional provisions. Recall that at the time the Constitution was framed, colonial criminal laws were already in existence, along with the network of 'special' legislation, which we have discussed above. The governing logic of colonial criminal law was the maintenance of order through the preservation of coercive State power.

In this context, it becomes crucial to ask the question: what was the governing logic of the *constitutional* provisions? Because if the Constitution was meant to be transformative—and if the philosophy underlying Articles 20–22 was a philosophy of *redistributing* power between the State and the individual through the vehicle of rights—then the existing criminal codes and criminal jurisprudence would have to be tested upon a new anvil, and a new touchstone (it should be immediately obvious that much of it would be found wanting).

However, if the governing logic was *still* a logic of order through power, then existing (colonial) jurisprudence was already consistent with the (new) Constitution. In such a situation, the interpretation of the constitutional provisions would be such as to *preserve* the existing architecture of State power and the relationship between the State and the individual[21] by reading down these provisions so as to bring them in line with the existing legal landscape (rather than testing the latter upon the touchstone of the former).[22]

In the next three sections, we shall examine the terrain of contestation around these provisions, keeping in mind the role played by Articles 20–22 in redistributing—or rebalancing—power between the State and the individual: ostensibly through the creation of walls around a zone of individual autonomy, safe from the incursion of State power.

II. Article 22: The Authoritarian Enclave

Preventive detention has a long lineage, going back to the 1818 Bengal Regulation. As Hallie Ludsin notes, the British government adopted preventive detention as a 'paramilitary mode of policing ... structuring the police [in a manner so as to] perpetuate British rule'.[23] Preventive detention was an embodiment of the 'rule of colonial difference'. As Indian judges would note immediately after Independence, although liberally used by the British in the colony at all times, in Britain itself, it was only used for a limited purpose, during a period of war.[24]

Occupying an ambiguous zone between the (formally) extraordinary and the (practically) ordinary, preventive detention was thoroughly embedded into the Indian legal landscape at the time of Independence: so much so that facing a situation of 'communal tensions, communist uprisings, and the partition of Pakistan from India', it turned into a public order tool under the newly independent federal and provincial governments.[25] As the Constituent Assembly met to frame the Constitution between 1947 to 1950, the provinces framed—and wielded—increasingly strict preventive detention laws.[26] Meanwhile, at the central level, the wartime Defence of India Regulations guided the exercise of preventive detention powers.[27]

The source of authority for these provincial preventive detention laws was the 1935 Government of India Act, which authorized provincial legislatures to enact preventive detention legislation in the interests of public order, but which notably did not have a bill of rights. In the absence of a rights framework, the pre-Constitutional

Federal Court refused to review the 'subjective satisfaction' of the executive that detaining an individual was, indeed, necessary for the maintenance of public order.[28] The Court limited its intervention only to a scrutiny of whether the grounds of detention were 'relevant' to its objective.[29]

The Constituent Assembly's decision to retain preventive detention was controversial. Its history as a tool of colonial oppression was brought up repeatedly (and perhaps somewhat ironically, given that provincial governments under the 1935 Government of India Act, many of whom were run by the Indian National Congress, had proven equally, if not more, adept at using it). It was justified in the language of emergency—the precarious and communally charged situation prevailing at the time, and the need for extraordinary powers to deal with extraordinary situations. It was also justified, however, on the basis that the problem was not with the existence of the power, but by its *misuse* by an alien colonial government; misuse that would no longer occur under an elected sovereign government.[30]

This background to the Constituent Assembly Debates deepens our analysis of Article 22 as a terrain of contestation. Article 22 was framed as a Janus-faced provision, incorporating the elements of due process and then excluding them from the scope of preventive detention laws; as both a power-constraining and a power-enabling provision; and as both a provision of the state of exception, and one of 'normalcy'.

Almost immediately after the framing of the Constitution, the question of how to interpret Article 22 came before the Supreme Court—indeed, the first time the Supreme Court was called upon to interpret the Constitution. *A.K. Gopalan vs State of Madras* is one of those judgments that is now studied as an element of legal history and a cautionary tale, rather than as an aspect of living jurisprudence. This is a mistake.

At the stroke of the midnight hour, A.K. Gopalan—a communist leader from Madras—famously went from being a detainee of the colonial government to a detainee of the new independent Indian government. His detention was eventually sanctioned under the newly enacted Preventive Detention Act of 1950 (PDA), purportedly passed under the authority of Article 22 of the Constitution. As Ujjwal Kumar Singh notes, with the enactment of a preventive detention legislation immediately after the entrenchment of preventive detention under the Constitution, it was clear that this was a framework '[not] to deal with an emergent or aberrant situation, but in fact enunciating a basic policy'.[31] The need for the law was publicly justified by reference to 'the Telangana disturbances, the recurrent labour troubles, and the fact that a large number of detenus under colonial laws were being released by courts on the ground that the laws were not consistent with the Constitution'.[32] The PDA thus was a statement of continuity both with respect to the colonial period, as well as the deployment of preventive detention as a public-order tool during the Independence period of 1947–50. The only significant difference now was the existence of the Indian Constitution.

The question that A.K. Gopalan posed to the Supreme Court was whether that made any difference.

Gopalan challenged several provisions of the PDA. Among the many arguments that he made, two are relevant for our purposes. First, that the term 'procedure established by law' under Article 21 articulated a *substantive* constraint upon the State: laws that took away an individual's life or liberty had to conform to a certain basic requirement—that of providing notice, a hearing, an impartial tribunal, and a just procedure—to pass constitutional muster; and *secondly*, that the provisions of the detention law violated certain fundamental rights, such as the rights to free speech and especially the right to freedom of movement under Article 19.[33]

A majority of the Supreme Court rejected both arguments.[34] The exact reasoning of the Court has long been a matter of some debate, but at least as interpreted through subsequent judgments, the Court did two things.[35] First, it held that the term 'procedure established by law' under Article 21 did not contain substantive content.[36] Thus, as long as a law stipulated *a* procedure, and executive action complied with it, it was constitutionally compliant. Secondly, the Court held that a preventive detention law could not be challenged on the grounds of Article 19. Subsequent judgments extended this to mean that the limited ground of challenge to a preventive detention law *was non-compliance with the requirements of Articles 22(3)-22(7) itself.*

In *A.K. Gopalan*, therefore, the Supreme Court turned Article 22 into what we can call an 'authoritarian enclave'. While a preventive detention law admittedly violated an individual's personal liberty (Article 21), and a bouquet of other constitutional rights (to free movement, in particular), it was insulated from complying with the constitutional constraints otherwise imposed upon State power when dealing with those rights. In the Fundamental Rights chapter, Article 22 stood alone, self-defining and complete. As P.K. Tripathi trenchantly noted—writing in 1960—*Gopalan* (and its progeny) stood for the proposition that when Article 13 of the Constitution stated that 'any law' inconsistent with the Bill of Rights would be void and unconstitutional, what it really *meant* was 'any law other than a law of preventive detention'.[37] For Tripathi, this position reflected 'the evolution of a judicial policy towards preventive detention laws, that verges on total abandonment of the unfortunate individuals who happen to fall under their shadow'.[38]

Moreover, the 'authoritarian enclave' informed the Court's interpretation of Article 22 itself. Other than relying upon Articles 19 and 21, Gopalan also made a third set of arguments: namely, that the internal requirements of Article 22 had not been met. For example, the act empowered the State to detain an individual for longer than three months without having their detention reviewed by an advisory board, as required by Article 22(4). To justify this, Article 22(7) was invoked, which allowed Parliament to dispense with the advisory board for certain 'circumstances' and 'classes' of cases.

What were these 'circumstances' and 'classes'? It turned out that Parliament had simply copied the subjects set out in Schedule VII, with respect to which it was *competent* to pass preventive detention laws (such as 'public order'), and made no further effort to identify 'circumstances' and 'classes'. The Court split 4–2 on whether this was constitutional, and the split reflected a fundamental difference in interpretive approach. For the two dissenting judges, Article 22(7) was clearly an *exception* to Article 22(4) (itself an exception to the safeguards under Articles 22[1] and [2]), and had to be treated as such. As Justice Fazl Ali noted, 'I do not think that it was ever intended that Parliament could at its will treat the normal as the abnormal or the rule as the exception.'[39] And given that it was an exception, Parliament had to clearly state what those 'classes' and 'circumstances' were that were so grave so as to justify dispensing with the advisory board.

For the majority, on the other hand, Articles 22(4) and (7) were simply independent sources of power, and there was no warrant to read Article 22(7) narrowly. Parliament could, therefore, pass a law that would remove all detentions from Article 22(4)'s requirement of advisory board review, and attain complete executive impunity: thus turning the *exception to the exception* into the rule.[40]

Gopalan empowered Parliament to promptly extend the Preventive Detention Act (initially meant to last for only one year), which it did in 1951, and then again, through a 'series of extending and modifying Acts,'[41] up until 1969.[42] And, as noted above, subsequent judgments followed *Gopalan*—or at least, interpreted *Gopalan* in the manner described above.[43] In *Ram Singh vs State of Delhi*, for example, Ram Singh and his colleagues of the Hindu Mahasabha were detained for allegedly making communally incendiary speeches.[44] They argued that the detention order referred to the maintenance of 'public order' as a ground of detention. However, 'public order' was not (at the time) a ground for the State to restrict speech under Article 19(2) of the Constitution.[45] It was therefore argued that as the detention order was a response to the exercise of the Fundamental Right of freedom of speech, it would have to meet the test of Article 19(2), which it did not.

The Supreme Court rejected the argument by relying upon *A.K. Gopalan*. It held that while State action imposing censorship, or otherwise 'directly' infringing Article 19(1)(a), would have to comply with the requirements of Article 19(2), a law that infringed personal liberty—even if it was *for* restricting an individual's (future) speech—need not do so. In other words, the Supreme Court strengthened the authoritarian enclave by interpreting *A.K. Gopalan* to hold that even where the grounds of detention directly pertained to the exercise of a constitutionally protected right, there was no need for compliance with the legal tests laid down for when such a right could be validly restricted by the State.[46] All that was needed was procedural compliance with the provisions of Article 22 itself.

Apart from the constitutional issues with such reasoning, the result of such a position was, of course, that the preventive detention law could—and would—be deployed as a 'matter of convenience' in order to incarcerate an individual without the State having to run the gauntlet of Fundamental Rights compliance if the 'ordinary' criminal justice procedure of prosecution and punishment had been deployed instead.[47]

Indeed, this was evident right from the earliest operation of preventive detention. In *Sahadat Ali vs State of Assam*, the State elected to withdraw a criminal case against an undertrial, Sahadat Ali, leading to his release from prison.[48] However, Sahadat Ali 'had hardly gone some paces from the jail' when he was re-arrested under a preventive detention order that had been issued *while he had still been incarcerated*.[49] Despite the clear indication that the State was using preventive detention law as a substitute to accomplish what it had not been able to through the criminal legal process, the High Court declared that its hands were tied by the deferential judicial standards under Article 22, and upheld the detention order.

The logic of the High Court was subsequently affirmed by the Supreme Court when dealing with the issue of whether a person already incarcerated could be subjected to a preventive detention order. The Supreme Court held that this was permissible, while retaining the right to scrutinize the order on a case-by-case basis.[50] This is not a one-off: as we shall see below, preventive detention often serves as a tool in keeping individuals incarcerated through cycles or webs of confinement.[51] Bail in an ordinary criminal case is followed by arrest under a preventive detention order, the expiry of the order is followed by re-arrest in another criminal case, and so on.[52] The roots of this lie in *Gopalan*, and the logic of *Gopalan*, that set the jurisprudence of preventive detention in independent India along the path of the authoritarian enclave as early as 1950.

In the mid-1970s, the Supreme Court apparently had a change of heart. In *Maneka Gandhi vs Union of India*, relying upon its own previous judgment in *R.C. Cooper vs Union of India*, the Court apparently 'overruled' *A.K. Gopalan.* It did so on two grounds: first, that contrary to both the text of Article 21 and its drafting history, the phrase 'procedure established by law' *did* actually mean 'due process'. In other words, it required procedure to be 'just, fair and reasonable'. And secondly, that Fundamental Rights in the Constitution were not to be read in isolation from each other, but as an interconnected whole.[53] In the annals of Indian constitutional scholarship—and in the history of the Supreme Court as recounted by the Supreme Court—the judgment in *Maneka Gandhi* corrected the historical mistake made in *Gopalan*, and moved the Court into a new era of rights protection.[54]

Or did it? As Abhinav Sekhri notes, even as *Maneka Gandhi* claimed that henceforth all rights would be read together, one of the judges—Justice Beg—took time out to specify that this would *not* apply to Article 22.[55] Five years later, the question came up squarely before the Supreme Court in *A.K. Roy vs Union of India*, where the constitutionality of the National Security Act—one of the four central preventive-detention laws in existence—was challenged.[56] Many challenges were raised in *A.K. Roy*, including the argument that the provisions of the NSA—which were virtually identical with the pre-Emergency and Emergency-era Maintenance of Internal Security Act (MISA)—were unconstitutional because they violated other Fundamental Rights. Thus, in *A.K. Roy*, the Supreme Court had the opportunity to make good on the rhetoric of *Maneka Gandhi*: in this new rights-protecting era, to test—for the first time—a preventive detention law on the anvil of due process (Article 21) and reasonableness/proportionality (Article 19).

The Supreme Court, however, refused to do so. In a paragraph that is difficult to decipher, it first held that 'a law of preventive detention which falls within Article 22 must also meet the requirements of Articles 14, 19, and 21';[57] but then went on to hold held that 'the question whether a law of preventive detention is unconstitutional for the reasons that it violates freedoms conferred by Articles 14, 19, 21, and 22 of the Constitution is also concluded'—in the negative![58] How these two sentences are to be reconciled is anybody's guess, but notably, the Court relied on pre-*Maneka Gandhi* judgments for the proposition that preventive detention laws in general (and MISA in particular, which was the basis of the NSA), could not be held unconstitutional for violating other Part III rights.

The Court's analysis had a downstream effect on its consideration of the constitutionality of specific provisions of the NSA. For example, it rejected the argument that a detenu had a constitutional right to be represented by a lawyer during preventive detention proceedings, on the basis that the language of Article 22 (specifically, Article 22[3][b]) excluded it. The internal contradiction that we have pointed to above appeared in the Court's reasoning here too. While observing that in the light of *R.C. Cooper* and subsequent cases (such as *Maneka Gandhi*), a preventive detention law had to satisfy the standards of Article 21 as well, in this case, 'the Constitution itself has provided a yardstick for the application of that standard, through the medium of the provisions contained in Article 22(3)(b)'.[59]

In sum, therefore, and notwithstanding the judgment in *Maneka Gandhi*, the Supreme Court in *A.K. Roy* refused to effectively test preventive detention laws on any anvil other than the requirements of Articles 22(3) to 22(7). The Court's analysis gave an even starker meaning to 'authoritarian enclave'. Even as the rest of the Fundamental Rights chapter was now to be read as an integrated whole, Articles 22(3) to 22(7) would stand apart, a truly 'complete code' for detention without trial.

A.K. Roy vs Union of India thus is an inflection-point judgment in the sense that the term is used in this book. Because of the judgment in *Maneka Gandhi*, for the first time in two and a half decades, the Supreme Court had a clear interpretive choice before it: acknowledge that preventive detention affects a range of rights, and subject it to constitutional scrutiny accordingly; or retain and further entrench the 'authoritarian enclave' of Article 22. It chose the latter, and thus foreclosed—for the foreseeable future—the path of interrogating and mitigating the exercise of State power in the domain of administrative detention.[60]

The survival of Article 22 as an authoritarian enclave creates a further irony, one that existed pre-*A.K. Roy*, but has grown starker since. On the one hand, the *use* of administrative or preventive detention has long been normalized as a regular, non-exceptional part of the criminal justice system. It is no longer treated as something to be deployed only in 'exceptional' cases, where the regular criminal justice machinery is insufficient (that is, if it ever was). However, judicial *scrutiny* of preventive detention continues to be conducted on exceptional terms.

Thus, a result of the *A.K. Roy* line of cases—as Ludsin points out, for example—is that the Court has consistently refused to subject preventive detention to the test of proportionality (even as proportionality has become an embedded feature of judicial review of violations of other Fundamental Rights).[61] The executive is not required to demonstrate, for example, that it resorted to preventive detention because the usual mechanisms of the criminal justice system were proving insufficient to deal with a particular threat.[62] Indeed, quite the opposite: preventive detention orders have been upheld in situations where incarcerated individuals *might* be granted bail through the regular process, in order to ensure that they are not set free (the Supreme Court has upheld minimalistic scrutiny of such cases);[63] in situations where the regular courts *have* already 'granted the same person bail on largely the same set of allegations,'[64] or even where an individual has been acquitted for the very offence on the basis of which he is (subsequently) subjected to preventive detention.[65]

This position—where preventive detention simultaneously functions as a *substitute* for the ordinary criminal process, but also as an *exceptional* mechanism where deprivation of liberty can be accomplished by the State without the safeguards of that process or the rigours of judicial scrutiny—was taken to its logical extreme in *Dropti Devi vs Union of India*.[66] Here, the Supreme Court upheld preventive detention in the context of the regulation of foreign exchange, even where violation of the substantive foreign exchange law was no longer a criminal offence (it was now a civil offence). The Court invoked the distinction between preventive and punitive detention to hold that the absence of the latter had no bearing upon the former. This, however, is counter-intuitive: if the *violation* of a law is not treated as an offence worthy of depriving an individual of their personal liberty, how can the *anticipatory violation* of the law be a ground for the deprivation of personal liberty? This is, in essence, the thin edge of the wedge in treating preventive detention as entirely exceptional and untethered from the logic of the criminal justice system.

The authoritarian enclave thus turns into a proverbial constitutional blackhole. Article 22 is, in effect, a rightless zone within the Constitution, sanctioning the deprivation of liberty on its terms alone. Apart from the thin procedural safeguards offered by Articles 22(3) to 22(7), preventive detention in India manifests itself as a near-unchecked exercise of State (and primarily, executive) power over the individual.[67]

III. Article 20: Comforting the Comfortable

The Indian Supreme Court has tended to look at the Fundamental Rights chapter through the lens of trinities. The most famous 'trinity' is that of Articles 14 (equality), 19 (fundamental freedoms) and 21 (life and personal liberty). But another—somewhat lesser examined—trinity is constituted by the three clauses of Article 20.[68] Article 20(1) bars retrospective conviction or enhanced punishment. Article 20(2) bars double jeopardy: 'No person shall be prosecuted and punished for the same offence more than once.' Article 20(3) grants the right against self-incrimination: 'No person accused of any offence shall be compelled to be a witness against himself.'

A first look at Article 20 makes it clear that it is intended to put certain brakes or constraints upon what the law and law-enforcement agencies may do in their quest to prevent, investigate, prosecute, and punish crime. These constraints will interfere with the otherwise legitimate exercise of State power to achieve these goals. Indeed, that is their point. So, even when fresh evidence is discovered after an individual has been acquitted, which clearly points to their guilt, the Constitution seeks to prohibit the State from a second bite at the cherry. Even when an individual is in sole possession of incriminating information—necessary to secure a conviction—the Constitution bars compelled testimony. And so on.

The underlying policy justifications for the rights under Article 20 are often debated, and vary across jurisdictions.[69] Let us consider two prominent justifications, relevant for our argument. The first is that these rights are, in a sense, designed to save the State from itself. If individuals could be prosecuted multiple times for the same offence, or if they could be coerced into yielding up incriminating information, police officers would become lax and shoddy in their investigations.[70] Furthermore, compelled testimony, with its propensity towards falsehood, could be as likely to lead the investigation astray as to aid it. On this justification, these brakes are in aid of efficient investigation and crime-solving, and should be interpreted keeping that goal in mind.

The other justification views these provisions through the lens of power. Stripped of its adornments, the police station (and subsequently, the criminal legal process) is the space where the State's physical coercive power over the individual is revealed in its starkest, most naked form. It is there where the individual body is most vulnerable to State power, and where an individual is *physically* deprived of their freedom. As Thakur Das Bhargava eloquently noted during the Constituent Assembly Debates:

> What happens after a person is arrested or detained? His troubles begin then. When he is detained or arrested and he is in the clutches of the police, he is alone in the world, and the forces of the Police, the forces of the Crown and all other forces combine against him and he is helpless.[71]

Article 20, thus, should indeed be about breaks and constraints. The purpose of these constraints is to recognize the power imbalance between the State and the individual, and to mitigate it. The scope and meaning of Article 20—so the argument goes—ought to be interpreted in service of this philosophy.

The language of Article 20 leaves enough space for these questions to turn into salient, interpretive issues. Consider, first, the Article 20(3), the famous 'right against self-incrimination',[72] which the framers of the Indian Constitution borrowed (with some modifications) from the Fifth Amendment of the Constitution of the United States.[73] The text reads: 'No person accused of any offence shall be compelled to be a witness against himself.' The phrase 'to be a witness' has been invoked to challenge a range of policing techniques—from the taking of fingerprints to voice samples, from document seizures to seizures of devices, and from lie-detector tests to narco-analysis—with varying degrees of success.[74] This is a fascinating story in its own right, but for the purposes of this chapter, we are more concerned with another phrase in Article 20(3): 'person accused of any offence.'[75]

The Supreme Court first had occasion to consider this question in *M.P. Sharma vs Satish Chandra*, a case that is more famous because of the Court's ostensible refusal to recognize a right to privacy under the Indian Constitution. In *M.P. Sharma*, petitioners invoked Article 20(3) to challenge a seizure of their books of accounts and other documents as part of a police investigation into fraudulent corporate transactions. The Supreme Court had to therefore consider whether, as a starting point, the phrase 'accused of any offence' included proceedings *outside* the courtroom. The Supreme Court held that it did, noting that the phrase meant, at the very least, 'a person against whom a formal accusation relating to the commission of an offence has been levelled which in the normal course may result in prosecution'.[76]

While on the one hand the Supreme Court appeared to expand the scope of the protection under Article 20(3), as Sekhri notes, its linking of the availability of the right to the eventual possibility of legal prosecution, would create problems.[77] Future judgments would build upon this to link the availability of the right *only* to the eventual possibility of legal prosecution.

But the other ambiguous term was 'a formal accusation', which again the *M.P. Sharma* court left uninterpreted. Soon afterwards, in *Raja Narayanlal Bansilal vs Maneck Phiroz Mistry*, the Court was confronted with a challenge to Section 240 of the (then) Companies Act, which required officers and employees of companies that were under investigation for irregularities to provide 'books and papers' relating to the company to the investigator.[78] Section 242, helpfully titled 'Prosecution', specifically stated that the government could, on the basis of the investigator's report, initiate criminal proceeding against individuals. The compelled production of documents was challenged on grounds of Article 20(3). However, the Court rejected the challenge, noting that what Section 240 envisaged was a mere 'inquiry' by the inspector into alleged irregularities in a company's books of account: in effect, according to the Court, nothing more than a 'fact-finding commission'.[79] It, therefore, did not fall within the contours of 'a formal accusation', even though it might eventually lead to a prosecution.[80]

Maneck Phiroz Mistry laid the framework for an approach to Article 20(3) that was grounded in a formal or technical understanding of 'formal accusation', while failing to consider the manner of State power that Article 20(3) was meant to protect an individual from.

Soon afterwards, this framework was taken to its logical extreme in the case of *Romesh Chandra Mehta vs State of West Bengal,* which, as we shall see, constitutes an 'inflection-point judgment' as we are using the term in this book.[81]

In *Romesh Chandra Mehta,* a combination of interrogation, search, and seizure—under the provisions of the Sea Customs Act—led to the recovery of certain allegedly smuggled goods. At the trial, confessional statements made by Mehta to the customs officer were tendered as evidence against him. Mehta challenged the admissibility of these statements on two interrelated grounds: first, that confessions made to a police officer were inadmissible under Section 25 of the Evidence Act, and that customs officers were 'police officers' for this purpose; and *secondly,* that under Article 20(3), Mehta—who stood accused of an offence—had a constitutional right against self-incrimination.

The Supreme Court noted that the purpose of Section 25 of the Evidence Act was to prevent the police from extracting confessions through 'coercion, torture, or ill-treatment'.[82] Immediately after that, however, it went on to note that a customs officer was *not* a 'member of the police force', as he was not entrusted with a duty to maintain law and order, but rather was tasked with powers relating to the collection of customs duties, and the prevention of smuggling.[83]

Mehta argued that customs officers were clothed with powers that were identical to the powers vested in police officers under criminal law: the powers of search, of screening, of arrest, of summons, and of the collection of evidence. These were, in essence, the *coercive* powers of the State. For the Supreme Court, however, this did not matter, as the *purpose* for which these powers were vested was not maintaining law and order or investigating offences, but securing compliance with the Sea Customs Act (such as checking the smuggling of goods and the realization of customs duties, among other things).[84] Mehta pointed out that this notwithstanding, the nature of the powers—of detention, arrest, remand, custody, and so on—was precisely that which raised an apprehension that confessions could be extracted through coercion or ill-treatment.[85] The Supreme Court, however, dismissed this as irrelevant, noting that it was not the nature of power that mattered, but that this power was vested 'qua the *investigation of an offence*, including the power to submit a report under Section 173 of the Code of Criminal Procedure' (emphasis supplied).[86] In simple language, the Court chose to define 'police officer' by reference to which law was applicable to a given set of facts, and not the actions undertaken, or the powers enjoyed, by the functionaries of the State.

The Court then deployed similar logic to the Article 20(3) claim. It held that when the Customs Office arrested a person on finding him in possession of smuggled goods, or upon the suspicion that he was involved in smuggling, that person was nonetheless not 'accused of an offence' within the meaning of Article 20(3). How, one might wonder, could an individual be *arrested* without being *accused*? The Court made the same self-referential argument that it had made with respect to the confessional statements: i.e., that the arrest was for the purpose of holding an enquiry under the Sea Customs Act, and not for the purpose of initiating a trial before a magistrate.[87] In this, as we have seen above, the Court carried forward the seeds of the logic that had first been planted in *M.P. Sharma*: that is, a formalistic approach that linked *accusation* with *future prosecution*.

This technical distinction, however, masks a deeper deference to State power. In an ordinary criminal proceeding, the 'formal accusation' comes in the First Information Report (FIR) filed by the police, which also marks the commencement of the investigation.[88] There exist, however, a number of 'special laws' (euphemistically referred to as socio-economic laws), where this process is flipped. Under these laws, investigatory bodies staffed by State agents conduct 'enquiries' into allegations of crime. These State agents are formally not called 'police officers' (even though they are clothed with all the coercive powers granted to police officers, as we have seen above), and their enquiries are not called 'investigations' (even though they resemble the post-FIR investigation conducted by the police).[89] The upshot of this is that the 'formal accusation' under such laws comes at the end of the 'enquiry', when the report is filed.

As a result of this, *Romesh Chandra Mehta* is much more than a holding about the technical meaning of the terms 'police officer' and 'accused of an offence'. Its interpretation had the effect (subsequently confirmed) that the protections under Article 20(3), as well as the protection against confessional statements, are simply unavailable to those who fall within the coercive arm of the State, as long as the law under which that coercive arm acts, as a definitional matter, stipulates that State officers are not 'police officers', and are only conducting an 'enquiry'.[90] This is notwithstanding the fact that during this process, individuals can be summoned, interrogated, detained, and placed in custody, *on the lines of what the police would do in the course of investigating an ordinary crime*. Over the years, thus, the Supreme Court entrenched the *Romesh Chandra Mehta* holding into 'a nearly unassailable position that Article 20(3) didn't extend to the questioning of persons before filing of formal complaints in socio-economic offences' and that officers conducting the interrogation were not '*police officers*'. Therefore, confessions made to these officers would not be hit by Section 25 of the Indian Evidence Act.[91]

A few decades later, this logic culminated in the case of *Directorate of Enforcement vs Deepak Mahajan*, where the Supreme Court observed that custody under Foreign Exchange Regulation Act (FERA) did not trigger the right against self-incrimination, even though the legal warrant for such custody came from Section 167 of the Code of Criminal Procedure, which specifically used the term 'accused'.[92] The Court drew a distinction between the word 'accused' as used in Section 167 ('… no Magistrate shall authorise detention in any custody under this section unless the *accused* is produced before him…' [emphasis supplied]), and as used in Article 20(3). It held that the former had a wider meaning (in the sense of an individual being *in* custody), while—following *Romesh Chandra Mehta*—under Article 20(3), the word 'accused' was used in a *narrower* sense. One may call this being Schrödinger's accused: accused enough for the purposes of the CrPC and the FERA, but simultaneously not accused enough to invoke the protections of Article 20(3).

There is, of course, an irony here. It is normally constitutional rights that are read broadly, and with a view to protecting the individual from State power, rather than statutory provisions—and not the other way around. And if the statutory provision is broader than the constitutional provision with respect to the State coercion that it authorizes, one would expect it to be struck down for not conforming to the Constitution—and not the other way round!

Formal meaning does not, of course, change the reality of State coercion, whether the coercive agent is a police officer or a customs officer. Indeed, as we have just seen, the effect of *Romesh Chandra Mehta* was to enable the State to escape the constraints of Article 20(3) through an exercise of technical labelling, a position that has only become further entrenched in the five decades since. It is a position continues till today, most starkly visible in legal cases around the powers of the ED.

In sum, therefore, *Romesh Chandra Mehta*—both in its own right, and in its gloss upon *M.P. Sharma*—interpreted Article 20(3) (and also Section 25 of the Evidence Act) as being not about redressing the coercive imbalance of power between the State and the individual, but as a checkbox provision whose protection was limited to cases where there was a formal overlap between the terms used in the Constitution ('accusation'), and the terms used in criminal statutes. This brings us back to the framing with which we began this chapter. Rather than applying the Constitution (here, Article 20) as a constraint upon State power, the Court allowed the exercise of State power to shape constitutional interpretation. In the process, it ensured that constitutional interpretation worked to *conserve* State power over the individual rather than redress it.

Addendum: A Comparative Note

The approach of the Indian Supreme Court towards the interpretation of the phrase 'accused of any offence' stands out in stark perspective when compared with a very similar interpretive dispute that arose in Kenya. The Kenyan Criminal Procedure Code authorized magistrates to require individuals to execute 'peace bonds' where, according to the police, it appeared that the individual was 'likely to commit a breach of the peace or disturb the public tranquillity'.[93] Failure to execute the bond would lead to imprisonment.

Such 'peace bonds' are a colonial holdover, based entirely upon the 'jurisdiction of suspicion' that governed British colonies across the world. Their Indian equivalent was found in Section 107 of the Code of Criminal Procedure (titled 'security for keeping the peace'). In *Anthony Njenga Mbuti and Ors vs Attorney-General and Ors*, the constitutionality of these 'peace bonds' was challenged before the High Court of Kenya by individuals who had never been accused or charged with any offence but nonetheless been forced to execute peace bonds on pure suspicion (one of them had spent time in prison for being unable to do so).[94]

The Constitution of Kenya grants a right to a 'fair trial' to everyone 'accused' of an offence.[95] The petitioners argued that the 'peace bond' provisions grossly violated this right. The State responded with precisely the same linguistic trick that had worked so well in India in *Romesh Chandra Mehta* and its progeny. Individuals compelled to execute 'peace bonds', it argued, were not 'accused' of anything. They were merely 'suspects'. They were, therefore, not entitled to the constitutional safeguards guaranteed to 'accused persons'.

The trick did not work. The Kenyan High Court immediately asked: 'Who or what is a suspect? What is his place within our new constitutional dispensation based on human rights, non-discrimination and the rule of law?'[96] In other words, the State could not simply classify a set of individuals out of constitutional protections. What mattered was not *formal* status, but the balance of power between the State and the individual. With that governing philosophy in mind, the Kenyan High Court declined to *level down* the Constitution in order to conserve State power within the existing framework of the criminal law. Rather, it tested the 'peace bond' provisions on the touchstone of the Constitutional imperatives of constraining the arbitrary exercise of coercive State power over all individuals, and thus found them to be unconstitutional.

The identical nature of the State's contentions in both India and Kenya (attempting to narrowly read the word 'accused' in a constitutional text so as to limit the scope of constitutional safeguards), and the diametrically opposite judicial responses to the argument, highlights the central argument of the book: that when it comes to the question of power, the constitution is a terrain of contestation, and that interpretive disputes always present the Court with a choice about which vision of power to commit the constitution to. There was nothing inevitable about the Supreme Court of India's interpretation of the word 'accused' in *Romesh Chandra Mehta,* and there was nothing inevitable about the Kenyan High Court's interpretation of the same word in *Anthony Njenga Mbuti*. These are judicial choices that reflect how the Court elects to navigate a constitution's power maps, and how it engages with a constitution's cartography of power. *Anthony Njenga Mbuti* show us how there is always the possibility of an alternative reading to the centralizing drift that has come to dominate Indian constitutionalism.

IV. Article 21: The Forever War

As we have seen, personal liberty was not one of the priorities of the colonial criminal codes. One of the ways in which this attitude manifested itself was through the provisions for bail, i.e., the conditions under which an accused individual could be set free pending their trial (what, in common parlance, we refer to as 'undertrials'). In the 1898 Code of Criminal Procedure, for example, a magistrate was prohibited from releasing an individual on bail 'if there appear reasonable grounds for believing that he has been guilty of the offence of which he is accused'.[97] In other words, apart from examining whether the accused was a flight risk, or might tamper with the evidence or intimidate witnesses (which were reasons *relevant* for not releasing him pending trial), the magistrate also had to examine the merits of the case itself, before having the benefit of a full trial.

This did not mean, however, that the magistrate had to decide the question of bail only on the basis of the police version. The 1898 Code also had what were known as 'committal proceedings': that is, prior to the framing of charges, the prosecution had to examine the witnesses it was planning to rely on, and the defence had an opportunity to cross-examine them. Thus, when deciding a bail application, the magistrate would have had some access to the defence version, and also had an opportunity to watch the defence cross-examine the prosecution's witnesses.[98]

This regime of bail was extant at the commencement of the Second World War. In the section discussing preventive detention, we flagged the Defence of India Rules, 1942. These rules are a classic example of the law of the state of exception: they were passed during World War II, the quintessential emergency of emergencies. And yet, elements of these rules would persist after the war and beyond.

Among other things, the Defence of India Rules stipulated what is now known as the 'twin test' for bail.[99] These rules provided that 'bail cannot be given unless the prosecutor is heard and the Magistrate is satisfied that there are *reasonable grounds* for believing that [the accused] is *not* guilty' (emphasis supplied).[100] In other words, apart from introducing the requirement of hearing the State before granting bail, the rules changed the substantive requirement from reasonable grounds for belief that the accused *is* guilty of the offence, to reasonable grounds for believing that the accused is *not* guilty of the offence. The introduction of the word 'not', however, upended the entire structure of the bail clause. The default starting position now placed the burden upon the defence to convince the Court that the accused was not guilty in order to get bail, as opposed to the prosecution affirmatively *establishing* reasonable grounds for guilt.[101] Given the limited materials that were before the Court at this stage of the criminal process, this was an onerous burden to discharge. As the Calcutta High Court would note in its examination of the 'twin test' a few years later:

> ... under Section 497, Criminal P. C., what prevents bail is the reasonable ground for believing that the accused is guilty. That in actual practice works more favourably to the accused in the sense that at the early stages, before the regular trial has started, it is easier for the Court without the full materials to say that there are no reasonable grounds for believing that he is guilty and thus admit him to bail. But in a case, however, under Section 13A, Essential Supplies Act, it is the converse and more difficult case of reasonable ground for believing that the applicant for bail is not guilty. It is difficult because in actual practice it is bound to be unfavourable to the applicant for bail in the sense that at the early stages, before the regular trial bas started, it will ordinarily be difficult and may in some cases be impossible for the Court to say without sufficient materials that there are reasonable grounds for believing that he is not guilty.[102]

This was not all that the rules did. Crucially, in the Defence of India Rules, there was no committal process. Thus, the application for bail would have to be decided on the basis of the *record* before the Court. While this may seem a technical omission, when placed alongside the 'twin test', it turned the bail regime into what we have been referring to in this book as the 'Frankenstate', or, to be more precise, a 'Frankentest' for bail.[103]

Let us take a step back and pause for a moment to understand why. An application for bail is, for the most part, made before a criminal trial commences. Its underlying logic is that an individual should not be deprived of their liberty until they are convicted by a court of law, and that includes the period during which investigation and trial are ongoing. For this reason, in a bail hearing, a judge is not expected to scrutinize, in detail, the merits of the case. In our criminal justice system, that scrutiny can take place only at the culmination of trial, during which both sides have had equal opportunity to subject each other's evidence and witnesses to cross-examination.

The second element of the 'twin test' makes this logic redundant by requiring the defence to satisfy the judge that the accused is not guilty. How is the defence expected to do such a thing, since it cannot lead its own evidence in a bail hearing, or subject the prosecution's witnesses to cross-examination (it can only do this at the stage of the trial)? Until the passage of the Defence of India Rules, this problem was *partially* offset by the committal process, which is, in essence, a mini-trial. But with the abolition of committal, this safeguard was removed. Without committal, at the stage of bail, a judge would only be presented with the prosecution/police's version of events: a chargesheet or a police report, which the police have almost unbridled power to shape and construct (including the choice of offences).[104] The highest that the defence could do, then, is to point out internal inconsistencies within the police's version, or to show that *even if* taken to be true, at its highest, the police version does not satisfy the ingredients of the criminal offence.

The 'twin test', combined with the removal of committal, thus upended the fundamental principle—the so-called 'golden thread'—of criminal law: the presumption of innocence (or, 'innocent until proven guilty').[105] It authorized the deprivation of liberty on the basis of the State's version of events, until such time that the accused was able to displace that version through the long course of a criminal trial.[106] Exceptional in every sense, it finding a place in wartime emergency colonial legislation, thus, was unsurprising.

The 'twin test', however, would survive the war, the Emergency, the colony, and the Constitution. Less than a month after Independence, amidst the violence of Partition, the provincial government of East Punjab issued the East Punjab Armed Bands (Arrest and Detention) Ordinance. Soon converted into an act, this law reintroduced the 'twin test' into Indian law.[107] Other provincial laws followed suit.

And soon after, the 'twin test' would reappear in central legislation as well. In 1950, even as the Constituent Assembly doubled up as the provisional Parliament—debating the draft Constitution in the morning and enacting legislation in the afternoon—the latter enacted an amendment to the Essential Services Act (ESA). The ESA itself was originally a wartime law, designed to control the practice of hoarding during war. The law continued even after the war and Independence, but the provisional Parliament found it an increasingly ineffective check against the practices of hoarding and black marketing. In a bid to make the law 'stricter', the twin test for bail was introduced. In the teeth of fierce opposition in the provisional parliament, K.M. Munshi admitted its wartime emergency-era provenance, but insisted that the country was still under emergency conditions, and still at war (against hoarders).[108] Attempted amendments to reverse the burden of proof under the twin test were, ultimately, not moved, as they were certain to be defeated.

The ESA entrenched the 'twin test' into the post-Constitutional legal landscape, but it is K.M. Munshi's language that is most telling. Invoking Emergency (without the formal proclamation of one) and a war (without the formal declaration of one), he substituted legal categories with metaphors, and substituted a defined state of exception (with a defined starting point and end point, and accompanying safeguards) with an open-textured, open-ended, and interminable situation where the normal and the exceptional blurred into each other (as we saw with Article 22).[109] The entrenchment of the 'twin test' into peacetime non-emergency legislation was one of the hallmarks of this blurring, of this 'forever war'.[110]

Because it would, indeed, turn out to be forever. The Defence of India Rules themselves made a temporary return during the 1962 war with China, along with the 'twin test', which was upheld on the basis of it being an extraordinary measure in a time of actual war.[111] But it did not stay confined there. Long after the threat of hoarding and black marketing had disappeared, and long after the war was over, the 'twin test' endured, finding its way into various 'extraordinary laws'. Meanwhile, while committal came back with the end of the World War II, it was radically watered down in 1955, when the right to cross-examine the prosecution's witnesses was removed; and it was then done away with for good in the new Code of Criminal Procedure, which was enacted in 1973. This had the collateral effect that the primary material a court would consider in an application for bail would be statements recorded by the police—which, ironically, were themselves inadmissible at trial.[112] The 'Frankentest' for bail, thus, was set in stone.

What, then, of the courts?

Thirty-four years after the Constitution was born, the constitutionality of the 'twin test' was challenged for the first time before the Supreme Court. The legal context was the Terrorist and Anti-Disruptive Activities (Prevention) Act (TADA). The constitutional context, as we have noted above, was that the judgment in *Maneka Gandhi* had (apparently) fundamentally changed the landscape, with the incorporation of due process into the Constitution. Was the twin test 'just, fair, and reasonable' in its balancing of State power and human freedom?

In *Kartar Singh vs State of Punjab*, the Supreme Court held that it was.[113] Notably, it used an almost identical rhetoric of war to what K.M. Munshi had deployed many decades ago. Terrorists had created a 'warlike' situation in India, and extraordinary times called for extraordinary measures. Among a slate of other such provisions, the constitutional validity of the twin test was also upheld, with its impacts on personal liberty being relegated to an *enforcement* problem, rather than a constitutional issue.[114] As an additional, buttressing point, the Court also noted the 'twin test' existed in other laws as well, such as the FERA and the Customs Act, and that *therefore* it 'cannot be said to be an unreasonable condition infringing the principle of Article 21 of the Constitution'.[115]

Missing from the Court's rhetoric about terrorism and war and the ubiquity of the twin test, however, was any serious analysis of how the post-Independence changes to criminal procedure (in particular, the repealing of committal, and the concomitant reliance on police statements to determine the existence of a prima facie case at the stage of bail) had created a 'Frankentest' that stocked the decks entirely against the liberty of the accused, in a manner that even the colonial wartime law had not done.[116] The rushed and ahistorical nature of the Court's examination of the twin test's constitutionality (it occupied exactly one page comprising four paragraphs, of the law report) belied the seriousness of the issue: none of the wealth of historical material that we have discussed above was referred to, or examined, in the judgment.

While the highly unpopular TADA itself lapsed soon after and was not renewed, in a familiar story, the twin test endured. It endured in the 2008 amendments to the Unlawful Activities Prevention Act 'UAPA', TADA's successor, and in a range of other 'special laws' such as the Prevention of Money Laundering Act (PMLA), the Narcotic Drugs and Psychotropic Substances Act (NDPS; with some variation), and others.[117] While the constitutional validity of the test has not been adjudicated again, in a set of infamous cases, the Supreme Court has made its application even stricter, making the grant of bail extraordinarily difficult once an individual is arrested under these laws.[118] At the time of writing, India's jails are full of individuals arrested under the UAPA and the PMLA, imprisoned for years without trial, with their bail applications rejected by every court on the basis of the 'twin test'.

Kartar Singh thus was an inflection point in the constitutional history of personal liberty. Although the forever war—that began with the Defence of India Rules in 1942 before iterating into more restrictive versions after Independence—had long been legally entrenched, *Kartar Singh* was when it received *constitutional imprimatur* and in its worst form. in doing so, the Supreme Court sanctioned a legal landscape where, notwithstanding Article 21, the balance of power between the State and the individual, on the question of individual liberty, was—and remains—radically skewed towards the State.

V. Conclusion: The Perfect Storm

In 2022, the Supreme Court heard a comprehensive challenge to the provisions of the Prevention of Money Laundering Act. The PMLA is one of the 'special statutes' that we have discussed above, and its investigating agency—the ED—has been particularly active in recent years. The record speaks for itself: while the case was being heard, a detailed investigative report revealed a sharp rise in the use of the ED, including the targeting of opposition politicians.[119]

The Supreme Court upheld the provisions of the PMLA, including the powers of arrest, search, and seizure, and the 'twin test' for bail. While the judgment was decried for the effective carte blanche that it gave to a centrally controlled investigative agency in exercising its coercive powers, the Supreme Court's reasoning marks the culmination of the legal doctrines that we've discussed above, rather than a break with the past.[120] In essence, the Court subordinated the *reality* of the coercive power enjoyed by the ED over the individual to the *formal* terminology used by the law (au courant with its doctrinal history under Article 20(3)), and to the continuing existence of an ordinarily extraordinary state of affairs in order to justify that power (consistent with its doctrinal history under Articles 21 and 22).

Thus, the ED's powers of arrest—including the power not to reveal the grounds of arrest to the individual—were upheld on the basis that the PMLA was not *really* a penal statute, and that the ED was not *really* akin to the police (despite having all the powers of the police, and wielding them with much greater enthusiasm).[121] The same reasoning was then used by the Court to exclude the applicability of the right against self-incrimination as well as the bar on confessions to police officers under the Evidence Act to the PMLA and the ED: the ED's officials were not *really* police officers, and the persons they were questioning in custody were not *technically* 'accused of an offence'.[122] The 'twin test' for bail was not itself challenged on substantive grounds, but rather on grounds of procedural arbitrariness, and was likewise upheld.[123]

Vijay Madanlal Choudhary, therefore, was only the latest milestone along a road that the Supreme Court had been walking for a long time, marked by inflection points such as *Romesh Chandra Mehta*,

Kartar Singh, and other such judgments. *Vijay Madanlal Choudhary* saw a convergence of these paths upon one overarching doctrine of subordinating the constitutional guarantees of individual freedom to the logic of State power. As Sekhri summed up the state of play in the immediate aftermath of the judgment:

> ... *Vijay Madanlal Choudhary* is a conservative decision, inasmuch as the Supreme Court has simply remained faithful to its inglorious past of taking away all semblance of safeguards to personal liberty and property when it comes to socio-economic offences. Restrictive bail conditions in independent India first came for the essential supplies law before they became famous for anti-terror laws; reverse burdens were held good in 1964 when it came to gold smuggling; the guarantee of Article 20(3) was held inapplicable till customs officials or those from the registrar of companies concluded their inquiry given the theoretical possibility that such inquiries might, till that stage, not end in prosecution ... what the PMLA does, is that it weaves together all the restrictive, rights-effacing clauses from this illustrious past in one fine blanket, and it then goes a step further. It is not restricted to just the smuggler or hoarder, but to practically anyone ... in its reach and deleterious impact on basic freedoms, the PMLA is truly a *sui generis* law unlike any other. The judgment in *Vijay Madanlal Choudhary* was an opportunity to trim it down to size and prevent it from becoming another MISA from the 1970s; instead, the Court has, for now, green-lit that very outcome.[124]

In his famous book, *The Jurisprudence of Emergency*, Nasser Hussain challenges us to examine how 'the concept of emergency cannot be separated from the logic of a rule of law'.[125] While Hussain's arguments are located within the context of colonial constitutionalism—in particular, how racial difference contributed to the 'interplay between norm and exception'[126] —as he himself notes, the blurred lines between the two concepts have had a long afterlife in the post-colony. In this chapter, we have seen how the Indian Constitution is a stark illustration of this: Articles 20 to 22 represent what Hussain calls 'attempt[s] to regulate the claim of necessity by rules ... to locate [such claims] within a normative legality'.[127]

The interpretive borders of this finely wrought scheme, however, were left porous by design, and ill-suited for containing what the 1818 Bengal Regulation first referred to as 'the reasons of State'. In this context, Articles 20 to 22 have been a terrain of contestation between the 'contrary impulses' enabling the exercise of State power upon the individual, and constraining it. Through various inflection points, the courts have contracted the boundaries of constitutional constraint, allowing—in effect—an eternal state of necessity, a permanent exception. The courts thus have taken what was originally a colonial justification of a permanent emergency, and sanctified it with the authority a post-colonial Constitution.[128]

Vijay Madanlal Choudhary is the most striking and most recent example of this tradition. But it is, at the end of the day, a *tradition* of constitutional interpretation as old as the Constitution itself, and deeply embedded in its structure, design, and vision of State power.

6

Power Unbound: The People

'WE THE PEOPLE OF India ... do adopt, enact, and give to ourselves this Constitution.'[1] With these ringing words, the Preamble casts 'the People' as the primary actors in India's constitutional drama. The Constitution—both as national vision and as a blueprint for governance—claims to draw its legitimacy from the people; in particular, through the consent of the people, who authorized the Constituent Assembly to frame the Constitution on their behalf.

As in all constitutions that invoke 'the People', this story involves at least a degree of fiction[2], or evasion.[3] In what manner, and to what degree, were the people actively involved in the drafting of the Indian Constitution? The predominant view, entrenched over decades, has been: *not very much.* The Constituent Assembly was not constituted through universal adult suffrage. Rather, its members were 'elected' under the highly restrictive franchise rules of the Government of India Act of 1935. Nor was the draft Constitution affirmed by the people in a referendum.[4] There was, therefore, a democratic deficit both 'upstream' and 'downstream' in the making of the Indian Constitution, leading scholars to view it as an elite, top-down document, imposed upon a relatively passive population.[5]

More recent scholarship has challenged this assumption. Upon a careful study of the archives, Rohit De and Ornit Shani argue that beyond the Constituent Assembly Debates, the Constitution-making process saw a wide and deep engagement across the newly forming country. De and Shani urge us to understand the making of the Indian Constitution as an 'assemblage' of several other smaller-scale constitution-making processes, taking place across a variety of diverse publics: from constitutional reform movements in the princely states, to direct engagement with the Constituent Assembly by the judiciary, to representations and critiques from tribes and other indigenous groups.[6] While in some situations there is a direct link between the intervention and the final form of the constitutional text, in most other contexts, the key issue was not so much the impact on the *text*, as the creation of a vocabulary of *constitutionalism* through participation. This participation and this articulation of constitutional vocabulary in turn contributed to the legitimation of the Constitution, despite the absence of upstream or downstream 'popular' ratification.[7]

This contested history is reflected in the Constitution itself, and is the focus of this chapter. What role do the people have in the story that the Constitution tells about itself, beyond the ritual invocation in the Preamble?

To understand the context, let us begin with Uday Mehta's important insight: 'Constitutional founding moments express that inescapable circularity in which they are authorized by the people, but which, by the structures that constitutions put in place, reconstitute the people as subjects.'[8] In other words, the people—having given to themselves the Constitution—then shuffle off the stage, leaving the rest of the drama to be enacted by other players: representative bodies, administrators, judges, commissions, and so on. According to the preambular fiction, 'the People' are the authors of the Constitution, but their role as authors ends once the Constitution comes into force.[9]

To what extent does Mehta's observation hold true for the Indian Constitution? In this chapter, I will consider the roles that the Constitution envisages for the people, in the processes of constitutional change, of law-making, and of administration. I will begin with a conceptual and comparative overview of the different ways in which the people may be involved in constitutional governance, at three levels: at the level of constitutional change, at the level of law-making, and at the level of executive action **(I)**. I will then consider the constitutional text and constitutional silences (there are a *lot* of silences), and examine the history of the Constitution as a terrain upon which the struggle for broader, deeper, and more inclusive public participation played out over the years leading up to the framing of the document **(II)**.

Unsurprisingly, the courts have had an important part to play in the articulation of constitutional meaning, especially in cases involving textual silences. I will argue that the courts have been constrained by the limitations of the constitutional text, but *also*—when faced with an inflection point where more than one reading of the Constitution was interpretively possible—they have chosen a path that closes off the possibilities of public participation, rather than opening them up **(III)**. At present, therefore, the role of the people as constitutional actors is fragile and tenuous. Built upon a foundation of easily amended executive orders, patchwork legislation, and ambiguous constitutional provisions, it lives in a precarious present, facing an uncertain future **(IV)**.

I. Overview

In studying the relationship between political institutions and the people, Roberto Gargarella draws a useful distinction between 'internal constraints' and 'external constraints' upon those institutions. According to classical separation of powers theory, a constitution ought to distribute power in a way that the different wings of State act as checks and balances *upon* each other (a prime example of this is the multiple 'veto points' under the US Constitution). As long as political institutions are granted this 'checking' power, they will ensure that no one institution encroaches too far into another's domain, prevent excessive centralization or concentration of power, and in this way, preserve the rights and freedoms of the people.[10] Gargarella labels this a system of 'internal constraints': the people, as a collective body, do not exercise oversight or control over political institutions, but the institutions do so, inter se, among themselves.

'External constraints', on the other hand, do involve the people exercising oversight and control over political institutions. External constraints exist across a spectrum. The thinnest form is a guarantee of universal, periodic, adult suffrage ('electoral democracy'). After having given to themselves the Constitution, the people re-appear on stage at periodic intervals to vote in or vote out their representatives.[11]

A combination of internal constraint and the thinnest form of external constraint—electoral democracy—is found in most modern democratic constitutions.[12] Cohen and Fung therefore refer to this as 'conventional democracy', which they define in familiar terms:

> ... systems of competitive representation, in which citizens are endowed with political rights, including the rights of speech, association, and suffrage; citizens advance their interests by exercising their political rights, in particular by voting for representatives in regular elections; elections are organized by competing political parties; and electoral victory means control of government, which gives winning candidates the authority to shape public policy through legislation and control over administration.[13]

But for all its dominance, this form of conventional democracy has long been critiqued for its minimalism, its concentration of power in the hands of the political elite, its exclusion of citizens from having any meaningful say in the issues that affect them, and for how elections themselves are flawed instruments for the determination of popular will (not to mention that electoral processes in contemporary democracies are often skewed towards entrenched power structures).[14] As a representative critique notes: 'However central to democracy, elections occur intermittently and only allow citizens to choose between the highly aggregated alternatives offered by political parties, which can, especially in the early stages of a democratic transition, proliferate in a bewildering variety.'[15]

Various strands of democratic theory, therefore, have long advocated for conceptualizing democracy in a way that is thicker or richer than simply electoralism and representation and which, crucially, would mitigate the difference in power between representatives and the people whom they formally represent.[16] Constitutionalism has responded: many constitutions (especially those that have been drafted relatively recently) accord a role to 'the People' that goes *beyond* the fiction of constitutional authorship and periodic participation through voting.[17]

This thicker role of 'the People' can be typologized in the following (non-exhaustive) way, on a spectrum of abstract to concrete: participation in *constitutional change*, participation in *law-making* and oversight over *lawmakers*, and participation in *administrative decisions or governance*.

At the highest level, the process of constitutional change may or may not accord a role to the people. Certain constitutions choose to limit participation in constitutional amendment processes to parliamentary bodies, while putting into place supermajority rules, in order to distinguish between ordinary legislation and constitutional amendments. Other constitutions, however, involve the people in constitutional amendments, primarily through the guarantee of referendums. Referendums themselves are of many different kinds, ranging from straightforward up-down votes on proposed constitutional amendments to highly complex procedures that attempt to 'refine' popular opinion (inter alia, through deliberative organs such as citizens' assemblies).[18]

One example of this is Article 257 of the Kenyan Constitution, which sets out a ten-step procedure for the amendment of certain entrenched constitutional provisions, known as the 'Popular Initiative'. This procedure requires the involvement of the people at multiple stages and in multiple ways: from initiation (a 'Popular Initiative' requires one million signatures to get off the ground), to consultation and engagement (through measures of civic engagement at the level of county assemblies), to a final referendum.[19]

It can be seen, therefore, that a provision such as Article 257 introduces an element of direct democracy into the processes of constitutional change, which sits alongside—and potentially in tension with—representative institutions. The reconciliation between these elements and the carving out of a *meaningful* role for the people in constitutional change was at issue before the Kenyan courts in the famous *BBI* set of cases, in 2020–21. In simple terms, the BBI Bill was a 'package deal' of seventy-four proposed amendments to the Constitution of Kenya. It was an initiative driven by the then President of Kenya and the then principal Opposition leader. Mid-way through the ten-step procedure outlined under Article 257, its constitutionality was challenged. The constitutional challenge went to the heart of what it meant for people to *participate* in constitutional change, and whether the direct involvement of political actors in a process titled 'the Popular Initiative' would render that participation illusory.

The Kenyan judiciary held that it would and struck down the BBI Bill. The commitment to direct democracy under Article 257, the court(s) held, would be hijacked if representative organs were allowed to co-opt the process. The vision underlying public participation was that of an *active* citizenry, and not simply a passive population that was presented a binary choice in a yes/no referendum, where the choices themselves had been framed and crafted by the political elite.

In articulating this reading of Article 257, the three courts that considered the issue—the High Court, the court of appeal, and the constitutional court—held, in their own ways, that the nature of the public involvement contemplated under Article 257 went beyond simply *ratification* at a referendum. It required something deeper and richer, where the people had a genuine opportunity to consider and engage with the proposed changes to the constitutional order. It was a process that would necessarily have to entail civic education about, and demonstrable public participation with respect to, the substance of the proposed changes. The ratifying referendum was simply the end point of this process, but it was not meant to exhaust the constitutional commitment to public participation.

Interestingly, and on a similar point, two of the three courts also held that public participation would be defeated if multiple amendments, on topics unrelated to one another, were presented to the public in a single up-down vote: to do so would be nothing more than an illusion of choice (the Kenyan Supreme Court declined to rule one way or another on the ground that the referendum stage had not yet been reached, leaving the question open for another day).[20]

The *BBI Case* is a microcosm of the issues that arise when a constitution seeks to involve the people as a collective agent in the processes of constitutional change. There is an ever-present danger of even the most carefully drafted provisions for public participation turning illusory; or—what is worse—being co-opted by the political elite into top-down projects where the role of the people is reduced to little more than formally ratifying (or acclaiming) a pre-determined and pre-decided political project. But the *BBI Case* also reveals how a combination of careful constitutional drafting, a history of active public participation in constitution-making that is still fresh in everyone's minds, and an alert judiciary can nonetheless *preserve* a certain space, within the constitution, for meaningful public participation.

We then come to the stage of law-making, which shares some of the concerns discussed above. Representative democracy exists upon the premise that the actual task of law-making is delegated by the people to their representatives, whom they vote into (and out of) legislatures, on a periodic basis. There is, therefore, a degree of tension between the claims of public participation in the law-making process on the one hand, and the fundamentals of representative democracy on the other.

In some constitutions, this tension is addressed by thinking of the relationship between the people and their representatives not as *periodic*, but as *continuing*.[21] These constitutions thus either contain provisions obligating the State to facilitate the participation of the people in decisions that affect them,[22] or obligating legislative bodies to consider submissions from the public in their deliberations.[23] In more specific terms, the South African Constitution calls upon its legislative organ (the National Assembly) to have 'due regard' for 'public involvement' while framing its rules of business.[24] The Constitution of Kenya makes this a mandatory requirement, requiring Parliament to 'facilitate public participation and involvement in … *legislative* and other business' (emphasis supplied).[25] In both jurisdictions, these constitutional provisions have been used as hooks to argue for a greater role of the people in the legislative process, and have formed part of constitutional challenges to laws that allegedly have fallen below a minimal threshold of participation.

Thus, in *Doctors for Life International* case—its landmark decision on the scope of public participation the law-making process—the Constitutional Court of South Africa noted that the purpose of the Constitution was to go beyond voting as the sole expression of public participation, and facilitate a more 'expansive role of the public in the conduct of public affairs'.[26] For this reason, the Constitution enshrined participation elements, which were meant to be read complementary to the representative elements (of course, as the case of Kenya shows, this is not always possible).[27] The court also saw participation as an *equalizing* principle, which—because of its transparent and open character—would help counteract 'secret lobbying and influence peddling', especially in a context in which there were vast disparities of wealth and power.[28]

While the precise contours of public involvement and participation were the subject of legislation, the South African Constitutional Court did note that any such legislation would have to be consistent with two core duties: that of providing 'meaningful opportunities' for public participation, and that of ensuring that people had the *ability* to meaningfully participate.[29] Thus, giving notice and information about a proposed bill, ensuring that it was made accessible in multiple languages, granting enough time for people to study and engage with it, and providing spaces within which public engagement could take place, were all issues that a court could consider in adjudicating whether or not meaningful public participation had taken place.[30]

As with constitutional change, public participation in the law-making process raises its own set of issues. Thus, in his dissenting opinion in *Doctors for Life International*, Justice Van der Westhuizen wondered how a court would respond if the legislators simply 'decide to pursue the policies of their political party and in the process reject or ignore submissions made to them by a member of the public'.[31] In other words, given that the people (admittedly) had no *veto* on the legislative outcome, what was to prevent 'mechanically holding public hearings for every piece of legislation';[32] thus turning the ideals of participatory democracy 'cosmetic and empty'?[33] The majority judgment had noted that public participation lay on a continuum between simple communication of *information* about legislation to the people on the one end, and partnership in decision-making on the other, but what was to prevent the legislature from assuming the least onerous obligations upon itself, and limiting the exercise to a simply communication of information?

While there are potential solutions, such as, for example, requiring the legislature to demonstrate that it has actively considered the inputs received from the public participation process, and to provide reasons for the inputs that it has chosen to reject (as the High Court of Kenya recently did)—the difficulty in enforcing them (especially through courts) remains a live one.[34]

There are other ways as well that legislatures can get around public participation requirements: for instance, by substantively amending a bill after one round of public participation, and passing the amended bill without a second round. Kenyan courts have discussed, at some length, whether in such a case, the judiciary ought to strike down the law, thus creating the possibility of a long and time-consuming cycle where even responsive amendments have to be put through another round of public participation.[35] Once again, the problem is not insoluble. Judicial tests can be devised that test amendments on the touchtone of whether they are entirely, or at least substantively new, and on subjects upon which the people have not yet had a chance to engage. Given the (understandable) hesitancy on the part of courts to intervene too deeply into legislative processes, however, there do exist limits as to how far a constitution's public participation provisions can constrain the actions of a legislature determined to breach them (at least in spirit).

That said, nonetheless, explicitly spelling out the obligation of public participation within the constitutional text creates the kind of gravitational force that we have discussed before in this book. The terrain of the debate then becomes what *manner* of public participation is sufficient to discharge the constitutional obligation, and how the relevant constitutional provisions are to be interpreted in the context of the overall constitutional design and history. On the other hand, in a constitution where there are no entrenched provisions for public participation, the debate first becomes about establishing the *existence* of the right. This inevitably affects downstream debates about content and enforcement.

Let us move on. Oversight over representative institutions is not only about participation in legislative process, but also about the legislators themselves. The most common and hoary form that this takes is a *right to recall*: subject to meeting certain threshold requirements (the exact nature of which varies by jurisdiction), the people—acting as a collective body—can 'recall' legislators mid-term, and without waiting for the next election cycle.[36] A somewhat lesser-known variant is the *right to instruct*—i.e., where, on a particular issue, a majority of constituents can direct their representative to vote a particular way.[37] In our discussion so far, the right to instruct is most directly opposed to the fundamentals of representative democracy, something that perhaps explains its absence from most contemporary constitutions.[38,39]

Finally, there is the question of public participation in administrative decisions.[40] This can take many forms. One of its most famous iterations, for example, is participatory budgeting in the Brazilian city of Porto Alegre, often held up as a model of participatory democracy in practice.[41] In the case of Porto Alegre, empirical research has demonstrated that there is a direct link between public participation and the redistribution of power, something that democratic theory has often been sceptical about. As Hilmer notes, for example, Porto Alegre's participatory budgeting model 'enables all members of society to participate, traditionally underrepresented groups are able to exercise real political power. And in so doing citizens have curtailed the power of the elite-driven institutions of the state'.[42]

Historically, however, issues of participation in this domain have been at their starkest—and most poignant—in the clash between the 'developmental' aims of the State, and indigenous and collective rights over land. Some constitutions have sought to resolve this conflict by guaranteeing a right of prior, free, and informed *consultation* with all individuals and communities 'affected' by an administrative decision, in specific domains (such as activities that have 'environmental impacts').[43]

Consultation does not, of course, equate to consent; and despite longstanding demands, constitutions do not generally provide a right of veto to affected individuals and communities.[44] This has led to scepticism about whether the consultation framework serves any meaningful goals, or whether it is little more than window-dressing, or even—what is worse—on certain occasions, a delegation of functions that the State does not wish to perform, to 'community groups'.[45] Constitutional rights to consultation have, however, served as a terrain upon which these affected groups have made both procedural and substantive arguments for greater involvement with State developmental projects, and in defence of their continued individual—and collective—rights over the land, and to stewardship of the environment.[46]

As with the case of law-making, the struggle has been between a State that seeks to minimize the enforceable content of the obligation, limiting it to an obligation solely of *information dissemination* (about the relevant project, to the people affected) on the one hand. On the other are the people, seeking to ensure that even if they do not have the right of veto, their views are genuinely considered as a part of the participation process. Upon the State lies the burden of demonstrating, if it rejects those views, *why* they have been rejected.[47] Often—or at least, so it is hoped—the obligation to transparently set out its reasons will itself constrain the range of options that the State can use in response to the inputs of the participatory process.[48]

By way of conclusion, it is important to note that a constitution may contain one or more (or other) forms of popular participation alongside representative democracy and its institutions. For example, in a remarkable document produced in the build-up to the drafting of the Bolivian Constitution, the alliance of social movements called the Pacto Unidad proposed a vision of participatory democracy that would comprise of '[a] constituent assembly, popular vote, referendum, popular indigenous community councils, plebiscites, popular indigenous communal assemblies, citizens' legislative assemblies, and other mechanisms of direct democracy and recall'.[49] While this bouquet of demands was eventually diluted in the Bolivian Constituent Assembly,[50] in his analysis of the Bolivian Constitution, Tockman notes that it nonetheless 'articulate[d] the combination of three dimensions of democracy—representative, participatory, and communitarian'—a phenomenon called 'demodiversity'.[51] How these different dimensions relate to each other within the text and the structure of the constitution, and in judicial decisions, will go some way towards determining the exact role that 'the People' will play in the working of constitutional democracy.

II. Exit, the People: The Silences in the Indian Constitution

A glance at the text of the Indian Constitution reveals that it establishes the familiar political structures of a representative democracy. It may therefore be argued at the outset that this design choice precludes any attempt to read in elements of public participation (read: direct democracy), or a role for the people, back into the Constitution. That choice, so the argument goes, had been made at the moment of the founding, and cannot now be unmade.

However, as we have seen in the previous section, the choice of representative democracy does not necessarily erase the space for the people as constitutional actors, beyond their role as voters. Constitutions have devised a variety of ways to bridge what Gargarella calls the 'distance' between the people and their representatives. These various ways include the participation of the people in different manners and to different degrees, in processes of constitutional change, of law-making, and of administrative action.

A deeper look at the provisions of the Indian Constitution, however, reveals a more restricted vision of the people as constitutional actors, and a structure of representative democracy that combines internal restraints (the separation of powers between the wings of State) within the thinnest form of external restraints (periodic suffrage). While constitutional change is limited to supermajorities in Parliament (and, for some subjects, majorities in state legislatures) the Constitution is silent on all other forms of public participation in the practice of constitutionalism.[52] In Sandipto Dasgupta's elegant formulation, 'there [are] no structures that enable [the people] to emerge as a collective agent outside of electoral aggregations.'[53] As we have seen, this is unlike some of its more recent counterparts from South Africa to Kenya, from Bolivia to Ecuador. The text of the Indian Constitution thus seems to vindicate Partha Chatterjee's observation about nationalist struggles that simultaneously invoke popular authority ('We the People') while 'distancing … those elements from the structure of the State'.[54]

To understand this not simply as an omission, but as a question of constitutional design, we must consider the intellectual history that led up to the framing of the Constitution. As Nazmul Sultan points out, late-nineteenth century British liberals justified British dominion over India on the basis that the mass of Indian people, because of its condition, was not yet ready to constitute itself into 'the People': a collective agent that could—and had the right to—exercise political sovereignty.[55] The role of the Empire was to guide Indians until they *were* ready at some indeterminate point in the future. It was at that (indeterminate) point that the question of self-government would be considered. Thus, as Sultan sums up: 'The aim of British rule, then, was not simply to train the Indians into self-government. More fundamentally, it involved the challenge of transforming its amorphous masses into a people fit for self-government.'[56]

As Sultan goes on to note, in the initial years, the Indian National Congress accepted this formulation, and restricted its demands to incremental representation within the existing institutions of government. However, this changed with the Swaraj movement (first articulated by Dadabhai Naoroji in 1906). The argument now was that it was only self-government (swaraj) that could bring the Indian people to the point where they could become sovereign political agents. In other words:

> Naoroji and his colleagues readily accepted that the Indian masses were not developed enough to exercise sovereignty: the state of Indian peoplehood failed to meet the demand of the democratic norm. Still, they refused to leave the task of transforming the masses to the British. Instead of deriving the claim for self-government from the prior ground of popular sovereignty, they proposed that the practice of self-government would pave the way for the development of the sovereign authority of the Indian people.[57]

The liberal Imperial argument was thus turned on its head, but—as Sultan observes above—its *premise*, namely that the Indian masses were not yet ready to exercise political sovereignty, was maintained. The debate now was whether swaraj was conditional on them achieving that readiness under British tutelage, or whether swaraj was to be the instrument to create the conditions of readiness.

The result of this was, however, that the evolving vision of the post-independence State was one where the role of the people was a limited one. That this post-independence State would be a constitutional and parliamentary democracy was not in question. However, it was a democracy in which the people's role was to periodically *authorize* the government to act on their behalf (through elections), and the role of the government was to accelerate national development (primarily through planning and other technocratic devices).[58] As Sultan writes:

> ... the role of universal suffrage and legislative representatives was to keep the planners in touch with the people and allow the latter to have some control over the process, albeit via the means of elections. The result was a form of democratic project that sought to *carry the people and yet be authorised by them* (emphasis supplied).[59]

I suggest that this history and this political vision (which was championed by Nehru and the other dominant figures in the Constituent Assembly)[60], explains the marginalization of the people as political actors within the Constitutional text.[61] After all, visions of a more expanded role for the people in the processes of constitutional governance were not unknown to Indian anti-colonial political thought. In previous chapters, we have studied the arguments of the radical federalists, and the many visions of decentralized power that accommodated public participation and the practices of direct democracy to a much greater degree.[62] Some of these visions also found their way into political life, as parts of the many experiments with constitutionalism that took place in various parts of India, from the 1920s onwards. For example, as Tejas Parasher sums up some of the striking features of a draft

Constitution for the princely state of Mysore, which was prepared (on invitation) by the philosopher Brajendra Nath Seal:

> It proposed *a network of local citizens'* assemblies under an overarching central authority, a 'federal' state 'suited to the genius (and the socio-economic condition) of the Indian people'. His guiding philosophy, Seal declared, was that 'the people must be put en rapport with the Government *in various ways, other than the mere machinery of constitutional representation in the Legislature*'.[63] (Emphasis supplied.)

As Parasher argues, Seal's ideas did not emerge from a vacuum, but were a part of a *tradition* of political thought in late-colonial India, which sought to locate the history of Indian constitutional governance (and, by extension, its future) beyond *merely* representative institutions, and through forms such as 'participatory citizens' councils at the local level',[64] in order to 'find arrangements of sovereignty more participatory than representative institutions could ever be'.[65] Importantly, these visions were directly at odds with the dominant vision of self-government espoused by the Indian National Congress through the freedom struggle which, even as it drew its legitimacy from mass public participation,[66] was 'aimed resolutely towards a ventriloquizing of the voice of the masses, anchored in the indirect, electoral institutions of government which made legislators the primary agents of popular will'.[67]

Furthermore, nor were these visions unknown to, or unarticulated within, the Constituent Assembly. Even as there was agreement that—contrary to Gandhian thought—the Indian Constitution would enshrine *representative* democracy as its bedrock, a survey of the Constituent Assembly Debates reveals that ideas around bridging the gap between the people and their representatives were well known to the framers, and indeed, given an airing in the Assembly.[68] Lokanath Misra, for example, proposed inserting a right to recall as part of a broader set of rights to 'suffrage and election', explicitly arguing that bottom-up democracy would not be possible without bridging that gap between the legislator and the constituent.[69] The Constituent

Assembly did not accept this, with the only response—from Sardar Patel—being the rather unconvincing claim that legislators would voluntarily step down if they' lost the confidence of their electors.[70]

Proposals for incorporating referendums met with a similar fate. From K.T. Shah's suggestions of non-binding referendums initiated by the executive, to Brajeshwar Prasad's mandatory referendums for constitutional amendments, they were all rejected without any substantive discussion.[71] And the 'thin' set of external constraints that finally found their way into the Indian Constitution were specifically critiqued in the assembly for the absence of the people. Commenting on the final draft of the Constitution, T.J.M. Wilson noted, for instance, that the right to vote was only the most 'elementary requisite of democracy', but that the 'essence' of democracy lay in the 'effective participation of the individual in the actual government of the country'.[72]

The absence of specific participatory provisions in the Constitution, therefore, was not an accident, or a product of lack of knowledge, or a lack of awareness of comparative experience.[73] It was the product of conscious *constitutional design*. As we have seen above—at least as far as the thought of some of the prominent framers of the Constitution, such as Jawaharlal Nehru and B.R. Ambedkar, went, and as far the written text reflected—the vision of democracy that the Indian Constitution was committed to was governance through internal constraints (institutions checking institutions), combined with thin external constraints, limited to periodic voting as a means of *authorizing* government, but not *participating* in it.[74]

Needless to say—and as we shall see—the text and the framers' intent did not and could not, of course, exhaust the range of interpretive possibilities that remained open when it came to reading public participation into the Constitution. However—and this has been a recurring theme of the book—the text and context *facilitated* interpretations that would close off public participation in constitutionalism, while throwing up barriers against interpretations that would expand it.

III. A Patchwork Quilt

The absence of constitutional guarantees of public participation does not translate into their absence from the legal landscape altogether. Decades of social movements' claims have resulted in the inclusion of specific public participation guarantees in various legal instruments. In themselves, however, these guarantees are insufficient, for the following reasons. First, they remain isolated and limited to the specific contexts in which they operate; secondly, without a constitutional anchor, the exact scope and nature of these guarantees remains subject to legislative or executive discretion; and thirdly, legislation—and even more so, executive orders—are particularly easy to amend or repeal, leaving the right to public participation at the mercy of either the government, or (at present) a Parliament that has increasingly become subordinate to the executive, for structural and institutional reasons that we have previously discussed.[75]

A. Environment, Extractivism, Displacement

These inadequacies become evident when we study some of the judgments dealing with the scope of public participation. Consider, for instance, two of the landmark judgments on the subject, where the argument of public participation actually succeeded. In *Hanuman Laxman Aroskar vs Union of India*, the grant of an environmental clearance for building an airport in the state of Goa was suspended by the Supreme Court. The clearance was suspended on multiple grounds, one of which was the absence of public participation. The basis of the Court's judgment was the government's non-compliance with a notification that had been issued by the Ministry of Environment and Forests, and in accordance with which public consultation was mandatory. Notably, however, that very notification exempted a whole range of projects from the requirement of a public consultation, at the government's discretion. During its analysis, the Court, indeed, repeatedly indicated that '*subject* to the exceptions' set out in the 2006 notification, prior public consultation was mandatory.[76]

The Court—in some of its observations—attempted to place public participation on a constitutional footing, noting for example that it was 'an important facet of governance based on the rule of law'[77] and a part of environmental governance rooted in the Constitution.[78] It held the government to strict account when it came to fulfilling the detailed criteria for public participation set out in the notification.[79] The Court was also clear that the analysis was, at all times, within the four corners of the notification *itself*. Without the existence of the notification, there would be no independent hook from which to hang the guarantee of public participation.

This is not a criticism of the judgment in *Hanuman Laxman Aroskar*. Indeed, the Court ought to be credited for reading a broad and rigorous set of criteria for public participation under the 2006 notification. The point, however, is that by necessity, the Court's analysis remained pegged to the notification (i.e., an executive order). It would thus be impossible to extrapolate the analysis in *Hanuman Laxman Aroskar* into a context where a similar notification did not exist, or where one of the exemptions was attracted, or indeed, in an event that the government decided to simply withdraw it.

In fact, something of the kind did happen: a few months after the judgment in *Hanuman Laxman Aroskar*, the Ministry of Environment and Forests returned to the Court, asking that the embargo be lifted on the grounds that the procedural flaws pointed out in the judgment had now been addressed by Expert Appraisal Committee. On this occasion (*Hanuman Laxman Aroskar-II*) the Court accepted the arguments of the ministry and lifted its embargo, allowing the construction of the airport to go ahead.[80] Notably, public participation played no role in the Court's analysis. Its approach was oriented towards broad administrative law principles of judicial deference to the expert body, rather than grounded in constitutional principles, that might have justified more rigorous scrutiny.[81] The absence of constitutional entrenchment thus precludes a constitutional hook on which the Court could have pegged its analysis even in round two, allowing for a regression to a more deferential mean.

A similar example is the Supreme Court's judgment in *Orissa Mining Corporation vs The Ministry of Environment and Forests*, which is popularly known as the 'Niyamgiri judgment'. Here, the Court upheld a decision of the ministry in refusing environmental clearance for a bauxite mining project in the Niyamgiri Hills of Odisha. The relevant legal instruments were—once again—executive orders: in particular, the Ministry of Tribal Affair's guidelines passed under the Forest Rights Act (FRA), which required consultation with vulnerable forest dwellers. Beyond this, the FRA itself required the active participation of gram sabhas (i.e., self-governing institutions at the village level) before land could be acquired for developmental purposes. The Supreme Court found that this procedural requirement of gram sabha participation in settling a certain set of claims had not been carried out, and that, therefore, the ministry's decision to withhold the clearance was justified.[82] Here again, the case was determined within the four corners of the statutory guidelines and the parent enactment.[83]

Admittedly, both *Hanuman Laxman Aroskar-I* and *Orissa Mining Corporation* achieved the right outcome for those who sought public involvement and participation, especially in the context of large-scale, environmentally destructive developmental projects (although, as we have seen, *Hanuman Laxman Aroskar-I* was largely undone by *Hanuman Laxman Aroskar-II*). However, the inadequacy of the *framework* within which they were decided is clear.

This inadequacy is further entrenched by a seemingly innocuous, even attractive, judicial doctrine. In its environmental cases, the Supreme Court has often articulated the doctrine of 'public trust' which is, in essence, a doctrine meant to *protect* the environment from degradation by treating certain natural resources as being held 'in trust' by the State for the people. In certain cases, however, this doctrine of public trust has been deployed not as a shield to protect the environment, but as a sword in cases involving the question of *exploiting* mineral or petroleum resources. As recently as 2024, in a case involving a federal dispute over taxing mineral rights, the Court specifically used the doctrine in the context of extractivism, holding that 'the *State* holds all natural resources, including minerals, as a trustee of the public and must deal with them in a manner consistent with the nature of such a trust' (emphasis supplied).[84]

This sounds intuitively plausible until you consider the logical corollary: the State's power of disposal of natural resources, especially the ones that require large-scale extraction, such as minerals, is a power to *exclude* affected people from a share in the decision-making authority.[85] Indeed, this is written into legislation. The Mines and Minerals (Development and Regulation) Act of 1957 (MMRDA)—India's umbrella legislation for regulating mining throughout the country—creates a detailed regulatory regime that, among other things, requires *State* agencies to account for environmental impact in granting mining leases, but has no statutory provisions for *public* participation in any of those decisions.[86] Even in dealing with the establishment of bodies called the District Mineral Foundations, whose ostensible goal it is to 'work for the interest and benefit of persons, and areas affected by mining related operations', the rule-making prerogative is with the state government; the law only asks it to be 'guided' by the provisions of participatory legislation such as the Forest Rights Act.[87]

We can therefore see that without a counterveiling, constitutionally entrenched, and effective right to participation, the doctrine of public trust—as the Court has read it into laws such as the MMDRA—in essence sanctifies top-down, State-led extractivist projects that foreclose meaningful involvement of the people most affected by them.[88]

B. Evictions and Housing

The inadequacy of the existing framework becomes even clearer when we consider the fate of cases where there was no existing statutory regime that covered the case, and where, therefore, the claimants did have to resort directly to the Constitution for making their arguments.

The most famous of these cases is *Olga Tellis vs Bombay Municipal Corporation*.[89] *Olga Tellis* concerned the forced evictions of pavement and slum-dwellers from the streets of Bombay. Before the Supreme Court, the case against the evictions was grounded in Articles 21 (the right to life and personal liberty) and 19(1)(e) (the right to reside and settle in any part of India) of the Constitution. While accepting that the right to life included within it the right to livelihood and that the right to livelihood was infringed through forced evictions, when it came to deciding the remedy, the Court articulated an extremely thin concept of public participation, limited to holding that *if* the city commissioner decided to exercise their discretion to dispense with the requirement of giving adequate notice before an eviction, *then* this discretion would have to be exercised reasonably.[90] Thus, let alone articulating substantive elements of public participation within the Constitution, the Court stopped short of even holding that notice was mandatory in the event of evictions.

The strict proceduralism of *Olga Tellis*, which continues to govern and limit the contours of public participation as a constitutional guarantee, is in stark contrast with the law as it has developed in the comparative jurisdictions that we have studied. For example, in the previous part of this chapter, we have considered comparative constitutional jurisprudence in South Africa and Kenya on the role of the people in constitutional change and in law-making. A combination of expressly guaranteed socio-economic rights within the Constitution (in particular, the right to housing) and the constitutional principle of public participation has enabled these jurisdictions to fashion a detailed right to public participation in cases of proposed evictions and relocations.

In South African constitutional law, this takes shape through the famous doctrine of 'meaningful engagement'. The statutory authority and the individual residents are required to engage with each other as a necessary prerequisite for any eviction or relocation. The terms of the meaningful engagement—often crafted through a judicial order—can include the need for relocation (and proposals for in situ rehabilitation), the timelines for relocation, the adequacy of the alternative provided (including its impact on the rights of vulnerable groups, such as children, the aged, and the disabled), among other things.[91]

The goal of the process is that both parties arrive at a settlement, on equal terms, which does not fall below the 'constitutional floor' when it comes to housing.[92] The doctrine of meaningful engagement has allowed the South African courts to put the brakes on arbitrary and sudden evictions and demolitions, but also—as has been repeatedly noted—to ensure that individuals have a degree of *agency* when it comes to fundamental issues such as relocation, alternative housing, and the like. The Kenyan judiciary has followed suit.[93]

The reason why it is important to *constitutionalize* the process is explained by Rosalind Dixon: 'The idea of engagement-style remedies is also to constitutionalize a requirement of consultation of this kind—both as a sign of respect for those parties and as a means of enlisting and empowering them to help protect and promote relevant constitutional guarantees and *assist in defining their content* (emphasis supplied).'[94]

In other words, therefore, public participation in such contexts also provides an avenue for people to participate in fleshing out the constitutional content of rights (such as the right to housing): that is, to become participants in the project of constitutional interpretation.

In 2019, in a landmark judgment called *Ajay Maken vs Union of India*, the High Court of Delhi incorporated these principles into Indian jurisprudence, pegging them both on the existing municipal policy, as well as on the Constitution.[95] Drawing upon both international law and South African constitutional jurisprudence, the court highlighted the importance of:

> … deliberative democratic practices through the device of 'meaningful engagement.' In this model, the Court becomes both a democratic space where such dialogue can take place and also

> the Constitutional authority that facilitates it. The State is obliged to take into confidence the affected groups about the schemes for rehabilitation it proposes for them and is prepared to review and re-shape them based on their inputs.[96]

However, despite the depth and detail of the reasoning of *Ajay Maken*, the principles that it articulates have not yet become entrenched in Indian jurisprudence. From 2021 onwards, for example, a spate of demolitions and evictions have taken place across the country. Some of these are standard examples of demolitions of urban informal settlements, carried out with a view to 'beautification' (that is, gentrification) of the urban environment. Courts—including the Supreme Court—have enthusiastically upheld these demolitions without paying any attention to the constitutional standards that we have discussed above; they have, instead, endorsed a minimal State offer of resettlement without inquiring into its suitability, or into the constitutional rights of those affected.[97]

Other instances, however, are examples of what is now called 'bulldozer justice', or 'bulldozer raj'. These demolitions come on the heels of public disturbances or violence, involve a disproportionate destruction of Muslim dwellings and homes, and are characterized by the State speaking in a forked tongue. While political figures claim that the demolitions are being undertaken to 'punish' perpetrators (without any trial or finding of guilt), municipal authorities claim that they are only pulling down 'illegal structures'.[98]

Whether demolitions and evictions have been undertaken with a view to gentrification or whether—more disturbingly—they belong to the category of State-sponsored vigilantism and collective punishment, authorities do little more than fulfil the formal *Olga Tellis* requirements of notice, and courts have been unwilling (or unable) to hold them to a higher standard.[99] In either event, *Ajay Maken's* attempts to elevate meaningful public participation to a constitutional guarantee has been more the exception rather than the norm.

This, indeed, is most clearly evident from the Supreme Court's recent judgment in *Rajeev Suri vs Delhi Development Authority*, where a divided Court upheld (2:1) the central government's scheme to redesign a substantial part of the national capital ('the Central Vista'). One of the core arguments before the Court was that the absence of public participation before necessary clearances had been granted to the project constituted grounds for setting it aside. As there was no statutory regime in place, petitioners' arguments rested *explicitly* on a constitutional guarantee of public participation, framed in general terms: the rights of affected people to participate in administrative decisions.[100]

The Supreme Court examined the argument over twenty-five paragraphs in its judgment, but appeared to return no clear finding.[101] It went into some of the constitutional history that we have discussed previously, and observed that from the time of the Indian Councils Act in 1861, the evolution of democratic institutions had always been *representative* in character, and that this was a clear choice made in and by the Constituent Assembly (as we have seen, the history is slightly more complex than this). That said, the Court nonetheless held that public participation was a constitutional value—but that its contours were to be decided and articulated through legislation. It was, therefore, not open to the Court to develop the concept of public participation in *constitutional terms*, in the absence of enabling legislation. But even so, the Court did appear to set out a cramped and narrow vision of public participation, one that was limited to 'information dissemination' by the State, as we have discussed above: '... such public participation is not to supplant the discretion of the Government or to retard the development work. It is only for inviting constructive suggestions/objections from all stakeholders for effective implementation of the policy of the Government, to subserve public interest.'[102]

In other words, public participation was not a constitutional *value* in its own right, one that could *inform* public policy, but only an instrument towards more effective *implementation* of an already decided policy. With such a narrow articulation in place, it is unsurprising that the Court went on to hold that the Central Vista Project cleared whatever abstract threshold for public participation that *was* there in the Constitution.

No doubt—and for the reasons set out above—it was more than open to the Court to read the Constitution in this way. As we have just seen, the Court relied upon both the constitutional text (in particular, its silences), and one reading of history to argue that the vision of democracy under the Constitution was meant to be primarily representative in character, with departures from that rule being in the nature of narrow and firmly limited exceptions, prescribed specifically by the legislature.[103] However, it is equally important to note that this was not the *only* interpretive option that was open to the Court. After all, judgments such as *Ajay Maken*, in their reading of *Olga Tellis*, had—implicitly—read in a right to public participation into Article 21 of the Constitution. Judgments like *Hanuman Aroskar* had fleshed out the details of what public participation required, albeit within the four corners of an executive instrument. It remained possible, then, for the Court to read these judgments together, and find in them authority, both for the proposition that public participation was a constitutional principle, *and* that even where there was no statutory scheme in existence, it had enough content—or purchase—so as to form the basis of meaningful judicial review.

In this way, the judgment in *Rajeev Suri* is a constitutional 'inflection point', in the sense that this book discusses. Faced with an invitation to constitutionalize the right to public participation, the Court declined to do so—and thus, perhaps, closed the door on a possible reading of the Constitution that would have done so. No doubt, doing so would have been, in a way, reading the Constitution against the grain, but—and this is important—in my view it remained possible for the Court to do so while remaining faithful to the canons of constitutional interpretation. Text and context perhaps indicated a particular outcome but did not *determine* it. That determination, at the end of the day, was made by the Court.

IV. Conclusion

In their journey through the archives, Rohit De and Ornit Shani sum up the uniquely participatory nature of the Indian Constitution-making process in the following words:

> Indians at different sites and in different positions of power were thinking about the constitution, framing their claims within this language and transforming what constitutionalism would mean in independent India … while diverse groups had indeed petitioned and made constitutional demands during colonial times, in 1946 new kinds of claims and involvements, on a far greater scale, turned the constitution-making process into a public experience, with the public beginning to own the constitution as a political practice, as a means of asserting themselves.[104]

When we consider the nature of this participation, in its breadth and depth, it rivals the lauded and famous examples of participatory constitution-making in more recent decades, from Bolivia[105] to Kenya.[106] What, then, explains the absence of the people in Indian constitutional jurisprudence, and the resistance of courts towards constitutionalizing public participation?

There are, I believe, two reasons for this. The first is that the involvement of the people in the crafting of the Indian Constitution was not translated into the text and design of the Constitution. It is here, perhaps, that the upstream and downstream exclusion of 'the People' becomes significant. While participation—as De and Shani demonstrate—was both broad and deep, ultimate control (including the manner and extent of engagement with the public) remained within the hands of the Constituent Assembly. And the assembly itself remained sceptical about the value of public participation.

Secondly, this history of public participation and involvement with the Constitution-making process was quickly lost and submerged within a narrative that privileged the Constituent Assembly as the pre-eminent site of constitution-making. This created what we have referred to, in this book, as a 'constitutional common sense': a widespread, almost unarticulated set of assumptions about the Constitution, which nonetheless informs constitutional interpretation and adjudication (and is often revealed at moments of crisis).

This constitutional common sense takes the absence of participatory mechanisms within the Constitution—and their rejection within the Constituent Assembly—as evidence of a constitutional vision limited to the forms and procedures of representative democracy, with the role of the people being limited to the periodic exercise of suffrage. It is this that explains judgments like *Rajeev Suri*. The judgment's reasoning was based in absence: the absence of 'the People' in the constitutional text, and their absence from the narrow (and incomplete) history of constitutional evolution that the Court sanctioned. Relying upon these absences and silences, the Court resisted the 'reading in' of public participation into the constitutional provisions. It is this also that explained the patchy and uneven jurisprudence around environmental and housing rights, where a *partially* constitutionalized right to participation is at perennial risk of clawback and regression.

This loss of constitutional history is what sets apart Indian constitutional interpretation with its counterpart in, for example, a jurisdiction such as Kenya, where the participatory nature of constitution-making has become part of constitutional folklore, and has therefore contributed towards building an opposite constitutional common sense: one where judges are expected to draw on a history of participation to interpret the provisions of the present Constitution.[107] Indeed, one striking feature of the Kenyan *BBI Judgments*, which we discussed previously in this chapter, is how much a shared pride in a history of public participation as an integral element of constitution-making contributed to, and informed, the courts' analysis of how to understand and interpret the Constitution's provisions.

Of course, this task is made much easier by the fact that a constitution such as Kenya's or Bolivia's specifically encodes a right to public participation, at multiple levels. We, therefore, come back to the core issue of constitutional text and design. While text and design do not exhaust the scope for constitutional interpretation, when combined with the constitutional common sense mentioned above, they make it far more likely that at the moment of a constitutional inflection point, the judiciary will be more inclined to adopt a reading of the constitution that excludes public participation, rather than one that includes it. And this is what happened in a case like *Rajeev Suri*, where the question was posed squarely to the Court.

As a final point, it is important not to overstate the case. There is an easy—and flawed—attraction to romanticizing public participation or presenting it as an easy solution to a climate of State impunity, enabled by thin representative democracy. Despite constitutional provisions and judicial doctrine, evictions remain a serious problem in South Africa and Kenya, with the 'meaningful engagement' requirements—as we noted in the introduction—often subverted or undermined by powerful actors. In Ecuador and Bolivia, the requirements for 'prior and informed consultation' were inserted in order to dilute more radical demands from indigenous people, that insisted upon a right of co-governance of the commons (including natural resources found beneath the soil), and a community veto upon large-scale extractivist projects.[108]

In the case of Bolivia, for example, the Pacto Unidad had specifically urged the idea of consultation being tied to the ideas of co-decision and veto, in case of the exploration and exploitation of natural resources.[109] However, the diluted final text of the provisions has allowed the State to argue that ultimate and final control over natural resources—including decisions on their extraction and exploitation—rests *with* the State.[110] But that said, it is these very provisions that have also allowed these communities to contest and challenge State decisions *upon* the terrain of the Constitution—something that would not be possible from a baseline of absence.

In the Indian Constitution, the baseline is one of absence.[111] In this chapter, I have argued that amidst this sound of silence if we do wish to constitutionalize public participation both as a right and a norm, perhaps the first task is to recover the submerged histories of popular constitution-making—pace De and Shani—and to chip away at encrusted constitutional common sense, in order to break open a space for another alternative reading of the Constitution: one that brings the people *back* into the Constitution.

Interlude: Yesterday's Tomorrow

IN A BOOK TITLED *Yesterday's Tomorrow*, Bini Adamczak takes us on a journey through the 'departure points' of twentieth-century history: forks in the road and moments of inflection, where 'the past [might have been] a different one and with it the present, palpably, perhaps a little, maybe even significantly'.[1] It is a journey that seeks to imagine a future not just 'in the moments of the present that point beyond it', but also in 'dislodge[ing] it from the moments of the past in which it is anchored'.[2]

What might such a journey look like for Indian constitutionalism? Were there 'departure points' where an alternative future to that of the centralizing Constitution glimmered with possibility? In this Interlude, I follow Adamczak in traveling back through time, moment after moment, to illumine these departure points: the end of the Emergency in 1977 **(I)**, the alternative constitution-making projects of 1944–48 **(II)**, and the constitutional experiments in India's princely states from the 1920s onwards **(III)**.

The windows opened up in these moments were decisively closed. In the words of Adamczak, these imagined futures 'were incapable of materialising themselves in lasting, visible traces, of institutionalising themselves in architecture, laws, customs, thought patterns, manners of speaking. They are only—almost only—present as absences. In brief: they are gone'.[3] But even in the absence of those futures—and in the impossible memory of 'something that never happened'—such a journey of restoration can provide us with 'a dream of something that could have come true'.[4]

Constrained by space, the elegy that follows is necessarily sketchy in nature. A fuller project of excavating the buried constitutional futures of the past is awaited, although—as we have seen at various points in this book—parts of it have begun. This Interlude is meant to provide a moment of illumination, a (hopeful) prelude to a longer-lasting light.

I. The Emergency

Reams have been written about India's 'first dictatorship', the twenty-one-month Internal Emergency that lasted from 25 June 1975 to 21 March 1977.[5] Under Prime Minister Indira Gandhi, democracy was suspended, the political opposition arrested and imprisoned, civil liberties violated with impunity (including mass demolitions), and the Constitution eviscerated. But ultimately, it was the People who repudiated this attempt to establish a constitutional dictatorship, handing Indira Gandhi a stunning political defeat in the general election of 1977. The victorious Janata Party—a hastily cobbled-together coalition of opposition forces—had explicitly campaigned upon a platform to restore democracy and to undo the damage wrought by the Emergency. Their sweeping victory affirmed that they had a mandate to do just that.

At the heart of the Emergency Regime's assault upon the Constitution had been the 42nd Amendment, much of which was enacted on 3 January 1977.[6] The 42nd Amendment was principally about power: the shifting of power to the Prime Minister, and to the executive-dominated Parliament, away from other institutions. Its primary target was the judiciary, and especially the recalcitrant high courts, many of whom had proven to be a thorn in Indira Gandhi's side by frequently ordering the release of detained dissidents and opposition leaders. To serve this goal, the powers of high courts to invalidate central laws was removed (and vested solely in a more amenable Supreme Court), the power of constitutional amendment was placed explicitly beyond judicial review, and supermajorities were required if a court wished to invalidate a law for being unconstitutional.

There were, however, other significant changes to the constitutional structure. Subjects such as education were shifted from the State List to the Concurrent List, thus subordinating the legislative and executive powers of the states in key domains to that of the Union's. A new Article—Article 257A—was inserted stating that 'the Government of India may deploy any armed force of the Union or any other force subject to the control of the Union for dealing with any grave situation of law and order in any State'.[7] To supplement this, the competence to enact laws requiring the deployment of central forces in the states was explicitly inserted into Schedule VII.

The Emergency provisions themselves were amended. One key change was that while under the pre-Emergency Constitution, the default position was that laws enacted during the Emergency would lapse unless expressly affirmed. According to the new position, these laws would continue unless expressly repealed. This blurred the line between an Emergency as an explicitly *temporary* event with a defined starting point and end point, and the Emergency as a *continuing* event whose effects would linger in the legal landscape even after it was formally revoked.

However, it is important to understand that even as the 42nd Amendment accelerated the Constitution's centralizing drift, much of what defined the Emergency did not *need* formal constitutional amendments. After all, the Emergency had been declared under the existing Constitution, and many of the human rights violations were explicitly sanctioned by the 'rights-less zone' that the Constitution's Emergency provisions contemplated. The widespread use of administrative detention under national security legislation hearkened back to the long 1950s and 1960s, and the lasting shadow of *A.K. Gopalan*. Home demolitions—carried out at the instance of Indira Gandhi's son, Sanjay Gandhi—were also a legacy of times past, now accelerated under conditions of greater impunity. In short, not just the formal changes, but even the conduct of the State during the 'declared Emergency' reflected the blurring of lines between the state of exception and the state of normalcy that we have discussed in the previous paragraph and elsewhere.

Thus, whether by constitutional amendment or otherwise, the defining features of the Emergency implicated many of the strands of the web of power considered in this book, and illustrated the inability of the existing constitutional arrangements to stand as a bulwark against an authoritarian centralizing of power without accountability.

The end of the Emergency, and its comprehensive repudiation by the People, opened up a window of opportunity for the first time in the two-and-a-half-decades of the functioning of the Constitution: an opportunity to undo not just the excesses of the Emergency, but reconsider the very centralizing drift embedded within the Constitution, of which the Emergency was only the most recent and most virulent symptom.

The 44th Amendment was the Janata Party's main response. The Statement of Objects and Reasons of the Constitution Amendment Act hit some of the right notes, invoking the need to protect Fundamental Rights, to place checks upon emergency powers, to give the people an 'effective voice', and to correct the 'distortions' in the Constitution that had been wrought during the Emergency.[8]

And yet, the amendment itself was only a partial rollback of these 'distortions'. The power of the courts was restored. The threshold for triggering an internal emergency was heightened, and (some of the) older limits were restored. It was stipulated that even during an emergency, the rights under Articles 20 and 21 could not be suspended (a direct riposte to the Supreme Court's infamous habeas corpus judgment). And—perhaps most significantly, in a sign that the 44th Amendment contemplated something deeper than *simply* reversing the Emergency amendments—additional procedural safeguards were added to the preventive detention provisions under Article 22. The stipulated period for which a person could be detained without confirmation by an advisory board was brought down to two months, and the advisory board itself was to consist of serving or retired high court judges.

But the inadequacy of the 44th Amendment stares the reader in the face. Changes in the legislative lists remained intact. Another crucial change that the 44th Amendment left untouched was the fate of laws after the end of an Emergency. The 44th Amendment conspicuously *did not* restore the pre-Emergency position that laws passed during an Emergency would cease unless explicitly affirmed.[9] Thus, the line between the state of exception and the state of normalcy remained blurred, and many years later—as we have seen in Chapter 1—it allowed the Supreme Court to endorse the near-limitless powers of the Union during the pendency of an internal emergency, leaving the very existence of states at the mercy of the Union. And finally, the amendments to Article 22 were never notified by the government, and thus never came into force. An attempt to compel the Union to do so was rejected by the Supreme Court in 1980—the very Court whose powers the 44th Amendment had so enthusiastically restored, in the hope that it would stand as a bulwark against the State's encroachment upon the rights of the People.[10]

The character of the 44th Amendment is perhaps summed up by the following: the 42nd Amendment's Article 257A (mentioned above) which authorized the central government to deploy armed forces in the states was repealed. But Entry 2A of List I (*also* a 42nd Amendment product, which authorized Parliament to legislate for the deployment of armed forces 'in aid' of the civilian authority in a state) was left intact, as was the mirror provision in List II taking this competence away from states. Twenty years later (as we saw in Chapter 1) the Supreme Court seized upon this to uphold the constitutional validity of the Armed Forces (Special Powers) Act.

Beyond these deficiencies, the partial and incomplete nature of the 44th Amendment reflected an almost exclusive concern about the *symptoms* (the Emergency and the 42nd Amendment), rather than the *cause* (the Constitution's centralizing drift). True, not all of this can be laid at the feet of the Janata Party; Indira Gandhi continued to enjoy large numbers in the Upper House, which allowed her to block a part of the proposed changes. Even in its moment of victory, the Janata Party was thus constrained in how much it could accomplish by way of constitutional amendment. Had it managed to sustain the wave of popular support that it brought it to power in 1977, perhaps a time would have come, indeed, for those conversations.

But history—as W.H. Auden wrote, and later regretted writing—cannot help nor pardon.[11] Riven by its internal contradictions, the Janata Party fell apart by 1980. In the elections that ensued, Indira Gandhi was returned to power. One of the first acts of the second Indira Gandhi regime was to legislate the National Security Act of 1980 (NSA), which legalized preventive detention (once again) under a central law. The Supreme Court, like the French Bourbons, had learned nothing and forgotten nothing.[12] It upheld the NSA soon after.[13]

And so, the brief window that had been opened up in 1977 to reconsider the centralizing drift of the Constitution, and to reflect upon the design choices that had brought the country its first post-Independence dictatorship, was closed once more. In the fifty years since the Emergency, it has not opened again.

If, therefore, there is a moment of regret in our post-Independence constitutional history, a moment where an alternative future for constitutionalism flickered into existence before being snuffed out, it is perhaps the brief heady days of 1977.

II. The Framing

In this book, we have studied the dissenting voices within the Constituent Assembly, which spoke in opposition to the centralizing vision espoused by the leaders of the Indian National Congress.

These voices, however, were not limited to internal dissent. Outside of the Constituent Assembly, there were other individuals—representing different intellectual and political currents, and unencumbered by an oppositional role within the assembly—who embarked upon constitution-writing projects of their own. A perusal of these documents reveals the existence of alternative constitutional visions, visions that served as a collective counterpoint to that of the Constituent Assembly. It shows us that at the time of Independence, there *were* other ways and vocabularies of articulating constitutionalism.

Consider, for example, M.N. Roy's 1944 *Constitution of India: A Draft*, endorsed by the Radical Democratic Party.[14] Drawing from Roy's historical engagement with popular movements across the world, the Draft tackled multiple prominent axes of power.[15] Most importantly, it sought to make the people central to the constitutional imaginary. It did so by according a prominent role to elected bodies called the People's Committees, which would be established in villages, towns, and cities. The People's Committees would nominate candidates seeking election to both the federal and the provincial legislatures, but also—crucially—could recommend the recall of legislators, and demand that legislative and executive measures at either level be subject to a referendum.

Thus, through a set of complex and interlocking provisions, Roy imagined a constitution where authority sprang *bottom-up* from the People's Committees, with the central and provincial legislatures acting as delegates, rather than the top-down, representative-oriented vision of the Indian Constitution. To this, Roy linked a highly devolved federal scheme, where 'fully autonomous' provinces constituted on the basis of *ethnic* and *linguistic* lines, rather than the British-era administrative divisions, could volunteer to become a part of the main federal union, hive off to form federal unions of their own (while remaining loosely bound within the overall constitutional scheme). And once this Constitution was in force, they could even secede, as long as such a proposal was approved by a referendum.

One can question, of course, whether Roy's Constitution would have worked; a question to which there will never be a definitive answer. Reading his draft Constitution, however, one sees glimpses of a constitutionalism and a constitutional vision where the primary locus of power is not embedded within the central executive, but distributed more equitably along the strands of the web.

A reversal of the default 'top-down' constitutional structure was also at the heart of what came to be known as the 'Gandhian Constitution', drafted by Shriman Narayan Agarwal (and endorsed by Gandhi in a Foreword) in 1946.[16] Gandhi's idea of a governance structure radiating outwards from a conglomeration of 'village republics', which he articulated in *Hind Swaraj*, was famously—or notoriously—lampooned by Ambedkar in the Constituent Assembly. While the Gandhian Constitution replicated some of the romanticization of the 'village republic' that Ambedkar had no patience for, it was also a carefully crafted document, which had given significant thought to the question of power, and drew upon a range of sources—from the anarchist thinker Prince Kropotkin to the federalist scholar Radhakumood Mookerjee—in building its arguments. Thus, its ideas deserved to be studied and engaged with, instead of being summarily dismissed.

At the outset, the Gandhian Constitution declared itself opposed to the centralized State, drawing categorical links between centralization, violence, and the curtailment of individual liberties—as we have discussed in this book. Its own proposal for constitutional design was strikingly similar to M.N. Roy's Constitution. The Gandhian Constitution envisaged a federal pyramid where the basic unit was the 'village republic', the governing panchayat of which would be elected through popular structure. Moving up the pyramid, the Gandhian Constitution delineated the structures and functions of the taluka, the district, the province, and the central government, with each successive administration playing the role of *coordination* (of the administrative units directly below it), and not *command*: this was consistent with the principle of guaranteeing the 'largest measure of local autonomy for the federating units'.

At the heart of this structure was a core idea that we have discussed in this book: how could one meaningfully guarantee a role for *the People* in governance, and combat the alienation that inevitably creeps into the relationship between people and their representatives in a parliamentary structure? For the Gandhian Constitution—quoting a contemporary classic of political theory—this was to be accomplished by making it 'possible for the individual to belong to a variety of small bodies possessing executive powers, dealing both with production and with local administration'.[17] *Nodes of public participation,* to use a term that coined in this book.

Other than this, like M.N. Roy, the Gandhian Constitution called for a strengthening of the federal structure by reorganizing the provinces along linguistic lines, as opposed to the British policy of dividing them up according to administrative convenience. Like M.N. Roy, the Gandhian Constitution incorporated provisions for recall (with a supermajority), to ensure that office-bearers further up the pyramid remained accountable at all times.[18] And most interestingly, like M.N. Roy, the Gandhian Constitution forswore compelling any federal unit to stay in the federation against its will. While Shriman Narayan Agarwal stopped short of specifically spelling out a right to secession, he did everything other than that, clearly stating that 'no territorial unit could be compelled to join the All-India Federation against the declared and established will of the adults of that territory'.[19]

It is interesting to note that even though M.N. Roy and Shriman Narayan Agarwal came from very different political traditions, their constitutional drafts were motivated by the same spirit: of pushing back against the centralizing drift that had come to define colonial constitutionalism, and that would soon be embedded within independent India's Constitution. While the wisdom behind specific individual provisions can always be debated, taken as a whole, their drafts represented an alternative constitutional imagination in its truest sense: a different way or organizing and structuring power, with different normative principles at its heart.

The third 'alternative' constitutional draft was produced by the Socialist Party of India, its Foreword authored by the man who would become the hero of the resistance to Indira Gandhi's Emergency two and a half decades later, Jayaprakash Narayan.[20] The Socialist Party's primary disagreement with the Indian National Congress was about the extent to which economic models could or should be entrenched within the Constitution. On the question of the structuring of public power, the Socialist Party's Constitution overlapped in substantive degree with the Constituent Assembly.

This overlap, however, would make some of the departures even more striking. Three such departures stand out as relevant to our discussion in this book. First, the Socialist Constitution made the *consent* of the state legislature a condition precedent to any alteration of state boundaries or other forms of reorganization of the states, thus tilting significantly towards the states when it came to the federal structure. Secondly, this Constitution exhaustively defined the features of a money bill, and had no omnibus clause (as exists in the Indian Constitution) under which all bills could be sneaked in because they had something to do with money. And thirdly, the ordinance-making power was not left to the sole discretion of the executive, but featured the involvement of a statutory committee, whose members were to be elected through proportional voting, by the state legislatures. While at first blush these might seem minor technical departures, we have seen throughout this book how it is precisely through these technical clauses that the power shifts in significant ways between different bodies.

A final alternative draft was the Constitution of the Hindusthan Free State Act, produced under the auspices of the Bhopatkar Satkar Nidhi, a group affiliated with the Hindu Mahasabha.[21] As with the Socialist Party's Constitution, when it came to constitutional design and questions of power, this constitution was strikingly similar to the Constituent Assembly, but once again with a few fascinating variations.[22] Primary among these was a provision for a popular initiative (a proto-version of the 'popular initiative' that we have discussed in the context of the 2010 Constitution of Kenya). This was accompanied by a provision for recall, as well as a referendum in the case of constitutional alterations.

Reading the four Constitutions together—M.N. Roy's Constitution, the Gandhian Constitution, the Socialist Party's Constitution, and the Hindusthan Constitution—we see a common concern with the power map of colonial constitutionalism, and the eventual shape of the Indian Constitution. In their own separate ways, these four Constitutions attempted to put forth their own power maps, which would address this concern. Thus, even as the Constituent Assembly crafted an executive-trusting Constitution with a centralizing drift, a contrapuntal constitutional canon came into being alongside it. There it remains, at a forking of the roads in our constitutional history.

III. The States

When we now think of the princely states, we think of the challenging process of their integration into the Indian Union; or perhaps we think of the constitutional politics around the abolition of the 'Privy Purses', two decades later. However, beyond their fraught relationship with democratic India, there was a time when the princely states were the sites of some fascinating experiments in constitutionalism.

From the 1920s onwards, as representative institutions began to take root in British India, the princely states responded in two ways. Some held on to autocratic governance, while others set off on their own journeys towards democratization and constitutionalism. As early as 1922–23, Brajendranath Seal wrote a draft Constitution upon the invitation of the dewan of Mysore. The draft Constitution self-consciously distanced itself from unitary representative government, and opted, instead, for a system based on direct democracy and local citizens' assemblies, with a view to securing effective public participation in governance. As Tejas Parasher notes, Seal's draft Constitution was an expression of an intellectual and political current in early twentieth-century India that actively sought an alternative to parliamentary structures in a more decentralized, federal, and directly democratic set of institutions.[23] While, ultimately, this Constitution was not enacted—with Mysore opting for a more traditional arrangement in 1940, modelled upon the 1935 Government of India Act—it demonstrated that in the decades leading up to Independence, there was an alternative intellectual and political trajectory that did not bind itself to the constitutional evolutions traced through the 1919 and 1935 Government of India Acts, and culminating in the Indian Constitution; but rather, sought to *re-imagine* what a democratic constitution might look like, and how it might address the question of power.

Another constitutional experiment that did come to fruition was the 1939 Constitution of the princely state of Aundh.[24] The Aundh Constitution is one of the few examples in Indian history of the ruler of a princely state voluntarily abdicating significant powers to the people (while—in the tradition of a constitutional monarchy—retaining certain powers for himself). The Aundh Constitution of 1939 was a precursor to Shriman Narayan Agarwal's later Gandhian Constitution, albeit not decentralized to the same degree. It stipulated the existence of popularly elected Panchayats in every town and village, with significant devolved powers (education and justice being the two most significant categories); moving up the ladder, there were the talukas, and then the Legislative Assembly of each state and these assemblies did retain legislative powers.

As with the three constitutional drafts we have discussed in the previous section, we can see that these experiments in the princely state of Aundh were likewise concerned with the question of power, and with a strong undercurrent of confronting the centralizing drift within parliamentary and representative structures (especially in the distorted form that they took under colonial constitutionalism).

More than that, however, these initiatives signalled the possibility of a possible future for *constitutional pluralism*: in the 1940s, as Independence neared, many princely states drafted their own Constitutions in the anticipation of a future federal arrangement along the lines of the United States. Previously in this book, we have also discussed the draft Constitutions prepared by the Naga and the Mizo people. Ultimately—barring the case of Jammu and Kashmir—none of these experiments lasted beyond Independence, as all the princely states were integrated into the Union, and the demands of constitutional autonomy rejected out of hand, in favour of the legal safeguards of Schedules V and VI.[25]

One can imagine how a more capacious and generous vision of constitutional pluralism within the Constituent Assembly might have yielded a different history, where constitutional experiments within an overall democratic structure were not only tolerated, but celebrated as an instance of Indian pluralism.[26] There was, as we have seen, a history of constitutional thought that allowed for such a future to come into being. The Constituent Assembly's homogenizing vision of the nation-state, however, ensured that the birth of the Indian Constitution also saw the end of these constitutional experiments. These varying hues and shades of constitutionalism were erased and painted over by a constitution of monochrome.

It is that world of monochrome that we live in today, with all its submerged yesterday's tomorrows.

Epilogue: State, Power, and the Future of Constitutionalism

THIS BOOK HAS PROPOSED a new way of understanding the Indian Constitution, through the lens of power. Its core argument rests on three mutually supporting pillars: first, that the Indian Constitution, like any other constitution, is a terrain of contestation between different and competing visions of power; secondly, that the Constitution has been characterized by a 'centralizing drift' towards a statist, homogenous, and executive-oriented vision of power at the cost of a more decentralized, plural, and distributed vision; and thirdly, this 'centralizing drift' is both embedded in the Constitution's text and design, and has been accelerated through the judgments of the Supreme Court at various 'inflection points' in our constitutional history.

In this concluding chapter, I seek to do two things. By way of completing my account, I will flag some of the axes of power that I have not discussed in this book. These include forms of economic and social power that the Constitution largely avoids addressing in detail (which is why they have not been discussed in *this* book), but which are nonetheless highly relevant for constitutionalism (**I**).

Secondly, I will return to the four themes that I highlighted in the Prologue, and reconsider them in light of our discussion through the course of this book. These are—to recall—colonial constitutionalism, constitutional common sense, the relationship between constitutionalism and politics, and the idea of the Frankenconstitution. With respect to the Frankenconstitution, I will bring together the discussion in the various chapters of this book to show how the centralizing drift reinforces and entrenches itself *across* axes of power, and how recent, glaring examples of executive overreach are enabled by this overlap across axes. In understanding and assessing the Constitution, then, Granville Austin's image of the 'web' is instructive (as we have noted previously), but not quite in the way that he presents it. The Constitution is a web of power; to understand how it works, we must consider each strand separately, but *also* as co-constitutive of the web as a whole (**II**).

This book is a project of diagnosis and critique, not a blueprint. I end, therefore, by posing two questions: is an executive-trusting, centralizing power map the power map that we want for our Constitution? And if not, then given the structure and design of the Constitution (consciously chosen, in full awareness of the alternatives), and given encrusted judicial interpretation over the last seven decades, is it possible to rewrite that power map on the terrain of *this* Constitution? The answers to these questions are left for another day **(III)**.

I. Other Axes

In large part, the Indian Constitution follows a certain historical and ideological model, according to which the purpose of constitutional documents is primarily, if not exclusively, to address 'public power'. As a foundational text tells us, 'most commonly we think of the Constitution as the law that defines and limits the reach of the State'.[1] The model is sustained through the construction of the 'public/private divide', with the domain of constitutionalism primarily confined to the 'public' side of the divide.[2]

This construction has long been understood to be artificial and has been subjected to detailed critique over the years. Scholars have noted how, historically, the public/private divide was conceptualized to insulate a rising bourgeoisie from egalitarian demands, and to similarly insulate the patriarchal institution of the family from claims of gender equality.[3] In essence, right from its inception, the public/private divide has contributed towards entrenching and perpetuating power structures and hierarchies within the so-called 'private domain'.

A critique of the Indian Constitution for (largely) replicating the public/private divide is a task for a different project. Here, I will briefly note the result of this: in particular, two axes of power that the Constitution either omits to address, or addresses sketchily. The first is that of economic power. Formally, the Indian Constitution is agnostic about the question of economic structure. This, however, was not an inevitability. The famous Indian National Congress Resolution of 1929 explicitly attributed Indian poverty to foreign exploitation *and* the 'economic structure', and called for a revolutionary change to the 'economic and social structure', towards the removal of inequalities.[4] Proto-constitutional documents produced by the Congress, such as the Karachi Resolution of 1931, contained enforceable socio-economic rights and redistributive taxation provisions.[5] Early drafts of the constitution—especially one put forward by Dr B.R. Ambedkar, called *States and Minorities*—proposed explicitly writing State socialism into the Constitution.[6] In a brief Memorandum accompanying *States and Minorities*, Ambedkar also observed that while hitherto Constitutions had been about protecting individuals from the dictatorship of the State, the Indian Constitution would also focus on protecting individuals from the dictatorship of the *private employer*. In his words, which are best quoted in full:

> Constitutional lawyers assume that the enactment of fundamental rights is enough to safeguard their liberty and that nothing more is called for. *They argue that where the State refrains from intervention in*

> *private affairs—economic and the social—the residue is liberty.* What is necessary is to make the residue as large as possible and State intervention as small as possible. It is true that where the State refrains from intervention what remains is liberty. But this does not dispose of the matter. One more question remains to be answered. To whom and for whom is this liberty? Obviously this liberty is liberty to landlords to increase rents, for capitalists to increase hours of work and reduce rate of wages. This must be so. It cannot be otherwise. *For in an economic system employing armies of workers, producing goods en masse at regular intervals some one must make rules so that workers will work and the wheels of industry run on. If the State does not do it the private employer will ... In other words what is called liberty from the control of the State is another name for the dictatorship of the private employer.*
>
> How to prevent such a thing happening? How to protect the unemployed as well as the employed from being cheated out of their *fundamental rights to life, liberty and pursuit of happiness*? The useful remedy adopted by democratic countries is to *limit* the power of Government to impose arbitrary restraints in political domain and to *invoke* the ordinary power of the legislature to restrain the more powerful individual from imposing *arbitrary restraints* on the less powerful in the economic field. The inadequacy nay the futility of the plan has been well-established ... [this] plan follows quite a different method. It seeks to limit not only the power of Government to impose arbitrary restraints but also of the more powerful individuals or to be more precise to eliminate the possibility of the more powerful having the power to impose arbitrary restraints on the less powerful by withdrawing *from the control he has over the economic life of the people.* There cannot be the slightest doubt that of the two remedies against the invasion by the more powerful of the rights and liberties of the less powerful the one contained in the proposal is undoubtedly more effective. Considered in the light of these observations *the proposal is essentially a proposal for safeguarding the liberty of the individual.*[7] (Emphasis supplied.)

Had these proposals been carried through, the Indian Constitution would have radically rewritten the map of economic power. But what form this rewriting would finally have taken we do not know, as by the end of the Constitution-drafting process, Ambedkar had done a complete volte face. Responding to objections that the Constitution had *not* entrenched socialism, he argued that the choice of economic structure was something for each generation to determine, instead of being bound by the founding generation. In other words, decisions about economic structure were to be taken through ordinary political contestation, and not through constitutional prescriptions.[8]

The final Constitution thus remained largely silent on political economy, and placed socio-economic rights within the non-enforceable 'Directive Principles of State Policy', where the State was expected—but not legally bound—to advance them.

Of course, there were provisions in the Constitution that placed limits upon redistributive or egalitarian measures. These were, most notably, the provisions governing compensation for land expropriation, which were wielded by the early Supreme Court to fetter the government's ambitious land redistribution programme.[9] Over two decades, however, these provisions were more or less amended out of existence (even though, as a by-product, they gave rise to the famous basic structure doctrine). Another possible fetter—the fundamental right to property—was removed by the Janata Government in 1978. The removal of these provisions further entrenched the position that questions of political economy—and especially, questions around redistribution and equality—would be primarily *political* questions, and not constitutional questions.

It is important to recall, however, that economic and political power are deeply intertwined in the modern nation-state.[10] A constitution that is agnostic towards economic power is, as we have seen, a constitution that leaves existing economic power structures and hierarchies intact. It is also true that those with economic power wield a disproportionate influence over the political process. It is therefore worth asking whether a constitution that refrains from affirmatively *intervening* into the economic sphere (in a redistributive and egalitarian direction), and instead elects to relegate questions of economic power to the political process will only end up ensuring that the economically powerful are able to use the political process to entrench and perpetuate their own power. In other words, constitutional agnosticism about economic power is not neutral. By absenting itself from the field, a constitution does privilege one vision of power over another.[11]

Notably, this was something Ambedkar realized and articulated with particular clarity in his Memorandum, as well as in the explanatory notes to *States and Minorities*, when he argued for inscribing the economic structure into the Constitution, so as to insulate it from parliamentary majorities.[12] Not doing so, he argued, would ensure that '... the political structure is completely set at naught by the forces which emerge from the economic structure which is at variance with the political structure'.[13]

This understanding, however, was not inscribed into the text and design of the Constitution.

When we consider, next, the question of social power, we find something similar at play. In drafting the Constitution, the primary concern of the framers appeared to be to ensure that the document did not act as a *barrier* towards the breaking down of existing social power structures and hierarchies. The Constitution, however, stopped there. It did not *affirmatively* seek to intervene into the social domain, reshape these structures and hierarchies, and rewrite the social power map.

Consider, for example, the issue of gender equality. The Constitution contains a standard non-discrimination clause, which includes 'sex' as one of the prohibited grounds (Article 15(1)).[14] In order to avoid the non-discrimination guarantee from being invoked to invalidate affirmative action for women, Article 15(3) expressly enables—but does not mandate—the State to make 'special provisions' for women (and children).[15] The exact scope of Article 15(3) has been subject to some interpretive debate over the years.[16] More recently, the Constitution was amended to provide for women's reservations in Parliament, although this amendment has yet to come into force.

Consider, next, the most prominent and virulent axis of social power in India—the institution of caste. As with gender, it is noteworthy that although the Constitution explicitly bans the practice of untouchability (the most pernicious expression of the caste system), its chosen method of overcoming caste discrimination—that is, through reservations—is framed in *enabling* terms, and not in *mandatory* terms.[17] That is, the Constitution *allows* reservations, but does not *require* them.[18] The Supreme Court's expansive interpretation of the equality clause has given rise to a legitimate argument that a necessary corollary of substantive equality is a *right* to caste-based affirmative action.[19] However, the same Supreme Court has also repeatedly quashed these claims when they have come before it.[20]

Here again, B.R. Ambedkar had a specific vision of overcoming caste hierarchies through the exercise of political power, as well as through enforceable rights. In the political domain, the chosen remedy was the mechanism of separate electorates. As is well known, Ambedkar was blackmailed into dropping this demand at the 1932 Poona Pact[21] and separate electorates were not considered thereafter.[22] Instead, what did find its way into colonial constitutional instruments was *joint* electorates (i.e., reserved constituencies for the 'depressed classes', but as part of the common electoral roll). In *States and Minorities*, Ambedkar produced a detailed critique of this scheme. Through an analysis of the statistics, he noted that 'depressed-class' candidates vying for elected office could not succeed without the support of upper-caste Hindus, thus defeating the entire purpose of the scheme. He advocated for a return to separate electorates—something that the Constituent Assembly was unwilling to accept.[23] Ultimately, the Constitution does have reserved *constituencies: a* partial acknowledgement that it could not entirely fail to address caste hierarchies in the political domain—but only partial, at best.[24]

In *States and Minorities*, Ambedkar also proposed an extensive set of enforceable rights, dealing specifically with social power. The most prominent of these proposals was a detailed anti-boycott provision, which would have prevented dominant castes from using their economic, social, and political power to exclude the submerged classes[25] from equal participation in the economic and social life of the community.[26] This, once again, would have been a substantive rewriting of the social power map, had it found its way into the Constitution.

The Constitution kept a kernel of Ambedkar's idea, but substantially watered it down. In both the economic and the social sphere, there are certain specific provisions of the Constitution that move beyond enabling/facilitating affirmative action measures, and guarantee enforceable rights against other *private* actors ('direct horizontality'). We have already considered the prohibition of untouchability, which is one example. Others include Article 15(2), which prohibits discrimination in access to certain sites of economic and social commerce (such as shops, hotels, and public restaurants),[27] and Article 23, which prohibits forced labour.[28]

Undoubtedly, direct horizontality represents a significant attempt to rebalance power relations within the private sphere using the vehicle of rights. However, the sparse and isolated nature of the direct horizontal provisions of the Indian Constitution (especially when compared with the extensive and coherent proposals in Ambedkar's draft constitution), and the absence of any theory or principled account linking these provisions to each other, has meant that their impact has been sporadic. The jurisprudence around them is limited to the odd case spread out over many decades.[29]

In *States and Minorities*, Ambedkar invited the Constituent Assembly to seriously consider the consequences of both economic and social power, and to craft a constitutionalism where these (intersecting) axes of power would be addressed on the terrain of the constitution. The Constituent Assembly, however, declined this invitation. As a result, ultimately, the dominant tenor of the Constitution remains one of agnosticism, with all its consequences for private power.

II. Four Themes

Let us return, in the end, to the beginning: to the four themes with which we started this book. The first theme was that of 'colonial constitutionalism'.

From its birth, the Constitution has been haunted by its colonial antecedents. This was a point of significant contestation in the Constituent Assembly, compelling Ambedkar to stand up and explicitly defend the extent to which the Indian Constitution borrowed from the 1935 Government of India Act. Ever since then, the critique that the Constitution is colonial in character has never quite gone away. As Dasgupta astutely notes, however, the surface-level borrowings from colonial legal instruments—which have been the primary focus of the colonial critique—are 'the effects rather than the roots of the [colonial] continuity'.[30] To get to the roots, we must frame the question another way: did the Constitution rewrite the power map, and the vision of power, that had long characterized colonial constitutionalism?

We must answer with some care. There is no doubt that the decision to establish universal adult franchise—in one sweep—was a significant alteration of the power map. It accorded to every citizen power that they did not earlier have, exercised through the processes of electoral democracy. This was a hard-won achievement, and we should not trivialize it, or take it for granted.[31] Elections have served as important spaces for the making of collective claims upon the State. They have empowered individuals and groups in ways that were unimaginable before Independence. And of course, more than once in our post-colonial history, popular elections have been the vehicle through which would-be authoritarians have been cut down to size.

Beyond that, however, we have seen that in many crucial ways, the power map of the Indian Constitution resembles that of colonial constitutionalism. It does so in how it centres the executive, in its weak oversight and accountability mechanisms, in its thin concept of representation, in its resistance to meaningful decentralization or distribution of power, in its homogenizing vision, and in its normalization of the state of exception. When, therefore, it comes to the organization of power, the edifice of the Constitution appears to be upheld, at least in part, by pillars of a colonial vintage.

This understanding helps us to see Ambedkar's defence of borrowing from the 1935 Government of India Act in a new light. Ambedkar famously insisted that what was being borrowed only pertained to the 'details of administration'.[32] But if there is one thing we have learned through the course of this book, it is that the 'details of administration' make up a constitution's power map—to a much greater extent than programmatic declaration of rights. Perhaps unintentionally, Ambedkar thus revealed something crucial about the relationship of the Constitution's structure and design with its colonial antecedents.

Another equally unintentional revelation can be found in the opening paragraphs of the very first Supreme Court judgment on fundamental rights, authored by the first Chief Justice of India. In *A.K. Gopalan vs State of Madras*, the Chief Justice began by asking himself how the new Constitution differed from the 1935 Government of India Act, which he called 'the previous Constitution of the Government of India'.[33] His answer was that 'the material points substantially altering the edifice are first in the Preamble Part III of the Constitution is an important innovation. It is headed "Fundamental Rights"'.[34] In other words, the 'new' Constitution was new with respect to its dogmatic part (to use Gargarella's term). When it came to the *organic* part—the structure and the design—the Chief Justice's silence told its own story of continuity.

Let us turn to the second theme: the idea of constitutional common sense. The structure and design of the Constitution that we have just discussed has been supported by a constitutional common sense that has, at key inflection points, underpinned a centralizing drift in constitutional interpretation. We have seen examples of this constitutional common sense at play in contestations over each of the six axes of power. In *State of West Bengal vs Union of India*, the Supreme Court operated upon an unarticulated premise that Indian federalism is not a normative principle, or an end in itself, but an instrumental goal towards sustaining a national unity anchored by the Centre. In *Kihoto Hollohan*, the Court had proceeded on an assumption that the primary vehicle of parliamentarianism was the *political party*, consequently marginalizing the role of the *representative*. In *Re: Article 370 of the Constitution* (and indeed, in the Article 370 cases that came before it), the Court equated 'integration' with 'homogeneity' and 'unity' with 'uniformity' in order to deny normative salience to constitutional pluralism. Indeed, one of the interesting features of *Re: Article 370* was the Court's refusal to countenance the possibility that the Constitution of Jammu and Kashmir could occupy a status complementary to that of the Indian Constitution (and not subordinate to it), even though the existence of state and federal constitutions is one of the most standard features of federalism across the world. In *Jaya Thakur*, the Court was unconvinced that there was any constitutional principle requiring the independence of fourth-branch institutions (such as the Election Commission) from the executive. In *Rajeev Suri*, the Court believed that the Indian Constitution's choice of the representative system excluded forms of direct democracy and public participation in governance decisions. And all the cases on Articles 20–22 that we have discussed operate on the presumption that the Constitution is meant to preserve the investigatory and coercive powers of the State against the due process claims of the accused.

It is particularly striking that in each of these examples, and others that we have discussed in this book, constitutional common sense has been deployed in service of the centralizing drift. In our discussions, we have attempted to critically interrogate the basis of this constitutional common sense, and to show that there are alternative readings of constitutional history, as well as of the constitutional text and design, which should prompt deeper reflection about some of its assumptions.

However, what we have also seen is that this constitutional common sense, at least in some ways, can be plausibly traced back to the document itself. The Constitution and constitutional common sense then act in mutually supporting ways, each entrenching the other, and making alternative constitutional interpretations and visions of power particularly difficult to come to the forefront.

This is also closely connected to the intersection between constitutionalism and politics, our third theme. This is a book that is primarily about the Constitution, and about constitutional interpretation (reflecting the expertise—and limitations—of the author!). And so, it is important to acknowledge that the Constitution neither determines, nor exhausts, the domain of politics. Indeed, in some cases, such as the balance of political forces in the Centre and in the states, constitutional interpretation *follows* politics (think, for example, of the *S.R. Bommai* judgment delivered at the dawn of the coalition era). But what we have seen throughout the course of this book is that constitutional interpretation *facilitates* certain exercises of political power, and *constrains* others. Politics is *shaped* by the Constitution, and politics, in turn, shapes the Constitution.

Once again, the relationship is mutually entrenching. Constitutional interpretation that contributes towards a centralizing drift will create a more powerful executive, which will then advance its own centralizing reading of the Constitution and attempt to use its power to inscribe that reading into constitutional common sense. As we have seen, with a few exceptions, the history of Indian constitutionalism can be seen through the lens of this mutual reinforcement.

Our analysis of the relationship between the Constitution and politics has also revealed something else that is interesting. When confronted with political reality, there are times when the Supreme Court takes it into account in how it interprets the Constitution, and there are times when it ignores it. Perhaps unsurprisingly, there appears to be a positive correlation between the Court's decision and the centralizing drift. The most obvious example of this is *Kihoto Hollohan*, where the Court somehow managed to *both* acknowledge political reality and ignore it within the same judgment, and *both times* in service of the centralizing drift. The Court acknowledged the reality of large-scale, unprincipled political defections in justifying the anti-defection law, but ignored the structural non-neutrality of the speaker while repelling the challenge to the provision authorizing the speaker to adjudicate disqualification petitions.

Examples abound, from the cases that we have discussed. The Court chose to ignore how an executive-controlled appointments process would compromise the independence of the Election Commission (ironically, the Court was *extremely* alive to this possibility when choosing to insulate *itself* from executive control in the *Judges Appointments Cases*). The Court acknowledged the political reality of 1980s Punjab in justifying the need for a special anti-terrorism law in *Kartar Singh*, but ignored the workings of criminal law and its impact on liberty when it came to the twin test (here, the Court used a very old get-out-of-jail card that it always uses when it wishes to avoid inconvenient reality—it said that the potential *abuse* of a law was no ground to impugn its *constitutionality*). The Court also ignored the workings of criminal law and its impact on liberty in *Re: Article 370*, where the reality of mass detentions and crackdowns on civil liberties did not even register on its radar while interpreting a provision that was fundamentally about the *consent* of two parties to a constitutional relationship.

While the Court's inconsistency in choosing to acknowledge or ignore political reality is one thing, at the same time, the Court has been *very* consistent in evading questions of power in its interpretation of the Constitution. There are a few standard techniques that the Court uses to accomplish this, as we have seen. Sometimes, the Court treats the problem as being one of *individual* bad actors occupying constitutional offices, and expresses either a hope or a belief that these actors will comport themselves in accordance with the spirit of what the Constitution demands.[35] We have seen this in the Court's approach towards the independence of fourth-branch institutions, the speaker and the governor, and so on. On other occasions, the Court invokes formalism to mask the underlying questions of power. We have seen this most starkly in how it has excluded individuals from the protective shield of Article 20 through various acts of definitional fiat (are you an 'accused' or not?). On still other occasions, the Court treats the Constitution as a neutral field, ignoring the fact that an existing asymmetry of power will be reinforced and entrenched by how it interprets the constitutional text. We have seen this in various issues around federalism and constitutional pluralism.

Throughout its history, thus, the Supreme Court has frequently shut its eyes to how power works in and through the constitutional text and structure, and it has refused to acknowledge how its interpretation of constitutional provisions is bound up with the question of power. One of the tasks of this book has been to strip away that veneer of neutrality from the Court's judgments, and to show how the Court is, at the end of the day, a *participant* in constitutional battles over power, and not merely a detached arbiter. And as a participant the Court has, far too often, been partisan towards the centralizing drift.

With that, we come to our final theme, the Frankenconstitution.

The centralizing drift—to use a term familiar to Indian constitutionalism—does not exist in silos. Centralization around one axis of power bleeds into other axes, and affects the shape and structure of Austin's 'constitutional web'. To illustrate how, let us return to the case of the 'toppling' of the Maharashtra state government in 2022, which we discussed in Chapter 2 of this book. I discuss this case not by way of passing judgment on the political forces involved, but because it presents an excellent example of the Constitution's centralizing drift across multiple axes underlying what appeared to be a major political upheaval.

The beginnings of the 'Maharashtra political crisis' lay in an internal rebellion and effective split within one of the parties of the ruling coalition. There is now more than enough correlational evidence to show that defections and splits are frequently engineered under threat of prosecution and imprisonment, especially under the Prevention of Money Laundering Act.[36] This immediately implicates two of the six axes of power discussed in this book. The non-independence of investigation authorities (who are *meant* to be independent fourth-branch institutions), and their effective control by the executive, renders such threats credible when they are made at the instance of whichever is the ruling force at the Centre. And the existence of the 'twin test'—upheld and given teeth by the Court—ensures that a credible threat of prosecution is accompanied by a credible threat of lengthy incarceration without bail.[37] Brought together, these two factors create a very powerful incentive to 'defect'; an incentive that would be substantially weakened if fourth-branch institutions were independent, and/or if prosecution under laws such as the PMLA did not result in an immediate and indefinite period of incarceration.

Once the 'rebellion' had commenced in Maharashtra, events moved to the Legislative Assembly, where two partisan authorities, the governor and the speaker, came to play crucial roles, in succession. We have met the governor when discussing the federal axis, and we have met the speaker when discussing the parliamentary axis. The governor's order of a floor test (upheld by the Supreme Court) led to the fall of the government, and the new speaker (appointed by the new government) was able to simply avoid deciding pending disqualification petitions (notwithstanding some rather gentle prompting by the Court), until the issue was effectively infructuous. Meanwhile, there were parallel proceedings before the Election Commission—another fourth-branch institution—on which was the 'real' political party entitled to the party symbol and the name. The decision (perhaps unsurprisingly) came in favour of the initiators of the party split.

We can therefore see how the entire 'Maharashtra political crisis' was underlaid by four axes of power: federalism, parliamentarianism, fourth-branch institutions and rights. The centralizing drift within each axis reinforced the others, and their combined effect was to bring about a 'toppling' of the government to the benefit of the ruling political force at the Centre. As a corollary, we can also see how the centralizing drift in constitutional interpretation directly contributes to centralizing *politics*, where the ruling force at the Centre is given the tools to entrench and perpetuate its power, at the cost of other institutions and political forces. Needless to say, this fundamental *interlinkage* between different axes of power was ignored by the Court when it considered—and ruled on—the constitutional dispute that arose out of all these actions.

The Kashmir case saw a similar reinforcement of multiple axes of power. The constitutional alterations to Article 370 were made possible because the relevant fourth-branch institution (the Election Commission) had simply refused to hold elections after the fall of the previous coalition government, thus leading to the absence of the state Legislative Assembly, and its replacement by the centrally appointed governor. The tools used to bring about this change were Article 356 and Article 3, which implicate the heart of the federal scheme. These tools were further enabled by a history of judicial interpretation that had subordinated the asymmetric federal relationship between Jammu and Kashmir and the Union to the prevailing balance of political forces (rather than strengthening constitutional autonomy). And this was done in a climate of a mass curtailment of civil liberties, which denied the people an effective voice, as well as violating core rights to life and personal liberty. All six axes of power thus came together to enable what was very evidently an abuse of Union power. Once again, these interlinkages escaped the attention of the Court when it decided to uphold the effective abrogation of Article 370. And so, one wonders what a constitutional jurisprudence would look like where the Court would be keenly aware of how its decision with respect to one axis of power would reverberate throughout the strands of the constitutional web—and would factor those reverberations into its decisions.

Examples could be multiplied, but through these two instances, it should be clear that the Constitution's centralizing drift operates through specific axes of power, but in doing so, it shapes the Constitution *as a whole*. It is therefore important not simply to study our inflection-point judgments as contributing to the centralizing drift in one domain, but to understand how judgments—across seemingly disparate and unconnected constitutional provisions—nonetheless relate to each other the construction of a *centralizing Constitution*. That has been the task of this section, and the larger task of this book.

III. Untidy Endnotes

> 'Indeed, if I may say so, if things go wrong under the new Constitution, the reason will not be that we had a bad Constitution. What we will have to say is, that Man was vile.'[38]
>
> —Dr B.R. Ambedkar

On 4 November 1948, B.R. Ambedkar introduced the Draft Constitution to the Constituent Assembly, and finished his speech with these ringing words. He was to reprise this theme a little over a year later in his last speech to the Constituent Assembly, a speech most famous for his observations on the 'grammar of anarchy'. Ambedkar had said:

> However *good* a *Constitution* may be, it is sure to turn out *bad* because those who are called to work it, happen to be a *bad* lot. However, bad a Constitution may be, it may turn out to be good if those who are called to work it, happen to be a good lot. The working of a Constitution does not depend wholly upon the nature of the Constitution.[39]

These oft-quoted passages have become something of an article of faith for Indian constitutionalists, and for understandable reasons. This book is an attempt to question that faith, and to reconsider the easy dichotomy between a 'good' Constitution and the 'bad' people who have administered it from time to time. Just as human beings make their own history, but not under circumstances chosen by themselves, thus people act for good or for ill, but their actions are shaped and constrained by institutions, structures and encrusted patterns of thought and belief.[40] So it is with constitutions.

This is not to say that human agency does not matter. It matters. Nor are constitutions self-administering. They need human beings to administer them. But constitutional design is not a neutral field, within which people act as they may. Human action is shaped by constitutional structure and by the architecture of constitutional institutions.

And so, is it too much of a surprise that a centralizing constitution has often thrown up centralizing executives, who have been entirely comfortable working with and through the document to achieve their goals? Is it all that surprising that judges have interpreted the Constitution to accelerate and entrench a latent centralizing drift, rather than take the more difficult route of counteracting it? Of course, these judges have had a choice, and a part of the project of this book has been to demonstrate that these choices have always existed, that alternate non-centralizing visions of power have always been *possible*. But these choices—to repeat the point—are not made in a neutral field. Constitutional history, constitutional text and design, and constitutional common sense all come together to make one set of interpretive choices seem more *plausible* than others, at a given time. And that has been the story of the Indian Constitution and its centralizing drift over the last seventy-five years.

Thus, to those for whom this centralizing vision of power is an unpalatable one, it is not sufficient to critique bad judgments and judges (and struggle for better ones), or to critique bad politicians and administrators (and struggle for better ones). The critique must begin with a conversation about the *Constitution*, about the historical choices that were made before and at the time of its framing, about its language and its architecture, and above all, about its 'power map'. And it is a conversation that must not be 'afraid of the results it arrives at and ... just as little afraid of conflict with the powers that be'.[41]

This book is offered up as an initiation of that conversation. If it can serve as a starting point or a signpost, then its goal will have been accomplished.

Acknowledgements

I AM THANKFUL TO the editorial and administrative staff at HarperCollins India for their work on this manuscript; in particular, to Udayan Mitra and Amrita Mukerji for their editorial work, Sashi Aiyer for copy edits, and Veer Misra for the cover design.

The ideas underlying this book germinated and took shape during a post-doctoral fellowship at the SCRIPTS Centre in Berlin in 2021–22. I'm grateful to Philipp Dann for bringing me to Berlin and giving me an obligation-free year to simply think and write about the Indian Constitution.

Various parts of this book have been informally 'workshopped' at various places. My thanks to Philipp Dann's research group at Humboldt University; Sandy Fredman's research group at the University of Oxford; Adrienne Stone, Cheryl Saunders and everyone at the Centre for Comparative Constitutional Studies at Melbourne University; Rosalind Dixon's comparative constitutional law seminar at the University of New South Wales; Balveer Arora's Planning Group on Federal Democracy; and students in my elective seminar courses at the National Law School of India University and the Jindal Global Law School. The feedback was involved, and disagreements sometimes sharp, but always constructive. This book is the better for these engagements.

As with my previous work, a large part of this book was smelted, tempered, and refined in the furnaces of the Bar. I was involved with some of the cases discussed in the chapters that follow, and a ringside spectator for others. You truly begin to understand how power works through the Constitution when you experience it play out before you, in the urgency of the draft due tomorrow and the written submissions due yesterday, in grappling with constitutional text and design with material consequences at stake, and in the many losses and failures that accompany attempts to contest State power upon the terrain of the Constitution. My thanks, in particular, to comrades at the Bars—too many to name—and fellow travellers on that often frustrating, sometimes seemingly futile, but occasionally exhilarating journey. It has been difficult at times, but never lonely.

And, as always, my gratitude to the many scholars, past and present, whom this book is in conversation with and against, and whose presence fills the notes.

Notes

Prologue: A Question of Power

1. Four and a half years later, on the eve of the next general election, the Supreme Court would uphold the constitutionality of these moves. See infra, Chapter 3.
2. Mark Tushnet, 'Constitutional Hardball' (2004) 37 *J. Marshall L. Rev.* 523.
3. Bodyline bowling is a term in cricket, referring to a tactic where the bowler aims a fast short-pitched ball into the body of the batter. When it was first used by the English cricket team in its 1932–33 tour of Australia, bodyline bowling was considered to be at the edges of legality, and in the grey area between the 'laws of the game' and conventions of sporting behaviour.
4. As more than one commentator has noticed, many of the weapons perfected by the executive in 2019–24 were initially forged in the 1970s.
5. It is also arguable that the frequent resort to constitutional amendments in order to get over inconvenient court judgments under India's first post-Independence government—that of Prime Minister Nehru—was its own form of constitutional bodyline-bowling.

6. Stronger versions of this approach might even see the phenomenon as one of constitutional subversion: that is, the use of formal constitutional methods to undermine constitutionalism itself. See, e.g., Tarunabh Khaitan, 'Killing a Constitution with a Thousand Cuts: Executive Aggrandisement and Party-State Fusion in India' (2020) 14(1) *Law and Ethics of Human Rights* 49.
7. The metaphor of the 'web' is not new to Indian constitutional studies. Granville Austin famously called the Constitution a 'seamless web', whose three strands were strong democratic institutions, social revolution, and national unity and integrity. See Granville Austin, *Working a Democratic Constitution: A History of the Indian Experience* (Oxford University Press, 2003). As will become obvious in the course of this book, I do not subscribe to Austin's hagiographic story of the Indian Constitution.
8. This is not to say, of course, that studies of this period for its own sake are not valuable; that is just not the project of this book.
9. Ivo D. Duchacek, *Power Maps: The Comparative Politics of Constitutions* (Oxford University Press, 1973).
10. Gunther Frankenberg, *Comparative Constitutional Studies: Between Magic and Deceit*, (Edward Elgar, 2018), [ix].
11. For a summary of this critique, see 'Introduction' in Gautam Bhatia, *The Transformative Constitution* (HarperCollins India, 2019), .
12. See, e.g., Parliament of India, *Constituent Assembly Debates,* Vol. XI (21 November 1949) (speech of Mahboob Ali Baig Sahib), available at http://164.100.47.194/Loksabha/Debates/cadebatefiles/C21111949.html; Parliament of India, *Constituent Assembly Debates,* Vol. XI (22 November 1949) (speech of Dr P.S. Deshmukh), available at http://164.100.47.194/Loksabha/Debates/cadebatefiles/C22111949.html.
13. Most notably, *State of Gujarat vs Vora Fiddali Badruddin Mithibarwala* 1964 6 SCR 461; *M.P. Sharma vs Satish Chandra*, 1954 SCR 1077
14. Sandipto Dasgupta, '"A Language Which is Foreign to Us": Continuities and Anxieties in the Making of the Indian Constitution' (2014) 34(2) *Comparative Studies of South Asia, Africa and the Middle East* 228.
15. In many ways, this story owes its origins to Granville Austin's accounts of the Indian Constitution. See: Granville Austin, *The Indian Constitution: Cornerstone of a Nation,* (Clarendon Press, 1966); Granville Austin, *Working a Democratic Constitution: A History of the Indian Experience* (Oxford University Press, 1999). It would perhaps not be too much of

an exaggeration to say that Austin's initial work set the frame for future discussions about the Indian Constitution. As I have noted above, this book takes issue with Austin's heroic ode to the Constitution and seeks to break away from that way of thinking about the document. For a previous critique, see Upendra Baxi, 'Saint Granville's Gospel: Reflections' (2001) 36(11) *Economic and Political Weekly*, 921.

16. See, e.g., Upendra Baxi, 'Taking Suffering Seriously: Social Action Litigation in the Supreme Court of India' (1983) 4(6) *Third World Legal Studies* 107.
17. Ujjwal Kumar Singh, *The State, Democracy, and Anti-Terror Laws in India* (Sage Publications, 2007).
18. See e.g. Anuj Bhuwania, *Courting the People: Public Interest Litigation in Post-Emergency India* (Cambridge University Press, 2016).
19. A point advanced perhaps most eloquently by K.G. Kannabiran. K.G. Kannabiran, *The Wages of Impunity: Power, Justice, and Human Rights* (Orient Blackswan, 2004).
20. See, e.g., the discussion of transformative jurisprudence as a 'contrapuntal canon' in Gautam Bhatia, *The Transformative Constitution*, supra.
21. See the discussion in Aditya Nigam, 'A Text Without an Author: Locating Constituent Assembly as Event' (2004) 39(21) *Economic and Political Weekly* (2004) 2107.
22. Part IV, Constitution of India.
23. See, e.g., Ranojoy Sen, 'Life of a Nation's Text: The Travels and Travails of the Indian Constitution' (2021) 94(4) *Pacific Affairs* 707.
24. Granville Austin, *The Indian Constitution: Cornerstone of a Nation*, supra.
25. See Sandipto Dasgupta, *Legalizing the Revolution: India and the Constitution of the Posctolony* (Cambridge University Press, 2024) 205, for an identification—and critique—of exactly this phenomenon. In *A.K. Gopalan vs State of Madras*, [1950] S.C.R. 88—the very first case on Fundamental Rights that was heard by the Supreme Court—the Court enthused about the unique changes brought in by the new Constitution through the Preamble and the Fundamental Rights chapter. As Justice Mahajan noted, the declaration in the Preamble 'makes our Constitution sublime and it is the guarantees mentioned in the chapter on Fundamental Rights that make it one of the greatest charters of liberty and of which the people of this country may well be proud'. We shall study *A.K. Gopalan* in greater detail in Chapter 5.

26. See also the categorization in The Bar Council of India, 'Rules of Legal Education,' available at http://www.barcouncilofindia.org/wp-content/uploads/2010/05/BCIRulesPartIV.pdf
27. Sujit Chaudhry, Madhav Khosla and Pratap Bhanu Mehta (eds), *The Oxford Handbook of the Indian Constitution* (Oxford University Press, 2016).
28. I return to this idea in (**II**).
29. Roberto Gargarella, *Latin American Constitutionalism 1810–2010: The Engine Room of the Constitution* (Oxford University Press, 2013) 135.
30. Ibid., viii.
31. Ibid., 106–07.
32. Uday Mehta, 'Indian Constitutionalism: Crisis, Unity, History' in *The Oxford Handbook of the Indian Constitution*, supra 38, 54.
33. Ibid. See also Sandipto Dasgupta, *Legalizing the Revolution*: India and the Constitution of the Postcolony (Cambridge University Press, 2024) 10.
34. See Madhav Khosla, (*India's Founding Moment: The Constitution of a Most Surprising Democracy* (Harvard University Press, 2020).
35. Louise Tillin, 'Building a National Economy: Origins of Centralised Federalism in India' (2021) 51(2) *Publius: The Journal of Federalism*, 161.
36. Vatsal Naresh, 'Pride and Prejudice in Austin's Cornerstone: Passions in the Constituent Assembly of India' in Udit Bhatia (ed.) *The Indian Constituent Assembly: Deliberations on Democracy* (Routledge, 2018) 58, 74.
37. Article 1, Constitution of India 1949.
38. See the discussion in Gunther Frankenberg, *Comparative Constitutional Studies*, supra.
39. Article 22, Constitution of India.
40. Preamble, Constitution of India 1949.
41. See e.g., Article 257, Constitution of Kenya 2010.
42. Article 10, Constitution of Kenya 2010.
43. Article II, Constitution of California 1879.
44. Nirvikar Singh, 'Fiscal Federalism' in *The Oxford Handbook of the Indian Constitution*, supra 521.
45. The original Constitution, of course, vested in the President the power to appoint constitutional court judges, until, in the 1990s, the Supreme Court took this power for itself in a controversial act of interpretive fiat.

46. See, e.g., Philipp Dann, 'Choices and Contexts in India's Constitutional Founding' (2022) 4(25) *Jus Cogens*, 25.
47. Roberto Gargarella, *Latin American Constitutionalism*, supra.
48. Madhav Khosla, *India's Founding Moment*, supra.
49. For the most recent iteration, see Arghya Sengupta, *The Colonial Constitution* (Juggernaut, 2023).
50. Kim Lane Scheppele, 'The Rule of Law and the Frankenstate: Why Governance Checklists Do Not Work' (2013) 26(4) *Governance: An International Journal of Policy, Administration, and Institutions*, 559.
51. See, e.g., Tanja Herklotz, 'Legal Cultures' in *The Max Planck Encyclopaedia of Comparative Constitutional Law*, (Oxford University Press, 2023) 1; Pierre Legrand, 'Comparative Legal Studies and the Matter of Authenticity' (2006) *Journal of Comparative Law* 365; Reva Siegel, 'Constitutional Culture, Social Movement Conflict and Constitutional Change: The Case of the De Facto Era' (2006) 94(5) *California Law Review* 1323; Andre Siegal, ' Constitutional Theory, Constitutional Culture' (2016) 18(4) *Journal of Constitutional Law*, 1067.
52. Cheryl Saunders, 'Constitutional Cultures' in Tom Gerald Daly and Dinesha Samararatne (eds), *Democratic Consolidation and Constitutional Endurance in Asia and Africa* (Oxford University Press, 2024) 158, 174.
53. Or, in the words of David Kenny: '... a set of suppositions about what [the Constitution] means, what it does, what it allows, what it prohibits—that actually animates its institutions, drives its development, resolves case.' David Kenny, '"It's Just the Vibe of the Thing": Mapping the Role of Culture in Comparative Constitutional Law' Paper No. 18/2023, *Trinity College School of Law Legal Studies Research Paper Series*, available at https://www.tcd.ie/law/researchpapers/David.Kenny-It's_just_the_vibe_of_the_thing.pdf 2.
54. See also Oran Doyle, 'Conventional Constitutional Law' (2015) 38(2) *Dublin University Law Journal* 311. While Doyle's conceptualisation of conventional constitutional law is similar to what I call 'constitutional common sense', Doyle limits his discussion primarily to judges. For another account focusing on the role of constitutional culture in the use of comparative law by judges, see Dennis M. Davis, 'Constitutional Borrowing: The Influence of Legal Culture and Local History in the Reconstruction of Comparative Influence' (2003) 1(2) *International Journal of Constitutional Law* 181. See also the definition of 'judicial culture' as 'a crucial subset of the legal and political culture within the

judicial branch will set the limits of judging, the level of openness to new ideas and influences, and a great deal more that will shape the constitutional law that the judiciary makes'. Kenny, '"It's Just the Vibe of the Thing"', supra, 26.

55. As Saunders perceptively notes—and as we shall repeatedly see in the course of this book—assumptions about national history often play a pivotal role in constituting this 'constitutional imaginary'. See Saunders, 'Constitutional Culture', supra, 174.
56. I borrow the term from Albert M. Kales, '"Due Process," the Inarticulate Major Premise and the Adamson Act' (1917) 26(7) *Yale Law Journal* 519.
57. I experienced this first-hand during the proceedings in 'the Article 370 case' (discussed in Chapters 1 and 3 of this book), in particular, on the question of the relationship between the constitution of the state of Jammu and Kashmir and the Constitution of India. The constitutional imaginary—or the constitutional 'common sense' that the judges of the Court subscribed to make it impossible—to frame this relationship in any other terms than the subordination of the former to the latter, thus hamstringing the range of arguments open to the petitioners. Of course, none of these 'upstream considerations' appear in the final judgment of the Supreme Court; they can, however, be momentarily glimpsed through a close observation of the archive of oral arguments.
58. As the example in the previous endnote shows, the practitioner's standpoint can help illumine aspects of constitutional 'common sense' that are more prominent upstream, and therefore do not always make it to the final judicial opinion. The promises and perils of the practitioner's standpoint are summed up by Doyle, with whom I find myself to be in complete agreement:

> Specifically, I approach these issues as someone who has been an insider in Irish constitutional law, partly as an academic commentator but more relevantly as a barrister preparing and sometimes arguing constitutional cases before the Irish superior courts. A practitioner learns (whether through bitter experience or the instruction of those more senior, i.e., more internal to the practice) which arguments will work and which will not. Court advocacy involves marshalling the posited rules and constitutional

> common law in support of conclusions that are beneficial to one's client while feeling right to judges. This experiential knowledge precludes me from adopting a wholly detached perspective on Irish judicial decision making – I am fated to understand the practice partly through my own experience of it. See Doyle, 'Conventional Constitutional Law', supra, 327.

See also David Kenny, '"It's just the vibe of the thing"', supra, who discusses this as an instance of 'constitutional ethnography'.

59. Social action and social movements also shape our understanding of the Constitution, and often bear upon both political action and judicial interpretation. The focus of this book upon the courtroom should not be taken as devaluing the shaping of the Constitution *outside* of the court.

1: Power Decentralized: Federalism

1. Interestingly, Kerala's suit came soon after the German Federal Constitutional Court handed down a hugely controversial ruling striking down a significant portion of the German government's funding plan for dealing with climate change and clean energy, on the basis that it violated the German Basic Law's 'debt brake' provision (something quite similar to the net borrowing ceiling). While the German case did not involve a federal element, as it does here, the constitutionalization of this particular political economy debate is evidently not unique to India.
2. As with many provisions of the Constitution, Article 293—complete with its skew towards central power—mirrored a provision of the 1935 Government of India Act: in this case, Section 163.
3. For a copy of the Original Suit, see *State of Kerala vs Union of India*, Original Suit No. 1 of 2024, available at https://www.scobserver.in/wp-content/uploads/2024/04/Kerala-Original-Suit-Petition_compressed.pdf
4. *State of Kerala vs Union of India*, (2024) INSC 253, para 6.
5. Ibid., para 9.
6. At the time of writing, the case has not yet been decided.
7. Ibid., para 31.
8. Ibid., para 32.

9. Of course, its 'prima facie' determination had very real and tangible economic impact on the state of Kerala. An impact that, given the glacial pace at which the Indian Supreme Court decides disputes, can go on for a long time. At the time of writing, the issue had not yet been adjudicated.
10. Article 1, Constitution of India.
11. See, e.g. Nirvikar Singh and Govinda Rao, *The Political Economy of Federalism in India* (Oxford University Press, 2005).
12. As we shall see, it is this centralizing reading that formed the unarticulated premise of the Supreme Court's interim order in *State of Kerala vs Union of India.*
13. For a detailed analysis of the interplay between constitutional federalism and political federalism through the course of independent India's history, see R. Mohan, *India's Federal Setup: A Journey through Seven Decades* (Aakar, 2023). For an early, briefer examination of the same topic, see C.H. Alexandrowicz, 'Is India a Federation' (1954) 3(3) *International and Comparative Law Quarterly* 393.
14. Part IX, Constitution of India. For a discussion, see, e.g., K.C. Sivaramakrishnan, 'Local Government' in Choudhry et al. (eds), *The Oxford Handbook of the Indian Constitution* (Oxford University Press, 2016) 560. See also: Malavika Prasad, 'Decentralization and the Third Tier of Governance' in *The Cambridge Handbook of the Indian Constitution* (forthcoming), for a detailed account of the mechanics of how local government is constitutionalized under the broad control of the state legislature. Prasad makes a strong argument that notwithstanding the text of Part IX, the powers of the state legislature should be constrained in accordance with the principles of democratic self-governance that underlie Part IX, and that the principle of 'interdependence' should be deployed to structure the relationship between the second and third tier. This is, essentially, an argument of implied limitations. As we shall see, however, courts have been reluctant to accept arguments from constitutional structure and design as limiting power in the absence of any express proscriptions. This is borne out by some of the judgments that Prasad cites in her article. We do not have the space to go into the third tier in detail in this chapter, but interested readers may see Prasad, 'Decentralisation and the Third Tier of Governance', ibid.

15. For an examination of the federal structure under the Government of India Act of 1935, see Frederick Whyte, *India, A Federation?* (Leopold Classic Library, 2016). The antecedents of this model go further back in the history of British colonial constitutionalism, in particular to the Constitution Act of 1867, which created the federal dominion of Canada.
16. A significant shift in this arrangement was achieved through the 101st Constitutional Amendment, which introduced the General Sales Tax (GST). A detailed discussion of the GST is beyond the scope of this chapter, but at present it is the source of significant conflict between the Union and the states, on issues of collection and distribution of sales tax revenue.
17. Albeit not without a degree of ambiguity. See the discussion in Singh and Rao, *The Political Economy of Federalism in India*, supra, on the bureaucracy.
18. Singh and Rao thus observe that when it comes to finances—as in the sphere of administration and politics—the Constitution has a 'centripetal bias'. Singh and Rao, *The Political Economy of Federalism in India*, supra.
19. For a summary, see—for example—Mohit Bhattacharya, 'The Minds of the Founding Fathers' in *Federalism in India: Origins and Development* (Vikas Publishing, 1992) 87.
20. See, e.g., Asok Chanda, *Federalism in India* (George Allen & Unwin, 1965).
21. Singh and Rao, *The Political Economy of Federalism in India*, supra. In his analysis of the Government of India Act 1935, Ambedkar had openly confessed his 'partiality for unitary government'. See: B.R. Ambedkar, *Federation Versus Freedom* (Gokhale Institute of Politics and Economics, 1939) 156.
22. 'Second Report' of the Union Powers Committee, Constituent Assembly, in B. Shiva Rao, *The Framing of India's Constitution: Select Documents,* Volume 2 (Universal Publishing, 1967) 776. See below for a more detailed account of the Cabinet Mission Plan.
23. See Louise Tillin, 'Building a National Economy: Origins of Centralised Federalism in India' (2021) 51(2) *The Journal of Federalism* 161. This rationale was strongly echoed by the Supreme Court in its first significant decision concerning inter-state trade and commerce.

In *Atiabari Tea Co. Ltd. vs State of Assam*, (1961) 1 SCR 809, the majority opinion repeatedly stated that the need for *economic unity* within a federal structure was the guiding principle for interpreting the Constitution's chapter on inter-state trade and commerce. See also *Automobile Transport (Rajasthan) Ltd. vs State of Rajasthan*, (1963) 1 SCR 491.

24. Madhav Khosla, *India's Founding Moment: The Constitution of a Most Surprising Democracy* (Harvard University Press, 2020). For a detailed account of the framers' preference for centralisation as a necessary requirement for overcoming entrenched, localized power structures, see Sandipto Dasgupta, *Legalizing the Revolution: India and the Constitution of the Postcolony* (Cambridge University Press, 2024) 86–90 and 99–103. The possibility of decentralization leading to the dominance of local elites and private interests (including corporate interests) has long been a concern in political theory. For a classical treatment, see e.g. Grant McConnell, *Private Power and American Democracy* (Alfred A. Knopf, 1966). For a discussion of how this took the language of constitutionalism—specifically, 'regional autonomy' in one specific country (Bolivia), see, e.g., Ximena Soruco Sologuren, 'El Porvenir, the Future That Is No Longer Possible: Conquest and Autonomy in the Bolivian Oriente' in Nicole Fabricant and Bret Gustafson (eds), *Remapping Bolivia: Resources, Territory, and Indigeneity in a Plurinational State*, (SAR Press 2011) 68.
25. Uday Mehta, 'Indian Constitutionalism: Articulation of a Political Vision' in Chakrabarti, Majumdar and Sartori (eds), supra.
26. On the terminology of 'quasi-federation', which has gained substantial currency, see: K.C. Wheare, *Federal Government* (Oxford University Press, 1951), and the critique in C.H. Alexandrowicz, 'Is India a Federation?' (1954) 3(3) *International and Comparative Law Quarterly* 393.
27. For a broad agreement with *State of West Bengal vs Union of India* being one of the inflection points in the sense discussed here, see also Singh and Rao, *The Political Economy of Federalism in India*, supra.
28. Schedule VII, Constitution of India.
29. Entry 42, List III, Schedule VII, Constitution of India.
30. *State of West Bengal vs Union of India* (1964) SCR (1) 371, para 23.
31. Ibid., para 24.

32. Ibid., para 25.
33. Ibid.
34. Ibid.
35. Ibid., para 36 (regarding the Court finding no 'positive interdict')
36. Ibid., para 46.
37. *Babulal Parate vs State of Bombay*, (1960) SCR (1) 605; see also *Pradeep Chaudhary vs Union of India* (2009) 12 SCC 248, where this view was reaffirmed.
38. Ibid.
39. Ibid.
40. Its starkest articulation is perhaps in *State of Rajasthan vs Union of India*, (1978) SCR 1. For another example, see *Kuldip Nayyar vs Union of India*, AIR (2006) SC 3127, holding that representatives to the Council of States (the 'Upper House') need not be domiciled in the state that they purport to represent.
41. Perhaps a many-volumed one.
42. *Mullaperiyar Environmental Protection Forum vs Union of India*, (2006) 3 SCC 643.
43. Section 108, States Reorganisation Act, 1956.
44. Article 4(1), Constitution of India.
45. Article 4(2), Constitution of India.
46. *Mullaperiyar Environmental Protection Forum vs Union of India*, para 21. Subsequently, the attempt of the Kerala legislature to assert its legislative competence by passing a law prohibiting the raising of the water level on safety grounds was struck down by the Supreme Court in *State of Tamil Nadu vs State of Kerala*, (2014) 12 SCC 810.
47. This is, indeed, somewhat ironic, as many years before—in *Mangal Singh vs Union of India*, (1967) SCR (2) 109, which had concerned the creation of the states of Punjab and Haryana—the Supreme Court had insisted that the power under Article 4 could not be used to 'override the constitutional scheme', and had rubbished fears that Article 4 could be invoked to justify the creation of a state without effective legislative, executive or judicial organs. Four decades later, however, when the situation did involve depriving a state of legislative power (albeit not its legislative organ), the Supreme Court suggested that the power under Article 4 was, after all, 'paramount' and 'unfettered'. The contradiction remains unresolved.

48. *Naga People's Movement of Human Rights vs Union of India* (1998) (2) SCC 109.
49. Interestingly, many decades before, Ambedkar had recognized the links between federalism and civil rights. In his analysis of the federal scheme of the 1935 Government of India Act, he noted how the criminal law fields in the legislative lists were vital subjects, as they 'affect the liberties of the people in the provinces'. Ambedkar, *Federation Versus Freedom* (1989) 84.
50. *Naga People's Movement of Human Rights vs Union of India*, paragraph 24.
51. Ibid., paragraph 25.
52. This might not have mattered in any event, as the Court also had a back-up argument: that even if Entry 2A didn't exist, competence could be traced back to the Union's residuary law-making competence, set out under Entry 97 of List I. Ibid., paragraph 24.
53. Ibid., paragraph 26.
54. See, e.g., S.G. Vombatkere, 'AFSPA: Criminal Misuse for Decades', *Frontline,* 29 September 2021, available at https://frontline.thehindu.com/the-nation/human-rights/afspa-criminal-misuse-of-law-for-decades/article36542410.ece
55. *I.T.C. Ltd. vs The Agricultural Produce Market Committee* (2002) 9 SCC 232.
56. Entry 52, List I, Schedule VII, Constitution of India.
57. Entries 26–28, List II, Schedule VII, Constitution of India.
58. *I.T.C. Ltd. vs The Agricultural Produce Market Committee*, supra. For the prior development of these doctrines in the early years of the Supreme Court, see the landmark judgments of *Tika Ramji vs State of Uttar Pradesh*, (1956) SCR 393 and *Hingir-Rampur Coal Co. vs State of Orissa*, (1961) SCR (2) 537.
59. Ibid. This doctrine—like many others—was borrowed from colonial constitutional jurisprudence around the interpretation of the 1935 Government of India Act. See, e.g., *United Provinces vs Atiqa Begum* (1940) 2 FRC 110. The Court appeared not to notice that, or if it noticed chose not to deem important, the fact that the partial federal structures under the Government of India Act of 1935, where the will of the Imperial Viceroy remained overriding, might not map out very cleanly on the Constitution of India.
60. Ibid.

61. Ibid.
62. The problem highlighted in this section was compounded in *Hoechst Pharmaceuticals vs State of Bihar*, (1983) 4 SCC 45, where the Court appeared to hold that the principle of 'federal supremacy' in legislative relations meant not only that Union law would prevail over state law in case of conflict, but also that if there was an irreconcilable conflict between the *entries* in List I and II, Parliament's exercise of power would prevail over that of the states. But there is no warrant within the constitutional text for holding that a List I entry would prevail over a List II entry in case of a conflict: the entries in the Lists only set out *fields* of legislation, and not powers. This reading was most recently referred to (albeit without much discussion) by the Supreme Court in *Mineral Area Development Authority vs M/S Steel Authority of India* (2024) INSC 554.
63. On the other hand, the Court's interpretation of the *taxing* entries has been more protective of state power. As early as *M.P.V. Sundararamier vs State of Andhra Pradesh* (1958) SCR 1422, the Court held, first, that a general legislative field could not be invoked to justify taxing competence; and secondly, that the taxing entries in Lists I and II had no overlap. This interpretation, most recently affirmed in *Mineral Area Development Authority*, ibid., has acted to prevent a creeping assumption of taxation powers by the Union, through using broad, legislative fields in List I (or, for that matter, its residuary powers).
64. For a judicial attempt to temper the centralizing drift of the GST—something of an outlier in the cases that we have discussed—see *Union of India vs Mohit Minerals* (2022) 10 SCC 700.
65. For a history of the pushes and pulls regarding decentralisation of public finance during the colonial period, see B.R. Ambedkar, 'The Evolution of Provincial Finance in British India: A Study in the Provincial Decentralisation of Imperial Finance' (1925) in *Dr. Babasaheb Ambedkar: Writings and Speeches* Vol. 6 (Vasant Moon [ed.], (3rd edition, Dr. Ambedkar Foundation, 2020); available at https://www.mea.gov.in/Images/CPV/Volume6.pdf
66. See, e.g. Attiya Warris, 'Kenya's Fiscal Accountability Revisited: A Review of the Historical Erosion of the Country's Fiscal Constitution from 1962 to 2010' in Morris Kiwinda Mbondenyi et al. (eds), *Human Rights and Democratic Governance in Kenya: A post-2007 Appraisa*l (Pretoria University Law Press, 2015) 301.

67. Article 280, Constitution of India.
68. See the discussion in Rao & Singh, *The Political Economy of Federalism in India*, supra. The discussion here is relevant to another axis of power—that of 'Fourth Branch' institutions. See Chapter 4 of this book.
69. Ibid.
70. *Bhim Singh vs Union of India*, (2010) 5 SCC 538.
71. Ibid.
72. Article 282, Constitution of India.
73. The judgment in *Bhim Singh vs Union of India* is in striking contrast to the judgment of the Supreme Court of Kenya in *The Institute for Social Accountability and Anr vs The National Assembly and Ors*, Petition No. 1 of 2018, popularly known as the 'CDF Case'. The case involved a constitutional challenge to the Constituency Development Fund, which was extremely similar, in all material respects, to the MPLADS fund. Despite the fact that the Kenyan Constitution is not federal, but has a weaker system of *devolution* of power to county governments, the Kenyan Supreme Court nonetheless took the implications for the division of powers very seriously, and struck down the CDF. This demonstrates a point that we have made in this book: the constitutional text impacts, but does not exhaust, the terrain of constitutional interpretation; and a *formally* weaker decentralized system can nonetheless see stronger *protection* of decentralisation of power, depending on the history, constitutional culture, and the Court's approach. For an analysis of the CDF Case (and a more detailed comparison with *Bhim Singh*), see Chapter 3 in Gautam Bhatia, *Law-Making, Political Process, and the State: Transformative Constitutionalism and Kenya 2010–2025* (James Currey, forthcoming), Chapter 3.
74. Ibid.
75. Ibid.
76. Here, for example, one sees the linkages between constitutional interpretation and the direction of political power.
77. Katharine Adeney, *Federalism and Ethnic Conflict Regulation in India and Pakistan* (Palgrave, 2007).
78. Lloyd I. Rudolph and Susanne Hoeber Rudolph, 'Federalism as State Formation in India: A Theory of Shared and Negotiated Sovereignty' (2010) 31(5) *International Political Science Review*): 553, 559.

79. Ibid., p. 560. In fact, Frederick Whyte—in a book analysing the history of Indian federalism up until the Government of India Act of 1935—specifically cited the evolution of the Presidency Towns in order to argue that the historical origins of 'central government' in India was similar to its counterparts in the 'classical' federations of the United States and Switzerland. In other words, it began with the existence of distinct state-level entities, which then had to give up some of their powers to a central government in order to solve coordination problems at scale. See Frederick Whyte, *India, a Federation?*, supra, 5.
80. Rudolph and Rudolph trace representative governance in the imperial era further back, to the provision for non-official Council members under the 1861 Indian Councils Act, and federalism to the subsequent introduction of elected municipal councils and rural district boards between 1880-1884. Ibid., 560. For a similar claim, see K.R. Bombwall, *The Foundations of Indian Federalism* (Asia Publishing House, 1967).
81. See the discussion in Arvind Elangovan, *Norms and Politics: Sir Benegal Narsing Rau in the Making of the Indian Constitution, 1939–1950* (Oxford University Press, 2019).
82. Stephen Legg, *Round Table Conference Geographies: Constituting Colonial India in Interwar London* (Cambridge University Press, 2023) 19.
83. Indeed, as is well known, the Cabinet Mission Plan of 1946 proposed a federation with a weak Centre, retaining powers only over defence, external affairs, and communications. This was the understanding upon which the Constituent Assembly initially began to work. However, after Independence, Partition, and the departure of the Muslim League, the constraints that had initially required the Indian National Congress to accept the contours of the Cabinet Mission Plan no longer existed. It was at this stage that the centralizing vision of leaders such as Nehru took concrete shape via the Constituent Assembly.
84. One odd omission in the majority judgment in *State of West Bengal vs Union of India* is its failure to engage with the princely states in its account of pre-Independence India. As Ambedkar himself noted—albeit, not in a positive sense—there had always been a difference in the 'theory of federation as regards British India and as regards the Indian States'. B.R. Ambedkar, *Federation Versus Freedom*, supra.

85. For an account of the debates around federalism at the Round Table Conferences, see Legg, *Round Table Conference Geographies*, supra. For an account of Nehru and the Indian National Congress' scepticism towards this form of federalism as an impediment to the anti-colonial freedom struggle, see Rama Sundari Mantena, 'Anticolonialism and Federation in Colonial India' (2018) 3 *Ab Imperio* 36.
86 Ambedkar, *Federation Versus Freedom*, supra. For an account of how the Federal Court attempted to expand the powers of provincial governments under the 1935 Government of India Act, see Rohit De, 'Constitutional Antecedents' in *The Oxford Handbook of the Indian Constitution* (Oxford University Press, 2016) 17.
87. In the Constituent Assembly Debates, a speaker's name is immediately followed by the name of the province that he or she is representing (if applicable).
88. H.M. Seervai, *Constitutional Law of India*, Vol. 1 (4th edition, Universal Law Publishing, 1991) 288.
89. Singh and Rao, *The Political Economy of Federalism in India,* supra.
90. Such a reading was indeed advanced by a Constitution Bench of the Supreme Court in *Govt of NCT of Delhi vs Union of India*, (2018) (8) SCC 501. It is also a point made, albeit implicitly, by Alexandrowicz, in a very early piece on Indian federalism. See C.H. Alexandrowicz, 'Is India a Federation?' supra.
91. *State of West Bengal vs Union of India*, supra, para 82 (Justice Subba Rao, dissenting). For a detailed critique of treating the historically contingent US Constitution as a normative baseline for 'federalism'—and labelling alternative constitutional arrangements as 'quasi-federal' or otherwise—see Stephen Tierney, *The Federal Contract: A Constitutional Theory of Federalism,* (Oxford University Press, 2022). Indeed, the very trap that Tierney warns against is the trap that Indian judicial and scholarly approaches towards federalism have invariably fallen into since the days of *State of West Bengal vs Union of India*: that is, examining Indian federalism as a foil to the American, rather than on its own terms. Interestingly, Justice Subba Rao's own articulation of federalism is, in many ways, similar to Tierney's normative defence of the concept: that is, a system of constitutional governance designed to accommodate territorial pluralism.

92. Seervai, *Constitutional Law of India*, supra, 284.
93. *State of West Bengal vs Union of India*, supra, para 98 (Justice Subba Rao, dissenting).
94. *S.R. Bommai vs Union of India*, (1994) 3 SCC 1.
95. *NCT of Delhi vs Union of India*, supra.
96. Ibid.
97. For an account of the constitutional skulduggery that has significantly diluted the original judgment, see Gautam Bhatia, 'Judicial Evasion, Judicial Vagueness, and Judicial Revisionism: A Study of the NCT of Delhi vs Union of India Judgment(s)', in Swati Jhaveri et al. (eds), *Constitutional Resilience in South Asia* (Hart 2023).
98. *Government of NCT of Delhi vs Union of India* (2023) 9 SCC 1.
99. While it took the government of the National Capital Territory of Delhi eight years and multiple Supreme Court hearings to finally get a definitive judgment in its favour, it lost its newly regained powers within a month—and at the time of writing, it has been more than a year since the latest set of constitutional challenges were filed before the Supreme Court. The Court's repeated delays in hearing the case—and especially the last round, where the challenge, in effect, argues that it is the Court's *own* judgment that has been unconstitutionally undone—reveals a dimension that we cannot go into in detail in this book, but which is crucial nonetheless: how the Supreme Court's failure to hear cases (what I call 'judicial evasion') has the effect of entrenching and perpetuating executive power, and facilitating the centralising drift *through* non-hearing and evasion. See Gautam Bhatia, 'Judicial Evasion, Judicial Vagueness, and Judicial Revisionism', supra.
100. See Presidential Order C.O. 272/2019; Presidential Order C.O. 273/2019; Jammu & Kashmir Reorganisation Act, 2019.
101. Article 370, Constitution of India (as it stood before 5 August 2019).
102. The Election Commission's persistent refusal to schedule fresh elections speaks to another axis of power—the independence (or absence thereof) of the fourth-branch institutions. See Chapter 4.
103. Jammu & Kashmir Reorganisation Act, 2019.
104. Article 3, Constitution of India.
105. For a detailed exploration of this argument in the Article 370 Case, see *Muzaffar Iqbal Khan vs Union of India*, WP (C) 1104 of 2019, written

submissions of Mr Gopal Subramanium, Sr Advocate, available at https://drive.google.com/file/d/1cC-KuNV1iURm8qkcTweyV8e7a7xlsnH_/view, and drafted, in part, by the present writer.

106. For a detailed exploration of this argument in the Article 370 Case, see *Inder Salim @ Inderji Tikoo and Satish Jacob vs Union of India*, WP (C) No. 1062 of 2019, available at https://drive.google.com/file/d/1hedlt530sJWPafFCkGOcIDSo_U0oucMC/view, and drafted, in part, by the present writer. Incidentally, the language of Article 3—as with many other centralizing provisions of the Constitution—was almost directly taken from the Government of India Act, 1935. See Section 290, Government of India Act, 1935.

107. Discussed at some length in Chapter 3.

108. For a critique of the Court's mischaracterization of the petitioners' case, see Gautam Bhatia, 'Federalism, "Permanent Changes" and the Article 370 Judgment: an Interpretive Note', *Indian Constitutional Law and Philosophy Blog* (12 December 2023), available at https://indconlawphil.wordpress.com/2023/12/12/federalism-permanent-changes-and-the-article-370-judgment-an-interpretive-note/

109. Of course, perhaps no amount of conceptual vocabulary could rectify the intellectual dubiousness of accepting an open-ended 'assurance' from the executive in a constitutional challenge.

110. For an argument that the heavily interdependent nature of the state-Centre fiscal relationship would require, on occasion, the exercise of unitary control, see Chapter 5 in Malavika Prasad, (n.d.), 'The Promise of Central Planning,' unpublished diss., NALSAR University of Law, on file with the author.

111. In particular, in the decade after 2014, when a single-party majority government replaced an uninterrupted period of coalition rule at the Centre. The latter (through the 1990s and 2000s) had allowed a certain degree of breathing room for the states *politically*, although—as many observers point out—this had not been accompanied by any pro-federal *structural* reforms to the Constitution. Reasserting central dominance after 2014 thus presented no great challenge.

112. See *State of Chhattisgarh vs Union of India*, original plaint available at https://images.assettype.com/barandbench/2020-01/a986997f-b4b1-4d2d-b32a-4686b367cd3b/Final_Draft_NIA_Original_Suit.pdf. Shortly prior to this challenge, the NIA Act was amended and expanded.

113. For a comprehensive account, see Alpa Shah, *The Incarcerated: BK-16 and the Search for Democracy in India* (William Collins, 2024).
114. The lack of *independence* of an agency such as the NIA from the central government/executive is another, related, pathology, which we will examine in Chapter 4. We can see, however, the linkages between multiple axes of power: federalism, civil rights, and institutions, in this case.
115. See, e.g. Abdul Khader Kunju S., 'Explainer: Here's How Handing Over UAPA Cases to the NIA Affects the Federal System', The Wire (29 January 2020), available at https://thewire.in/government/uapa-nia-act-centre-state.
116. *Pragyasingh Chandrapalsingh Thakur vs State of Maharashtra*, (2014) 1 Bom CR (Cri) 135.
117. Entry 8, List II, Schedule VII. Ironically, the words 'and investigation' were a late addition to the draft Constitution—as late as 29 August 1949—by Dr B.R. Ambedkar. Precisely the objections raised in Chhattisgarh's plaint were raised in the assembly by Naziruddin Ahmed. Ambedkar defended the new insertion on the basis that the word 'investigation' only meant investigation for the purposes of *assisting* state police, and not usurping their functions. Naziruddin Ahmed asked why, then, was the word 'enquiry' not used instead. He received no answer. While nobody can tell the future, one wonders, however, at the striking lack of foresight in inserting such ambiguous language within an overall centralizing Constitution, and not accounting for how it might be interpreted by executives and courts down the line—a problem that, as we have seen and shall continue to see—runs throughout the Constitution. See Parliament of India, *Constituent Assembly Debates,* Vol. IX (29 August 1949), available at https://eparlib.nic.in/bitstream/123456789/763258/1/cad_29-08-1949.pdf
118. Entries 1 and 2, List III, Schedule VII.
119. Ibid., para 89. As a coup de grace, the Court held that even if competence could not be traced to any specific entries in the List, the field of residuary powers under Entry 97 of List I was always available to the Union!
120. Just a few months later, the High Court of Gauhati—in a rare instance of the federalizing approach—struck down the government resolution constituting the Central Bureau of Investigation (CBI), accepting the

same federalism-based arguments that the Bombay High Court had rejected: in particular, the limited scope of the word 'investigation' under Entry 8 of List I, drawing on the Constituent Assembly Debates, and the absence of any other applicable field under List I or List III. See *Navendra Kumar vs Union of India*, (2014) 1 GAU LT 351. However, in a development that will surprise no one who has observed the Supreme Court of India for a length of time, the Court immediately stayed the operation of the judgment, without providing reasons: a centralizing Court for a centralizing Constitution! At the time of writing, twelve years have passed, and the Supreme Court has not deigned to hear the case substantively. The CBI has effectively operated for a decade on the basis of an unreasoned Supreme Court stay order, something that raises very serious concerns about the rule of law.

121. Border Security Force Act, 1968.
122. Or for that matter, any other concern, including that of civil rights.
123. Entry 33, List III, Schedule VII, Constitution of India.
124. For example, in an interview in 2024, Tamil Nadu Minister Palanivel Thiagarajan pointed out that public medical educational institutions are invariably affiliated with a public hospital.
125. *Dr. Preeti Srivastava vs State of Madhya Pradesh* (1999) 7 SCC 120.
126. Entry 66, List I, Schedule VII, Constitution of India.
127. *Christian Medical College, Vellore vs Union of India* (2013) 14 SCC 539.
128. Indeed, Justice Dave's dissenting opinion in the 2013 NEET judgment stressed upon the benefits of uniformity and centralization in the conduct of examinations. In one of the internal flips that happens frequently in the Supreme Court, after the two majority judges retired, it was Justice Dave who headed the review bench that recalled the 2013 judgment.
129. One issue that we have not discussed in this chapter is that the central skew has been reflected within the functions of the judiciary itself. Over the years, the Supreme Court has—for the most part, informally—expanded its own power and jurisdiction, and incrementally stripped state High Courts from hearing substantive constitutional cases, frequently by 'transferring' such cases to itself (often at the behest of the executive). Often, such 'transfers' have been justified on the ground that multiple High Courts are hearing the same issue. The

assumption seems to be that this is a duplication of time and effort—and not that the Supreme Court would actually benefit from having multiple reasoned judgments before it when it finally considers the issue. One of the more egregious recent examples of this was when the Supreme Court stopped the High Courts of Delhi and Kerala from hearing cases on the legalization of same-sex marriages, brought the case to itself, fast-tracked it, and then dismissed it! This, coupled with the Supreme Court's expanded jurisdiction under Article 32 of the Constitution under the guise of 'public interest litigation', which often prompts litigants to bypass High Courts and directly approach the Supreme Court, has created a situation where the Supreme Court has become the 'first and final tribunal' for most constitutional issues. As—to reiterate—most of this has happened informally, it is difficult to subject it to a constitutional analysis, other than pointing to the constitutional provisions involving transfer of cases to the Supreme Court, that have facilitated this drift. It is also a little difficult to map the aggrandizement of power by the Supreme Court to the continued persistence of the centralizing approach, as there is no iron-clad separation between the High Courts and the Supreme Court in terms of personnel (a similar 'constitutional common sense' is likely to percolate throughout the judicial hierarchy). Here, we can only flag some of these issues, in the hope that political science literature might take them up in the future.

2: Power Divided: Parliamentarianism

1. See infra, Chapter 4.
2. In one of the more farcical aspects of the incident, one of the suspended MPs was not physically present in Parliament on the day he was supposed to have created disorder. His suspension was later revoked, on the basis of misidentification.
3. This is discussed in greater detail subsequently in this chapter.
4. For accounts of the Indian Parliament, see, e.g.: Arun Agarwal, 'The Indian Parliament'in Devesh Kapur and Pratap Bhanu Mehta (eds), *Public Institutions in India* (Oxford University Press, 2007) 77; B.L. Shankar and Valerian Rodrigues, *The Indian Parliament: A Democracy at Work* (Oxford University Press, 2011); Vernon Hewitt and Shirin

M. Rai, 'Parliament' in Niraja Jayal and Pratap Bhanu Mehta (eds), *The Oxford Companion to Politics in India* (Oxford University Press, 2010) 28.

5. For an account of some of the factors contributing to Parliament's decline that lie outside of Parliament's institutional character itself (such as the increasing role of international treaties in constraining law-making, the increasing complexity of administration requiring increasing delegation, and institutionally weak political parties), see Devesh Kapur and Pratap Bhanu Mehta, 'The Indian Parliament as an Institution of Accountability', *Democracy, Governance and Human Rights Programme Paper Number 23* (United Nations Research Institute for Social Development, 2006).
6. There is a generally held viewpoint that the stature and quality of Parliament was at its highest during the premiership of Jawaharlal Nehru, and then progressively declined under Indira Gandhi (who initiated a process of 'deinstitutionalization'), and her successors. See e.g., Arthur G. Rubinoff, 'The Decline of India's Parliament', 4(4) *The Journal of Legislative Studies*, (1998) 13, for a chronological account. The history traced by Rubinoff supports the point being made here: if the importance and role of the legislature depends upon the will and inclination of the head of government, that speaks to a structural flaw in the executive-legislature relationship.
7. A few decades later, Supreme Court would go so far as to say that the 'Westminster system' was part of the basic structure of the Constitution: *Madras Bar Association vs Union of India* (2014) 10 SCC 1.
8. The formal head of the executive under the Indian Constitution is, of course, the President.
9. It is important to note that this is not a necessary feature of parliamentarianism *in general*. See, e.g., the discussion in Loewenberg about the German political system, where the cabinet and the parliamentary party leadership are occupied by different sets of individuals. Gerhard Loewenberg, *Parliament in the German Political System* (Cornell University Press, 1966).
10. For a detailed account of legislation as practice, see: Vasudev Devadasan, 'From Idea to Act: The Indian Legislative Process' (2022) (unpublished article on file with the author).

11. This was not always the case and is a product of developments in the late nineteenth century. Executive dominance within the Westminster system was widely recognized by the middle of the twentieth century. For a bibliography and a historical account, see: Matthew Vincent Flinders, 'Shifting the Balance? Parliament, the Executive and the British Constitution' (2002) 50 *Political Studies* 23–42. For a contemporary mid-twentieth century account, see, e.g.: Harold J. Laski, *Parliamentary Government in England: A Commentary* (Viking Press, 1938). Laski nonetheless argued that parliamentary deliberation was intrinsically important, even if the chances of it changing legislative outcomes was scant.
12. See the discussion in Anthony King, 'Modes of Executive-Legislative Relations: Great Britain, France, and West Germany' (1976) 1 *Legislative Quarterly* 11–36.
13. For examples of governing party backbench influence in British politics, see e.g.: Anthony King, 'Modes of Executive-Legislative Relations: Great Britain, France, and West Germany', (1976) 1(1) *Legislative Studies Quarterly* 11, 15.
14. Ibid., 18.
15. Needless to say, in cases of a minority government, or a government ruling under a 'confidence and supply arrangement', or even a coalition government, the power of the Opposition is significantly stronger.
16. In this classification I follow, but also depart from, Anthony King's taxonomy of executive-legislature relations: intra-party, opposition, cross party, and non party. See Anthony King, 'Modes of Executive-Legislative Relations: Great Britain, France, and West Germany' (1976) 1 *Legislative Studies Quarterly,* 11.
17. Ibid.
18. Indeed, as is common with many Constitutions, the Indian Constitution does not mention political parties at all.
19. This is not a new point. As Kapur and Mehta have noted, in a similar context, the practical reality—where the Opposition uses Parliament as a forum for impugning the government rather than exercising substantive oversight—is because of a distorted incentive structure. When thinking about Indian institutions of governance, therefore, practice and the constitutional framework exist in a somewhat uneasy

tension. See Devesh Kapur and Pratap Bhanu Mehta, 'The Indian Parliament as an Institution of Accountability', *Democracy, Governance and Human Rights* (United Nations Research Institute for Social Development, 2006), available at https://casi.sas.upenn.edu/sites/default/files/bio/uploads/The%20Indian%20Parliament.pdf

20. See Brian Galligan and Scott Brenton (eds), *Constitutional Conventions in Westminster Systems* (Cambridge University Press, 2015).
21. Madhav Khosla, *India's Founding Moment; The Constitution of a Most Surprising Democracy* (Harvard University Press, 2020) 22–24.
22. For an early account of some of these issues, see W.H. Morris-Jones, *Parliament in India* (Longmans, 1957).
23. Parliament of India, *Constituent Assembly Debates,* Vol. VII (4 November 1948) (speech of Dr B.R. Ambedkar), available at https://eparlib.nic.in/bitstream/123456789/762996/1/cad_04-11-1948.pdf. This choice was first made by the Union Constitution Committee. For a summary of the records, see Shiva Rao, *The Framing of India's Constitution*, (1967) 433–677 ('Principles of the Union and Provincial Constitutions').
24. Parliament of India, *Constituent Assembly Debates*, Vol. VII (10 December 1948) (speech of K.M. Munshi), available at https://eparlib.nic.in/bitstream/123456789/762994/1/cad_10-12-1948.pdf Alladi Krishnaswmai Ayyar backed this point, noting prior experiences with dyarchy and then with the provincial governments under the 1935 Government of India Act.
25. This latter point is echoed by scholars as well. See, e.g., Rubinoff, 'The Decline of India's Parliament', supra, 16.
26. For a similarly sceptical account to the one that follows, see Sandipto Dasgupta, *Legalizing the Revolution: India and the Constitution of the Postcolony* (Cambridge University Press, 2024) 117.
27. Indian Councils Act, 1861. The act provided allowed the viceroy to nominate Indian members to sit on the legislative council.
28. See, e.g., The Indian Councils Act, 1892, which expanded the size of the central and provincial legislative councils and allowed discussion on the budget; The Indian Councils Act, 1909 ('Morley-Minto Reforms'), which, for the first time, provided for indirect elections.
29. Government of India Act, 1919.

30. Government of India Act, 1935.
31. Githu Muigai, *Power, Politics, and the Law* (Kabarak University Press, 2022). See also Ken Ochieng' Opalo, *Legislative Development in Africa: Politics and Postcolonial Legacies* (Cambridge University Press, 2019) 101, making the same point in the context of colonial Zambia.
32. Tellingly—as Sandipto Dasgupta noted—one of the major demands of the Indian National Congress was of an executive *accountable* to the legislature. Sandipto Dasgupta, *Legalizing the Revolution* (Cambridge University Press, 2024) 411, fn 50. This, of course, did not come about even in the 1935 Government of India Act.
33. For a detailed discussion, see Frederick Whyte, *India, a Federation?* (Leopold Classic Library, 2016)
34. Section 37(3), Government of India Act, 1935.
35. Section 38(d), Government of India Act, 1935.
36. Section 44, Government of India Act, 1935.
37. Section 12, Government of India Act, 1935.
38. Section 32, Government of India Act, 1935.
39. For many decades this would be the exact dispute between the National Capital Territory of Delhi and the Union of India. Despite the advent of a constitution in the intervening years, the more things changed, the more they stayed the same.
40. This included, for example, denying the legislature even a consultative role on the financing of reserved subjects.
41. B.R. Ambedkar, *Federation Versus Freedom* (Gokhale Institute of Politics and Economics, 1939) 82, 92.
42. See, for example, the powers of the secretary of state, discussed in Whyte, *India, a Federation?* Supra, 37. On another note, R.J. Moore has a fascinating account, for example, how the question of whether—and when—to announce dominion status for India was determined by internal political calculations within the British Parliament and Whitehall. See R.J. Moore, *The Crisis of Indian Unity: 1917-1940*, (Clarendon Press, 1974).
43. As Dasgupta notes, 'whatever hallowed place the legislature occupied in the British constitutional system, the colonial government was a model of unfettered executive authority.' Dasgupta, *Legalizing the Revolution*, supra 182.

44. For a history, see Rohit De, 'Constitutional Antecedents' in Sujit Chaudhra, Madhav Khosla and Pratap Bhanu Mehta ed. *The Oxford Handbook of the Indian Constitution (*Oxford University Press, 2016) 17.
45. Madhav Khosla, *India's Founding Moment*, supra. This was something that did not escape the attention of the Court either. Very early on, in *A.K. Gopalan vs State of Madras*, (1950) S.C.R. 88, Justice Kania noted that 'in contrast to the American Constitution, the Indian Constitution is a very detailed one. The Constitution itself provides in minute details the legislative powers of the Parliament and the State Legislatures. The same feature is noticeable in the case of the judiciary, finance, trade, commerce and services'.
46. In the context of the leader of the Opposition, Elliot Bulmer notes that this is something common to 'older' Westminster Constitutions (such as Australia and Malaysia, among others), where the role and function of the leader of the Opposition was considered to be a matter for convention, and not codification. Elliot Bulmer, 'Opposition and Legislative Minorities: Constitutional Roles, Rights and Recognition', *International IDEA Constitution-Building Primer 22*, (2021) 15.
47. This is with respect to Parliamentary privileges, which—according to the original text of the Constitution—were to be the same as those enjoyed by the British House of Commons on the date of the commencement of the Constitution.
48. Parliament of India, *Constituent Assembly Debates*, Vol. VII (10 December 1948) (speech of Kazi Syed Karimuddin), available at https://eparlib.nic.in/bitstream/123456789/762994/1/cad_10-12-1948.pdf
49. See, e.g., Parliament of India, *Constituent Assembly Debates*, Vol. IV (23 July 1947), available at https://eparlib.nic.in/bitstream/123456789/762949/1/cad_23-07-1947.pdf, where the speeches of the members treated the decision on the form of government as settled. See also Parliament of India, *Constituent Assembly Debates*, Vol. IV (28 July 1947) (speech of Jawaharlal Nehru), available at https://eparlib.nic.in/bitstream/123456789/762946/1/cad_28-07-1947.pdf, where Nehru introduced a draft amendment to codify the existence of the Council of Ministers, and noted that the choice between the American and British systems had been made, with the House now 'committed' to the latter. See also Parliament of India, *Constituent Assembly Debates*, Vol. VII (10 December 1948) (speech of Dr B.R. Ambedkar), available

at https://eparlib.nic.in/bitstream/123456789/762994/1/cad_10-12-1948.pdf, treating this question as settled in response to a proposed amendment by K.T. Shah seeking to introduce American-style separation of powers into the Constitution.

50. This provision was criticized throughout the Constituent Assembly Debates. See, e.g., Parliament of India, *Constituent Assembly Debates*, Vol. IV (23 July 1947) (speech of Hriday Nath Kunzru), available at https://eparlib.nic.in/bitstream/123456789/762949/1/cad_23-07-1947.pdf; ibid., speech of Pandit Lakshmi Kanta Maitra; ibid., speech of Hussain Imam, warning of 'autocracy'. The elected governor was eventually replaced by one nominated by the President, thus replacing semi-presidentialism with centralism. See, e.g., the debates in Parliament of India, *Constituent Assembly Debates,* Vol. VIII (31 May 1949), available at https://eparlib.nic.in/bitstream/123456789/763981/1/cad_31-05-1949.pdf
51. See, e.g., Parliament of India, *Constituent Assembly Debates,* Vol. IV (28 July 1947) (speech of Kazi Syed Karimuddin), available at https://eparlib.nic.in/bitstream/123456789/762946/1/cad_28-07-1947.pdf arguing that parliamentarianism under the 1935 Government of India Act had 'miserably failed'; Parliament of India, *Constituent Assembly Debates,* Vol. VII (10 December 1948) (speech of Prof. Shibban Lal Saksena), available at https://eparlib.nic.in/bitstream/123456789/762994/1/cad_10-12-1948.pdf noting the propensity of parliamentarianism to devolve into a 'one-man Government'; Parliament of India, *Constituent Assembly Debates,* Vol. XI (18 November 1949) (speech of Babu Ramnarayan Singh), available at https://eparlib.nic.in/bitstream/123456789/763231/1/cad_18-11-1949.pdf
52. Jawaharlal Nehru, *Toward Freedom* (John Day, 1941) 324.
53. Nazmul Sultan, *Waiting for the People: The Idea of Democracy in Indian Anticolonial Thought*, (Harvard University Press, 2024) 164. See also Sudipta Kaviraj, *The Imaginary Institution of India: Politics and Ideas* (Columbia University Press, 2010); Sandipto Dasgupta, 'Parliamentarianism, not Presidentialism: Democracy and Development in India' (2018) 53(33) *Economic and Political Weekly* 43.
54. Udit Bhatia, 'The Pedagogical Account of Parliamentarianism at India's Founding' *The American Journal of Political Science*, (2023) 1, 2. For a more detailed account of Nehru's political thought, see,

e.g. Partha Chatterjee, *The Nation and its Fragments: Colonial and Postcolonial Histories* (Princeton University Press, 1993).

55. Dasgupta calls it the role of being an 'accomplice' to the administrators. See Dasgupta, *Legalizing the Revolution*, supra, 201.
56. Ibid. That this would be the ultimate goal of the parliamentary system was echoed by other members of the Constituent Assembly as well. See, e.g., Parliament of India, *Constituent Assembly Debates,* Vol. VII (10 December 1948) (speech of K. Santhanam), available at https://eparlib.nic.in/bitstream/123456789/762994/1/cad_10-12-1948.pdf.
57. See e.g. Paras Diwan, 'Aaya Ram, Gaya Ram: The Politics of Defection' (1979) in *Journal of the Indian Law Institute,* 291.
58. Y.B. Chavan, 'Report of the Committee on Defections' (The Ministry of Home Affairs, 1969), available at https://indianculture.gov.in/reports-proceedings/report-committee-defections
59. Schedule X, Constitution of India, 1949.
60. Ibid.
61. For a list, see: Kenneth Janda, 'Laws Against Party Switching, Defecting, or Floor-Crossing' Working Paper 2: The Legal Regulation of Political Parties, 2009, available at https://www.partylaw.leidenuniv.nl/uploads/wp0209.pdf
62. Interestingly, almost two decades before the insertion of Schedule X into the Indian Constitution, the Fifth Amendment to the Kenyan Constitution had introduced a very similar anti-defection law. Its goal was to quell rising dissent within the ruling KANU party of the newly independent Kenyan nation, and solidify the leadership of President Jomo Kenyatta. The Fifth Amendment is now widely understood to be one of a set of amendments that sought to marginalize the Kenyan Parliament, at the cost of increasing the powers of the executive presidency.
63. Udit Bhatia, 'Cracking the Whip: the Deliberative Costs of Strict Party Discipline' 23(2) (*Critical Review of International Social and Political Philosophy*, 2020) 254–79.
64. Ibid.
65. Schedule X contributes to, but is not constitutive of, the highly centralized nature of Indian political parties: there are reasons for this that go beyond the Constitution. For a discussion, see Eswaran Sridharan, 'India's Democracy at 70: The Shifting Party Balance'

(2017) 28(3) *Journal of Democracy* 76. For a more detailed treatment of the concept of 'intra-party democracy' and a survey of literature, see Samuel Bagg and Udit Bhatia, 'Intra-Party Democracy: A Functionalist Account' (2022) 30(3) *The Journal of Political Philosophy* 347–69.

66. *Prakash Singh Badal vs Union of India*, AIR 1987 P&H 263.
67. *Kihoto Hollohan vs Zachillhu*, (1992) Supp (2) SCC 651.
68. Ibid.
69. Ibid. As we have seen throughout the course of this book, when it comes to inflection-point judgments, in significant part, the centralizing drift is caused by a gap between the Court's exhortation of what would be *desired* behaviour on the part of constitutional functionaries on the one hand, and the behaviour that is actually *incentivized* by the constitutional design and structure on the other. A particularly stark example is the Court's assumptions about the independence of election commissioners appointed by the executive, which we discuss in Chapter 4 of this book.
70. For an examination of how a set of conventions guarantee speaker independence in the United Kingdom, see Charith Reddy and Shagun Bhargava, 'For Laws May Come and Laws May Go, But Defections Go On Forever: A Critical Analysis of the Role of the Speaker in Indian Anti-Defection Laws', 10(1) (*NLIU Law Review*, 2022) 328, 340.
71. *Kihoto Hollohan vs Zaichilhu*, supra, paragraph 118. The Supreme Court also went on to note—bizarrely—that 'the robes of the Speaker do change and elevate the man inside'. Ibid. Not only did the Court provide zero empirical evidence for what was a factual assertion, but—as anyone with the slightest knowledge of Indian politics will agree—this statement has aged like milk. For an express judicial acknowledgement of this, see *Keisham Meghachandra Singh vs The Hon'ble Speaker, Manipur Legislative Assembly* (2020) 2 SCR 132, where the Supreme Court took note of the Manipur speaker's continued refusal to decide a disqualification petition, and finally directed the speaker to decide within four weeks.
72. A very similar form of flawed reasoning plagued the 2024 debate around the selection of election commissioners, which we shall consider in Chapter 4. It is worth flagging at this point, however, that a factor behind the centralizing drift has been the Court's inability—

or unwillingness—to seriously engage with the constitutional design, when it comes to cases like this.

73. Ibid. The Court appeared to believe—and this was echoed in later judgments (most recently, the Maharashtra judgment, discussed below)—that judicial review would be an adequate safeguard against abuse of the speaker's powers. This is, however, not the case, as post facto review is often insufficient where partisan action can irrevocably change the political terrain, long before the Court has a chance to consider the issues. Indeed, the Maharashtra case (below) is a classic example of exactly this.
74. Ibid.
75. Ibid.
76. This was subsequently expanded in *Ravi Naik vs Union of India* (1994) SCR (1) 754, where the Supreme Court held that the phrase 'voluntary giving up of membership' could be *inferred* through conduct as well.
77. For a recent instance, see *Subhash Desai vs Principal Secretary, Governor of Maharashtra*, WP (C) 493 of 2022 (11 May 2023).
78. *Shrimanth Balasaheb Patil vs The Hon'ble Speaker, Karnataka Legislative Assembly*, W.P. (Civ) No. 992 of 2019 (13 November 2019), paragraph 12.
79. Ibid.
80. *Shivraj Singh Chouhan vs Speaker, Madhya Pradesh Legislative Assembly*, W.P. (Civ) No. 439 of 2020 (13 April 2020).
81. This was based on a few stray observations in previous cases, which the Court (wrongly) took to have settled the issue.
82. *Subhash Desai vs Principal Secretary, Governor of Maharashtra*, WP (C) 493 of 2022 (11 May 2023). There were a range of other issues in this case that we shall not discuss here.
83. In *Nabam Rebia vs Deputy Speaker* (2017) 13 SCC 332, the Supreme Court placed extensive constraints upon the scope of discretionary action that the governor could take with respect to the internal business of the state legislatures, restricting such action only to the calling of a floor test. While did this contain certain forms of central meddling, as we have seen, even within this limited scope, there is a lot that governors can do to destabilize state governments, through a device as simple as the timing of calling for a floor test.
84. Indeed, before these three judgments, *Nabam Rebia*, ibid., is a good example of this: in Arunachal Pradesh, rebel legislators from the ruling

party were alleged to be working along with the Opposition (also the central ruling party) *and* the governor, resulting in the moving of a no-confidence motion against the speaker, as well as the governor summoning the legislature to vote on the no-confidence motion, *and* also ordering that, in the meantime, the speaker could not change the composition of the House (in practical terms, that is, injuncting the speaker from acting on disqualification petitions). This resulted in the fall of the chief minister. The Supreme Court found all of the actions of the governor to be illegal, and restored status quo ante. It also held, however, that a speaker facing a no-confidence motion could not decide on disqualification petitions. This part of the ruling was at issue in the Maharashtra case, as described in the next note, and was ultimately referred to a larger bench for resolution.

85. In the Maharashtra case, this tension within Schedule X was particularly stark. One issue before the Court was that the 'rebel' legislators purported to elect their own chief whip of the party, who could then issue directions to the legislators about how to vote in the House. The new speaker of the House—elected under the changed government—recognized the 'rebel' legislators' whip. The Supreme Court held that this was illegal, on the basis that the power to appoint the party whip lay with the *political party* and not the *legislature party* (that is, the collective of legislators from the political party during a specific term of the assembly). In other words, the Court accorded prominence to the *political party* (which would, of course, be dominated by the formal party leadership) over the *legislators of the party*, when it came to questions such as the appointment of the party whip. In line with our discussion in the previous section, this holding undermined intra-party democracy; however, according to our discussion in *this* section, it constituted another important safeguard for institutionally weaker, regional parties from internal coups, instigated by the institutionally stronger ruling party at the Centre in alliance with a section of that party's legislators.

    Similarly, another issue in the case was whether the speaker could rule on disqualification petitions while there was a pending motion for his removal—initiated by some of the very legislators whose disqualification petitions he was considering (see *Nabam Rebia*, note 84). Once again, in line with our discussion about the speaker's office in this chapter, constraint upon the speaker's powers—especially when it comes to disqualifications—would appear to be desirable. Here, however, the motion for removal was evidently an attempt by the 'rebel' legislators to insulate themselves from the consequences of their defection. Consequently, and again, affirming the speaker's powers to rule on disqualification petitions in cases like this would be a method of protecting state governments from being toppled through the kind of internal coup that we have referred to above. At present, the question is pending before a seven-judge bench, although the Court put into place an interim arrangement that *would* allow the speaker to decide (but subject to judicial review).

86. Bulmer, 'Opposition and Legislative Minorities', supra 26, discussing the Constitutions of Portugal, Mozambique, Tunisia, and Georgia.
87. The basis of the controversy was the failure of the Indian National Congress as the largest opposition party to secure 10 per cent of the membership of the House in the 2014 and 2019 general elections.
88. See Meenakshi Ramkumar and Aishwarya Singh, 'The Road Not Taken: India's Failure to Entrench the Rights of the Opposition' (2022) 6(2) *CALJ* 55.
89. Ibid., 56, flagging the constitutions of Mauritius, Barbados, Sri Lanka, and South Africa. The last of these is discussed in some detail. See also Bulmer, 'Opposition and Legislative Minorities', supra, 17.
90. The Salary and Allowances of Leaders of Opposition in Parliament Act, 1977, s. 2.
91. Ramkumar and Singh, 'The Road Not Taken' supra, 62–64.
92. Parliament of India, *Constituent Assembly Debates,* Vol. IV (28 July 1947) (speech of Kazi Syed Karimuddin), available at https://eparlib.nic.in/bitstream/123456789/762946/1/cad_28-07-1947.pdf
93. See, e.g., Bulmer, 'Opposition and Legislative Minorities', 16, on the importance of 'future-proofing' opposition rights through constitutional entrenchment, *especially* in the absence of favourable conditions.
94. Ramkumar and Singh, 'The Road Not Taken', supra.
95. See Anirudh Burman, 'Legal Framework for the Parliamentary Oversight of the Executive in India', (2013) 6 *NUJS Law Review* 387, 398.
96. For a discussion of the Committee system, see Arthur G. Rubinoff, 'India's New Subject Based Parliamentary Committees' (1996) 36 *Asian Survey* 723; Anirudh Burman, 'Legal Framework for

Parliamentary Oversight', supra 399. The problem is compounded by the fact that oversight over the powers of standing committees to issue summons vests in the speaker—the same partisan official whom we have discussed at some length in this chapter. See, e.g., Rule 270, *Rules of Procedure and Conduct of Business in the Lok Sabha* (fifteenth edition, Lok Sabha Secretariat 2014); Kapur and Mehta, 'The Indian Parliament as an Institution of Accountability', supra 13.

97. For a detailed examination of the role of committees in the power relationship between the executive and the legislature, see Bert A. Rockman, 'Legislative-Executive Relations and Legislative Oversight' (1984) 9(3) *Legislative Studies Quarterly* 387.
98. Rubinoff, 'The Decline of India's Parliament', supra 28. Elliot Bulmer notes that certain Constitutions entrench the existence, composition, and role of Parliamentary Committees, at least to a degree (e.g. Tunisia, Sierra Leone, and Papua New Guinea). See Bulmer, 'Opposition and Legislative Minorities', supra 25. Bulmer also points out that in certain constitutions, the convention that the chair of the Public Accounts Committee will be a member of the Opposition is also constitutionally entrenched (e.g. Trinidad and Tobago). Ibid., 26.
99. Tarunabh Khaitan, 'The Real Price of Parliamentary Obstruction' (2013) 642 *Seminar*, available at https://india-seminar.com/2013/642.htm The phrase parliamentary 'state of nature' is borrowed from Gary W. Cox, 'The Organisation of Democractic Legislatures' in D. Wittman and B. Weingast (eds), *The Oxford Handbook of Political Economy* (Oxford University Press, 2006).
100. For a discussion of the office, see Hari Chand, 'Powers of the Speaker' 16 (1) *Journal of the Indian Law Institute* (1974) 128.
101. For example, in the opening session of the Lok Sabha after the 2024 general election, the speaker expunged substantive portions of the speech of the leader of the Opposition, leading to significant controversy.
102. Reddy and Bhargava, 'A Critical Analysis of the Role of the Speaker in Indian Anti-Defection Laws', supra 328–337-8.
103. Matthew Laban, 'More Westminster than Westminster? The Office of Speaker across the Commonwealth' 20(2) *The Journal of Legislative Studies* (2014) 143. Laban points out, however, that problems around partisan and party-political speakers are found in numerous

commonwealth countries, with the strict neutrality demanded by the original Westminster system often missing in practice.

104. See also Ramkumar & Singh, 'The Road Not Taken', supra 65–66. It should be noted that the problem went back to the Government of India Act, which also failed to secure the independence of the speakers of the colonial legislatures. See e.g. Section 22, Government of India Act, 1935.
105. Vijaya Bhaskar Reddy, 'Sabotage of Anti-Defection Law in Telangana' (2015) 1 *Economic and Political Weekly* 50.
106. *Subhash Desai vs Principal Secretary, Governor of Maharashtra*, supra.
107. Ambedkar, *Federation versus Freedom*, supra 82.
108. Ibid.
109. This is another problem that goes back to the Government of India Act, 1935.
110. Article 110, Constitution of India.
111. Ibid.
112. Aadhaar Act, 2016.
113. *Justice K.S. Puttaswamy (Retd) vs Union of India* (2019) 1 SCC 1.
114. Ibid. (Dissenting opinion of Justice Chandrachud.)
115. Article 89, Constitution of India.
116. This has happened increasingly in recent years; and as Ramkumar and Singh note, refusing a division when asked for is expressly contrary to the Speaker's obligations under the Rules of Procedure and Conduct of Business in Rajya Sabha, 2016. See Ramkumar and Singh, 'The Road Not Taken', supra 64.
117. Article 123, Constitution of India.
118. Ibid.
119. Ibid.
120. Article 210, Constitution of India.
121. See, e.g., John M. Carey and Matthew S. Shugard (eds), *Executive Decree Authority* (Cambridge University Press, 1998); Josse Antonio Cheibub and Fernando Limongi, 'Legislative-Executive Relations' in Tom Ginsburg and Rosalind Dixon (eds), *Comparative Constitutional Law*, (Edward Elgar, 2011) 211, 226–29.
122. See, e.g., Madhav S. Aney and Shubhankar Dam, 'Decree Powers in Parliamentary Systems: Theory and Evidence from India' (2021) 83(4) *The Journal of Politics* 1432–49.

123. See Shubhankar Dam, *Presidential Legislation in India: The Law and Practice of Ordinances* (Cambridge University Press, 2014), Chapter 1.
124. Section 23, Indian Councils Act, 1861.
125. Section 72, Government of India Act, 1915.
126. Dam, *Presidential Legislation in India*, supra 42.
127. In the 1935 Government of India Act, the word 'emergency' was replaced by 'circumstances render[ing] it necessary ... to take immediate action', a term of considerably wider import.
128. *Bhagat Singh vs King-Emperor*, 1931 55 Ind App 169, c.f. Dam, *Presidential Legislation in India*, ibid. 47.
129. For a summary of the debates, see Dam, *Presidential Legislation in India*, ibid. 54–59.
130. *R.K. Garg vs Union of India*, (1981) 4 SCC 675.
131. Shubhankar Dam, *Presidential Legislation*, supra.
132. In the Constituent Assembly, members strongly objected to the persistence of the ordinance-making power as a colonial relic, and noted its deleterious impact upon democracy. See, e.g., Parliament of India, *Constituent Assembly Debates*, Vol. IV (28 July 1947) (speech of Prof. Shibban Lal Saksena), available at https://eparlib.nic.in/bitstream/123456789/762946/1/cad_28-07-1947.pdf
133. *Dr. D.C. Wadhwa vs State of Bihar* (1987) SCR (1) 798.
134. *State of Orissa vs Bhupendra Kumar Bose* (1962) SCR Supl. (2) 380; *T. Venkata Reddy vs State of AP* (1985) 3 SCC 198.
135. It was even held that the executive proroguing Parliament solely to make room for an ordinance was permissible. See *Re Kalyanam Veerabhadraya* 1949 MWN (Cri) 185 (Madras High Court), considering the ordinance-making powers under the Government of India Act 1935 (page 201):

> We do not see anything, wrong in the Governor proroguing the Assembly and the Council with a view to enable himself to issue an ordinance under Section 88. It is a well-known fact that the legislature, which is democratically constituted, *is very slow to move in the matter of legislation*, having regard to the rules of procedure laid down in that behalf, and if urgent action is necessary, at any rate, when His Excellency the Governor has reasons to believe that immediate action is

> necessary, *it will be more expedient* to have resort to the power of issuing an ordinance under Section 88 rather than approach the Legislature for the necessary legislation. The section itself requires that the Governor should be satisfied that circumstances exist which render it necessary for him to take immediate action. Of this necessity, the Governor is the sole judge. The satisfaction is that of the Governor. It is not open to a Court to canvass and find out whether in fact there could or could not have been the satisfaction. The power of the Governor under this section is analogous to the power of the Governor-General to promulgate Ordinances in case of emergency. (Emphasis supplied)

This judgment was then followed by other High Courts in interpreting the Constitution, essentially sanctioning the use of ordinances as a parallel law-making power on grounds of 'expediency'. See, e.g., *Vishwanath Agarwal vs State of Uttar Pradesh*, AIR 1956 All 557, where prorogation with a view to passing a tax ordinance was upheld on the basis that to bring it in Parliament might have triggered speculation and black marketing. But see *Satya Pal Dang vs State of Punjab* (ILR 1968) 2 P&H 42, where two judges out of five noted that this view could not hold in a democratic Constitution, as it would effectively subordinate the state legislature to the governor.

It is instructive to compare this line of cases with the landmark judgment of the UK Supreme Court in *R (Miller) vs The Prime Minister*, (2019) UKSC 41, where—even in the absence of a written constitution—the UK Supreme Court held that a prorogation would be set aside if its effect was to deprive Parliament of the chance to scrutinise important legislation.

136. *Krishna Kumar Singh vs State of Bihar* (2017) 3 SCC 1.
137. Ibid.
138. Ibid.
139. Notice that while this has become an accepted fact of Indian constitutional practice, it is a significant distortion in its own right. The Supreme Court's inability—or unwillingness—to hear urgent constitutional questions *urgently* has basically defanged judicial review as a meaningful check or constraint upon time-sensitive challenges to State action. There is no reason why this *has* to be so: by way of

comparison, see for example the practice of issuing conservatory orders by the High Court of Kenya in urgent constitutional challenges. These orders (whether in favour of the petitioner or the respondent) are invariably issued in under a week, after a specific hearing on urgency, and accompanied by reasons. The Supreme Court of India's refusal to do the same is a matter of choice, and not one of compulsion. For an analysis of some recent instances, see Gautam Bhatia, 'The Mysterious Disappearance of the Stay Hearing', *Constitutional Law and Philosophy* (13 January 2024), available at https://indconlawphil.wordpress.com/2024/01/13/the-mysterious-disappearance-of-the-stay-hearing/

140. Precisely the same trajectory took place in response to the Supreme Court's 2023 judgment declaring the powers of the legislature and executive of the NCT of Delhi. Very soon after the judgment, the President issued an ordinance stripping the NCT's legislature and executive of some of these powers, and vesting them in the central executive nominee (the lieutenant-governor). There was no reason why this could not have waited until the next session of Parliament, in two months' time, where the ordinance could—and indeed, was—replaced by an act.
141. For a classic, if slightly dated, set of debates on the issue, see Arend Lijphart (ed.), *Parliamentary versus Presidential Government* (Oxford University Press, 1992).
142. The relationship between the systems of government and the bureaucracy/administrative state is also a subject of debate. In this chapter, we have not considered the civil service; interested readers can consult Terry M. Moe and Michael Caldwell, 'The Institutional Foundations of Democratic Government: A Comparison of Presidential and Parliamentary Systems' (1994) 150(1) *Journal of Institutional and Theoretical Economics* 171.
143. Kim Lane Scheppele, 'The Rule of Law and the Frankenstate: Why Governance Checklists Do Not Work' (2013) 26(4) *Governance: An International Journal of Policy, Administration, and Institutions* 559, 560.
144. Opalo, *Legislative Development in Africa*, supra, 131, referring in particular to the fiscal relationship, where legislators become dispensers and patrons of developmental services in their constituencies, which in turn makes them reliant upon the executive. In India, we see a similar phenomenon playing out through the MPLADs funds, discussed briefly in Chapter 2. For more on the African perspective,

see B. Ojwang, 'Legislative Control of Executive Power in Africa: New Insights' (1986) 19(4) *Verfassung un Recht in Ubersee* 421.

145. Cheibub and Fernando Limongi, 'Legislative-Executive Relations', supra 215.
146. Although very different in context, when considering executive governance with very few effective checks and balances, the closest analogy might be the executive Presidencies of the late nineteenth and mid-twentieth-century Latin America. Roberto Gargarella, *Latin American Constitutionalism, 1810–2010: The Engine Room of the Constitution* (Oxford University Press, 2013).
147. We have discussed some of these costs—in particular, the reciprocal cycle of parliamentary disruption and mass expulsions that characterized the December 2023 session of the Lok Sabha. It may also be worth considering whether the disempowerment of legislators within the house has, in part, contributed to the self-definition of the role of the MP as not being that of 'legislation, deliberation, and oversight', but that of a dispenser of patronage within the constituency. As Kapur and Mehta note, 'MPs are not often seen as *lawmakers* ... most MPs and their constituents look upon MPs primarily as distributors of patronage ...' Kapur and Mehta, 'The Indian Parliament as an Institution of Accountability', supra 19-20. This is not unique to India: the changing emphasis of the role of MPs from *legislative* to *administrative* has been a feature of many post-colonial democracies. It is also worthwhile to note that in Chapter 2, we looked at the MPLADs case and the Supreme Court's understanding of the role of the legislator: we can now see the linkages between that judgment and our present discussion, along the intersecting power axes of federalism and parliamentarianism.

3: Power Dispersed: Pluralism

1. For an account of asymmetric federalism under the Indian Constitution, see Louis Tillin, 'Asymmetric Federalism' in Sujit Chaudhra, Madhav Khosla and Pratap Bhanu Mehta (eds), *The Oxford Handbook of the Indian Constitution* (Oxford University Press, 2016); Alfred Stepan, Juan Linz, and Yogendra Yadav, *Crafting State-Nations: India and Other Multinational Democracies* (John Hopkins University Press, 2011).

2. The term was coined by Charles Tarlton. See Charles Tarlton, 'Symmetry and Asymmetry as Elements of Federalism: A Theoretical Speculation' (1965) 27(4) *Journal of Politics* 861.
3. Ferran Requejo, 'Federalism in Plurinational Societies: Rethinking the Ties Between Catalonia, Spain and the European Union' in D. Karmis and W. Norman (eds), *Theories of Federalism: A Reader*, (MacMillan, 2005).
4. Louis Tillin, 'United in Diversity? Asymmetry in Indian Federalism', (2006) 37(1) *Publius: The Journal of Federalism* 45, 47.
5. See, for example, the arguments in Stepan, Linz, and Yadav. The authors argue for India to be understood as a 'robustly multinational society', where asymmetrically federal arrangements ought to reflect its character as a 'state-nation' rather than a nation-state. Stepan, Linz, and Yadav, *Crafting State-Nations: India and Other Multinational Democracies*, supra.
6. But see Tillin, ibid., who contests whether Article 370 can be considered to be an example of asymmetric federalism, as its existence is owed to the specific political and historical expedients that involved the accession of Jammu and Kashmir into the Union of India, at the time of Independence. We will consider this in greater detail in the course of the chapter.
7. See Sumantra Bose, *Kashmir: Roots of Conflict, Paths to Peace* (Harvard University Press, 2003), and the discussion in Madhav Khosla, *The Indian Constitution: A Very Short Introduction* (Oxford University Press, 2012).
8. For a historical analysis, see Kavita Datla, 'Origins of Indirect Rule' (2015) 33 (2) *Law and History Review* 347.
9. For a discussion, see Raja Sekhar Vundru, *Ambedkar, Gandhi, and Patel: The Making of India's Electoral System* (Bloomsbury, 2017).
10. One of the exceptions, unsurprisingly, was Jaipal Munda, himself an Adivasi.
11. For a summary of the points raised by both sides, see J. Zahluna, 'Constituent Assembly and the Sixth Schedule: With Special Reference to Mizoram' (2010) 71(4) in *The Indian Journal of Political Science* 1235; for a brief discussion tracing contemporary controversies to the debates in the Constituent Assembly, see Kham Khan Suan Hausing, 'Putting Asymmetric Federalism in a Tinder-Box in India', *Outlook India* (18

February 2022), available at https://www.outlookindia.com/national/putting-asymmetric-federalism-in-a-tinder-box-in-india-news-182801

12. See V.P. Menon, *Integration of the India States* (Orient Blackswan, 2014).
13. Ministry of States, Government of India, White Paper on Indian States, Part IV: Instrument of Accession (1950), available at https://en.wikisource.org/wiki/White_Paper_on_Indian_States_(1950)/Part_4/Instrument_of_Accession
14. Taylor C. Sherman, 'The Integration of the Princely State of Hyderabad and the Making of the Postcolonial State in India, 1948–56', (2007), *Indian Economic and Social History Review* 44(4): 489.
15. A.G. Noorani (2011), *Article 370: A Constitutional History of Jammu and Kashmir*, (Oxford University Press, 2011) 37–41.
16. 'Letter dated 17 May 1949, by N. Gopalaswami Ayyangar to Vallabhbhai Patel Enclosing Jawaharlal Nehru's Draft Letter to Sheikh Abdullah for his Approval', in Noorani (2011), *Article 370*, pp. 51–53.
17. Article 370, Constitution of India (as enacted).
18. Ibid.
19. Ibid.
20. Ibid. In quite an extraordinary act of interpretive legerdemain, the Supreme Court, in its Article 370 judgment, ignored the plain imports of the words 'shall be necessary' to hold that the President had *unilateral* power to abrogate Article 370. This is discussed in the chapter.
21. Technically, the requirement of double consent, of course, is a principle applicable across the board: for example, states can authorize the Union legislature to legislate on List II subjects by passing a resolution to that effect. In that sense, the difference in the case of Jammu and Kashmir was more a matter of degree than of principle.
22. The incarceration of Sheikh Abdullah midway through the process cannot, of course, be ignored in this story.
23. The Constitution (Application to Jammu & Kashmir) Order, 1954 (C.O. 48). See the discussion in Tillin (2016), 'Asymmetric Federalism'.
24. See Noorani (2011), *Article 370*, Chapter 1.
25. Ibid.
26. Jammu and Kashmir Preventive Detention Act, 1964.
27. See Chapter 5.

28. *Sampat Prakash vs State of Jammu and Kashmir*, (1969) SCR (3) 574.
29. Ibid.
30. Ibid.
31. Ibid.
32. Noorani (2011), *Article 370.*
33. Ibid.
34. In effect, this was a situation where the Constitution would *follow* politics, and be subordinate to it.
35. *Mohd Maqbool Damnoo vs State of Jammu and Kashmir*, (1972) SCR (2) 1014.
36. Ibid.
37. See Chapter 2 and ongoing chapter, of this book.
38. See the discussion in Stepan, Linz, and Yadav, *Crafting State-Nations*, supra, Chapter 3.
39. C.O. 272.
40. C.O. 273.
41. In *Re: Article 370 of the Constitution*, (2023) INSC 1058.
42. This argument emerged with greatest force in the oral submissions of Harish Salve, SA.
43. This argument was pressed, in particular, by the attorney general for India and the solicitor general of India.
44. Note, however, that under Article 371, nine other states have a 'special status' of different kinds, which we will consider below. The claim for 'equivalence', therefore, was arguably always a myth.
45. In *Re Article 370 of the Constitution*, (2023) INSC 1058.
46. Ibid.
47. A silencing that was both literal and metaphorical. One striking point about the Supreme Court's judgment is its refusal to acknowledge that the events of 5 August 2019 were accompanied by mass detentions of political leaders, a military clampdown, and an internet shutdown that would last months.
48. Another striking thing about the judgment was that the Supreme Court granted to the Union a unilateral power that it *itself* did not believe it possessed, at least not when it issued C.O. 272 and C.O. 273. The legal path that the Union took to achieve abrogation involved the conversion of 'Constituent Assembly' in Article 370(3)

to 'Legislative Assembly', something that the Supreme Court found to be unconstitutional. However, the Court then went on to hold that even though the manner in which abrogation was accomplished was unconstitutional, it didn't matter, as it *could* have been accomplished through the unilateral actions of the President. This is, therefore a rare case where State action is upheld not on the basis of what the State did, but because the State *could* have done it another way.

49. See the Written Submissions on behalf of Gopal Subramanium SA, filed in *Muzaffar Iqbal Khan vs Union of India*, W.P. (C) 1104/2019, available at https://drive.google.com/file/d/1cC-KuNV1iURm8qkcTweyV8e7a7xlsnH_/view. This author (Gautam Bhatia) was involved in the drafting of these Written Submissions.
50. In the picturesque image used by Zafar Shah, counsel for the Jammu and Kashmir bar, 'I will shake you by the hand, but I will not embrace you.'
51. Article 371, Constitution of India.
52. Article 371D, Constitution of India. See, e.g., *A.V. Narasimha Rao vs State of Andhra Pradesh*, [1970] 1 SCR 115; *C. Surekha vs Union of India*, (1988) 4 SCC 526; *V. Jagannadha Rao vs State of Andhra Pradesh*, 2001 10 SCC 401.
53. Article 371C, Constitution of India.
54. For an account, see, e.g., Bela Bhatia, 'The Struggle for Self-Rule in Manipur's Hill Districts' in *India's Forgotten Country: A View from the Margins* (Penguin Random House India, 2024), 504, 516.
55. Sekhola Kom, 'Identity and Governance: Demand for Sixth Schedule in Manipur', *The Indian Journal of Political Science,* (2010) 71(1): 313.
56. Ibid., 519.
57. Article 371I, Constitution of India.
58. Article 371F, Constitution of India. In *R.C. Poudyal vs Union of India*, AIR (1993) SC 1804, the Supreme Court rejected a basic structure challenge to some of the (asymmetrically federal) terms on which Sikkim had been admitted to the Union via Article 371F, such as a departure from the one-person-one-vote principle.
59. Tillin, 'United in Diversity?', supra, where she argues that the application of these provisions to states in the north-east—which are regarded by the Indian State as being on the 'peripheries'—demonstrates that in

constitutional imagination, asymmetric federalism is an exception to the norm.

60. During the colonial era, the Naga Hills had been successively classified as Backward Areas in 1919, and Excluded Areas under the 1935 Government of India Act.
61. Naga-Akbar Hydari Accord (26–28 June 1947), available at https://peacemaker.un.org/sites/peacemaker.un.org/files/IN_470628_Naga-Akbar%20Hydari%20Accord.pdf
62. Discussed later in the chapter.
63. For a brief description, see Samrat Choudhury, *Northeast India: A Political History*, (HarperCollins India, 2023) 85–98. A few Naga testimonies can be read in Bela Bhatia, 'Awaiting *Nachiso*: Naga Elders Remember 1957', in Bela Bhatia, *India's Forgotten Country*, (2024) 529.
64. Ibid., 95.
65. For a critique of the exclusion of underground Naga leaders from the final stages of the negotiation of the sixteen-point agreement, see Bhatia, 'Awaiting *Nachiso*', supra 535.
66. 16 Point Agreement between the Government of India and the Naga People's Convention (26 July 1960), available at https://peacemaker.un.org/sites/peacemaker.un.org/files/IN_600726_The%20sixteen%20point%20Agreement_0.pdf
67. See, Kham Khan Suan Hausing, 'Asymmetric Federalism and the Question of Democratic Justice in Northeast India', *India Review* (2014) 13(2): 87.
68. Article 371A, Constitution of India. See Choudhury, *Northeast India*, supra 100, where he points out, interestingly, the objections to this 'special status' of Nagaland, which were made in Parliament, echoed a word that is familiar to us from the previous section: 'integration'.
69. See J. Zorema, *Indirect Rule in Mizoram: 1890–1954*, (Mittal Publications, 2007). This was a strategy that the British followed in certain other of their colonies, most notably in Africa.
70. Choudhury, *Northeast India*, supra 206, quoting the Bordoloi Report.
71. Ibid.
72. The Mizoram Peace Accord, 1986, available at https://www.satp.org/satporgtp/countries/india/states/mizoram/documents/papers/mizoram_accord_1986.htm Notably, the Mizoram Peace Accord was

signed at around the same time as the Rajiv-Longowal Accord, also designed to bring to an end another insurgency (in Punjab). Punjab, however, did not receive special constitutional safeguards along the lines of Articles 371A or G.

73. Article 371G, Constitution of India. For another history of both articles 371A and 371G, see Stepan, Linz, and Yadav, *Crafting State-Nations*, supra, Chapter 4.
74. They do not, of course, go as far as the original Article 370, in the sense that Nagaland and Mizoram were never accorded the right to frame their own Constitutions, and the subjects with respect to which they have the powers of self-governance are themselves set out in the Constitutional text (and thereby subject to alteration by a national legislative supermajority and a simple majority of state legislatures).
75. Article 371A, Constitution of India.
76. For the afterlife of the Naga insurgency, see Choudhary, *Northeast India*, supra 100–06.
77. Dr N. Jambemo Humtsoe, 'Special Powers of Nagaland Governor: Are His Actions Justified?', *EastMojo,* 8 July 2021, available at https://www.eastmojo.com/news/2020/07/03/special-powers-of-nagaland-governor-are-his-actions-justified/
78. Hausing, 'Asymmetric Federalism and the Question of Democratic Justice in Northeast India', supra 105. On the other hand, taking a more sympathetic approach to the issue, Jyotindra Dasgupta sees the figure of the governor as one part of a 'system of cascading linkages joining together various units of the federal polity in a complex system of coordination', involving the Centre, regional governments, and sub-regional units. See Jyotindra Dasgupta, 'Community, Authenticity, and Autonomy: Insurgence and Institutional Development in India's Northeast', *The Journal of Asian Studies* (1997) 56(2): 345, 362.
79. Article 371H, Constitution of India.
80. Article 371F, Constitution of India. With respect to the interpretation of Article 371F in its historical context, see *State of Sikkim vs Surendra Prasad Sharma*, (1994) 3 SCR 563.
81. See Chapter 2.
82. Schedule V, Constitution of India.
83. Schedule VI, Constitution of India.

84. I do not here go into the specific political histories of 'autonomous state within a state' movements. For an example discussing the prominent Bodoland movement, for instance, see Dasgupta, 'Community, Authenticity, and Autonomy'.
85. The Scheduled Districts Act 1874 (Act XIV of 1874).
86. Shaunna Rodrigues, 'Excluded Areas as the Limit of the Political: the Murky Boundaries of Scheduled Areas in India', *The International Journal of Human Rights* (2021) 25(7): 1126, 1129. This came one year after the introduction of the 'Inner Line', a moving colonial frontier whose purpose was to 'fence off the plantations and cordon off areas of clear, cemented colonial rule.' See Sanjib Baruah, (2020), *In the Name of the Nation: India and its Northeast,* (Navayana, 2020) 31; also see Choudhury, *Northeast India*. The Inner Line exists to this day.
87. For a comprehensive account, see Reeju Ray, *Placing the Frontier in British North-East India: Law, Custom, and Knowledge* (Oxford University Press, 2023). Ray notes that 'the violence of border-making was the core of imperial sovereignty as a governance strategy'. Ibid.: p. 73.
88. Stephen Legg, 'Dyarchy: Democracy, Autocracy and the Scalar Sovereignties of Inter-War India', *Comparative Studies of South Asia, Africa and the Middle East* (2016) 36(1): 44.
89. Saagar Tewari, 'Framing the Fifth Schedule: Tribal Agency and the making of the Indian Constitution (1937-1950)', *Modern Asian Studies* (2022) 56: 1556, 1558.
90. Legg, 'Dyarchy', supra.
91. For a discussion on this point, see Tewari, 'Framing the Fifth Schedule', 1558. See also Rodrigues, 'Excluded Areas as the limit of the political', 1135. Some of this history is discussed by the Supreme Court in *Samatha vs State of Andhra Pradesh* (1997) 8 SCC 191.
92. For a history of 'primitivism', see Uday Chandra, 'Liberalism and Its Other: The Politics of Primitivism in Colonial and Postcolonial Indian Law', *Law and Society Review* (2013) 47(1): 135.
93. The other basis—initially, at least—was the colonial imperative to quell rebellions in 'frontier' areas, which were, in part, caused by usurpation of land. For a discussion, see Pooja Parmar, 'Undoing Historical Wrongs: Law and Indigeneity in India', *Osgoode Hall Law Journal*,

(2012) 49(3): 491. This, ultimately, reinforced—and was reinforced by—the anthropological premise of protecting 'tribes' through a policy of isolationism. See, e.g., Tewari, 'Framing the Fifth Schedule', 1558. For an account of the construction of ethnic identity along both these lines, see Baruah, *In the Name of the Nation*, 28–29.

94. See Section 15(2) of the Government of India Act 1919, vesting legislative power in the Governor-General in Council for 'backward tracts'.
95. See, e.g.. Sections 91 and 92, Government of India Act, 1935. Under Section 92 of the Government of India Act 1935, for example, the Governor was granted the power to make regulations for the 'peace and good government' of excluded or partially excluded areas, and such regulations would override laws made by the federal and provincial legislatures.
96. Tewari, 'Framing the Fifth Schedule', 568.
97. Ibid. The fact that the Congress leadership was backtracking on its long-standing opposition to the existence of Scheduled Areas was not lost upon the members of the Constituent Assembly. See, e.g., the trenchant comments of Babu Ramnarayan Singh in the Constituent Assembly Debates. Parliament of India, *Constituent Assembly Debates*, Vol. XI (5 September 1949) (speech of Babu Ramnarayan Singh), available at https://eparlib.nic.in/bitstream/123456789/763207/1/cad_05-09-1949.pdf
98. Ibid.
99. See, e.g., Report of the Sub-Committee on North-East Frontier (Assam) Tribal and Excluded Areas, Annexure III, Appendix C in Parliament of India, *Constituent Assembly Debates*, Vol. VII (4 November 1948), available at https://eparlib.nic.in/bitstream/123456789/762996/1/cad_04-11-1948.pdf which uses both the terms. The word 'assimilation' was echoed by Shri Shibban Lal Saksena in the Constituent Assembly, during the debates on the Schedule V. See: Parliament of India, *Constituent Assembly Debates*, Vol. IX (5 September 1949) (Speech of Shri Shibban Lal Saksena), available at https://eparlib.nic.in/bitstream/123456789/763207/1/cad_05-09-1949.pdf
100. Interim Report of the Excluded and Partially Excluded Areas (Other than Assam) Sub Committee of the Advisory Committee (Constituent Assembly of India), Annexure III, Appendix D in Parliament of India,

Constituent Assembly Debates, Vol. VII (4 November 1948), available at https://eparlib.nic.in/bitstream/123456789/762996/1/cad_04-11-1948.pdf Also see: Tewari, 'Framing the Fifth Schedule', 1572–23. It is important to note, however, that on a reading of the Interim Report, even these recommendations were based at least as much on ideas of paternalism and 'protecting' the residents of these Areas, as they were on ideas of autonomy.

101. Parliament of India, *Constituent Assembly Debates*, Vol. IX (5 September 1949) (Speech of Jaipal Munda), available at https://eparlib.nic.in/bitstream/123456789/763207/1/cad_05-09-1949.pdf Munda was supported in this by Muniswamy Pillay.
102. Almost a mirror image of the colonial-era provisions.
103. *Constituent Assembly Debates*, Vol. IX (5 September 1949) (Speech of Jaipal Munda): Munda noted that despite being an Adivasi representative in the Constituent Assembly, he had not been consulted on this change, and that it had come as a 'bombshell'.
104. See, e.g., the speech of Shri Yudhishthir Mishra, from Orissa state, criticizing the element of 'discretion' that it introduced into Schedule V. *Constituent Assembly Debates*, Vol. IX (5 September 1949)
105. *Constituent Assembly Debates* (5 September 1949): Indeed, members of the Assembly such as Shri Shibban Lak Saksena and Brajeshwar Prasad were dissatisfied with Schedule V, because, in their view, it did not give the Centre *enough* powers. These members believed that the only way to achieve 'assimilation' was to bring Scheduled Areas under central control.
106. Ibid. In his speech introducing the Amendments, Ambedkar also refused to entrench Scheduled Areas within the Constitution; rather, the declaration of Scheduled Areas was left to the discretion of the President (i.e., the Union executive). This creates a curious situation where the *gatekeeper* of Schedule V autonomy is the Union executive.
107. Perhaps most aggressively by Biswanath Das, who called the TACs a 'racial virus'. Ibid. In slightly—but only slightly—milder language, K.M. Munshi argued that Schedule V ought not to create 'little republics to be perpetuated forever'. Ibid.
108. Paternalism was particularly evident in the speech of K.M. Munshi, who argued that one of the reasons why the TACs were being

given only an advisory role was the limited ability of the members of Scheduled Area to understand complex legislation, such as the Moneylenders' Act.

109. For a judicial account of the Constituent Assembly Debates around the framing of Schedule V, see the concurring opinion of Justice Saghir Ahmed in *Samatha vs State of Andhra Pradesh* (1997) 8 SCC 191.
110. Rodrigues, 'Excluded Areas as the Limit of the Political', supra 1138. According to Baruah, *In the Name of the Nation*, supra 39, Schedule VI marked a continuation of colonial 'indirect rule'.
111. Tellingly, the Report of the Committee placed the word *Constitution* within scare-quotes. See Report of the Sub-Committee on North-East Frontier (Assam) Tribal and Excluded Areas, Annexure III, Appendix C in Parliament of India, *Constituent Assembly Debates*, Vol. VII (4 November 1948), available at https://eparlib.nic.in/bitstream/123456789/762996/1/cad_04-11-1948.pdf
112. For more on this, see Choudhury, *Northeast India*, p. 83.
113. Ibid.
114. Report of the Sub-Committee on North-East Frontier (Assam) Tribal and Excluded Areas, Annexure III, Appendix C in Parliament of India, *Constituent Assembly Debates*, Vol. VII (4 November 1948), available at https://eparlib.nic.in/bitstream/123456789/762996/1/cad_04-11-1948.pdf
115. See Appendix A to the Part of North-East Frontier (Assam) Tribal and Excluded Areas Sub-Committee Report, Appendix C, Annexure V in Parliament of India, *Constituent Assembly Debates*, Vol. VII (4 November 1948), available at https://eparlib.nic.in/bitstream/123456789/762996/1/cad_04-11-1948.pdf
116. Report of the Sub-Committee on North-East Frontier (Assam) Tribal and Excluded Areas, Annexure III, Appendix C in *Constituent Assembly Debates*, Vol. VII (4 November 1948), available at https://eparlib.nic.in/bitstream/123456789/762996/1/cad_04-11-1948.pdf This idea of 'revenue sharing' as a solution to displacement would trickle over into post-constitutional legislation, and often limits the horizon of scholarly analysis as well. For an example of the latter, see Noronha, Ligia et al., 'Resource Federalism in India: the Case of Minerals', *Economic and Political Weekly* (2009) 44(8): 51.

Note also how this Constituent Assembly Debate foreshadowed future contestation in many different parts of the world between indigenous peoples insisting on exercising control over natural resources located on or under their land, and their national governments, which would invoke the 'larger national' interest in resisting such claims. This is especially true of Latin America: see the Conclusion to this chapter.

117. For a 'celebrated' judicial decision that replicated exactly this dichotomy, see *Samatha vs State of Andhra Pradesh* (1997) 8 SCC 191.
118. For a flavour of the debates, see Zahluna, 'Constituent Assembly and the Sixth Schedule', 1235.
119. Parliament of India, *Constituent Assembly Debates*, Vol. IX (6 September 1949), available at https://eparlib.nic.in/bitstream/123456789/763229/1/cad_06-09-1949.pdf; especially the speeches of Rohini Kumar Chaudhury, Lakshminarayan Sahu, Kuladhar Chaliha, and Shibban Lal Saksena.
120. Ibid.
121. Ibid. (speech of A.V. Thakkar).
122. Ibid. (speech of J.J.M. Nichols-Roy).
123. Ibid. (speech of B.R. Ambedkar).
124. Tewari, 'Framing the Fifth Schedule', 1590. See also, Xaxa, Virginius, 'Politics of Language, Religion, and Identity: Tribes in India', *Economic and Political Weekly,* (2005) 40(13): 1363, 1366. He, on the other hand, argues that the constitutional provisions reflect a normative philosophy of 'integration', which he understands as 'providing space for diversity'. Xaxa argues that the problem has been the gap between the constitutional provisions and social practice—especially in the domains of religion and language. Of course, with the Supreme Court having entrenched a narrow—and homogenizing—understanding of the word 'integration' in its Article 370 judgment, it is doubtful whether, in a constitutional sense, the word can still carry the weight that Xaxa intends it to carry.
125. Tillin, 'Asymmetric Federalism', calls it the 'paternalistic approach'.
126. Schedule V, Constitution of India.
127. Paragraph 5, Schedule V, Constitution of India.
128. At the time of writing, there does not appear to be an authoritative decision explicitly on the point of whether the governor, under

Paragraph 5, acts in their discretion. Some stray observations in *Samatha vs State of Andhra Pradesh* (1997) 8 SCC 191 suggest so (see paragraph 94), but there is no decision squarely on the point.

129. See Tillin, 'Asymmetric Federalism'.
130. Paragraph 5, Schedule V, Constitution of India.
131. Schedule V, Constitution of India.
132. Paragraph 7, V Schedule, Constitution of India.
133. Parmar, 'Undoing Historical Wrongs', 518.
134. For an analysis of the intersection of Schedule VI and political economy—especially in the context of mining —see Ray, Reeju, 'Terror in the Coal Mines of North-East India', *Jamhoor* (2021) 5, available at https://www.jamhoor.org/read/terror-in-the-coal-mines-of-meghalaya; for the intersection with criminal law, see Nandini Ramachandran, 'Exceptions' *FiftyTwo* (30 April 2022), available at https://fiftytwo.in/story/exceptions/
135. For a summary of the debates, see Hausing, 'Asymmetric Federalism', 90–91.
136. Schedule VI, Constitution of India.
137. It is important to note that the functioning of the ADCs has itself come under substantial criticism, with it being pointed out that ADCs are susceptible to capture by entrenched dominant interests at the local level, which transforms them into exclusivist bodies, often with specific costs to the environment, given their control over administering natural resources. For an example discussing mining in Meghalaya, see Baruah, *In the Name of the Nation*, Chapter 3.

    Another critique of the ADCs, which translates into a broader critique of asymmetric federalism, is how the devolution of law-making with respect to social customs can (and has) affected the rights of women. See, for example, Reeju Ray's critique of the ADC-enacted Khasi Custom of Lineage Act 2005, which 'imposed severe restrictions on women by controlling their sexual choices and their right of descent', in Ray, *Placing the Frontier in British North-East India*, p. 187.
138. Paragraph 15, Schedule VI, Constitution of India. In *Pu Myllai Hlychho vs State of Mizoram*, (2005) 2 SCC 92, the Supreme Court followed the '*Shamsher Singh* principle' of cabinet government to hold that except

where Schedule VI specifically provides that the governor may act in his discretion, he is bound by the aid and advice of the state's council of ministers. In doing so, it specifically departed from the dissenting opinion of Justice Hidayatullah in *Edwingson Bareh vs State of Assam*, (1966) 2 SCR 770. In that case, the majority had expressed no clear opinion on this issue. I am grateful to Shomona Khanna for helping me work through some of the implications of this.

139. Paragraph 15, Schedule VI, Constitution of India.

140. It is important to note that increased gubernatorial powers under Schedule VI have sometimes come about as a result of political demands. For example, the insertion of Paragraph 20BB into Schedule VI in 1988—which grants the governor discretionary power to nominate four members to the advisory council—followed demands from Mizoram asking for less control by the state government (i.e., the council of ministers), with the way to accomplish that being more power to the governor (i.e., the central government). This illustrates the interlocking nature of many of these provisions, and the fact that control by the central government may be seen as more conducive for local autonomy than control by (the more proximate) state government. For a discussion of some of these issues, see *Pu Myllai Hlychho vs State of Mizoram*.

141. Paragraph 16, Schedule VI, Constitution of India. This is not to say, of course, that the kill switch can be utilized at any point; naturally, it will be politics that will determine when—and whether—the kill switch is to be utilized. As we have argued throughout this book, however, the Constitution and politics exist in an intertwined relationship, with politics often taking place on the terrain of the Constitution. This is why focusing on the constitutional text is of crucial significance: the very fact that the Constitution formally creates a federal kill switch will, itself, shape the nature and the limits of the politics that is conducted around the issue of ADC autonomy.

142. *District Council of United Khasi and Jaintia Hills vs Sitimon Sawian*, (1972) 1 SCR 398.

143. Ibid.

144. Ibid.

145. Parmar, 'Undoing Historical Wrongs'.

146. Ibid. Of course, Jammu and Kashmir *did* have its own flag (and its own Constitution), something that was always particularly unpalatable to the nationalist wing of Indian public discourse.
147. Ibid. Interestingly, Bela Bhatia, 'Awaiting *Nachiso*', records the testimonies of Naga elders who understand the existence of two constitutions and 'internal autonomy' as being entirely compatible with federalism (something that, as we have seen, the Supreme Court was unable to imagine in its Article 370 judgment).
148. Or, to use a term beloved of the Supreme Court in the *Article 370 Case*, 'integration'.
149. Hausing, 'Asymmetric Federalism', 95. The 1928 Nehru Committee Report stated, for example, that 'the re-distribution of provinces should take place on a linguistic basis on the demand of the majority of the population of the area concerned, subject to financial and administrative considerations.' Article 86, *Nehru Report* (1928), available at https://www.constitutionofindia.net/historical-constitution/nehru-report-motilal-nehru1928/
150. Article 1, Constitution of Bolivia. Unsurprisingly, the drafting of this constitution saw extensive involvement by the indigenous peoples of Bolivia, the several 'nations' that are acknowledged by the word 'plurinational'. See, e.g., Mark Goodale, *A Revolution in Fragments: Traversing Scales of Justice, Ideology, and Practice in Bolivia*, (Duke University Press, 2019).
151. For precisely this link, see Nancy Postero, *The Indigenous State: Race, Politics, and Performance in Plurinational Bolivia*, (University of California Press, 2017) 55. For a discussion and critique of systems of indigenous territorial autonomy in a Latin American country that does not subscribe to plurinationalism, see Pablo Rueda-Saiz, 'Indigenous Autonomy in Colombia: State-building Processes and Multiculturalism', *Global Constitutionalism,* (2017) 6(2): 265.
152. Article 2, Constitution of Bolivia. One should be careful, however, not to overstate the case. As Nancy Postero notes in her critique of the Bolivian constitutional and State-building project, notwithstanding its public commitment to plurinationalism, the Bolivian Constitution 'subsumes indigenous local autonomy rights under a liberal government in which the central state retains decision-making power over most

significant matters, especially as regards the extraction of natural resources'. See Postero, *The Indigenous State*.

153. See Article 289, Constitution of Bolivia.
154. Aaron Augsburger and Paul Haber, 'Constructing Indigenous Autonomy in Plurinational Bolivia: Possibilities and Ambiguities', *Latin American Perspectives* (2018) 45(6): pp. 53, 54.
155. See, e.g., Pablo Regalsky (2010), 'Political Process and the Reconfiguration of the State in Bolivia', *Latin American Perspectives*, (2010) 37(172): 35; Nancy Postero and Nicole Fabricant (2019), 'Indigenous Sovereignty and the New Developmentalism in Plurinational Bolivia', *Anthropological Theory* (2019) 19(1): 95, 100. Augsburger and Haber, 'Constructing Indigenous Autonomy'. Also see Luis Tapia, 'Consideraciones Sobre El Estado Plurinacional', *Bolivian Research Review/Revista E* (2010) 8(2): 1, 14. Tapia (ibid.) notes that the indigenous demands for plurinationalism comprised three core elements: juridical pluralism, recognition of cultural diversity, and a non-hierarchical relationship between different forms of social organization. Ultimately, the Bolivian Constitution partially succeeds on the first two counts, but maintains a hierarchy of norms with the 'liberal State' subsuming other forms of social organization.
156. For a discussion, see Jason Tockman and John Cameron, 'Indigenous Autonomy and the Contradictions of Plurinationalism in Bolivia', *Latin American Politics and Society* (2014) 56(3): 46. I discuss some of these issues further, infra, in Chapter 6.
157. See, for example, Postero (2017), *The Indigenous State*, Chapter 7, where the author discusses how indigenous nations have attempted to work the autonomy clauses in the constitution.
158. This takes issue with the claim of Stepan, Linz, and Yadav (2011), who argue, in *Crafting State-Nations*, that Indian Constitutional arrangements do reflect a founding vision of India as a state-nation.
159. Parliament of India, *Constituent Assembly Debates*, Vol. II (25 January 1947) (speech of Jaipal Munda), available at https://eparlib.nic.in/bitstream/123456789/762961/1/cad_25-01-1947.pdf For a similar attempt to reconcile pluralism (i.e., non-uniformity) with unity, see Postero's discussion of the Pacto de Unidad's draft constitutional documents in the lead-up to the convening of the Bolivian Constituent Assembly, in Postero, *The Indigenous State*, 56.

4: Power Confronted: Institutions

1. The Right to Information (Amendment) Act, 2019. The history of the RTI movement is an example of one of the axes of power that we have not discussed in this book: social movements, invoking constitutional vocabulary, in order to bring about a change in the legal landscape. These social movements may not always be of a progressive bent, of course.
2. Aruna Roy, and MKSS Collective, *The RTI Story: Power to the People* (Roli Books, 2018).
3. See, e.g., Chapter V, RTI Act.
4. See, e.g., Sections 13 and 14, RTI Act.
5. Sections 13 and 16, RTI Act (replacing a fixed term of five years with a term fixed at the discretion of the central government, and replacing fixed remuneration with remuneration at the discretion of the central government, for both central information commissioners and state information commissioners.
6. PTI, 'Centre notifies RTI Act amendments, ignores civil society concerns', *Business Standard* (24 October 2019).
7. *Anoop Baranwal vs Union of India*, WP (C) No. 104 of 2015.
8. This obligation flows from Article 324 of the Constitution.
9. We will discuss the genesis of this committee subsequently.
10. Chief Election Commissioner and Other Election Commissioners (Appointment, Conditions of Service and Term of Office) Act, 2023.
11. *Dr. Jaya Thakur and Ors vs Union of India* (2024) INSC 246.
12. For a fuller discussion of this, see Chapter 6.
13. A Parliament that, as we have seen in the previous chapter, is structurally subordinate to the executive. This is an example of how the axes of power reinforce each other in service of the centralizing drift towards the executive.
14. In political theory, this distinction is generally traced back to John Locke's *Two Treatises of Government* and Baron Montesquieu's *The Spirit of the Laws*. See Baron de Montesquieu, *The Spirit of the Laws* (Colonial Press, 1899); John Locke, *Two Treatises of Government* (Peter Laslett ed., Cambridge University Press, 1970).
15. Heinz Klug, 'Transformative Constitutions and the Role of Integrity Institutions in Tempering Power: The Case of Resistance to State

Capture in Post-Apartheid South Africa' (2019) 67 *Buffalo Law Review* 701, 702.

16. Bruce Ackerman, 'The New Separation of Powers' (2000) 113(3) *The Harvard Law Review* 633, 638; Morgens Herman Hansen, 'The Mixed Constitution Versus the Separation of Powers: Monarchical and Aristocratic Aspects of Modern Democracy' (2010) 31(3) *History of Political Thought* 509.
17. Chapter IX, Constitution of South Africa, 1994; for a historical account, see Heinz Klug, 'Transformative Constitutions and the Role of Integrity Institutions in Tempering Power', supra, 705 – 7; for further discussion, see Charles M. Fombad, 'The Role of Emerging Hybrid Institutions of Accountability in the Separation of Powers Scheme in Africa' in Charles M. Fombad (ed.), *Separation of Powers in African Constitutionalism* (Oxford University Press, 2016).
18. Article 249, Constitution of Kenya 2010. See also the discussion in Constitutional Application No. 2 of 2011: *In the Matter of Interim Independent Electoral Commission*, [2011] eKLR, and in Advisory Reference No. 2 of 2014, *In the Matter of the National Land Commission*, [2015] eKLR.
19. Ibid. For a fuller list of such institutions, across jurisdictions, see Mark Tushnet, *The New Fourth Branch: Institutions for Protecting Constitutional Democracy* (Cambridge University Press, 2021).
20. Ackerman, 'The New Separation of Powers', supra.
21. Ackerman, 'The New Separation of Powers', supra; Charles M. Fombad, 'Designing Institutions and Mechanisms for the Implementation and Enforcement of the Constitution: Changing Perspectives in Africa' (2017) 25(1) *African Journal of International and Comparative Law* 66.
22. Although, of course, technical and domain-specific expertise is a relevant factor, which also explains why many of these functions cannot be performed by constitutional courts. See Tushnet, *The New Fourth Branch*, supra, 32.
23. Ibid.
24. For this, see also Chapter 8 of this book.
25. This checking function is articulated specifically by Christina Murray, in her discussion of South Africa's Chapter Nine Institutions. See Christina Murray, 'The Human Rights Commission et al: What is the Role of South Africa's Chapter IX Institutions?' (2006) 9(2) *PER* 10.

26. Heinz Klug, 'Transformative Constitutions and the Role of Integrity Institutions in Tempering Power', supra 703.
27. Christina Murray, 'The Human Rights Commission et al', supra. See also Dinesha Samararatne 'Sri Lanka's Constitutional ping-pong: the 20th Amendment in historical perspective', *Himal Magazine* (25 September 2020), for a teasing out of the intertwined concepts of institutional and discursive accountability.
28. Tarunah Khaitan, 'Guarantor Institutions' (2021) *The Asian Journal of Comparative Law* 1, doi:10.1017/asjcl.2021.19
29. For a discussion of some of these aspects, see the various opinions of the South African Constitutional Court delivered in *The New National Party of South Africa vs Government of the Republic of South Africa*, Case CCT 9/99.
30. Gregoire Webber, et al., *Legislated Rights: Securing Human Rights Through Legislation* (Cambridge University Press, 2018).
31. Mark Tushnet, *The New Fourth Branch*, supra.
32. Ibid.
33. Khaitan, 'Guarantor Institutions' supra.
34. Or, in the words of the Kenyan Supreme Court, these institutions serve as 'the People's Watchdogs'. See: *In the Matter of Interim Independent Electoral Commission*, supra.
35. Khaitan, 'Guarantor Institutions', supra.
36. Mark Tushnet, 'Institutions Protecting Democracy: A Preliminary Inquiry' (2018) 12(2) *Law and Ethics of Human Rights* 181, 183. This argument is developed further in Mark Tushnet, *The New Fourth Branch*, supra, where Tushnet expands the problem to include both conflict and convergence of interests.
37. Christina Murray, 'The Human Rights Commission et al', supra. For a similar argument in the US Constitutional context, see Jules Lobel, 'The Political Tilt of the Separation of Powers' in David Kairys (ed.), *The Politics of Law: A Progressive Critique* (Basic Books, 1998) 591, 607. The political theories Pierre Rosanvallon also makes a similar point in speaking of the 'multiplication of functional authorities' in liberal democracies, although he folds it within a more expansive conception of representation itself. Pierre Rosanvallon, in Samuel Moyn (ed.), *Democracy Past and Future* (Columbia University Press, 2006) 203.
38. Roberto Gargarella, *Latin American Constitutionalism*, supra.

39. See also the discussion in Advisory Reference No. 2 of 2014, *In the Matter of the National Land Commission*, [2015] eKLR, where the Land Commission's obligation to publish its reports was held by the Kenyan Supreme Court to be an integral element of public participation in the workings of independent commissions.
40. See Chapter 6 of this book.
41. See Éric Monnet, *Balance of Power: Central Bank and the Fate of Democracies* (University of Chicago Press, 2024); Quinn Slobodian, *Globalists: The End of Empire and the Birth of Neoliberalism* (Harvard University Press, 2018). I am grateful to Philipp Dann for raising this point in response to an early draft of this chapter.
42. See, for example, the judgment of the Supreme Court in *Vivek Narayan Sinha vs Union of India* (2023) 3 SCC 1, upholding the government's decision to 'demonetise' high-denomination currency notes with four hours' notice—a decision that caused a substantial amount of social chaos. One of the contentions in the case was that the Reserve Bank of India had not independently applied its mind to the proposal (as it was obligated to do, by law), and acted as a 'rubber stamp' for the executive. The majority judgment—which rejected the argument that the bank was supposed to act 'independently' of the government, in favour of an elastic idea of inter-institutional 'cooperation'—highlights the perilous nature of this terrain. While we do not want to *insulate* banks from democratic institutions, the demonetization case demonstrates the problem when the central bank (RBI) is arguably *subservient* to the political executive. For an analysis of the demonetization judgment from this perspective, see Gautam Bhatia, 'Every Noble Cause Claims Its Martyr: the Supreme Court's Demonetisation Judgment', *Constitutional Law and Philosophy* (3 January 2023), available at https://indconlawphil.wordpress.com/2023/01/03/every-noble-cause-claims-its-martyr-the-supreme-courts-demonetisation-judgment
43. Chapter V, Constitution of India, 1949.
44. Articles 315–323, Constitution of India, 1949; Article 338, Constitution of India, 1949. Civil services are under executive control. The Constitution expressly grants to the executive the power to dismiss civil servants, even without an opportunity to show cause where the executive wishes to dispense with it. See, e.g., Article 311(2), Constitution of

India, borrowed from its colonial antecedent, Section 240, Government of India Act, 1935.

45. Some of these had antecedents in the Government of India Act, 1935. For example, the CAG's antecedent was the auditor-general, who was appointed by British executive. See Section 166, Government of India Act, 1935.
46. Article 324(5), Constitution of India, 1949.
47. The Protection of Human Rights Act, 1993.
48. Delhi Special Police Establishment Act, 1946.
49. The Right to Information Act, 2005.
50. Digital Personal Data Protection Act, 2023.
51. The Internet Freedom Foundation (2021), '#DataProtectionTop10: On the importance of a strong, transparent, and independent Data Protection Authority', 28 May, available at https://internetfreedom.in/dataprotectiontop10-on-the-importance-of-a-strong-and-independent-data-protection-authority/
52. Fombad (2017), 'Designing Institutions and Mechanisms'.
53. *Vineet Narain vs Union of India*, (1998) 1 SCC 226.
54. Ibid., paragraph 48.
55. Otherwise known as the 'Vishaka formulation'. See *Vishaka vs State of Rajasthan*, AIR 1997 SC 3011.
56. *Alok Verma vs Union of India* (2019) 3 SCC 1.
57. Ibid., paragraph 26.
58. Ibid., paragraph 36.
59. Ibid., paragraph 37.
60. Ironically, in a swift sequel, Alok Verma was, as a matter of fact, removed by the Committee, perhaps demonstrating the limits of constitutional doctrine in the teeth of overwhelming political force.
61. The term 'constitutional statute' here ought not to be confused with the term 'constitutional statute' as used in the context of English administrative law.
62. That rights have a positive dimension has long been established in Indian constitutional jurisprudence. For a recent example, see *Indibility Creative Pvt Ltd vs Govt of West Bengal* (2020) 12 SCC 436.
63. See, e.g., *Hugh Glenister vs The President of the Republic of South Africa*, (2011) ZACC 6, where the South African Constitutional Court held that the obligation upon the State to establish an independent and effective anti-corruption body flowed from the positive component of

the Bill of Rights. See, specifically, paras 177 and 189. For analysis, see Rosaan Krüger, 'The Ebb and Flow of the Separation of Powers in South African Constitutional Law—the Glenister Litigation Campaign' (2015) 48(1) *Verfassung und Recht in Übersee/ Law and Politics in Africa, Asia and Latin America* 49; Melea Lewis and Philip Stenning, 'Considering the Glenister Judgment: Independence requirements for anti-corruption institutions' (2012) 39 *SA Crime Quarterly* 11;

64. See the discussion in *Glenister vs The President*, supra, para 191.
65. The Supreme Court, of course, is no stranger to legislating from the bench, on the occasion that it feels that it needs to; see, e.g., *Vishaka vs State of Rajasthan*, supra.
66. Lael K. Weis, 'Constitutionally Obligatory Legislation: A Case Study in Legal Constitutionalism', in Richard Albert and Joel I. Colon-Rios (eds), *Quasi Constitutionality and Constitutional Statutes: Forms, Functions, Applications* (Routledge, 2019) 204, 210.
67. *Glenister vs The President*, supra.
68. *Glenister vs The President* supra, paragraph 198.
69. The reasoning—especially the derivation of the obligation from the right to equality—is strikingly reminiscent of *Vineet Narain*.
70. *Glenister vs The President*, supra, paragraph 199.
71. *Glenister vs The President*, supra, paragraphs 188, 206.
72. *Glenister vs The President*, supra, paragraph 216.
73. *Glenister vs The President*, supra, paragraph 205.
74. For a similar case, which did not involve an institution, but did involve a derivative right, see *My Vote Counts NPC vs Minister for Justice & Correctional Services*, CCT 249/17. The constitutional court held that a combination of the right to information, the right to vote, and the freedom of expression (all expressly guaranteed by the South African Constitution) necessarily implied the right of voters to know about the funding of political parties and candidates. To the extent that the South African Promotion of Access to Information Act did not guarantee this right—and did not have in place an infrastructure for making it effective—it did not comply with the constitution. As the constitutional court held:

    > The right of access to information read with the entitlement to exercise or protect the informed right to vote, and the State's section 7(2) obligation to respect, promote and fulfil the rights in the Bill of Rights, implicitly demands that information on the

private funding of political parties and independent candidates be recorded, preserved and made reasonably accessible to the public. (*My Vote Counts*, ibid., paragraph 69.)

75. *State of UP vs Raj Narain*, (1975) 4 SCC 428.
76. Roy and MKSS Collective (2018), *The RTI Story*, supra.
77. See, e.g., the prescriptions of Privacy International in 'Independent Supervisory Authority', available at https://privacyinternational.org/sites/default/files/2018-09/Part%207-%20Independent%20Supervisory%20Authority%20copy.pdf
78. Article 324, Constitution of India.
79. Article 324(2), Constitution of India.
80. The most famous and controversial example of this, of course, is T.N. Seshan.
81. *Anoop Baranwal vs Union of India*, supra, paragraphs 15, 18, 25–26 (majority opinion of Joseph J).
82. Ibid., paragraphs 32–33 (majority opinion of Justice Joseph).
83. Ibid., paragraphs 21, 75 (concurring opinion of Justice Rastogi).
84. Ibid., paragraphs 135–36, 141 (majority opinion of Justice Joseph).
85. Ibid., paragraphs 150–60, 166–85. Indeed, some of these powers can sway electoral outcomes.
86. Under the Transaction of Business Rules, this effectively meant that appointments were at the instance of the Prime Minister.
87. This is why the details of such processes are always left to legislation, and not spelt out within the Constitution.
88. *Jaya Thakur vs Union of India*, supra, paragraph 9.
89. For a more detailed analysis of the Supreme Court's interim order, and its numerous shortcomings, see Gautam Bhatia, 'The Unexamined Law: On the Supreme Court's Stay Order in the Election Commissioners Case,' *Constitutional Law and Philosophy* (22 March 2024), available at https://indconlawphil.wordpress.com/2024/03/22/the-unexamined-law-on-the-supreme-courts-stay-order-in-the-election-commissioners-case/
90. It is a different matter, of course, that a later smaller bench of the Court being unwilling or unable to secure the enforcement of *its own* previous Constitution Bench judgment reflects none too well on the functioning of the Supreme Court as an institution.

91. *Dr. Jaya Thakur vs Union of India*, (2023) INSC 616.
92. Ibid., paragraph 91.
93. Arun Thiruvengadam notes that the absence of public participation in the CAG's proceedings more or less makes it a 'technocratic institution'. See Arun Thiruvengadam, *Constitution of India: A Contextual Analysis* (Hart Publishing India, 2017).

5: Power Contained: Rights

1. Now the Bharatiya Nagarik Suraksha Sanhita (BNSS).
2. As we shall see, however, the terminological question of what constitutes criminal law has attained some significance for the protection of rights in India today.
3. *Entick vs Carrington*, (1765) EWHC KB J98. A 'general warrant' refers to a warrant for search and/or seizure that does not specify what is being searched for, and on what probable cause: essentially, a fishing expedition in the hope or expectation of uncovering *some* incriminating material.
4. This right was recognized as common law in 1637, at the trial of John Lilburne. See Leonard W. Levy, *Origins of the Fifth Amendment: The Right Against Self-Incrimination* (Ivan R. Dee, 1999).
5. Section 25, Indian Evidence Act.
6. See, for example, the discussion around the Criminal Tribes Act of 1871 in Gautam Bhatia, *The Transformative Constitution* (HarperCollins, 2019), Chapter 9. The Supreme Court of India recognized this as well, in *State of Gujarat vs Shyamlal Mohanlal Choksi* (1965) 2 SCR 457, para 16.
7. See *Ahmed Mahomed Jackariah vs Ahmed Mahomed* (1888) ILR 15 Cal 109.
8. Sections 96–99, Code of Criminal Procedure, 1898; see also Section 91, Code of Criminal Procedure 1973.
9. For some of the classic discussions on this subject, see Elizabeth Kolsky, 'Codification and the Rule of Colonial Difference: Criminal Procedure in British India' (2005) 23(3) *Law and History Review* 631; Radhika Singha, *A Despotism of Law: Crime and Justice in Early Colonial India* (Oxford University Press, 1999).
10. Bengal Regulation (III) of 1818.

11. Hallie Ludsin, *Preventive Detention and the Democratic State* (Cambridge University Press, 2016), 87; for a catalogue of some of these laws, see Derek P. Jinks, 'The Anatomy of an Institutionalized Emergency: Preventive Detention and Personal Liberty in India' (2001) 22(2) *Michigan Journal of International Law* 311, 324.
12. For an account, see Nasser Hussain, *The Jurisprudence of Emergency: Colonialism and the Rule of Law* (University of Michigan Press, 2019); see also Ujjwal Kumar Singh, 'Democratic Dilemmas: Can Democracy Do Without Extraordinary Laws?' (2003) 38(5) *Economic and Political Weekly* 437.
13. Nasser Hussain, *The Jurisprudence of Emergency*: Colonialism and the Rule of Law (University of Michigan Press, 2003), 135.
14. In Lauren Benton's elegant formulation, the effect (of Imperial constitutional ordering) was 'less an epidemic of exceptionalism than a surfeit of legalism.' Lauren Benton, 'Just Despots: The Cultural Construction of Imperial Constitutionalism' (2011) 9(2) *Law, Culture and the Humanities* 213, 226.
15. See Article V, Constitution of the United States.
16. Article 25, Constitution of Kenya.
17. Article 21, Constitution of India.
18. See the discussion in Gautam Bhatia, *The Transformative Constitution*, supra.
19. Articles 22(1) and (2), Constitution of India.
20. Articles 22(3) – (7), Constitution of India.
21. See, e.g. K.G. Kannabiran, *The Speaking Constitution: A Sisyphean Life in the Law* (HarperCollins, 2023) 191, arguing against such a reading of constitutionalism.
22. For a similar discussion, see Sandipto Dasgupta, *Legalizing the Revolution: India and the Constitution of the Postcolony* (Cambridge University Press, 2024), Chapter 6.
23. Hallie Ludsin, *Preventive Detention and the Democratic State,* supra 208.
24. See *A.K. Gopalan vs State of Madras*, infra.
25. Ibid.
26. See Abhinav Sekhri, 'Calling Time on Preventive Detention' 9 *Indian Journal of Constitutional Law* 174, 178, for an illustrative list of provincial preventive detention laws. These are also extracted in the dissenting opinion of Justice Fazl Ali in *A.K. Gopalan vs The State of Madras*, infra.

27. Defence of India Rules, 1942.
28. For a more generous assessment of the Federal Court, see Rohit De, 'Emasculating the Executive: The Federal Court and Civil Liberties in Late Colonial India: 1942–1944' in Terence C. Halliday, Lucien Karpik, and Malcolm M. Feeley (eds), *Fates of Political Liberalism in the British Post-Colony: The Politics of Legal Complex*Cambridge University Press, 2012), 59.
29. *Machindar Shivaji vs The King*, AIR 1950 FC 129, involving the detention of a member of the Communist Party.
30. See the debates in Parliament of India, *Constituent Assembly Debates*, Vol. V (22 August 1947); *Constituent Assembly Debates*, Vol. IX (29 August 1949); *Constituent Assembly Debates*, Vol. IX (15 and 16 September 1949). The debates around preventive detention are discussed in greater detail in Gautam Bhatia, *The Transformative Constitution*, supra, Chapter 8.
31. Singh, 'Democratic Dilemmas', supra 438.
32. Ibid. Derek Jinks argues that a closer reading of the speeches accompanying the passage of the Preventive Detention Act of 1950 demonstrates that parliamentarians did not understand it to be an 'exceptional' legislation, but as something woven into the fabric of public order law, given the continuing conditions in post-Independence India—conditions with no definite expiry date. In other words, the invocation of a kind of Indian exceptionalism to normalize preventive detention. See Jinks, 'The Anatomy of an Institutionalized Emergency', supra 339–340.
33. *A.K. Gopalan vs The State of Madras*, (1950) SCR 88.
34. The Court split 4-2 on this point, with Justices Fazl Ali and Meher Chand Mahajan writing separate, dissenting opinions.
35. In particular, the debate has focused around whether a majority of the Court in *A.K. Gopalan* declared that Article 22 was a 'complete code', or whether this was a gloss put by later judgments. While scholarship predominantly espouses the former view, H.M. Seervai is a forceful proponent of the latter. For the purposes of the argument in this chapter, this particular debate is academic, and is therefore not examined in detail here.
36. At least three judges held this view. A fourth—Justice Sastri—did hold that Article 21 had substantive content, but that this content was

to be identified through gleaning the core principles of the existing criminal procedure code—that is, *colonial* criminal law. In other words, Justice Sastri proposed an interpretive approach where the *content* of Fundamental Rights would be *determined* by the content of colonial law, rather than colonial law being *tested* on the touchstone of fundamental rights. This approach as we shall see expanded to other domains as well.

37. P.K. Tripathi, 'Preventive Detention: The Indian Experience' (1960) 9(2) *American Journal of Comparative Law* 219, 226.
38. Ibid., 221.
39. *A.K. Gopalan vs State of Madras*, supra (dissenting opinion of Justice Fazl Ali).
40. This tactic—that of simply repeating the language of the Schedule VII or of the restrictions clauses under Articles 19(2) – (6) in legislation—would be used repeatedly in the future, and continue to be upheld by the Court; see, for example, cases involving film censorship, and the judgment of the Supreme Court in *K.A. Abbas vs Union of India*, (1971) SCR (2) 446; but see below.
41. Ibid., 222.
42. Subsequently, Parliament enacted the substantially similar Maintenance of Internal Security Act in 1971, and—following Indira Gandhi's return to power after the end of the Emergency in 1980—the National Security Act, 1980. The NSA continues to hold the field, marking the almost continued existence of a central, preventive detention law since the enactment of the Constitution in 1950.
43. See, e.g., *Haradhan Saha vs State of West Bengal*, (1975) 3 SCC 198. A limited exception is *Sambhu Nath Sarkar vs State of West Bengal*, (1974)1 SCR 1, where the Court did finally hold that a law seeking to extend the period of preventive detention without advisory board intercession under Article 22(7) for specific 'classes' or 'circumstances' (as required by the text of the Article), could not simply replicate the language of the legislative entries under Schedule VII; that is, the law would have to set out with greater specificity what 'classes' and 'circumstances' justified extended preventive detention without scrutiny. The Court held so on the basis that Article 22(7) was an exception to Article 22(4), and therefore had to be interpreted strictly.

44. *Ram Singh vs State of Delhi*, AIR (1951) SC 270. While the Court was unanimous on this point, it split on the issue of whether the detained individuals had been informed, with sufficient clarity, the reasons for their detention. Justices Mahajan and Bose, in dissent, noted that the constitutional right to make a representation against a detention order required a detained individual being informed of the grounds of his detention, at least in so much detail that he *could* make a representation. In this case, that would have required being informed of the gist of what the detaining authority considered offensive in the speeches that were made. It is striking, though, that even these two justices limited their dissents to a bare procedural right to *make* a representation against a detention order. Their dissents did not extend to whether the detaining power *itself* was limited, on the lines argued by the petitioners; indeed, Justice Bose, often considered to be an early hero of civil liberties from the bench, endorsed that power with some enthusiasm in his dissent.
45. Of course, 'public order' was introduced into Article 19(2) through the First Amendment of the Constitution.
46. In this case, this would have been the test of reasonableness under Article 19(2).
47. As early as 1960, Tripathi pointed this out in his discussion of the Allahabad High Court judgment in *Sarju vs Uttar Pradesh*, AIR (1956) All 589. See Tripathi, 'Preventive Detention', supra, 247.
48. *Sahadat Ali vs State of Assam*, AIR (1953) Gau 97.
49. Ibid., paragraph 4.
50. *Rameshwar Shaw vs District Magistrate, Burdwan* (1964) 4 SCR 921.
51. This pattern of State action has existed all over India but has been particularly and starkly evident in Jammu and Kashmir.
52. The present writer has been involved in cases where precisely this has happened.
53. *Maneka Gandhi vs Union of India*, (1978) 1 SCC 248.
54. See, e.g., *Justice K.S. Puttaswamy vs Union of India*, (2017) 10 SCC 1. This is also a story frequently told by the Court's hagiographers.
55. Sekhri, 'Article 22: Calling Time on Preventive Detention', supra 183. See also Jinks, 'The Anatomy of an Institutionalized Emergency,' supra 349.
56. *A.K. Roy vs Union of India,* AIR (1982) 1 SCC 271.

57. Ibid., paragraph 70.
58. Ibid.
59. Ibid., paragraphs 86–87. The Court placed great reliance on the provisions of the Constitution 'as enacted', reinforcing this book's argument about the centralizing drift within the Constitution's original structure and design.
60. While in *Haradhan Saha vs State of West Bengal*, (1975) 1 SCR 778 and *Khudiram Das vs State of West Bengal*, (1975) 2 SCC 81, the Court purported to test preventive detention provision of the Maintenance of Internal Security Act (MISA) on the touchstone of Articles 14 and 19, it did not do so in any substantive manner. In *Haradhan Saha*, the Article 14 challenge was repelled on the basis of the circular argument that 'preventive' and 'punitive' detention were 'different' in nature. And Article 19 was applied only to test whether preventive detention met a basic threshold of procedural reasonableness. *Khudiram Das*, supra, affirmed this.
61. Ludsin, *Preventive Detention and the Democratic State*, supra, 170.
62. Ibid., 203.
63. See *Union of India vs Dimple Happy Dhakad*, (2019) 20 SCC 609, and the analysis in Abhinav Sekhri, 'Dimple Happy Dhakad and Normalising Preventive Detention' *The Proof of Guilt* (20 July 2019), available at https://theproofofguilt.blogspot.com/2019/07/a-worrying-portent-supreme-courts.html. In such cases, the Court warns that such processes should not be used to short-circuit the ordinary criminal process, but does nothing to ensure that this will not actually be done.
64. Sekhri, 'Calling Time on Preventive Detention', supra.
65. See e.g. *Bhut Nath Mete vs State of West Bengal*, (1974) 3 SCR 315. In this case, the Supreme Court ordered the release of the detenu on the facts of the case, while affirming the proposition that a preventive detention order could be passed on the basis of a set of facts where the detenu had already been acquitted in criminal proceedings. As is often the case with such matters, as noted above, Justice Krishna Iyer wrote reams of pages cautioning the State against misusing or abusing the power of preventive detention to incarcerate people against whom it had failed to prove a criminal case, but none of this found its way into the actual jurisprudence of the Supreme Court.
66. *Dropti Devi vs Union of India* (2012) 6 SCR 307.

67. The 'blurring' of the state of exception and the state of normalcy, that is a staple feature of Article 22 jurisprudence, extends across the various domains of the Constitution. In Chapter 1, we discussed the Supreme Court's validation of AFSPA from the perspective of federalism. Another argument made in the case was that *in effect*, by virtue of the extraordinary powers it vested upon the armed forces, the AFSPA was a back-door method of exercising Emergency powers without going through the procedural requirements (and safeguards) needed to formally proclaim an Emergency. Counsel specifically pointed to how 'armed rebellion' was the trigger for proclaiming Emergency under the Constitution. The Supreme Court rejected this argument by holding that AFSPA was meant to be imposed in cases of 'internal disturbance' (ironically, 'internal disturbance' was the term used in a previous iteration of the Emergency provision, which had been *replaced* after its misuse by Indira Gandhi!)—a lower threshold than 'armed rebellion'. In this way, the Court entrenched the use of an Emergency-style law without an Emergency. See *Naga Peoples' Movement for Human Rights vs Union of India* (1998) 2 SCC 109, paragraphs 31–32.
68. Article 20, Constitution of India.
69. See, e.g., the detailed discussion by the Supreme Court of Canada *in R vs S (R.J.)* (1995) 1 SCR. 451, on the nature of the right against self-incrimination under the Canadian Charter.
70. This was the argument cited by Sir James Stephen, the drafter of thc Indian Evidence Act, for making confessions to police officers inadmissible under the law, although couched in racist overtones.
71. Parliament of India, *Constituent Assembly Debates*, Vol. IX (15 September 1949) (speech of Thakur Das Bhargava), available at https://eparlib.nic.in/bitstream/123456789/763310/1/cad_15-09-1949.pdf
72. For the origins of this right in common law, see John H. Langbein, 'The Historical Origins of the Privilege Against Self-Incrimination at Common Law' (1994) 92 *Michigan Law Review* 1047. For other histories of the right, see e.g. R.H. Helmholz, 'Origins of the Privilege against Self-Incrimination: The Role of European Ius Commune' (1990) 65 *New York University Law Review* 962; Eben Moglen, 'Taking the Fifth: Reconsidering the Origins of the Constitutional Privilege against Self-Incrimination' (1994) 92(5) *Michigan Law Review* 1086.

73. B.N. Rau, 'Notes on the Draft Report' in Shiva Rao, *The Framing of India's Constitution*, Vol. II (Universal Law Publishers, 1968) 147, 149
74. For a discussion of this line of cases, see Gautam Bhatia, *The Transformative Constitution* (HarperCollins, 2019), Chapter 8.
75. As noted above, the wording departs from its American ancestor. The Fifth Amendment to the US Constitution states that 'no person ... shall be compelled in any criminal case to be a witness against himself'. The Fifth Amendment thus applies to *all persons*, not simply to a person *accused* of an offence. Much then turns upon the interpretation of the phrase 'in any criminal case'. For example, for an argument advocating a narrower reading of that phrase, see Akhil Reed Amar and Renee B. Lettow, 'Fifth Amendment First Principles: The Self-Incrimination Clause' (1995) 93 *Michigan Law Review* 857. See also Harry J. Friendly, 'The Fifth Amendment Tomorrow: The Case for Constitutional Change' (1968) 37 *University of Cincinnati Law Review* 671.
76. Abhinav Sekhri, 'Whither the Right Against Self-Incrimination' in *The Proof of Guilt* (26 February 2016), https://theproofofguilt.blogspot.com/2016/02/wither-right-against-self-incrimination.html
77. Ibid.
78. *Raja Narayanlal Bansilal vs Maneck Phiroz Mistry*, (1961) SCR (1) 417.
79. Ibid., paragraph 26.
80. Ibid.
81. *Romesh Chandra Mehta vs State of West Bengal*, AIR (1970) SC 940.
82. Ibid., paragraph 5.
83. Ibid.
84. Ibid., paragraph 6.
85. Ibid., paragraph 10.
86. Ibid.
87. Ibid., paragraph 7.
88. Abhinav Sekhri, 'Wither the Right Against Self-Incrimination', supra.
89. Ibid.
90. See e.g., *Veera Ibrahim vs State of Maharashtra* (1976) 2 SCC 302; *Poolpandi vs Superintendent, Central Excise* (1992) 3 SCC 259; *Percy Rustam Basta vs State of Maharashtra*, (1971) 1 SCC 847.

91. Abhinav Sekhri, 'Detention, Deepak Mahajan, and Self-Incrimination' *The Proof of Guilt* (3 March 2016), available at https://theproofofguilt.blogspot.com/2016/03/aprevious-version-of-this-post-appeared.html
92. *Directorate of Enforcement vs Deepak Mahajan* (1994) 3 SCC 440.
93. Section 43, Criminal Procedure Code of Kenya.
94. *Anthony Njenga Mbuti and Ors vs Attorney-General and Ors*, Constitutional Petition No. 45 of 2014, [2015] eKLR.
95. Article 50, Constitution of Kenya, 2010.
96. *Anthony Njenga Mbuti*, paragraph 152. The 'new constitutional dispensation' refers to the 2010 Constitution of Kenya, which was won after a two-decades-long movement against authoritarian one-party rule.
97. Section 497(1), Code of Criminal Procedure, 1898. This regime was partially liberalized in 1923, as its scope was limited only to certain serious offences. See Abhinav Sekhri, ('Jail is Not the Rule: A History of Restrictive Bail Regimes Pre-Independence' *Proof of Guilt* (4 March 2024), available at https://theproofofguilt.blogspot.com/2024/03/jail-is-not-rule-history-of-restrictive.html
98. Ibid.
99. The 'twin test' originated in 1923 for certain offences triable by magistrates and was expanded under the 1942 Rules.
100. Defence of India Rules, 1942.
101. In *In Re V. Bhuvaraha Iyengar* 1942 ILR 414, this rule was challenged on the basis that it departed from the 'innocent until proven guilty' rule of common law (see below). The Court rejected this argument on the somewhat specious basis that the rule was only concerned with *bail*, and the 'innocent until proven guilty' presumption remained intact when it came to conviction or acquittal. See also *Nolan vs Emperor*, AR 1944 All 118. One wonders what is the value of the presumption, however, if an individual is kept in jail *until* they are proven innocent! This is yet another example of the Court taking refuge in formalism to avoid addressing the core question of power.
102. *Bodri Prasad vs State*, AIR 1953 Cal 28. For a more detailed discussion of the case, and of this extract, see Abhinav Sekhri, 'Jail is Not the Rule: Restrictive Bail Conditions, after Independence (Part I)' *The Proof of Guilt* (11 March 2024), available at https://theproofofguilt.blogspot.com/2024/03/jail-is-not-rule-restrictive-bail.html

103. For a brief and lucid explanation, see Abhinav Sekhri, 'Jail is Not the Rule – Stating the Problem (Interlude)' *The Proof of Guilt* (11 May 2024), available at https://theproofofguilt.blogspot.com/2024/05/jail-is-not-rule-stating-problem.html
104. Abhinav Sekhri, 'The New Supreme Court "Guidelines" on Bail', *The Proof of Guilt* (13 October 2021), available at https://theproofofguilt.blogspot.com/2021/10/the-new-supreme-court-guidelines-on-bail.html
105. While the Calcutta High Court in *Bodri Prasad* supra, emphatically stated that this was not the case, echoing the judgment in *In Re Bhuvaraha Iyengar*, supra, it is difficult to read the 'twin test' any other way, at least in terms of the effect it has on the question of bail. See also *Govindankutty vs State of Kerala*, AIR 1964 Ker 221, where the High Court of Kerala—examining the twin test under the 1962 Defence of India Rules—reiterated this reasoning.
106. Very soon after the passage of the Constitution, the Rajasthan High Court recognized this, in a case concerning a provincial legislation regarding essential supplies, where the twin test was replicated. The High Court observed that the twin test 'indirectly invests the prosecution with the power to allow or not to allow bail to an accused person'. See *Rajulal vs State*, (1950) RLW 168, 171. The High Court went on to note that this was an 'undesirable state of affairs', but that as a Court, it was not concerned with the desirability of legislation. One wonders if the trajectory of personal liberty in post-Independence India might have been different, had the High Court—in these early days—been persuaded to examine the constitutionality of the twin test!
107. Section 9, The East Punjab Armed Bands (Arrest and Detention) Act, 1947. For a discussion, see Abhinav Sekhri, 'Jail is Not the Rule: Restrictive Bail Conditions, after Independence (Part I)' *The Proof of Guilt* (11 March 2024), available at https://theproofofguilt.blogspot.com/2024/03/jail-is-not-rule-restrictive-bail.html.
108. Abhinav Sekhri, 'Restrictive Bail Conditions in Indian Criminal Procedure: Lessons from History' *The Proof of Guilt* (10 June 2019), available at https://theproofofguilt.blogspot.com/2019/06/restrictive-bail-conditions-in-indian.html
109. See, e.g., Article 352.
110. Joe Haldeman, *The Forever War* (St Martin's Press, 1974).
111. *Govindankutty vs State of Kerala*, supra.

112. For a detailed analysis of this paradox, see Abhinav Sekhri, 'Jail is not the Rule: Restrictive Bail Conditions, After Independence (Part 2)' *The Proof of Guilt* (6 May 2024), available at https://theproofofguilt.blogspot.com/2024/05/jail-is-not-rule-restrictive-bail.html
113. *Kartar Singh vs State of Punjab,* (1994) 4 SCC 569.
114. In language that is quite familiar to us, the Supreme Court exhorted prosecutors not to invoke the TADA for 'oblique motives' such as depriving accused people of bail, but did nothing to make its exhortation *enforceable* in any meaningful way. Ibid., paragraph 352.
115. *Kartar Singh, supra,* paragraph 349. Needless to say, this is an utter non-sequitur.
116. Sekhri, 'Jail is not the Rule (Part 2)', supra.
117. There are textual variations in the precise wording of the 'twin test' in these laws, with the PMLA version being more favourable to the State than the UAPA version, but for the purposes of our argument here, we can treat them as belonging to the same genus. For an analysis, see Abhinav Sekhri, 'Jail is Not the Rule', 10 June 2024.
118. *National Investigation Agency vs Zahoor Ahmed Shah Watali*, (2019) 5 SCC 1.
119. Supriya Sharma and Arunabh Saikia, 'How the Modi Government has Weaponised the ED to Go After India's Opposition', *Scroll,* (5 July 2022), available at https://scroll.in/article/1027571/how-the-modi-government-has-weaponised-the-ed-to-go-after-indias-opposition
120. Sekhri, therefore, picturesquely labels the judgment 'old wine in new bottles'. Abhinav Sekhri, 'Old Winc in New Bottles?: The Judgment in Vijay Madanlal Choudhary (Part 2)', *Proof of Guilt,* (29 July 2022) https://theproofofguilt.blogspot.com/2022/07/old-wine-in-new-bottles-judgment-in.html
121. *Vijay Madanlal Choudhary vs Union of India*, (2022) SCC OnLine SC 929.
122. Ibid.
123. Ibid.
124. Abhinav Sekhri, 'Old Wine in New Bottles?', supra
125. Hussain, *The Jurisprudence of Emergency*, supra 142.
126. Ibid., 136.
127. Ibid., 135–36.
128. Ibid. 94, discussed previously in this chapter.

6: Power Unbound: The People

1. Preamble, Constitution of India.
2. See, for example, the discussions of the concept of 'constituent power'. Joel I. Colon-Rios, *Constituent Power and the Law*, (Oxford University Press, 2020). For a discussion of the essentially non-unified, plural nature of 'the People' see, e.g. Claude Lefort, *Democracy and Political Theory* (David Macey trans., Polity Press, 1988)
3. Martin Loughlin, 'The Contemporary Crisis of Constitutional Democracy' (2019) 39(2) *Oxford Journal of Legal Studies* 435.
4. Compare, for example, the constitution-making processes leading up to the 1996 Constitution of South Africa and the 2010 Constitution of Kenya (to take two examples), both of which were ratified at a referendum. In the Kenyan case, this was at the second time of asking, with a previous version of the draft constitution having been rejected in a referendum. For a more recent example, see the two attempts at constitution-making in Chile, both of which were rejected in a referendum.
5. Sunil Khilnani, 'Arguing Democracy: Intellectuals and Politics in Modern India', Center for the Advanced Study of India *Working Paper Series*, no. 09-02 (Philadelphia, 2009).
6. Rohit De and Ornit Shani, 'Assembling India's Constitution: Towards a New History' (2023) XX *Past and Present* 1; Ornit Shani, 'The People and the Making of India's Constitution', (2022) 65(4) *The Historical Journal*, 1102. In the previous chapter on asymmetric federalism, we have made reference to draft Constitutions that emerged, for example, from the Mizo and the Naga People.
7. See e.g. Rohit De, *A People's Constitution: The Everyday Life of Law in the Indian Republic* (Penguin Random House, 2018).
8. Uday S. Mehta, 'Indian Constitutionalism: Crisis, Unity, and History' in Sujit Chaudhry et al. (eds) *The Oxford Handbook of the Indian Constitution* (Oxford University Press, 2015).
9. For a discussion, see Kalyani Ramnath, '"We the People": Seamless Webs and Social Revolution in India's Constituent Assembly Debates' (2012) 32(1) *South Asia Research* 57. Ramnath also complicates the idea of what constitutes 'the People', and points to the many fragmented segments of 'the People' that both played a role in the

framing of the Constitution, and as the subjects of constitutional imagination.

10. Gargarella, *Latin American Constitutionalism, 1810–2010: The Engine Room of the Constitution* (Oxford University Press, 2013). For another articulation of democracy as the ability of the People to exercise 'constraint' over their rulers, see Hannah Arendt, *On Revolution* (Viking Press, 1965) 265.
11. As Loughlin notes, this structure—as it first emerged in the federal US Constitution—was designed towards:

> ...maintaining the aristocratic basis of governing and protecting the order of property. The solution entailed conceiving democracy mainly as requiring the periodic election of representatives whose role was not so much to express the will of the people as to 'refine and enlarge the public views by passing them through the medium of a chosen body of citizens, whose wisdom may best discern the true interest of their country'. (Internal citations omitted)

    Loughlin, 'The Contemporary Crisis of Constitutional Democracy', supra 451. In other words, this structure was a response to fears on part of the framers of the Constitution of 'excessive democracy' at the level of the states, which was a potential threat (among other things) to the property-owning class. See Jules Lobel, 'The Political Tilt of the Separation of Powers' in David Kairys (ed.), *The Politics of Law: A Progressive Critique* (Basic Books, 1998) 591, 592.
12. This is sometimes referred to as 'Schumpeterian democracy', after the theories of Joseph Schumpeter. See, e.g., Joseph Schumpeter, *Capitalism, Socialism, and Democracy* (Harper Perennial Modern Thought Edition, 2008). For an equally influential, and slightly more expansive account (but which still falls short of what we are discussing here), see Robert Dahl, *Polyarchy: Participation and Opposition* (Yale University Press, 1971).
13. Joshua Cohen and Archon Fung, 'Radical Democracy' (2004) 10(4) *Swiss Journal of Political Science* 169, 169.
14. See e.g., Arrow's Impossibility Theorem and the Condorcet Paradox, discussed in Kenneth Arrow, *Social Choice and Individual Values* (third edition, Yale University Press, 2012).

15. Philippe C. Schmitter and Terry Lynn Karl, 'What Democracy Is... And is Not', (1991) 2(3) *Journal of Democracy* 78. For an argument of how political representation creates 'alienation' between constituents and their representatives, see Cornelius Castoriadis, 'The Hungarian Source' in David Ames Curtis (ed.), *Political and Social Writings:* Volume 3 (University of Minnesota Press, 1992) 261, and the discussion of Castoriadis in Christophe Premat, 'Castoriadis and the Modern Political Imaginary – Oligarchy, Representation, Democracy' (2006) 7(1) *Critical Horizons*, 251.
16. For expositions of 'participatory democracy', see, e.g., Carole Pateman, *Participation and Democratic Theory* (Harvard University Press, 1970); Benjamin Barber, *Strong Democracy: Participatory Politics for a New Age* (University of California Press, 1984); and the historical account in Jeffrey D. Hilmer, 'The State of *Participatory* Democratic Theory' (2010) 32(1) *New Political Science* 43. For an assessment of the tradition of 'council democracy', see James Muldoon, ed. *Council Democracy: Towards a Democratic Socialist Politics* (Routledge, 2018).
17. For a discussion of the range of roles that 'the People' might play—from citizens' assemblies to other forms of 'deliberation'—see, e.g., the discussion in Martin Loughlin, 'The Contemporary Crisis of Constitutional Democracy' supra 450; David van Reybrouk, *Against Elections: The Case for Democracy* (Bodley Head, 2016); James S. Fishkin, *When the People Speak: Deliberative Democracy and Public Consultation*, (Oxford University Press, 2009).
18. A famous recent example is the amendments to the Constitution of Ireland that legalized same-sex marriage and repealed the (effective) prohibition of abortion, both after successful (separate) referendums. These referendums were preceded by the deliberations of various 'Citizens' Assemblies', which had been established by the Parliament in 2016, and which sought to directly involve the people in deliberations around constitutional change. Citizens' Assemblies have not been entirely free of controversy. More recently, the same procedure—i.e., Citizens' Assemblies followed by a Referendum—to amend the Irish Constitution with respect to the definition of the 'family' and to replace language pertaining to the position of women within the home—was defeated. See, e.g., 'The Citizens' Assembly', *Report of the Citizens' Assembly on Gender Equality*, June 2021, available at https://

citizensassembly.ie/wp-content/uploads/2023/02/report-of-the-citizens-assembly-on-gender-equality.pdf

19. Article 257, Constitution of Kenya 2010.
20. For a more detailed analysis of this judgment by the present author, see Gautam Bhatia, 'The Hydra and the Sword: Constitutional Amendments, Political Process, and the BBI Case in Kenya', in *Global Constitutionalism* (forthcoming); Gautam Bhatia, *Law-Making, Political Process and the State: Transformative Constitutionalism and Kenya 2010–2025* (James Currey 2025), Chapter 2.
21. *Doctors for Life International vs Speaker of the National Assembly*, 2006 (12) BCLR 1399 (CC). See, in particular, the concurring opinion of Justice Albie Sachs (paragraph 230): 'Elections are of necessity periodical. Accountability, responsiveness and openness, on the other hand, are by their very nature ubiquitous and timeless. They are constants of our democracy, to be ceaselessly asserted in relation to ongoing legislative and other activities of government.'
22. See, e.g., Article 2 of the Constitution of Colombia (1991). See also the discussion, in *Doctors for Life International*, supra, of the Portuguese Constitutional Court's *Acordao* No. 609/94, where it was held that consultation with workers' bodies was mandatory before passing labour legislation (including accident legislation). *Doctors for Life*, supra, fn. 181.
23. Article 52, Constitution of the Portuguese Republic. For more examples, see *Doctors for Life International vs Speaker of the National Assembly*, supra, paragraphs 103 104.
24. Section 57(1)(b), Constitution of South Africa.
25. Article 118(1)(b), Constitution of Kenya 2010.
26. *Doctors for Life*, supra, para 108. In his concurring opinion, Sachs J. observed that 'although regular elections and a multi-party system of democratic government are fundamental to our constitutional democracy, they are not exhaustive of it. Their constitutional objective is explicitly'. Ibid., paragraph 228 (concurring opinion of Sachs J.).
27. Ibid., paragraph 115. Sachs J. referred to it as the goal of having a 'permanently engaged citizenry'. Ibid., para 230 (concurring opinion of Sachs J.).
28. Ibid., paragraph 115.
29. Ibid., paragraph 129.

30. Ibid., paragraphs 131–36, 171. However, *see* the dissenting opinions of Justices Yacoob and Van der Westhuizen, who held that public participation, as articulated in the judgment of the majority, could not be judicially enforced in a court. Justice Yacoob, in particular, held that the participatory elements in the constitution were fulfilled through the guaranteed rights of association, forming a political party, and participating in the electoral process: what we have referred to above as 'conventional democracy'. Ibid., paragraph 277.
31. Ibid., paragraph 244 (10) (concurring opinion of Justice Van der Westhuizen).
32. Ibid.
33. Ibid.
34. Joseph Enock Aura vs Cabinet Secretary, Ministry of Health, Constitutional Petition No. E473 of 2023 ('the SHIF Judgment'). For an analysis by this author, see Gautam Bhatia, 'Giving Meaning to Public Participation: The Kenyan High Court's SHIF Judgment', *Constitutional Law and Philosophy* (16 July 2024), available at https://indconlawphil.wordpress.com/2024/07/16/giving-meaning-to-public-participation-the-kenyan-high-courts-shif-judgment/. However, this position was subsequently rejected by the Supreme Court of Kenya in 2024.
35. In Chapter 1, we discussed a similar case with respect to the obligation under Article 3 upon Parliament to consult state legislators, and how—in *Babulal Parate's* case—the Supreme Court appeared to hold that there was no need to send even a radically amended bill for another round of consultation.
36. Article 240, Constitution of the Plurinational State of Bolivia 2009; Article 61(6), Constitution of Ecuador, 2008. For a brief discussion, see Jonas Wolff, 'New Constitutions and the Transformation of Democracy in Bolivia and Ecuador' in Almut Schilling-Vacaflor and Detlef Nolte (eds), *New Constitutionalism in Latin America: Promises and Practices* (Routledge, 2012) 183, 186.
37. Article 1(3)(a), Constitution of California.
38. Historically, it was an integral part of the programme of council democracy.
39. One can see a reference to this in the debates around the Election Commission, in the Constituent Assembly.
40. Latin American constitutionalism provides us with a particularly advanced jurisprudence on this point. For a summary and a bibliography,

see Cleide Calgaro, 'Latin American Constitutionalism: Comparative Law Study on Popular Participation for Urban Land Planning' (2023) 15(1) *Rev. Dir. Cid., Rio de Janeiro* 237. As noted previously, one of the most famous examples is the model of participatory budgeting in Porto Alegre, Brazil.

41. Leonardo Avritzer, *Participatory Institutions in Brazil* (The Johns Hopkins University Press, 2009).
42. Hilmer, 'The State of *Participatory* Democratic Theory', supra 62. Note, of course, that formal participation does not always entail redistribution of power; sometimes, it can have the opposite consequences. A lot depends on how participation is *structured*, including through institutions.
43. Article 395(3) and 398, Constitution of Ecuador 2008; for the most recent interpretation of these clauses, see *Sentencia No. 1149-19-JP/21*, Constitutional Court of Ecuador.
44. For a discussion of the slippages between consultation and consent in this context, see Juan C. Herrera, 'Judicial Dialogue and Transformative Constitutionalism in Latin America: the Case of Indigenous Peoples and Afro-descendants' (2019) 43 *Revista Derecho del Estado* 191. See also the Conclusion to this chapter.
45. See the nuanced discussion with respect to Bolivia, in Lorenza B. Fontana and Jean Grugel, 'The Politics of Indigenous Participation Through "Free Prior Informed Consent": Reflections from the Bolivian Case' (2016) 77 *World Development* 249.
46. See e.g. Thea Riofrancos, *Resource Radicals: From Petro-Nationalism to Post-Extractivism in Ecuador* (Duke University Press, 2020).
47. Ibid.
48. There is an interesting overlap here with our previous chapter on asymmetric federalism and constitutional pluralism. As Riofrancos notes in her book, many extractive projects affect indigenous communities, which are specifically recognized as constitutional actors in the very concept of the 'plurinational State' that these constitutions are committed to. Thus, in the words of Riofrancos:

   > ...in an enactment of the 'plurinational' state set forth in the [Ecuadorian] Constitution (itself a product of indigenous mobilization and theorization), consultations multiply the sites

> of democratic decision-making and disrupt the monolithic nation presupposed by state actors who claim to represent the public good ... If democracy in its radical form is enacted, and expanded, through the eruption of conflict over the terms of collective life, then the communities affected by resource extraction that claim the authority to decide the fate of extractive projects resonate with a long history of democratic contention. (Ibid., p. 117.)

We will consider this again in the conclusion to this chapter.

49. C.f. Luis Tapa, 'Consideraciones sobre el estado plurinacional' (2010) 8(2) *Bolivian Research Review/Revista E* 1, 8.
50. For a detailed account, see Fernando Garcés, 'The Domestication of Indigenous Autonomies in Bolivia: From the Pact of Unity to the New Constitution' in Nicole Fabricant and Bret Gustafson (eds), *Remapping Bolivia: Resources, Territory, and Indigeneity in a Plurinational State* (SAR Press, 2011) 46.
51. Jason Tockman, 'The Hegemony of Representation: Democracy and Indigenous Self-government in Bolivia' (2017) 9(2) *Journal of Politics in Latin America* 121, 122. For an example of communitarian democracy under the Bolivian Constitution, see the discussion of indigenous autonomy, flagged in Chapter 3.
52. Article 368, Constitution of India.
53. Sandipto Dasgupta, *Legalizing the Revolution: India and the Constitution of the Postcolony* (Cambridge University Press, 2024) 25.
54. Partha Chatterjee *Nationalist Thought and the Colonial World: A Derivative Discourse* (Zed Books, 1986) 51. See also Tejas Parasher, 'Federalism, Representation, and Direct Democracy in 1920s India' (2022) 19 *Modern Intellectual History* 444, invoking Chatterjee for a similar argument about the anti-colonial movement.
55. Nazmul Sultan, *Waiting for the People: The Idea of Democracy in Indian Anticolonial Thought* (Harvard University Press, 2024).
56. Ibid., 41.
57. Ibid., p. 70.
58. Readers will notice the link between this vision and the marginalization of Parliament within the constitutional design, which we have considered in Chapter 2 of this book.

59. Sultan, *Waiting for the People*, supra 164. For a detailed analysis, and an articulation of the idea that the dominant figure in the Constitution is the 'administrator', at the expense of 'the People', see Dasgupta, *Legalizing the Revolution*, supra 168–172.
60. Of Nehru specifically, Sultan writes:

> Though Nehru shared this conception of the people with his predecessors [i.e., of the People in terms of the starving masses], what he demanded from the people was different: the people did not have to prove their capacity for sovereignty but only had to express their readiness to authorise the acceleration of their own development. The desire for independence became one and inseparable from the popular authorisation for accelerated development.

(Sultan, *Waiting for the People*, 174.)
61. Most prominently, Ambedkar. However, as we have seen through this book, Ambedkar's impetus towards centralization was motivated by a different set of factors: among others, the belief that central authority would be in a better position to protect the rights of Dalits against entrenched and local caste structures and hierarchies. Sultan affirms this. (Ibid., 215.)
62. See Chapters 2 and 4.
63. Parasher, 'Federalism, Representation, and Direct Democracy', supra 444.
64. Ibid.
65. Ibid.
66. For an account of public participation through the freedom struggle, see Dasgupta (2024), *Legalizing the Revolution*, Chapter 3.
67. Ibid. Even the Indian National Congress, however, was not always like this. For an exploration of how, in the 1930s, the Congress leaders, including Nehru, considered a more expanded role for the people in constitutional institutions (ibid.).
68. For a nuanced exploration of decentralization and direct democracy in Gandhian thought, as part of the broader project of political non-violence, see Karuna Mantena, 'On Gandhi's Critique of the State: Sources, Contexts, and Conjectures', *Modern Intellectual History* (2012) 9(3): p. 535.

69. Parliament of India, *Constituent Assembly Debates*, Vol. VII (29 November, 1948) (speech of Lokanath Misra), available at https://eparlib.nic.in/bitstream/123456789/763032/1/cad_29-11-1948.pdf
70. This has never happened, of course.
71. See, e.g., Udit Bhatia, 'Precautions in a Democratic Experiment: The Nexus between Political Power and Competence' in Jon Elster et al. (eds), *Constituent Assemblies* (Cambridge University Press, 2018) 109.
72. Parliament of India, *Constituent Assembly Debates*, Vol. XI (23 November 1949) (speech of T.J.M. Wilson), available at https://eparlib.nic.in/bitstream/123456789/763263/1/cad_23-11-1949.pdf
73. It is worth noting, of course, that through the 73rd and 74th Amendments—which introduced local government into the Constitution—participatory mechanisms were introduced into the Constitution through the vehicle of Gram Sabhas. As noted in Chapter 1, however, the overall subordination of local governments to the states dilutes the force of these provisions to an extent. I thank Malavika Prasad for drawing my attention to this point.
74 Sandipto Dasgupta points out that Nehru rejected popular participation in the drawing of national boundaries at the time of the Partition of India, on the basis that ascertaining people's wishes would be too 'heavy and prolonged.' Sandipto Dasgupta, *Legalizing the Revolution* (Cambridge University Press, 2024) 390, fn. 201. One wonders: if you're not going to involve the people in a decision that would uproot them from their homes and make them refugees, what decision would you *ever* involve them in? Given that the Constitution came into being in the carnage of the Partition, we can perhaps think of this as one of the original sins of Indian constitutionalism, that has haunted us ever since.
75. See Chapter 2. This discussion, in certain ways, tracks our discussion of fourth-branch institutions, in Chapter 4.
76. See, e.g., *Hanuman Laxman Aroskar vs Union of India* (2019) 15 SCC 401, paragraphs 46, 51.
77. Ibid., paragraph 101.
78. Ibid., paragraph 141.
79. Ibid., paragraph 102.
80. *Hanuman Laxman Aroskar vs Union of India (II)*, (2020) INSC 49.
81. Indeed, objections were made both to the lack of qualifications of the expert body as well as its findings on merits; in both cases, the Court adopted a light-touch review.

82. *Orissa Mining Corporation vs Ministry of Environment and Forest*, (2013) 6 SCC 476, paragraph 60.
83. Indeed, the Forest Rights Act has occupied a vulnerable place since its enactment, with successive governments attempting to weaken it both through lackadaisical enforcement, and through amending other forest-related laws to curtail the rights of forest-dwelling tribes. See, e.g. Bela Bhatia, 'Forest Rights: Competing Concerns' in *India's Forgotten Country: A View from the Margins* (Penguin Random House, 2024) 216. It is of little doubt that the absence of constitutional entrenchment plays a significant role in the fragile landscape of public participation in the context of indigenous displacement. See also the Panchayat (Extension to Scheduled Areas) Act of 1996 ['PESA'].
84. *Minerals Area Development Authority vs M/s Steel Authority of India* (2024) INSC 554, paragraph 57.
85. The stated justification, of course, is that the State takes its decisions for the benefit of the people of the country as a whole, and not only for those who reside on the land that is being sought to be mined.
86. See the discussion in *Minerals Area Development Authority*, paragraphs 58–60. The Court in this case stated that the 'essence' of MMDR Act is to 'protect humankind' and the natural world from 'rapacious and unregulated mining', which is certainly a rather creative reading of the Act!
87. Section 9B, Mines and Minerals (Development and Regulation) Act of 1957. The provisions of Section 9B themselves primarily focus on the payment of royalty, taking us back to the 'revenue-sharing' model that the Constituent Assembly preferred over a meaningful autonomy model. For discussion of Section 9B as a 'social justice' provision, see *Federation of Indian Mineral Industries vs Union of India* (2017) 16 SCC 186.
88. Some of these tensions are reflected in *Samatha vs State of Andhra Pradesh* (1997) 8 SCC 191, also flagged in Chapter 3 of this book.
89. *Olga Tellis vs Bombay Municipal Corporation* AIR 1980 SC 186.
90. In one of those ironic moments that has come to characterize the history of the Indian Supreme Court, *Olga Tellis* has come to be known as a 'landmark' case in the evolution of housing rights under the Constitution, while the actual affected parties in the judgments—the pavement dwellers—got no relief, and were displaced (much like how *Maneka Gandhi* has come to be known as the 'landmark' case on

personal liberties, despite the fact that Maneka Gandhi did not, as a matter of fact, get back her impounded passport).

91. For the major judgments on the point, see *Port Elizabeth Municipality vs Various Occupiers* 2005 (1) SA 217 (CC); *City of Johannesburg vs Rand Properties (Pty) Ltd and Others* 2007 (6) SA 417 (SCA); *Occupiers of 51 Olivia Road, Berea Township, and 197 Main Street, Johannesburg vs City of Johannesburg and Others* 2008 (3) SA 208 (CC); *Dladla and Another vs City of Johannesburg and Others* [2017] ZACC 42. See also Sandra Liebenberg, 'Towards a Right to Alternative Accommodation? South Africa's Constitutional Jurisprudence on Evictions', *Housing and ESC Rights Law Quarterly* (2005) 2: 1; and Rishika Sahgal, 'Evictions and Participation Rights in India and South Africa', (2022), D. Phil Thesis, University of Oxford, available at https://ora.ox.ac.uk/objects/uuid:5384db59-946f-4275-ab07-7f84273439c7/download_file?file_format=application%2Fpdf&safe_filename=Sahgal_2022_Evictions_and_participation.pdf&type_of_work=Thesis
92. Considerations of location, accessibility, hygiene, the existence of disease vectors, affordability etc., all play a role in determining this 'constitutional floor'.
93. *Satrose Ayuma and Ors vs The Registered Trustees of the Kenya Railways Staff Retirement Benefits Scheme*, Petition No. 65 of 2010, [2013] KEHC 6003 (KLR)
94. Rosalind Dixon, *Responsive Judicial Review: Democracy and Dysfunction in the Modern Age*, (Oxford University Press, 2023).
95. *Ajay Maken and Ors vs Union of India and Ors*, W.P. 11616 of 2015 (High Court of Delhi).
96. Ibid., paragraph 77.
97. See, e.g., *Raju Sahu vs State of Uttar Pradesh* (SLP No. 7383/2024), which was about the demolition of the Akbar Nagar neighbourhood in Lucknow. After an initial progressive order by a single judge of the Allahabad High Court, the division bench of the High Court, and on appeal the Supreme Court greenlit the demolitions along with a minimal relocation package. Constitutional issues, although raised, were not considered. The present author was one of the counsels involved in the case and can personally testify to the Supreme Court bench's unwillingness to engage with the constitutional arguments. See also *Raju Sahu vs State of Uttar Pradesh*, 2024:AHC-LKO:20204-DB, for the judgment of the division bench; Gautam Bhatia, 'Pushing Back

Against Punitive Jurisprudence: The Allahabad High Court's Interim Order on Demolitions', *Constitutional Law and Philosophy,* 3 January 2024, available at https://indconlawphil.wordpress.com/2024/01/03/pushing-back-against-punitive-jurisprudence-the-allahabad-high-courts-interim-order-on-demolitions/, written before the present author's involvement in the case.

98. For an analysis of the judiciary's disingenuous approach to these demolitions, rejecting the evidence of their eyes and ears, see Gautam Bhatia, 'Home Demolitions and George Orwell's Supreme Court', *Constitutional Law and Philosophy,* 13 July 2022, available at https://indconlawphil.wordpress.com/2022/07/13/home-demolitions-and-george-orwells-supreme-court/. In October 2024, the Supreme Court did finally issue a set of guidelines aimed at stopping further instances of this kind of punitive demolition. Their impact remains to be assessed.
99. Sometimes—and especially in the collective punishment set of demolitions—even these standards are not fulfilled.
100. The present author was one of the counsels involved in the case.
101. *Rajeev Suri vs Delhi Development Authority*, (2021) SCC Online 7, paragraphs 173–98.
102. Ibid., paragraph 189.
103. Of course, as we have seen above in the context of Kenya, representative and direct democratic elements do not need to be in conflict within the same constitutional scheme. For a theoretical discussion of how elements of direct and representative democracy can be complementary to each other, see Premat, 'Castoriadis and the Modern Political Imaginary' supra, 269–270.
104. De and Shani, 'Assembling India's Constitution', supra 41–42.
105. See, e.g. Goodale, *A Revolution in Fragments*, supra.
106. See e.g., Mutua, Makau wa, *Kenya's Quest for Democracy: Taming Leviathan* (Lynne Rienner Publishers, 2008).
107. See, for example, the judgment of the High Court of Kenya in *David Ndii and Ors vs Attorney-General and Ors,* [2021] KEHC 9746 (KLR).
108. Tockman, 'The Hegemony of Representation', supra. In the same context, it has also historically been seen that public participation is sometimes conceded as a means of forestalling, or diluting, more radical demands for autonomy and self-determination. This is how scholars analyse, for example, the 1994 Law of Public Participation enacted in Bolivia, whose goal—under the guise of public involvement—was 'to

develop potential markets, privatize access to natural resources, and, especially, promote a market in land'. See Pablo Regalsky, 'Political Process and the Reconfiguration of the State in Bolivia' (2010) 37(172), *Latin American Perspectives* 35, 43. At the same time, whatever its intentions, the law *did* provide a space for certain claims to be made, that could not be made earlier. See Nancy Thede, 'Democratic Agency in the Local Political Sphere: Reflections on Inclusion in Bolivia' (2011) 18(1) *Democratization* 211; see also Bret Gustafson and Nicole Fabricant, 'Introduction: New Cartographies of Knowledge and Struggle' in *Remapping Bolivia*, supra, 1, 18.

109. C.f. Tapia, 'Consideraciones sobre el estado plurinacional', supra, 11.
110. Ibid. For an account of the State of Bolivia's attempts to weaken the constitutional guarantee through passing laws and executive orders that would weaken participation rights in the case of extractivist projects, see Nancy Postero and Jason Tockman, 'Self-Governance in Bolivia's First Indigenous Autonomy: Charagua' (2020) 55(1) *Latin American Research Review* 1, 11.
111. It is important to note that the absence of *constitutionalization* of public participation does not mean that public participation does not exist. In a fascinating account, Lisa Mitchell identifies the dharna, the hunger strike, the public assembly, the general strike, the rail roko and the yatra, among others, as specifically *Indian* practices, with a long genealogy, that commandeer public space in different ways, with a view to articulating claims and engaging with the State. These are all, of course, *extra-constitutional* practices, in that they take place without the sanction of the Constitution. Mitchell specifically discusses these as instances of democracy *between* elections, and as examples of 'an ongoing [democratic] *process* of engagement and communication that constantly expands recognition.' Lisa Mitchell, *Hailing the State: Indian Democracy Between Elections* (Duke University Press, 2023) 172.

Interlude: Yesterday's Tomorrow

1. Bini Adamczak, *Yesterday's Tomorrow: On the Loneliness of Communist Specters and the Reconstruction of the Future* (MIT Press, 2021) 109.
2. Ibid., 107.
3. Ibid., 109.
4. Ibid., 121.

5. Christophe Jaffrelot and Pratinav Atil, *India's First Dictatorship: The Emergency, 1975 – 1977* (Hurst, 2020).
6. The Constitution (Forty-Second Amendment) Act, 1976. The basis of the 42nd Amendment was the Swaran Singh Committee Report. For an analysis of the Report, praising it as a task of "remarkable expedition and wisdom," see Upendra Baxi, 'Constitutional Changes: An Analysis of the Swaran Singh Committee Report' (1976) 2 *SCC Journal* 17. Baxi concluded his peroration by noting that 'the prophets of doom who talked about the demise of constitutional democracy in India must now become partners in the sustenance of the new constitutional enterprise or face a self-imposed spiritual exile from the doorstep of a new India.' Ibid.
7. Article 257A, Constitution of India (repealed).
8. The Constitution (44th Amendment) Act, 1978.
9. Interestingly, even under the colonial Government of India Act, the default position was that laws enacted during an Emergency would cease two years after it ended, *unless* re-enacted. The post-44th Amendment position, thus, was even *more* centralizing than the colonial constitutional framework. See Section 44(5), Government of India Act, 1935.
10. *A.K. Roy vs Union of India*, AIR 1982 SC 710, discussed in Chapter 5 of this book.
11. W.H. Auden, 'Spain 1937' in *Another Time* (Random House, 1940).
12. A quote by the Chevalier de Panat, famously misattributed to Talleyrand.
13. *A.K. Roy vs Union of India*, supra. It is therefore particularly bewildering that popular histories of the period claim that the Supreme Court was chastened and regretful about its role during the Emergency and attempted to 'atone' by creating the jurisprudence of public interest litigation. Upholding a preventive detention law four years after an Emergency that was characterized by abuse of preventive detention seems a rather strange method of 'atonement'. No doubt, this is the story that the Supreme Court likes to tell about itself, but we might expect somewhat more critical scrutiny from those who write about it.
14. M.N. Roy, *Constitution of Free India: A Draft* (1944), available at https://www.constitutionofindia.net/historical-constitution/constitution-of-free-india-a-draft-m-n-roy-1944/
15. M.N. Roy broke bread with the Comintern, and founded the Communist Party of Mexico, among other things. Modern-day visitors to Mexico City can find a club named in his honour.

16. Shriman Narayan Agarwal, *Gandhian Constitution for a Free India* (1946), available at https://www.constitutionofindia.net/historical-constitution/constitution-of-free-india-a-draft-m-n-roy-1944/
17. Quoting C.E.M. Joad's *Philosophy For Our Times* (Thomas Nelson and Sons, 1940).
18. One of the most fascinating parts of the Gandhian Constitution was its proposal of partial sortition as a method of choosing representatives (i.e., selection through a draw of lots from among elected candidates): a method that has been discussed extensively in political theory as one way of dealing with the distortions that creep into electoral systems.
19. Agarwal, *Gandhian Constitution*, supra.
20. *Draft Constitution of the Republic of India* (Socialist Party, 1948), available at https://www.constitutionofindia.net/historical-constitution/draft-constitution-of-the-republic-of-india-socialist-party-1948/
21. *Constitution of the Hindusthan Free State Act* (1944), available at https://www.constitutionofindia.net/historical-constitution/the-constitution-of-the-hindusthan-free-state-act-1944-no-of-1944/
22. There were some alterations with respect to substantive rights: the Constitution did not, for example, provide for affirmative action.
23. Tejas Parasher, 'Federalism, Representation, and Direct Democracy in 1920s India' (2022) 19 *Modern Intellectual History* 444. See infra, Chapter 6.
24. Aundh State Constitution Act I of 1939, available at https://www.constitutionofindia.net/historical-constitution/aundh-state-constitution-act-1939/
25. See Chapters 3 and 6.
26. It is worth noting that the *nation-state* as the dominant post-colonial form was itself not an inevitability. There was a strong intellectual current of internationalism that existed in the first half of the twentieth century, and to which Indian thinkers contributed in important respects. See, e.g., Manu Goswami, 'Imaginary Futures and Colonial Internationalisms' (2012) 117(5), *The American Historical Review* 1461. For a more global history of internationalism during this period, see Frederick Cooper, *Citizenship between Empire and Nation: Remaking France and French Africa, 1945-1960* (Princeton University Press, 2016).

Epilogue: State, Power and the Future of Constitutionalism

1. Richard S. Kay, 'The State Action Doctrine, the Public–Private Distinction, and the Independence of Constitutional Law', (1993) *Constitutional Commentary* 10: 329, 338. For a critique of this model, see, Gautam Bhatia, *Horizontal Rights: An Institutional Approach* (Hart Publishing, 2023).
2. Dieter Grimm, *Constitutionalism: Past, Present, and Future* (Oxford University Press, 2016) 29.
3. See e.g. Seyla Benhabib, *The Claims of Culture: Equality and Diversity in the Global Era* (Princeton University Press, 2002); Carole Pateman, *The Sexual Contract* (Polity Press, 1988).
4. Sandipto Dasgupta, *Legalizing the Revolution: India and the Constitution of the Postcolony* (Cambridge University Press, 2024) 82.
5. 'Karachi Resolution, 1931', available at https://www.constitutionofindia.net/historical-constitution/karachi-resolution-1931-jawaharlal-nehru/
6. Ambedkar (1947), *States and Minorities.*
7. B.R. Ambedkar, 'Memorandum and Draft Articles on the Rights of States and Minorities' (24 March 1947) in B. Shiva Rao, *The Framing of India's Constitution*, Vol. II (Universal Law Publishing, 1968) 100-101.
8. For a historical account of this trajectory, see Sandipto Dasgupta, *Legalizing the Revolution: India and the Constitution of the Postcolony* (Cambridge University Press, 2024), Chapter 7. It is questionable, of course, to what extent Ambedkar had a choice in the matter, given the dominance of the Indian National Congress in the Constituent Assembly, the liberal use of the party whip, and Ambedkar's own future characterization of his role as being that of a 'hack'.
9. Ibid.
10. For a critique of the separation between the 'economic' and the 'political' in modern thought, see Ellen Meiksins Wood, *Democracy Against Capitalism: Renewing Historical Materialism* (Verso Books, 2016).
11. For the stronger claim that a vision of the bourgeois capitalist State is 'revealed' in the Constitution, see Sudipta Kaviraj, 'A Critique of the Passive Revolution' (1988) 23 (45/47) *Economic and Political Weekly* 2429, 2430.

12. This may also lead us to consider whether modern constitutionalism—in the forms that we recognize—actively constrains the horizons of the political economy to capitalist and market structures. See, e.g., Rob Hunter,'Constitutional Metaphysics' (13 June 2022), available at https://rhunter.org/blog/critique-socialist-constitutionalism-fetishism-domination/
13. Ambedkar (1947), *States and Minorities.*
14. Article 15(1), Constitution of India.
15. Article 15(3), Constitution of India.
16. For a discussion, see Gautam Bhatia, *The Transformative Constitution*, supra, Chapter 2.
17. Article 17, Constitution of India. B.R. Ambedkar's initial proposals for a far more detailed anti-boycott law did not finally make it to the Constitution.
18. See, for example, Article 16(4), Constitution of India. Indeed, the original Constitution did not enable reservations in educational institutions—something that the Supreme Court *did* treat as a barrier towards legislative provision of those reservations in *State of Madras vs Champakam Dorairajan*, AIR 1951 SC 226. Following this, the Constitution was amended to specifically allow reservations in educational institutions.
19. See the discussion in Gautam Bhatia, *The Transformative Constitution*, (HarperCollins, 2019), Chapter 3.
20. The Court has noted on multiple occasions that there is no 'right to reservation', a dictum seemingly in conflict with its jurisprudence that that the Constitution guarantees substantive equality (which means, in turn, that structurally disadvantaged individuals have a constitutional claim to remedial measures.
21. See, e.g., B.R. Ambedkar, *The Annihilation of Caste* (1936).
22. For a chronological account, see Raja Shekhar Vundru, *Ambedkar, Gandhi, and Patel: The Making of India's Electoral System* (Bloomsbury, 2017).
23. B.R. Ambedkar, *States and Minorities*, supra.
24. Article 334, Constitution of India.
25. The 'submerged classes' was Ambedkar's own term.
26. B.R. Ambedkar, *States and Minorities*, supra.

27. Article 15(2), Constitution of India.
28. Article 23, Constitution of India.
29. See, e.g., *Indian Medical Association vs Union of India* (2011) 7 SCC 179 (Article 15[2]); *PUDR vs Union of India* (1982) 3 SCC 235 (Article 23); *Indian Young Lawyers' Association vs Union of India*, W.P. (Civ.) 373/2006. All these cases are discussed in detail in Gautam Bhatia, 'Part Two: Fraternity', in *The Transformative Constitution* supra, Part II.
30. Dasgupta, *Legalizing the Revolution*, supra 152.
31. As Dasgupta notes, the grant of universal suffrage was one instance where 'the popular postcolonial political energy of the anticolonial struggle did ... translate into postcolonial institutions. Universal franchise was the clearest, most unambiguous, institutional expression of the anticolonial cause.' Ibid., 179
32. Parliament of India, *Constituent Assembly Debates*, Vol. VII (4 November 1948) (speech of B.R. Ambedkar), available at https://eparlib.nic.in/bitstream/123456789/762996/1/cad_04-11-1948.pdf
33. *A.K. Gopalan vs State of Madras*, (1950) SCR 88, paragraph 3.
34. Ibid.
35. Unkind critics have recently taken to calling this 'hope and faith jurisprudence'!
36. The most telling evidence of this is that politicians who 'cross over' have charges against them dropped, or placed in suspended animation.
37. Readers will be aware of multiple leaders of opposition parties who have spent substantial time in jail without bail, at the time of the writing of this book.
38. Parliament of India, *Constituent Assembly Debates*, Vol. VII (4 November 1948) (speech of Dr B.R. Ambedkar), available at https://eparlib.nic.in/bitstream/123456789/762996/1/cad_04-11-1948.pdf
39. Parliament of India, *Constituent Assembly Debates*, Vol. XI (25 November 1949) (speech of Dr B.R. Ambedkar), available at https://main.sci.gov.in/AMB/pdf/Closing%20speech%2025%20Nov%201949.pdf
40. Karl Marx, *The Eighteenth Brumaire of Louis Bonaparte*, (1852), available at https://www.marxists.org/archive/marx/works/1852/18th-brumaire/ch01.htm
41. 'Marx to Ruge', (1843), available at https://www.marxists.org/archive/marx/works/1843/letters/43_09.htm

Index

Aadhaar (Amendment) Ordinance, 71
Aadhaar Act, 66–67
Abdullah, Sheikh, 86
accountability, 74, 117, 121, 210
'accused of any offence', 161, 165
Ackerman, Bruce, 120–121
Adamczak, Bini, 207
Adeney, Katharine, 21
adjudication, viii, xxiv, 2, 54, 63, 204; disqualification petitions, 64, 233
Administration of Tribal Areas in the States of Assam, Meghalaya, Tripura and Mizoram' (as amended), 99
administrative: decisions, 181, 187, 201; detention, vii, xii, xx, xxii, 157, 210; public participation in, 187
affirmative action, 226–228
Agarwal, Shriman Narayan, 214–215, 218
Agricultural Produce Market Act, 17
Ajay Maken vs Union of India, 199–200, 202
A.K. Gopalan vs State of Madras, 150, 210, 230
A.K. Roy vs Union of India, 155–157
All-India Federation, 22, 215
Alok Verma vs Union of India/Alok Verma judgement, 128–130, 140
alternative constitutional draft, 215
Ambedkar, B.R., 6, 44, 47, 50, 64, 80, 102, 104, 147, 193, 214, 223, 225–230: characterization, 45; draft constitution, 228; on 'grammar of anarchy,' 237

Anoop Baranwal vs Union of India, 116, 119, 136–138, 141–142
Anthony Njenga Mbuti and Ors vs Attorney-General and Ors, 166–167
anti-defection law, xviii, 43, 51–53, 55–60, 74, 233
anti-money laundering law. *See* Prevention of Money Laundering Act, 2002 [PMLA])
arbitrary restraints, 224
Armed Forces (Special Powers) Act (AFSPA), 14–16, 32–33, 95, 211
asymmetric federalism, 75–77, 79–81, 83, 86–88, 92–99, 103, 107–109, 111; administrative, 93–94; centrally managed, 93, 98, 105, 108, 110, 113; legislative, 94
Auden, W.H., 212
Augsburger, Aaron, 112
Aundh Constitution, 218
Austin, Granville, xiv, 222; 'constitutional web,' 234
authoritarian enclave, 144, 149–158
autonomous district councils (ADCs), 104, 107, 109
autonomy, xix, 4, 24, 26, 32, 75–76, 102–105, 108, 111–112, 135

Babulal Parate vs State of Bombay, 11–12
bail, ix, 167, 170–171, 173–174; application for, 169, 172; commencement of regime of, 168; 'Frankentest' for, 169, 172; in ordinary criminal case, 155; twin test for, 168–174, 233, 235
Battle of Koregaon, 1818, 33
Beg, (J), 155
Bengal Regulation 1818, xx, 146, 149, 176
Bharatiya Janata Party (BJP), viii; in absolute majority, vii; 'toppling' of Opposition-led state governments, 56
Bhargava, Thakur Das, 160
Bhatia, Udit, 50, 52
Bhima-Koregaon case, 33
Bhim Singh vs Union of India, 19, 21
Bhopatkar Satkar Nidhi, 216
bicameralism, xvi, xviii, 41, 64
Bill of Rights, 133, 143, 149, 152
Bolivia, 189, 203, 205; Constituent Assembly, 188; Constitution of, 111; Tockman on, 188
Border Security Force (BSF) Act of 1968, 34
Bordoloi Committee Report, 94, 96, 106
British: colonies, 48, 166; parliamentarianism, 39, 44–46, 50; veto powers of governor-general, 47
budget, 1, 53, 64

Cabinet Mission Plan, 6
Calcutta High Court, 169
Central Bureau of Investigation (CBI), 118, 140; independence outside the Constitution, 125–131

centralizing drift, xi, xxi–xxii, 4, 36–37, 43–44, 53, 55–56, 145, 209–210, 212, 217–218, 221–222, 230–232, 234–236, 238; within Parliament, 68
Central Vigilance Commission (CVC), 127–129, 140
Central Vista Project, 202
Central Water Commission, 12
Centre–state transfers, 19–20
Chandrachud, (CJI), 31
Chatterjee, Partha, 189
Chief Election Commissioner, 135
Chief Justice of India, viii, 116, 137, 142, 230
China war 1962, 171
Choudhary, Vijay Madanlal, 174–176
civil liberties, 208; curtailment of, 233, 236
civil rights, xii, xx, 16, 32
Coal Bearing Areas Act of 1957, 8
coalition, 41, 59–60, 90
Code of Criminal Procedure, 144, 146, 163–164, 166–167, 171–172, *see also* committal proceedings
codification, 42, 48–49; constitutional, 61
colonial constitutionalism, xxiii–xxiv, 175, 215, 217–218, 222, 229
'colonial continuity', xii–xiii, xxiii–xxiv
colonial criminal codes, 167
the colony, 46, 147, 149, 170, *see also* post-colonial countries
'committal proceedings', 168–169; abolition of, 170, 172
communist riots/uprisings, 111, 149
comparative constitutional law, 69
Comptroller and Auditor General (CAG), xix, 121, 125, 127, 138–139, 142
Concurrent List, 8, 33–34, 209
confessional statements, 162–163; protection against, 164
Constituent Assembly, xii–xiii, 22–23, 44–46, 48–49, 61–62, 81–84, 89, 100–101, 110–111, 177, 191–, 203–204, 212–214, 216–217, 219, 227–229, 237; debates, xvi, 79, 83, 104–106, 136–137, 150, 160, 178, 192; sub-committees, 50; Union Powers Committee, 6
Constitution of India: during 2019–24, vii, x, xxv; 42nd Amendment, 208–209, 211–212; 44th Amendment, 210–212; 73rd Amendments, xviii, 5; 74th Amendments, xviii, 5; Article 1, xvii, 3, 29; Article 2, 111; Article 3, 6, 11–14, 27–31, 36–37, 91, 99, 236; Article 4, 13–14; Article 14, 156, 158; Article 15(1), 226; Article 15(2), 228; Article 15(3), 226; Article 19, 152, 156, 158; Article 19(1)(a), 154; Article 19(2), 153–154; Article 20, 144, 147–149, 158, 162, 164–165, 174–175, 231, 234;

Article 20(1), 159; Article 20(3), 159–165, 174–175; Article 21, xii, xvi, 144–145, 147–149, 151–152, 155–156, 158, 167–173, 175–176, 202, 231; Article 22, 84, 144, 147, 149–158, 171, 174–176, 211; Article 22 (3) (b), 156; Article 22(3), 148, 156–158; Article 22(4), 148, 153, 156–158; Article 35(c), 84; Article 110, 66; Article 123, 68, 70, 72; Article 131, 32; Article 155, 6; Article 210, 68; Article 239AA, 25; Article 245, 109; Article 246, 13; Article 254, 6; Article 257, 181–182; Article 257A, 209, 211; Article 280, 19–21; Article 282, 20; Article 293, 1–2, 6; Article 324, 119, 135–137; Article 356, 6, 25, 27–31, 36–37, 236; Article 368, 13, 86, 106; Article 370, xix, 4, 26–27, 30, 32, 76–77, 79, 81–92, 94–98, 107, 113–114, 231, 233, 236; Article 370(1), 86, 89, 94; Article 370 (1)(d), 86; Article 370 (3), 83, 89, 98; Article 371, 78, 80, 93, 95–98, 105, 108, 113; and Asymmetric Federalism. *See* asymmetric federalism; Article 371A, 94–95; Article 371A – I, xix; Article 371C, 93; Article 371 special provisions', 93; drafting the, 105, 226; federal character, 8; framers, xxii, 6, 39, 49, 78–79, 102, 112, 136, 160, 192–193, 226; framing of, 24, 39, 69, 80, 90, 94, 100, 144, 150, 190, 213; origins of, xvi; power map, xxiv, xxvi, 16, 167, 230; Preamble, xx–xxi, 177–178; as quasi-federal, 3, 7; Schedule V, xix, 77–78, 80, 99–102, 104–106, 108, 110, 113, 219; Schedule VI, xix, xxi, 77–78, 80, 94, 96, 99–100, 103–110, 113, 219; Schedule VII, 5–6, 8, 13, 15, 32, 34, 82, 109, 152, 209; Schedule X, 42–43, 51, 51–53, 55–60, 62–63, 65, 73

constitutional: amendments, xviii, xx, 19, 51, 82, 89, 181, 193, 209–210, 212; autonomy, vii, 219, 236; 'bodyline-bowling', ix–x, 31; 'common sense', xv, xx, xxii, xxiv, xxiv–xxv, 2–3, 80, 105, 109, 113, 204–206, 230–232, 238; constraints, 68, 128, 152, 159–160, 179–180, 193; conventions, 42, 48–49; design, 49, 54, 96, 99, 105, 105–108, 142, 147–148, 186, 190, 214, 216, 238; drafting process, 178, 203–204, 207, 225; governance, 179, 191–192; guarantees, 144, 175, 194, 198, 200–201; homogeneity, xix, 76, 102; institutions, 31, 122, 238; interpretation, x, xiv, 3, 5, 165, 199, 202, 204–205,

230, 232, 235; law, xiv, xxv, 3; lawyers, , xxiv, 223; pluralism, xvi, xviii–xix, 92, 94–99, 104–105, 108, 218–219, 231, 234; provisions, xxiv, 3, 7, 20, 36–37, 44, 82, 85–86, 148, 165, 204–205; reforms, 9, 22; rights, xv, 117, 123, 139, 152, 165, 187, 200; scheme, 10, 19, 31, 36, 87, 113, 126, 138, 213; silences, 23, 30, 42, 44, 60–61, 68, 92, 113, 118–119, 138–139, 179; statutes, 118–119, 125, 127, 131–135, 139, 142; text, xvi–xvii, xxi–xxii, 5, 36–37, 42, 105–108, 110, 113, 138–139, 142, 178–179, 202, 204–205, 231, 234

constitutionalism, xv, xvi–xvii, xxiii, 76, 87, 98, 110, 113, 167, 178, 181, 189, 191, 193, 207, 212–214, 217, 219, 221–223, 232, 234; Indian post-colonial, xxiv; 'progressive', xii, xiv; transformative, xii–xiii

constitutionality, 19, 155–156, 166, 182, 233; of 'twin test', 172–173

constitutional jurisprudence, xii, 2, 26, 127, 139, 199–200, 203, 236; centralizing approach, 11–21

Constitution of Hindusthan Free State Act, 216–217

Constitution of India, Roy, 213–214, 217

'cooperation': interpretation of, 15

Council of Ministers, 40, 51

Court, Constitution as neutral for, 234

criminal: codes, 144, 146, 148; jurisprudence, 148; justice system, xx, 154, 157–158, 169; legal process, 154, 159; proceeding, ordinary, 163

criminal law, 33, 145–146, 162, 170, 233; British codification of, 146; colonial, 148

Criminal Procedure Bill of 1872, 146

cross-examination, 169–170

CrPC, 165

Customs Officers, 162–163, 165

CVC Act, 128–130

CVC Committee, 140–141

Dam, Shubhankar, 44

Damnoo, Mohd Maqbool, 77, 84–88, 90, 113

Dasgupta, Sandipto, 189

Data Protection Act (DPA), 126, 134

Data Protection Authority, 126

De, Rohit, 178, 203, 206

'decree power,' 69

defections, 42, 51, 54– 57, 59, 63, 234

Defence of India Rules, 1942, 149, 168–171, 173

Delhi Special Police Act, 126

Delhi Special Police Establishment Act, 1946 (DSPE Act), 128–130

democracy: constitutional, 13, 51, 117, 121, 133, 188; direct, 182, 188–189, 191, 217, 231;

parliamentary, xviii, 39–42, 60, 66, 191; participatory, 185, 187–188; representative, 73, 183, 188–189, 192, 204; Westminster system of, 39
democratic: institutions, 201; theory, 11, 181, 187
democratization, 217
'demodiversity', 188
demolitions of home, ix, 199–200, 208, 210, *see also* evictions
depressed classes, 227, *see also* untouchability
'details of administration', 230
detention laws 149
Dhar Commission (Linguistic Provinces Commission headed by M.L. Dhar), 111
Directive Principles of State Policy, xiii–xiv, 225
Directorate of Enforcement vs Deepak Mahajan, 164
discrimination, xiv, 166, 226–228
dissent: intra-party, 40, 42, 52, 73; within Parliament, 65–68; within party, 51–60
District Council of United Khasi and Jaintia Hills vs Sitimon Sawian, 108
Dixon, Rosalind, 199
Dominion Government of India, 78, 45
Directory of Priority Crime Investigation (DPCI), 132–133
D.P. Wadhwa vs State of Bihar, 70
draft Constitution, 44, 103, 170, 177, 214, 217, 219, 237; Ambedkar's motion on, 49
Dr. Jaya Thakur vs Union of India, 140, 231
Dropti Devi vs Union of India, 158
Dr. Preeti Srivastava vs State of Madhya Pradesh, 35

East Punjab Armed Bands (Arrest and Detention) Ordinance, 170
economic structure, 223, 225–226
Ecuador, 189, 205; constitution of, 111
Election Commission, viii–ix, xix, xxii, 115–117, 119–122, 126–127, 134–138, 141–142, 231, 233, 235–236; entrenchment and , 135–138
election commissioners, viii, 116, 126, 135–136
Elections, 229, (*see also* General Election); indirect election procedure, 67; of President and vice-president of India, 67
Emergency, vii, x, xx, 27–29, 70, 90, 147, 155, 170–171, 207–210, 212, 216; internal, 210–211; and internet shut-down, vii; Provisions, 20, 28, 36, 107, 209
Enforcement Directorate (ED), ix, 140, 165; powers to arrest, 174
equality, 31, 127–128, 130, 132, 158, 225
escape clauses, xxi–xxii, 36
Essential Services Act (ESA), 171
evictions, ix, 197–200, 205
exceptional: cases, 40, 157; mechanism, 158; power, 71, 147, (*see also* power); situations, 28

executive: control, 41, 48, 50, 63–64, 119, 138–139, 141–142, 233; law-making, 68–72; in Parliament, 40; powers, viii, xvii, 3, 5, 43, 47, 104, 209, 215; trusting document, xxii, 119
'extraordinary laws', 146, 171

fact-finding commission, 161, *see also Commissions*; investigation
federal: kill switch, 78, 99, 107–108, 113; polity, 14, 111; scheme of Constitution, 2, 14–15, 32, 56, 236; state, 192; structure, xvii, 2–3, 5–7, 9, 19, 23–26, 30, 60, 75, 108, 215–216
federalism, vii, xiv, xvi, 3–4, 8–11, 18, 21, 23, 27–28, 33–36, 58, 60, 76–77, 88, 231, 234–235, (*see also* asymmetric federalism); approach, 8, 18, 24, 26, 28, 30–31, 36–37; and Article 3, 12–14; Asymmetric, 78; and human rights, 14–16; and Implied Limitations, 26–32; and legislative relations, 16–18; Nirvikar Singh on, xxi; and revenue, 18–21; and Text of Constitution, 5–8
Finance Commission, 19–21
First Information Report (FIR), 163
Foreign Exchange Regulation Act (FERA), 164–165, 172
Forest Rights Act (FRA), 196–197
formal accusation, 161, 163–164
fourth-branch institutions, xxii, xxv, 119–120, 125, 135, 138, 140–141, 231, 233, 235
Frankenberg, Gunther, xi
Frankenconstitution, xxiv, 74, 222, 234
Frankenstate, 169, 172; for bail, xxiv, 73, 169, 172; Scheppele on, 73
freedom of conscience, 52–54
freedom of speech, xiv, 134, 139, 153
fundamental rights, viii, xiii–xv, xx, 35, 84, 118, 131, 151–152, 154–158, 223–224, 230

Gandhian Constitution, 214–215, 217–218
Gandhi, Indira, x, 208–209, 216; returning to power, 212
Gandhi, Sanjay, 210
Gargarella, Roberto, xi, xv–xvi, xxiii, 124, 179, 189, 230
gender equality, 120, 223, 226
General Election, vii; of 1977, 208; of 2024, viii, 38, 116, 138
government: borrowing, 1–2; legitimacy of, xix; system of, 39, 44–45, 73
Government of India Act, 48–49, 64, 70, 97, 149–150, 218, 229–230; listing of Scheduled Areas, 100; of 1915, 69; of 1919, 46–48, 100, 218; of 1935, 5, 9, 46–49, 62, 64, 69–70, 97, 149–150, 218, 229–230; 'provincial autonomy' in, 22

Government of the National Capital Territory of Delhi Act, 25
'Governor,' 87–88, 90; of Gujarat, 93; of Maharashtra, 93; of Nagaland, 97
Governor-General's Acts, 47
guarantor institutions, xix, xx, xxi, 119, 122, 124–125, 127, 133, 135, 137, 139, 142

habeas corpus judgment, 210
Haber, Paul, 112
Hanuman Laxman Aroskar vs Union of India, 194–196, 202
Hausing, Kham Khan Suan, 97, 110
Hilmer, Jeffrey D., 187
Hind Swaraj, 214
Hindu Mahasabha, 153, 216
Hugh Glenister vs President of the Republic of South Africa, 132
Human Rights Commission, 120–121, 124, 126, 134
Hussain, Nasser, 147, 175
Hydari, Akbar, 94

identity, xiii–xiv, 53, 55
Independent review Committee (IRC), 127
Indian Councils Act, 1861, 69, 201
Indian Evidence Act, 146, 162, 164–165, 174
Indian National Congress, 46, 49, 100, 111, 150, 190, 192, 212, 216; Resolution of 1929, 223
Indian Union, 12, 24, 76, 81, 83–84, 93–95, 99, 112, 217
indigenous (Adivasi) territories, 78, 112, 187
individual freedom, xxiii, 175
information: commission, 117, 120–121, 123–124, 126, 134; dissemination, 188, 201
infrastructure of implementation, 122–123, 131, 134, 137
institutional independence, 133, 137–138, 140–141
Instrument of Accession, 81–82
investigation, 32–33, 38, 118, 126–127, 159, 161, 163, 169; authorities, 235. *See also* Central Bureau of Investigation (CBI)
I.T.C. Limited vs The Agricultural Produce Market Committee, 16, 20, 37

Jammu and Kashmir, viii, xix, 27, 29, 75–76, 79, 84–92, 231, 236; abolition of Article 370, 4, 30, 77, 82, 85, 89, 91, 114, 236; Constituent Assembly of, 77, 81–83; Constitutional amendments, 85; constitutional status, 98–99; Constitution of, 82–83, 85, 89, 231; Indian Constitution to, 85; remove the autonomy of, vii, 4; 'representative' of, 90; restoration of statehood, 31; 'special status' of, 26; strike of government employees and teachers in, 84; and the Union relations, 87

Jammu and Kashmir Preventive Detention Act 1964, 84, 87
Janata Party, 208, 210, 212, 225
judicial: adjudication, xxii; appointments cases, 233; decisions, xi, xiv, xxiii, 44, 68, 70, 72, 147, 188; doctrine, 108–110, 196, 205; interpretation, xiii, 72, 74, 110, 142, 145, 236; review, 41, 43–44, 67, 71, 121, 157, 209
judiciary, ix, xiii, xix, xxii, xxv, 108, 115–116, 119, 124, 131, 178, 205, 208
The Jurisprudence of Emergency, Hussain, 175
Justice K.S. Puttaswamy vs Union of India, 71
JVP Committee (Jawaharlal Nehru, Vallabhai Patel and Pattabhi Sitamaryya), 111

Karachi Resolution, 223
Karimuddin, Kazi Syed, 49, 62
Karnataka, 56–58; toppling of state government, 57, *see also* Maharashtra
Kartar Singh vs State of Punjab, 34, 172–173, 175, 233
Kashmir Preventive Detention Act of 1964, 84
Kenya, 19, 189, 203, 205, 216; Article 257 of, 181; Constitution of, 120, 147, 166, 182, 184, 216; Criminal Procedure Code, 166; High Court of, 166–167, 185; judiciary, 182, 199; jurisprudence, 198; participatory constitution-making, 204; Supreme Court of, 183
Kenyan Constitutional Court, 184–185; BBI Bill in, 182
Kerala, on 'net borrowing ceiling' case, 1–2
Khaitan, Tarunabh, 63, 122–123, 135
Khosla, Madhav, xxiii, 42, 48–49
Kihoto Hollohan vs Zaichilhu, 52, 54–56, 231–232
Klug, Heinz, 121
Krishna Kumar Singh vs State of Bihar, 70–71
Kropotkin, Prince, 214

Latin American constitutionalism, xv; 'social question' in, xvi
Latin American presidential systems, 69
law-making, 50, 62, 66, 69–70, 83–84, 179, 181, 183, 185, 188–189, 198; powers, xviii, 18, 47, 68, 70; public participation in, xxi, 184
leadership and legislators, 51–56, (*see also* leaders *under* Opposition); as rebels viii, 58
Legg, Stephen, 100
legislature, xvii, xxv, 23, 26–27, 29, 39–40, 44–48, 62, 64, 70, 72–74, 123–124, 129, 183–186; marginalisation of, 50; representatives, 50, 191

liberty, xi, 144–146, 151, 169, 172, 223–224, 233; deprivation of, 145, 158, 170
Lok Sabha, the lower house, xviii
Ludsin, Hallie, 149, 157
Lushai Hills, 96, 103

Madhya Pradesh cases, 56, 58, *see also under separate entries*
Maharashtra, 56, 58, 93; political crisis, 234–235, *see also* Karnataka
Maintenance of Internal Security Act (MISA), 155–156, 175
majority party, 40–41, 60–61, 63, 65–66
Maneka Gandhi vs Union of India, 155–157, 172
Manipur, 93–94
Manipur District Councils Act (and its various amendments), 93
Mehta, Uday, xvi–xvii, 162, 178–179
Members of Parliament Local Area Development Scheme (MPLADS), 19–20
Mikir and North Cachar Hills, 103
Mines and Minerals (Development and Regulation) Act of 1957 (MMRDA), 197
Misra, Lokanath, 192
Mistry, Maneck Phiroz, 161
Mizo National Front, 96
Mizoram, 77, 96, 99, 106, 113
Mizos, 80, 219
Mizo Union, 96
Mohd Maqbool Damnoo vs State of Jammu & Kashmir, 87, 89–90
money bills, xviii, 39, 41, 43, 65–67, 74, 216
Montesquiean branches [executive, legislature, and judiciary], 124
Mookerjee, Radhakumood, 214
M.P. Sharma vs Satish Chandra, 160–161, 163, 165
Muigai, Githu, 46–47
Mullaperiyar Dam, 12
Munda, Jaipal, 101–104, 106, 110, 114
Munshi, K.M., 45, 102, 171–172
Murray, Christina, 124

Naga Hills, 95, 103
Nagaland, 77, 94–96, 113; independence, 95
Nagaland Legislative Assembly, 95
Naga National Council (NNC), 94; plebiscite by, 95
Naga People's Movement of Human Rights vs Union of India, 14, 16, 34
Nagas, 80, 94–96, 219
Naoroji, Dadabhai, 190
Narayan, Jayaprakash, 216
Narcotic Drugs and Psychotropic Substances Act (NDPS), 173
Nariman, F.S., 129
National and state Commissions for Scheduled Castes and Scheduled Tribes, 126
national economy, 2, 32, 125
National Investigation Agency Act of 2008, (NIA), 32–33
national security, 34; legislation, xiii, 210

National Security Act of 1980 (NSA), 155–156, 212
nation-state, 75–76, 110, 112, 219; modern, 225
Nayyar, Kuldip, 65
NCT of Delhi vs Union of India, 25–26
NEET (nationwide examination for admission in undergraduate medical programmes), 35
Nehru, Jawaharlal, 6, 50, 91, 111, 193; on Article 370, 191
Nehru Committee Report of 1928, 111
non-electoral institutions, 119, 139
non-entrenchment problem, 118–119, 131–135
Noorani, A.G., 83, 86
North-East Frontier (Assam) Tribal and Excluded Areas, 103, 106

Olga Tellis vs Bombay Municipal Corporation, 198, 200, 202
Opposition, 34, 43–44, 65, 74, 208; arrested members of political, ix; 'disrupting' proceedings, 63; Khaitan on, 63; leaders of, viii, 49, 61, 63, 116, 137; mass suspension of MPs, 38; rights, 43, 60–61, 63, 65, 68; toppling, viii
ordinance-making power, 44, 48, 69–71, 216
ordinances, 25, 39, 43–44, 47, 68–72; shelf-life of, 71; for 'temporary legislation,' 70
Orissa Mining Corporation vs The Ministry of Environment and Forests (Niyamgiri judgment), 196

Panchayats, xviii, 5, 214, 218, *see also* gram sabhas
Parasher, Tejas, 191–192, 217
parliamentarianism, 38, 44–51, 65, 72–74, 231, 235; 'distortion' of, 62; full-blooded, 42, 49
parliamentary: decays, 39, 63; delays, 50; democracy, xviii, 39–42, 60, 66, 191, (*see also under* democracy); majorities, 65, 117, 226; Opposition, 40; party, 40; structures, 46, 62, 65, 215, 218; systems, 39–42, 45, 48–49, 73–74
Parliamentary Committees, 39–40, 61–62; on defections, 51
Parmar, P., 106, 110
participatory: budgeting in Porto Alegre, 187; citizens councils, 192; Constitution-making, 203; democracy, 185, 187–188 (*see also under* democracy); mechanisms, 204
Partition, 79, 111, 149; violence of, 170
party: leadership, 42–43, 51–52, 55–56, 59–60, 73; split in, viii, 235
the People, xx–xxi, 88, 100, 103, 121, 124, 177–186, 188–193, 196–198, 204, 206, 208,

210–211; in governance, 215; involvement of, 181, 197, 203
People's Committees, 213
Personal Digital Data Protection Act, 134
pluralism, xix, 75–76, 78, 91–92, 98–99, 105–106, 108, 113–114, 219
plurinationalism, 111–112
police officers, 146, 159, 162–165, 174
political: economy, 225; executive, 44, 55, 67–68, 72–74, 117–120, 126, 130, 132, 134, 141; forces, 33–34, 36–37, 59, 122, 140, 232, 234–236; institutions, 179–180; power, xvii, xxv, 19, 60, 225, 227–228, 232; rights, xii, 143, 180; sovereignty, 10, 190–191; theory, 215
Popular Initiative, 181–182, 216
power: axis of, xix, xxiii, 3–4, 43, 113, 143, 213, 221–223, 228, 230, 235–236; centralization of, xxiii, 55, 74, 214, 234; coercive, 143–145, 147, 159, 162–163, 174, 231; concentration, xviii, xxiii, 31, 72, 119, 180; definition of personal, 47; delegation of, 119; devolution of, 11, 93; distribution of, xviii, 5, 7, 10, 229; division of, 3, 13; economic, 221, 223–226, 228; emergency, 70, 210; of executive, xviii, 44, (*see also* law-making powers); of government, 121, 224; gubernatorial, xxi; imbalance, 30, 139, 160; organization of, xi, xv–xvii, xx, xxii–xxiii, 230; public, xvii, xxi, 3, 117, 119, 124–125, 139, 142–143, 216, 222; question of, xi, xvi, 4, 11, 76, 167, 214, 218, 234; redistribution of, 118; separation of, xiv, 20, 39, 119, 121, 124, 179, 189; of State, 104, 143–145; in taxonomy, xiv; visions of, xi, xvii, 221, 232, 238
Prakash, Sampat, 77, 84–88, 113
Prakash Singh Badal vs Union of India, 53
Prasad, Rajendra, 83
presidentialism, 44, 49, 67, 69, 72, 74
'Presidential legislation,' Dam on, 44
Presidential Orders/Constitutional Order (C.O.) xxiv, 48, 73, 75–76, 85, 87–90, 112, 183, 272–273; as Constitutional Amendments, 82–84; removed the constitutional autonomy, vii
President's Rule. *See* Emergency
Prevention of Money Laundering Act 2002 (PMLA), ix, 145, 173–175, 234–235
preventive detention, 84, 87, 144, 148–152, 154–158, 168; laws, 85, 150, 152–154, 156; legislation, 149, 151; order, 154–155, 157
Preventive Detention Act, 84, 87, 151, 153

Prime Minister, role of, 39–40, 74
Princely States, 22, 78–79, 81
Privy Purses, abolition of, 217
prosecution, 15, 32, 154, 161, 163, 168, 175, 234–235
Protection of Human Rights Act, 126
Provincial Constitution Committee, 45
public interest litigation (PIL), xii
'public order,' 15, 153
public participation, xxi, 103, 124–125, 179, 182–187, 189, 191–206, 215, 217; constitutionalizing, 203
public power and non-elected bodies, 119–125, *see also* power
Public Service Commissions, 139
Punjab and Haryana High Court, 53–54, 56

Raja Narayanlal Bansilal vs Maneck Phiroz Mistry, 161
Rajeev Suri vs Delhi Development Authority, 201–202, 204–205, 231
Rajya Sabha (Upper House), xviii, 41, 43, 65–66; chairperson of, 67–68; as Council of States, 40
Ramkumar, Meenakshi, 61
Ram Singh vs State of Delhi, 153
Rao, Govinda, 23
Rao, Subba (J), 4, 23–25, 29, 36
R.C. Cooper vs Union of India, 155–156
'the reasons of State,'. *See* Bengal Regulation 1818
Reddy, Charith, 63
redistributing/rebalancing power, 104, 148–149, 187, *see also* power
referendums, xx, 103, 177, 181–183, 188, 193, 213, 217
representatives, xxi, 22, 81, 90, 121, 124, 180–181, 183–184, 189, 192, 215
representative system, 231
resignations, 57–58, 60
Restrictive Bail Conditions, 175
Right to Information Act (RTI), 118, 126, 134–135, 139; amendments to, 115
Right to Life and Personal Liberty, xii, 147, 198
Romesh Chandra Mehta vs State of West Bengal, 162, 164–167, 174
Round Table Conferences, 22
Rowlatt Act of 1919, 146
Roy, A.K., 155
Roy, M.N., 213–215

Sadar-i-Riyasat, 87–88; replacement with Governor, 90
Sahadat Ali vs State of Assam, 154
Sampat Prakash vs State of Jammu and Kashmir, 84, 86–87, 89
Sawian, Sitimon, 108, 110
'Scheduled Areas,' 99–102, 108, 110; autonomy to, 106
Scheduled Caste and Scheduled Tribe Commissions, xix, 99, 126, 139
Scheduled Districts Act, 99

'Scheduled Offences' (provided for in the Act), 32
Scheppele, Kim Lane, xxiv, 73
Sea Customs Act, 162–163
Seal, Brajendra Nath, 192, 217
secessionism, 104
The Second Judges Case, 142
Seervai, H.M., 24, 29
Sekhri, Abhinav, 145, 155, 161, 175
self-governance, 76, 78, 82
self-incrimination, 146, 159, 162, 164, 174; right against, 160; in US Constitution, 147
semi-Presidential system, 49
separatism, 101, 104
Shah, K.T., 193
Shani, Ornit, 178, 203, 206
Shiv Sena: leadership, 58; split in, 58
Singh, Aishwarya, 61
Singh, Krishna Kumar, 70–72
Singh, Nirvikar, xxi, 23
Socialist Constitution, 216
Socialist Party of India, 215–217
social: movements, xiv, 139, 188, 194; power, 221, 226–228, *see also* power
socioeconomic rights, xii–xiii, 223
South Africa, 189; Constitution of, 120–121, 184; Constitutional Court, 132–133, 184, 199; constitutional law, 198; *Doctors for Life International* case, 184–185; evictions in, 205; jurisprudence, 198–199
South African National Prosecuting Authority Act, 132
South African Police Service Act, 132
speaker, 65, 233; absence of, 43; certification, 43, 67; control over the house, 64; executive-controlled, 73; powers, 53–54, 63; quasi-judicial functions, 64
special anti-terrorism law, 233
'special' legislation, 148
'special powers' (Articles 371A-I), 14, 77, 211
S.R. Bommai vs Union of India, 25, 232
Statement of Objects and Reasons of the Constitution Amendment Act, 210
State of Chhattisgarh invoked Article 131, 32
state of exception, xx, 144, 150, 168, 210–211, 230
State of Kerala, creation of, 12–13; Mullaperiyar Dam in 12
State of Kerala vs Union of India, 1, 3, 12, 18, 32
State of Mysore, Constitution for, 192
State of Sikkim, 94, 98
State of West Bengal vs Union of India, 7–12, 20–21, 23, 27, 29, 33, 36–37, 230; dissenting opinion in, 4
states ('provinces'), 2, 5, 15–17, 25, 28, 32, 34, 56–59, 84,

86, 217–219; boundaries, 11–12, 216; coercion, 77, 165; dismissal of, 6; power of, 7–8, 35–36, 124, 127, 142–144, 146–149, 152, 157, 159–161, 163, 165–167, 172, 175–176; reorganization of, 13, 112, 216; toppling of, viii
States and Minorities, 226–228; Ambedkar, 223
States Reorganisation Act of 1956, 12–13
Sub-Committee on Excluded and Partially Excluded Areas, 101
Sub-Committee on the North-East Frontier (Assam) Tribal and Excluded Areas (also known as the Bordoloi Committee), 106
Sultan, Nazmul, 50, 190–191
Supreme Court, vii–viii, 1–2, 9–22, 25, 32, 34–35, 44, 69–71, 77, 84–92, 108–110, 114, 116, 144, 150–152, 154–158, 160–165, 172–175, 196, 200–201, 210–212; judgments, xii, 43, 77, 113 jurisprudence of, xvi
swaraj (self-government) movement, 112, 190–191

Tamil Nadu, 1886 agreement, 12
Terrorist and Anti-Disruptive Activities (Prevention) Act (TADA), 172–173
Tewari, Saagar, 105
Tillin, Louis, 75
Tobacco Board Act of 1975, 16–17
trials, 33, 157, 162–163, 167–168, 172, 200; administrative, xx; criminal, 169–170; detention without, 146, 157, 173
'tribalstans,' 80, 104
Tribes Advisory Council (TACs), 101–102
trinities, 158–159
Tuensang Area, 95

UK House of Commons, 54
uncodified conventions, 49, 61
Union (Centre), 5; executive, 16, 25, 28, 31, 89, 93, 117; policing, 34; power, 7, 14, 26, 29, 236, *see also* power
Union–State: fiscal relationship, 1, 20; political balance of power between, 87; Public Service Commissions, 125–126; relations, 2–3, 5–7, 9–11, 13, 19, 22, 24, 29, 36 37
Union of States, xvii, 30
Union Parliament, 6, 11, 16–17, 26–28, 30, 109
Unique Identification Authority of India (UIDAI), 66–67, *see also* Aadhaar Act
Unitary State, 11, 19, 32–37
United States, xvi, 72, 219; Constitution of, xvi, 147, 179; constitutionalism, xvii; Fifth Amendment of the Constitution of, 160; presidentialism, 44–45, 50

universal adult franchise, 50, 191, 229
Unlawful Activities Prevention Act (UAPA) 1967, 33, 173; dissidents arrested under, ix
untouchability, 227; prohibition of, 228
upper house (Rajya Sabha, the council of states), xviii, 38–41, 43–44, 65–66, 68, 74, 212

Van der Westhuizen, Justice, 185
vice president, 43, 63, 67–68
Vineet Narain vs Union of India, 118, 127–130, 140–141
voting, 52–53, 63, 180–181, 184

Weimar Constitution, 73
Westminster: parliamentarianism, 40–41, 53–54, 62–63; system of democracy, 39
Wilson, T.J.M., 193
witnesses, 159–160, 168–171

About the Author

GAUTAM BHATIA IS A Delhi-based advocate and an Adjunct Professor at the Jindal Global Law School. He is the author of *The Transformative Constitution* (2019) and *Unsealed Covers* (2023). He has been involved in several contemporary constitutional cases, such as the challenge to the abrogation of Article 370, the electoral bonds case, the right to privacy case, and others. His work has been cited by the Indian Supreme Court, and by various High Courts. He has served as amicus curae on two occasions before the Supreme Court of Kenya. He is also the author of three science-fiction novels, *The Wall* (2020), *The Horizon* (2021), and *The Sentence* (2024).

HarperCollins *Publishers* India

At HarperCollins India, we believe in telling the best stories and finding the widest readership for our books in every format possible. We started publishing in 1992; a great deal has changed since then, but what has remained constant is the passion with which our authors write their books, the love with which readers receive them, and the sheer joy and excitement that we as publishers feel in being a part of the publishing process.

Over the years, we've had the pleasure of publishing some of the finest writing from the subcontinent and around the world, including several award-winning titles and some of the biggest bestsellers in India's publishing history. But nothing has meant more to us than the fact that millions of people have read the books we published, and that somewhere, a book of ours might have made a difference.

As we look to the future, we go back to that one word—a word which has been a driving force for us all these years.

Read.

Harper Collins 4th HARPER FICTION HARPER NON-FICTION HARPER BUSINESS HCCB HARPERCOLLINS CHILDREN'S BOOKS

HARPER DESIGN Harper Sport HARPER PERENNIAL HARPER VANTAGE हार्पर हिन्दी